Second Edition

COMPREHENSIVE SCHOOL COUNSELING PROGRAMS

K–12 DELIVERY SYSTEMS IN ACTION

Colette T. Dollarhide
The Ohio State University

Kelli A. Saginak
University of Wisconsin, Oshkosh

Boston   Columbus   Indianapolis   New York   San Francisco   Upper Saddle River
Amsterdam   Cape Town   Dubai   London   Madrid   Milan   Munich   Paris   Montreal   Toronto
Delhi   Mexico City   São Paulo   Sydney   Hong Kong   Seoul   Singapore   Taipei   Tokyo

Vice President and Editor in Chief: Jeffery W. Johnston
Senior Acquisitions Editor: Meredith D. Fossel
Editorial Assistant: Nancy Holstein
Vice President, Director of Marketing: Margaret Waples
Senior Marketing Manager: Christopher Barry
Senior Managing Editor: Pamela D. Bennett
Project Manager: Kerry Rubadue
Operations Supervisor: Central Publishing
Operations Specialist: Laura Messerly
Senior Art Director: Jayne Conte
Cover Designer: Karen Salzbach
Cover Art: Shutterstock
Project Management: Chitra Ganesan
Composition: PreMedia Global
Printer/Binder: Edwards Brothers
Cover Printer: Lehigh-Phoenix Color Corp.
Text Font: 10/12 Times

Credits and acknowledgments borrowed from other sources and reproduced, with permission, in this textbook appear on appropriate page within text.

Every effort has been made to provide accurate and current Internet information in this book. However, the Internet and information posted on it are constantly changing, so it is inevitable that some of the Internet addresses listed in this textbook will change.

Library of Congress Cataloging-in-Publication Data

Dollarhide, Colette T.
   Comprehensive school counseling programs: K–12 delivery systems in action / Colette T. Dollarhide, Kelli A. Saginak.—2nd ed.
     p. cm.
   Includes bibliographical references and index.
   ISBN-13: 978-0-13-705199-1
   ISBN-10: 0-13-705199-9
   1. Educational counseling—United States.   I. Saginak, Kelli A.   II. Title.
   LB1027.5.D55 2012
   371.40973—dc22

                                        2011001689

10 9 8 7 6 5 4 3 2 1

www.pearsonhighered.com

ISBN-10:   0-13-705199-9
ISBN-13: 978-0-13-705199-1

This book is dedicated to children, especially my grandchildren:
James Wesley and Cadence Colette. They remind me daily of how important
education is for the future, and this book is dedicated to the future of all
children whose school counselors work with passion, creativity, and faith.

—C.D.

I dedicate this edition to my children, Andrea, Riley, and Avery.
Thank you for teaching about school through your eyes, your feelings, and your
experiences. I also dedicate this edition to the school counseling graduate
students who exude a passionate determination to create schools where young
people can learn, thrive, and reach their fullest potential.

—K.S.

ABOUT THE AUTHORS

Colette T. Dollarhide, Senior Lecturer at The Ohio State University, earned her master's and doctorate degrees in counseling and educational psychology from the University of Nevada, Reno. She earned her bachelor's degree in political science from California State University at Fullerton. She has been a counselor for 22 years and a counselor educator for 16 years. For the past 10 years, Dr. Dollarhide's teaching and research focus has specialized in school counseling, but she has taught career counseling, college student development, theories and techniques of counseling, foundations of school counseling, special issues in school counseling (at elementary, middle, and secondary school levels), counseling through play, ethics, consultation, supervision, group counseling, pedagogy in counselor education, and practica and internships. She has coauthored a textbook on secondary school counseling, and she writes about school counseling leadership, professional development, supervision, and the work of school counselors. Dr. Dollarhide has presented papers at national ACA, ACES, and ASCA conferences and at state conferences on topics in school counseling, professional development, research, supervision, and leadership. She has coauthored a successful $400,000 grant for dropout prevention from the AT&T Aspire program and has served as President of C-AHEAD, one of the founding divisions of the ACA. Her editorial work includes over eight years as a reviewer for *Counselor Education and Supervision (CES)*, coeditor for a first-ever *CES* special section on school counselor supervision, four years as a reviewer for *Journal of Counseling and Development (JCD)*, and currently is in her first term as the Editor of the *Journal of Humanistic Counseling*, formerly the *Journal for Humanistic Counseling, Education, and Development*.

Kelli A. Saginak, Associate Professor in the Department of Professional Counseling at the University of Wisconsin, Oshkosh, earned her master's degree in counseling from Rollins College and her doctorate degree in counselor education from Idaho State University. Her involvement with schools as a teacher, counselor, prevention specialist, and consultant extends more than 20 years. As a counselor educator for over 13 years, she has specialized in school counseling, group counseling, life span development, counseling process, and addiction. Dr. Saginak has published and presented on a variety of subjects, including group counseling and group leadership development, school counseling leadership, systemic change and resistance to change, and service-learning in counselor education. She also coauthored a textbook on secondary school counseling. Dr. Saginak enjoys writing grants with student and community partners, and working collaboratively with schools on service-learning projects. Her current research focuses on students' experience in developing counseling process skills, group leadership development, and service learning in counselor education. Her editorial work includes over 10 years as a reviewer with *The Family Journal (TFJ)*, two years as a reviewer with *Professional School Counselor (PSC)* and *The Wisconsin Counseling Journal*, and recently she joined the *Journal for Humanistic Counseling* as a reviewer.

PREFACE

The second edition of any book is designed to address changes in the professional environment since the publication of the first edition, and to address content improvements that have become obvious since the first edition.

To understand this book, it is important to understand the context of professional school counseling. Two organizations have defined professional standards for school counselors—one for professionals-in-training in terms of curricular expectations for training programs, and the other for professionals in the field. The first, the Council for Accreditation of Counseling and Related Educational Programs (CACREP), represents the field's premier accrediting agency. The second, the American School Counselor Association (ASCA), is the national association for school counselors. This book has been written to reflect both the training and the professional standards applicable for school counselors.

NEW TO THIS EDITION

- In a major development, CACREP announced its revised accreditation standards in 2009. The new standards have been incorporated in this edition. In this major revision of school counseling standards for training, expanded requirements are detailed that contextualize what graduating new professionals should be able to do when they enter the school counseling profession. In addition to the foundation counseling training, the knowledge, skills, and practices inherent to school counselor training include:
  a. Foundation knowledge about schools, educational philosophy, ethics, preparation standards, models of school counseling practice, growth and development, diversity, and school emergency management planning;
  b. Counseling, prevention, and intervention for prevention of problems and maintenance of wellness through strengths-based approaches to maintain academic, career, and personal/social health;
  c. Diversity and advocacy as they relate to cultural, ethical, economic, legal, and political issues surrounding diversity and equity, as well as community, environmental, and institutional barriers and opportunities for students;
  d. Knowing the signs and symptoms of multiple negative events that impede the personal, social, career, and academic functioning of students, including various types of abuse;
  e. Knowing how to evaluate research, to conduct outcomes and program-related research, and ways to use data to inform decision making about the school counseling program;
  f. Understanding concepts, strategies, and practices designed to close the achievement gap, promote student academic success, and prevent dropout through understanding curriculum design, lesson development, classroom management, and differentiated instructional strategies for teaching counseling materials in the classroom;
  g. Ways to create, foster, and nurture healthy educational environments through family-school-community collaboration and through enhancing educational partnerships within various school professionals; and
  h. Leadership strategies that enhance professional functioning, programming, environmental improvement, and systemic change and growth.

  This edition of the book infuses these new competencies and standards into the foundation text that is written to help professional school counselors understand *why* what we do matters so much. We are not another "cog in the wheel of education"—we are critical to the learning process. Our efforts involve removing barriers to learning, enhancing resilience and strength, envisioning a brighter future, and helping kids see themselves as worthy, whole, and healthy—as you will see.

- The new ASCA School Counseling Competencies (which appeared in the July/August 2008 edition of *ASCA School Counselor,* pp. 64–73) provide great clarity about the competencies of professional school counselors. These Competencies itemize the various *knowledge, ability and skills,* and *attitudes* that school counselors need in order to:
  a. "plan, organize, implement and evaluate a comprehensive, development, results-based school counseling program that aligns with the ASCA National Model" (p. 64),
  b. "establish the foundations of a school counseling program" (p. 66),
  c. "deliver a school counseling program" (p. 68),
  d. "manage a school counseling program" (p. 70), and
  e. "monitor and evaluate the processes and results of a school counseling program" (p. 72).

  It is with these competencies in mind that we redesigned the Domains/Activities/Partners (DAP) Model and expanded our discussion of important topics such as accountability, collaboration, and advocacy (see figures below). It is our belief that most of the major topics for school counselor training are addressed in this book, and we have confidence that this book provides school counselors-in-training with content for reflection on each standard.

- A new chapter *Accountability, Action Research, and Data-Driven Outcomes* (Chapter 7) explains how data can drive decision making.
- A new chapter *The ASCA National Model* (Chapter 5) that reflects the model in action at the elementary, middle, and high school levels emphasizes application of the model for practice. Putting theory into practice is an ongoing challenge for new and evolving counseling professionals. Illustrating the implementation of the ASCA National Model provides school counselors in training and beyond with a visual and contextual glimpse of comprehensive school counseling in action.

DOMAINS/ACTIVITIES/PARTNERS MODEL

ACTIVITIES	DOMAINS					
	Academic Development	Career Development	Personal/Social Development			
Counseling	1a	1b	1c	5	6	7
Educating	2a	2b	2c	8	9	10
Consulting and Collaboration	3a	3b	3c	11	12	13
Leadership, Coordination, and Advocacy	4a	4b	4c	14	15	16
	Students			Parents and Caregivers	Colleagues in Schools	Colleagues in Community

PARTNERS IN THE PROCESS

DOMAINS/ACTIVITIES/PARTNERS MODEL DETAIL

Block	Description	Example
1a	Individual or group counseling with students about academic issues	Providing a group counseling experience in test anxiety
1b	Individual or group counseling with students about career issues	Providing individual counseling in career exploration
1c	Individual or group counseling with students about personal/social issues	Providing a group counseling experience for students who struggle with substance abuse
2a	Educating students in academic success issues	Providing a developmental curriculum lesson in study skills
2b	Educating students in career issues	Providing a developmental curriculum lesson in resume writing
2c	Educating students in personal/social issues	Providing a developmental curriculum lesson in healthy choices
3a	Consulting and collaborating with students about academic issues	Providing consultation to students who are working to establish a new award for academic excellence and collaborating with administration for the award
3b	Consulting and collaborating with students about career issues	Providing consultation to students who want to make application to specific colleges and collaborating with college counselors to provide information
3c	Consulting and collaborating with students about personal/social issues	Providing consultation to students about school policy on bullying and collaborating with teachers to promote a bully-free playground
4a	Leadership with students and advocacy on academic issues; Coordinating academic events with/for students	Advocacy with students to encourage all students to consider college and coordinating students in building a college file on the counseling website
4b	Leadership and advocacy with students on career issues, and coordinating career events with/for students	Leadership of students who want to petition the school board for more funds for technical education courses and coordinating a career fair for students
4c	Leadership with students and advocacy on personal/social issues; coordinating personal/social events with/for students	Leadership of students who are organizing a fundraising event for suicide awareness; coordinating the work of students to build a resource library on bullying
5	Counseling parents and caregivers	Short-term counseling with a grieving parent who has lost a child
6	Counseling with colleagues in the school	Short-term counseling with a colleague who has lost her teaching job
7	Counseling with colleagues in the community	Short-term counseling with a community colleague who is frustrated over budget cuts
8	Educating parents and caregivers	Providing a parent workshop on positive discipline
9	Educating colleagues in the school	Providing a workshop for school colleagues on psychopharmacology
10	Educating colleagues in the community	Providing a workshop for community counselors who work with your students on the school staffing process
11	Consulting and collaborating with parents and caregivers	Consulting with parents about student's academic progress
12	Consulting and collaborating with colleagues in the school	Consulting with teachers about classroom discipline issues with ADHD students

(Continued)

DOMAINS/ACTIVITIES/PARTNERS MODEL DETAIL (Continued)		
Block	Description	Example
13	Consulting and collaborating with colleagues in the community	Consulting with college admissions counselors on current graduation requirements
14	Leadership and advocacy with parents and caregivers; coordinating events for parents and caregivers	Leadership of a group of parents who are organizing a parent-teacher organization (PTO), or organizing a health fair for families of low-income kindergartners
15	Leadership, advocacy, and coordinating events with colleagues in the school	Leadership and advocacy for kids with teachers on issues of inclusion and bridging the achievement gap; coordinating a tour of a new college for the teachers in your school
16	Leadership and advocacy with colleagues in the community; collaborating with or coordinating events for colleagues in the community	Advocacy for your students with college admissions counselors in the area or coordinating a campus visit for students who are interested in a certain college or university

- The *Current and Emerging Trends* chapter (Chapter 13) is revised to emphasize the realities of school counseling today and explores topics such as crisis prevention and intervention, advocacy, changes in federal educational policies, and other relevant considerations. The field of counseling is advancing as new problems that affect children emerge. Although traditional therapy is not typically conducted in the schools, school counselors are nonetheless charged with helping to facilitate the academic, career, personal, and social development of all children, including those with mental health issues. In the continuum of prevention/intervention/treatment, school counselors must be educated in the ways that their work influences students, families, and entire school environments.
- *The Models of Delivery* chapter (Chapter 6) clarifies the differences between the DAP model and ASCA National Model and clearly articulates that the DAP model is one example of a Delivery System within the National Model.
- At least 50 percent of the case studies and exercises are new. The addition of new case scenarios will bring fresh issues and challenges for school counselors to consider during their education, training, and ongoing professional development.
- Expanded attention to multicultural and diversity issues in school counseling reflects the notion that as society and schools evolve demographically and the needs of students and their families increase across groups and populations, the importance of school counselors' multicultural competence likewise grows. Feedback from our readers suggested that the second edition provide greater emphasis on multiculturalism and diversity in school counseling. We hope the readers find the expansion in this area useful in their learning and development.
- The revised and updated *Instructor's Resource Manual with Test Bank* and *PowerPoint Presentation* (lecture outlines) parallels the revision to the main text. The *Instructor's Resource Manual* will present the crosswalk between the ASCA School Counselor Competencies, the CACREP Standards for School Counselors, as well as Application Activities and Portfolio Elements. We hope that instructors using the text will find the materials and information in the Instructor's Manual beneficial and useful to students' learning.

School counseling as a profession is at a crossroads. Old attitudes and old paradigms are still manifest in many schools, which makes new visions seem revolutionary. These new ideas are not radical; they are commonsense solutions to new problems. And they are practiced in many schools. The American School Counselor Association has articulated a coherent model for comprehensive school counseling programs, called the ASCA National Model®. This National Model is presented as the foundation of this book, and various delivery systems that align with the ASCA National Model are presented. One approach, the DAP model, will be used as the structure for exploring the activities of school counselors within the National Model. Both of these models are common sense, and they are attainable—but only when a critical mass of practitioners believes it is possible to change. That is the reason for this book—to promote a change in our profession and in our schools that will enable all students to be successful.

As with the first edition, this book is written with love—love for children, love for schools, and love for counselors-in-training, who we hope will benefit from the perspectives within. We are passionate about the need for all our children to have access to qualified counselors and quality comprehensive school counseling programs. In too many schools, the old answers to old problems are all that students are offered, and we find this troubling and tragic. It is troubling that some educational professionals have not bothered to keep up with new thinking in their chosen profession, and it is tragic that their lack of commitment will have an effect on the lives of their students. *Doing more of the same, the way we've always done it* is no longer working. It is our hope that this book and the vision of what school counseling *can be* will help generate new energy for the school counseling profession.

INSTRUCTOR SUPPLEMENTS

MyHelpingLab

MyHelpingLab is the online destination designed to help students in Counseling and Psychotherapy make the transition from their academic coursework to their professional practice. The online content consists of video clips of authentic practitioner-client sessions, video interviews with professionals in the field, an interactive case archive, and a licensing center with valuable information for students who are beginning their in-service career. For a demonstration of the website and to find out how to package student access to this website with your students' textbooks, go to www.myhelpinglab.com.

Instructor's Resource Manual with Test Bank

The Instructor's Resource Manual with Test Bank can be downloaded from our Instructor's Resource Center at www.pearsonhighered.com.

PowerPoint Presentation

The PowerPoint Presentation (lecture outlines) can be downloaded from our Instructor's Resource Center at www.pearsonhighered.com.

ACKNOWLEDGMENTS

Both the authors would like to gratefully acknowledge the contributions of several people to this book:

- To Charles Lindsey, University of Wisconsin, Oshkosh, who interviewed the counselors and wrote the information about Ford Elementary School, Tucson, Arizona
- To Phyllis Robertson, Western Carolina University, who interviewed the counselors and wrote the information about Sequoia Middle School, Fontana, California
- To Robert Urofsky, formerly of Clemson University and currently Director of CACREP, who interviewed the counselors and wrote the information about Wakefield High School, Raleigh, North Carolina. In addition, he contributed several sections for Chapter 13, *Emerging Issues for Schools and Students*, specifically, the content for "Educational Reform" and "Gender and Schools"
- To Bobbie Daul who helped organize and compile the references for this second edition

We would both like to thank our editor at Pearson: Meredith Fossel.

Finally, we are grateful to the reviewers of this book for their helpful suggestions: Charlene Alexander, Ball State University; Suzanne M. Dugger, Eastern Michigan University; Lynne Guiloot Miller, Kent State University; Shelley Jackson, Texas Women's University; and Rolla E. Lewis, California State University, East Bay.

—*Colette and Kelli*

No book is ever the sole intellectual property of the author or authors. There are countless people who serve as inspiration, whose thoughts influence the authors, whose presence makes the authors' lives more livable and more meaningful.

To acknowledge their many contributions, I would like to thank

- Mary Maples and Tom Harrison of the University of Nevada, Reno, who were there at the start of my journey in counseling and counselor education
- Norm Gysbers of Missouri, whose unflagging energy has transformed school counseling "services" into school counseling programs
- My former colleagues at the various programs where I was privileged to work (in chronological order): Emporia State University; the University of Wisconsin, Whitewater; the University of South Carolina; and The Ohio State University
- The many professionals in the American School Counselor Association, whose continuing work to shape and refine the profession reflect dedication, vision, and creativity
- All those whose works are cited in this book

I would be remiss if I did not give special acknowledgment to my colleague and coauthor. Kelli Saginak continues to be a constant source of inspiration, creativity, and energy. She helped me articulate and refine many of the ideas that are expressed in our first book, *School Counseling in the Secondary School: A Comprehensive Process and Program*, which now have provided the foundation for this second edition, *Comprehensive School Counseling Programs: K-12 Delivery Systems in Action*. Her faith in our collaboration on the first book provided fuel for its completion, and now I am blessed with this opportunity to collaborate with her again. She is a very special colleague indeed.

I would also like to thank my beloved family, who makes my life livable and meaningful.

—*C.D.*

Receiving the opportunity to develop a second edition of *School Counseling in the Secondary School: A Comprehensive Process and Program* is a privilege and honor. Writing the first edition was a dream. Writing the second edition has been beyond the imaginable. Many individuals were involved in my process of writing the second edition for which I am forever grateful. Simple words of "thanks" seem meager when compared to the assistance, support, encouragement, and occasional, yet gentle "kick in the pants" they gave to make this book possible.

Nonetheless, my most heartfelt thank you to

- Alan, Tom, Charles, Renae, Amney, and Paula, the Department of Professional Counseling at the University of Wisconsin, Oshkosh
- Kristen Nyholm, graduate assistant
- Bobbie Daul, graduate assistant, and *now* licensed professional school counselor
- Colette Dollarhide, patient, inspiring, and motivating coauthor, colleague, and friend
- Alan Saginak, husband, best friend, super dad, and lifelong companion

—*K.S.*

BRIEF CONTENTS

CONTENTS

1

The Profession of School Counseling

LEARNING OBJECTIVES

By the end of this chapter, you will

1. Have examined the professional and personal competencies and qualities that are needed by school counselors, including the qualities required for school counselors to be advocates for social justice and appreciation of diversity

2. Have examined and understand various philosophies of counseling so as to articulate your own philosophy of counseling

3. Have examined and understand the history and various philosophies of education so as to articulate your own philosophy of education

4. Have examined and understand the history and various philosophies of school counseling so as to articulate your own philosophy of comprehensive school counseling

5. Understand how the national association defines comprehensive school counseling programs

6. Understand the importance of the expectations and standards as defined by the national association for professional school counselors, including the professional organizations and credentials that are relevant to school counseling

CASE STUDY

The Best of Both Worlds?

Bobbi had been a teacher for 25 years in her inner-city school. In that time, she saw one of her best students lose a battle with cancer, two killed in a gang war in the neighborhood, and three die in a car crash the night before graduation. Fourteen left school after unplanned pregnancies, and far too few went to the college she encouraged everyone to attend. She felt that she had already given her best to her students, and now wanted to work with kids in a different way.

Today she was meeting with the faculty person in a school counseling graduate program to find out about their admissions process. It was her hope that she could continue working for the district in which her retirement fund was growing nicely.

"Tell me about why you want to become a school counselor, Bobbi," prompted the professor. "What can you bring to the students?"

"Well, I've been a teacher for many years. I know what students need and I know how to tell them to get to college. What more is there?"

"That's a start . . . What experience do you have with students' personal problems? For example, what would you say to a student who tells you she is thinking about suicide?"

"Goodness!" Bobbi said with a laugh. "I hope to goodness THAT never happens! That's ridiculous! When they have everything to live for, why would anyone think about suicide? I wouldn't even listen to such nonsense. I'll be too busy working with students to get them into the college-prep classes, getting information about colleges, getting scholarships for kids. I have listened to and cared about kids for 25 years, and I just don't know how much more I want to give . . ."

"But why do you want to be a school *counselor*?" pressed the professor.

"Because they have the best of all worlds! They work with kids AND they get to be in their offices all day, doing paperwork! I am tired of worrying about kids and their lives—I want to be able to relax in my last years before retirement."

CHALLENGE QUESTIONS

What do you see as the nature of the school counselor's job as Bobbi defines it? Are there limitations or problems with her definition? What are they? How do you think the principal and teachers would perceive the school counselor's job as Bobbi defines it? How do you think the parents of the students would perceive the school counselor's job as Bobbi defines it? What about the students—would they see registration, testing, and college recruitment as sufficient? Why or why not? What are YOUR reasons for coming to this profession? ▨

OVERVIEW OF THIS BOOK

This book is designed to provide you with a structure from which you will be able to design, implement, and evaluate your own comprehensive school counseling program for any educational level. Providing an overview of each level of education, this book is designed to meet the needs of today's new professional school counselors. For professionals, there is no such thing as a "cookbook" for programming; each activity of a school counselor is a creative application of best practices in the profession. This book presents readers with opportunities to reflect on why school counselors do what they do, how school counselors should function, and in what ways school counselors can create comprehensive programs to accomplish what they should. In this discussion, you, the reader, will be challenged to personalize your learning and to develop your own understanding of how you want to practice the art and science of comprehensive school counseling. You will also be challenged to examine your experiences with school counseling from your own K–12 education, to separate your prior understanding of "guidance" counseling from new visions of school counseling.

To help you do that, this book is written in the first person, directly to you, to connect with your heart and soul as well as your intellect. As you will see, the best school counselors are able to integrate and balance their *intellectual* understanding of school counseling, young people, and schools, with their empathic, *intuitive* understanding of learning, growth, and the conditions that facilitate healthy development. We need, therefore, to discuss both the professional skills and the personal qualities of effective school counselors.

REFLECTION MOMENT

Think about school counselors you have known in your K–12 education. Call to mind the image of the best school counselor you have known. How did that school counselor facilitate your learning, growth, and development? Now call to mind the image of the worst or least effective school counselor you have known, or recall stories of the worst school counselors others have known. How did that counselor, either actively or through a sort of "benign neglect," detract from the development of students? As you read this text, keep both the Super-Counselor and the Anti-Counselor in mind. Juxtapose those "role models" with your reading and reflection.

PROFESSIONAL COMPETENCIES AND PERSONAL QUALITIES OF SCHOOL COUNSELORS

In preparing to be effective school counselors, we must be prepared to demonstrate various *professional* skills and abilities and various *personal* qualities. Let's examine the professional skills first, looking at professional competencies and tests of professional competence. A good place to begin this exploration is with accreditation standards.

According to the 2009 Standards of the Council for Accreditation of Counseling and Related Educational Programs (CACREP) (Council for Accreditation of Counseling and Related Educational Programs, 2009), school counselors must be able to demonstrate significant professional knowledge and skills. These competencies comprise the essence of comprehensive school counseling. As you advance through your graduate program, you must remain aware of these competencies so that you can integrate them into your professional repertoire. In general, school counselors must be able to provide counseling through prevention and intervention efforts, advocate for diversity and equity in education, and use diverse and multicultural perspectives to help students to develop academically, vocationally, and personally. They must be able to understand the barriers to learning and be able to mitigate the causes and effects of these barriers, and they must be able to understand how to help students tap their strengths to support resilience. They must use data to improve student outcomes. They must design, implement, and evaluate comprehensive developmental school counseling programs, using a systems view of students' lives; design activities to help students attain academic, career, and personal/social competencies; and know legal and ethical standards and practices of counseling and school counseling. In addition, school counselors must be able to design and implement a school counseling calendar and must know strategies for integrating the school counseling program into the full school curriculum, strategies for seeking alternative funding, and ways to use technology in the comprehensive school counseling program.

The specific professional skills that school counselors must demonstrate include individual and small-group counseling; skills in individual, group, and classroom developmental curriculum; and skills in multicultural counseling issues. School counselors must understand and address conditions that impede the development and functioning of students, including assisting students with transitions, and techniques for prevention and early intervention of mental health challenges. School counselors partner with parents, families, and communities to promote the holistic development of all students using leadership, advocacy, and consultation strategies to enhance the school climate and promote effective teamwork across all systems.

As you can see, your skills in counseling, your understanding of young people, your learning about schools and families as systems, and your in-depth knowledge of comprehensive school counseling programs will all be required to attain the professional competencies of a school counselor. These skills are echoed in the American School Counselor Association (ASCA) School Counselor Competencies (American School Counselor Association, 2008b) and in the ASCA National Model (American School Counselor Association, 2005). This professional organization for school counselors represents the interests of professional school counselors in this country. The ASCA School Counselor Competencies (2008) and the CACREP Standards (2009) are addressed throughout the book.

External Tests of Professional Competencies

Currently, as accountability and outcomes assessments are increasingly emphasized, tests may be used in a number of ways to document professional attainment in school counseling. At the entry level, tests may be used to document the professional competencies of aspiring school counselors as a prerequisite for state licensure/certification as a school counselor. One example is the Praxis test in School Guidance and Counseling, published by Educational Testing Service (ETS). (More information on the test and the fees is available from their website at www.ets.org.) At the mid-professional level, a comprehensive documentation and skill reflection may be used to document the development of advanced or refined skills, as in the evaluation process for school counselors offered by the National Board for Professional Teaching Standards (NBPTS, 2006). This voluntary process of documentation of professional development enables school counselors to validate their professional attainment in the same way that teachers may choose to obtain their national professional teacher credential. (More information about the process, tests, and fees is available from their website at www.nbpts.org.)

In addition, many school counselors choose to become a National Certified Counselor (NCC) and a National Certified School Counselor (NCSC) through the National Board of Certified Counselors (NBCC). With the successful completion of the National Counselor Exam (NCE), payment of the required fees, and two years of full-time (or equivalent) experience, a school counselor may obtain the national school counselor certification status. (More information about the test and fees is available from the NBCC website at www.nbcc.org.) Being an NCSC is a laudable accomplishment; however, there is no current way to obtain school counseling licensure that is acceptable in all states. Each state defines its own requirements for licensure, and if you relocate to another state, you must contact that state's department of education to learn about requirements.

The desire of the profession to recognize and document professional competence is not born out of distrust of the counseling profession, but rather from a desire to ensure that only the best professionals work in our schools. This then begs the questions: How do schools define the "best" professionals? Do former teachers make better school counselors? Do all school counselors have to have teaching experience?

The perception has been (and in some states, continues to be) that former teachers make the best school counselors (Farwell, 1961; Fredrickson & Pippert, 1964; Hudson, 1961; Rochester & Cottingham, 1966; Tooker, 1957). Studies of the perceptions of administrators suggested that teaching experience was *not* a predictor of a counselor's success (Beale, 1995; Dilley, Foster, & Bowers, 1973; M. J. Olson & Allen, 1993). However, teachers themselves might still perceive counselors with teaching experience as more effective (Quarto, 1999). Rather than accept this conclusion fatalistically, school counselors should acknowledge that it is their expertise in academic issues that will establish their connection with the academic mission of the school and give them credibility within the school. Professional school counselors must develop this expertise for this reason.

Research suggests that teachers and nonteachers both face challenges in their professional development. In a study done by Peterson, Goodman, and Keller (2002), the challenges faced by interns who had not been teachers were compared with those faced by former teachers. They found that both groups faced challenges in the transition to becoming professional school counselors, but they faced different challenges. Teachers had to relinquish their old credibility (place in the school hierarchy), power (counselor role is less directive with fewer "perks" of prep time and breaks), and assumptions about education (need to learn about more age cohorts, need to learn how to negotiate for students' time out of class). Nonteachers had to learn about the school environment and culture, about the various stressors placed on all educators, and how to negotiate with teachers. The researchers' conclusions were that both teachers and nonteachers experienced a steep learning curve and had to make significant adjustments to fit in this new role.

Reflecting on the insights offered by Peterson et al. (2002), aspiring school counselors who do not have teaching experience could gain such experience through substitute teaching or working as a teacher's aide in the classroom. Additionally, aspiring school counselors who have been teachers might shadow a school counselor to learn more about the reality of the counselor's role, reflecting on the differences and similarities with the teacher's role.

REFLECTION MOMENT

Where are you in the development of your professional competencies? What do you need to do to develop and/or refine these competencies? (Ideas to attain these competencies include graduate coursework, attending workshops and/or courses on topics relevant to youth, reading the professional literature, joining professional associations, and attending professional conferences.) Are you preparing yourself now for the exams of professional licensure? If you are not currently a teacher, how will you develop your experience in the classroom? Substitute teaching can help tremendously to develop your empathy for teachers; it may be viewed positively by principals in the hiring process. Some states are moving toward the portfolio as documentation of the attainment of these professional competencies, and many principals and hiring committees in schools value portfolios as a way to evaluate the candidate's abilities. Consider starting a portfolio now to document your professional development. What would you insert into such a portfolio? Ideas for portfolio artifacts will be presented in the instructor's manual for this text.

PERSONAL QUALITIES OF A SCHOOL COUNSELOR

In addition to the professional competencies listed in the previous section, professional school counselors are also well served by personal qualities that enhance their ability to be effective. These personal qualities provide school counselors with passion for their work, energy, and resistance to burnout. An exhaustive list would be impractical, but some of the most notable qualities are provided in the following paragraphs.

Creativity and Imagination

Students, parents, teachers, administrators, and other professionals will bring questions, perspectives, issues, experiences, and challenges to us that we have never before encountered. Furthermore, as society changes over time, the needs of our students will change. We must have the creativity to respond to their various needs in an appropriate, ethical, and effective manner and the ability to imagine and design new approaches to old problems.

Flexibility

School counselors must be flexible in how they view their time, their activities, their students, and their students' needs over time. School counselors move from one activity to the next with little time to regroup, meaning that they need to move fluidly from one role to the next and from one activity to the next. Furthermore, school counselors address the needs of many different kinds of people (students, parents, teachers, administrators, school board members, and community members, to name a few), each with his or her own unique cultural, intellectual, emotional, and developmental signature. Highly flexible school counselors will be more fluid in response to those various needs. As needs change over time, flexible counselors will find themselves more comfortably adapting to new ways of looking at school situations.

Courage and Belief

School counselors address situations every day that challenge their courage and belief in others and in themselves, as well as in counseling itself. Daily we meet students engaging in dangerous risk taking, irate parents who don't understand why the counselor can't fix their child, and school board members who threaten to cut the counseling program because they don't understand what counselors do. Having courage in the face of these challenges comes from knowing that counselors make a difference, and that, while the larger pattern of meaning might not be immediately visible, all things do happen for a reason. This is not to say that school counselors must adopt a fatalistic worldview. A good example of courage and belief in the value of what we do is found in the story of the young girl who, when the tide was out, threw stranded starfish back into the sea. She knew she couldn't save them all, but she did what she could to make a difference for one at a time. She had the courage to try to help and the faith to know that it mattered. School counselors can't "save" any students, but they know they make a difference for those whose lives they touch. Knowing that school counselors make a difference in the lives of students is a powerful antidote to apathy and burnout.

Passion

Passion is not a word that is used in many counseling books. However, passion is a wonderful word that describes the feeling of profound commitment, the type of commitment and meaning described in existentialism (Frankl, 1984). The best counseling professionals are passionately and profoundly committed to clients, to the clients' best interests, and to their own personal and professional excellence. For counselors who work in the schools, this means that they are passionately committed to their students and to education. For some professionals, this might be a daunting challenge; if you've never worked in a school or around young people, how do you know you have that passion for kids and for schools? The answer is to find a way to work with kids in schools to see if there is "passion" in working with students in that setting.

Where do creativity, flexibility, courage, belief, and passion come from? After reading this book, thinking about the case studies in each chapter, reflecting on the questions posed throughout the text, and integrating the text with insights from your own life and experience, you will have the answers to that question.

REFLECTION MOMENT

How would you rate yourself on the preceding personal qualities? Reflect on the most important task or accomplishment of your life. In the completion of this task or accomplishment, how did each of the listed personal qualities manifest themselves? In what ways did you demonstrate your creativity, flexibility, courage, belief, and passion? How did each quality help you in your task or accomplishment? How would you document these qualities in a professional portfolio?

Commitment to Diversity and Social Justice

It is imperative that you are also willing to dedicate your professional energies to addressing the needs of our disenfranchised students and their families. Examples of disenfranchised students include those with gender diversity, cultural diversity, language diversity, religious diversity, learning and ability diversity, sexual orientation diversity, economic diversity, and many, many other constructs that delineate "normal" from what is perceived as "different," and often "less than." Each of these students brings unique gifts to the school community, and each student deserves the chance to learn, free of discrimination, disrespect, or intimidation. Such acts of exclusion may be individual or institutional, and it is our job as professional school counselors, as advocates for a culture of respect and inclusion, to address inequities when we see them on a personal and institutional level.

The reasons for this proactive perspective are based on both legislation and morality. While it is possible to debate the benefits and costs of legislation like No Child Left Behind (U.S. Department of Education, 2001), the intent behind the legislation was to "ensure that all children have a fair, equal, and significant opportunity to obtain a high-quality education" (U.S. Department of Education, Sec. 1001). According to the legislation, this purpose can be accomplished by "meeting the educational needs of low-achieving children in our Nation's highest-poverty schools, limited English proficient children, migratory children, children with disabilities, Indian children, neglected or delinquent children, and young children in need of reading assistance" to close "the achievement gap between high- and low-performing children, especially the achievement gaps between minority and nonminority students, and between disadvantaged children and their more advantaged peers" (U.S. Department of Education, Sec. 1001).

In addition to legislation, we have a higher calling based on the morals, ethics, and traditions rooted in our profession. Professional counselors in general and professional school counselors in particular are charged by the nature of the profession to be advocates for our clients. In the schools, this comes with being the guardians of school climate, in which we work to foster the conditions in which children can flourish. These conditions, as we will discuss in Chapter 2, are incongruent with discrimination, alienation, or exclusion.

REFLECTION MOMENT

For many of us, being an advocate for diverse others is a new role; for others, it is a familiar role. Before you can be an effective advocate, you must reflect on your own assumptions about others. This reflection goes deeper than just "what is your experience with persons of diversity"; it involves understanding what messages you have internalized about persons of diversity, persons of poverty, persons who have immigrated to this country, persons who live in very different ways than you were taught to live. Once you have attained self-awareness, the next task is to actively dispute those internalized messages that perpetuate exclusion, so that you are no longer blind to the myriad interpersonal and institutional ways that disrespect is shown to others who are powerless. Once you see how interpersonal and systemic oppression are manifest, you will empower yourself to address those examples of oppression. Start now to think about what you have been taught, and become aware of systems of oppression that you encounter in your journey to become a professional school counselor. As you further your training, you will learn skills of advocacy and empowerment.

PHILOSOPHIES OF COUNSELING

Imagine yourself outside on a cold, clear, moonless winter night, far from the lights of a city. When you look up, you see millions upon millions of points of light. How would you describe what you see?

Astronomers would talk about black holes, galaxies, and light years of distance; historians would contemplate how mariners navigated using the stars. Classical Greek scholars would describe the mythical origins of various constellations (Zimmerman, 1964), whereas astrologers would talk about those same constellations as related to personalities and birth signs. The Onondaga people would tell you that the stars are the Spiritual Beings of the Sky World (Wall & Arden, 1990). Poets would find divine inspiration; physicists would find inspiration from the possibility of discovering life somewhere else in the universe. And each of these persons would recommend that, to truly understand the points of light in the midnight sky, you need to study, as they have, in their philosophy, their discipline, and their culture.

We can use the example of how various people might describe the stars to understand how various people describe counseling. In this culture, it is generally agreed that the points of light in the sky are stars (as opposed to beliefs that the lights are millions of spacecraft, or evil demons, or campfires on the roof of the world). Similarly, we agree on certain qualities of a helping relationship that we call counseling (Brammer & McDonald, 1999; Corey, 2009; Hackney & Cormier, 1987; Hutchins & Cole, 1992; Kottler, 1991, 1993; Krumboltz & Thoresen, 1976; Meier & Davis, 1997; St. Clair, 1996). These qualities bind various theories of the counseling process into a constellation that we can map and navigate.

Counseling is a helping relationship, in which the primary focus is on the psychological healing, growth, change, and development of the client, with the goal that the client will be able to establish and maintain healthy relationships with self and others. The relationship is intentional, meaning that the counselor engages the client in activities that are thoughtfully chosen, with intentionality, for their potential to help the client heal, grow, and develop.

Counseling is a unique profession. It shares some common theoretical underpinnings with other disciplines such as psychology, psychiatry, and social work, but it is unique in its focus on developmental issues, interpersonal and intrapersonal relationships, and therapeutic milieu (F. J. Hanna & Bemak, 1997). As a profession, counseling is ethical, meaning helping behaviors are exhibited that adhere to moral, ethical, and professional guidelines as defined by the profession and the law (American Counseling Association, 2005; American School Counselor Association, 2004; Blackwell, Martin, & Scalia, 1994; Canon & Brown, 1985; Christopher, 1996; Corey, Corey, & Callanan, 1993; Herlihy & Corey, 1996; Huber & Baruth, 1987; Van Hoose & Kottler, 1988).

Counseling is both an art and a science, requiring intellect and intuition (Nystul, 1993). Intellectually, counselors need to understand various theories of change and the stages of development and maturation. Intuitively, counselors need to listen to the inner voice that whispers when to speak, when to be silent, when to intervene, and when to let go. Furthermore, to be ethical and effective, counselors must be sensitive to the values of the client's contexts of significance, as defined by the client and suggested by the client's culture, family system, gender, generation, abilities, health, and other diversity and values markers (Dollarhide & Haxton, 1999; Nichols & Schwartz, 1991; Sue & Sue, 1990).

Recall the various descriptions of the stars. Every time a counselor meets a client for the purpose of engaging in an intentional helping relationship, what will best facilitate change can be described in a variety of contexts based on theoretical orientation or philosophy. Some counselors would describe what they do in spiritual or intuitive terms, and other counselors would describe what they do in scientific or intellectual terms. Each theory describes change and those strategies that facilitate change: behavioral (Ellis, 1973), existential (Frankl, 1984), Rogerian (Carkhuff, 1987), Alderian (Dinkmeyer, Dinkmeyer, & Sperry, 1987), Reality Therapy (Glasser, 1965), and others.

How you see counseling is determined by your theoretical orientation, the lens of your philosophy. Whereas we can generally agree that the points of light in the night sky are indeed stars, descriptions of the stars vary widely. The profession of counseling generally agrees that the goal of counseling is to facilitate psychological healing, growth, change, and development to empower clients to experience healthy relationships with self and others. To be an effective counselor, you must have a method of bringing that healing, growth, change, and development to fruition with the client.

One useful way to conceptualize how to facilitate change with the client is to use the principles of learning, dealing with ambiguity, and reflective judgment. These are the same principles of learning described by Social Learning Theory (Bandura, 1977) and epistemological development (Dollarhide & Scully, 1999; Kegan, 1982; P. M. King & Kitchener, 1994; W. G. Perry, 1981). These theories constitute a description of counseling that includes a model of both the process of counseling and the process of change and growth, and using the language of learning, lends itself well to the educational setting.

In essence, both Social Learning Theory and counseling based on epistemological development begin at the same point—that counseling and learning are parallel constructs. If the point of counseling is to help clients learn how to develop and maintain healthy relationships with themselves and with others, then counseling strategies that use learning paradigms will be successful. In Social Learning Theory, that learning is the result of direct experiences, observation of models and vicarious experiences, and verbal persuasion (Bandura, 1977), which modifies the client's perception of self-efficacy and expectations of outcomes. From more positive perceptions of self-efficacy and more accurate expectations of outcomes, clients can choose healthier behaviors and attitudes. In counseling based on epistemological theory (Dollarhide & Scully, 1999), clients learn how to choose healthier behaviors and attitudes when they are allowed to encounter, struggle with, and resolve ambiguous life questions that have no clear answers. The counseling process entails allowing the client maximum freedom to explore existential questions, such as: What is the meaning of my life? What is my life direction? How do I establish healthy relationships? The counselor helps clients move from looking outside themselves for the answers to these questions, to looking within themselves for the answers, to ultimately, understanding how to look within for future answers.

REFLECTION MOMENT

What is your theory of counseling? How adaptable is that theory for use with children, adolescents, and young adults, recalling that verbal abilities and insight develop over time? How adaptable is that theory for use in the schools, considering that time for one-on-one counseling is often limited? What can you foresee as challenges in using your theory? What can you foresee as advantages in using your theory?

PHILOSOPHIES OF EDUCATION

To understand education, we must first understand the rationale for the design of educational experiences. These experiences are defined by the philosophy of education of state departments of education, superintendents, principals, parents, teachers, and district personnel. The style of the educational experience could be characterized by two basic camps on either side of a "pedagogical and philosophical divide" (L. Olson, 1999, p. 25): *progressive* versus *traditional* education. According to Olson, in its simplest form, traditional philosophy holds the primacy of subject matter, mastery of content, and preservation of the existing national cultural heritage. Progressive philosophy, on the other hand, has been characterized by primacy of the child, active learning, recognition of students' individual differences, the drive to relate school to real life, the "broad mission to address health, vocational, social and community issues" (p. 26), and an agenda that includes transforming the national cultural heritage. Each approach has significant problems as well as significant strengths.

What we see in schools today are the various combinations of a number of subtexts within the progressive movement, as well as the swing of the cultural values pendulum back and forth between progressive agendas and return-to-basics traditionalism (L. Olson, 1999). From 1873 through 1918, the pedagogical progressive movement was in vogue, emphasizing learning environments that were more informal and pupil oriented, and pedagogical approaches emphasizing active learning through meaningful, comprehensive projects and interdisciplinary teaching. The progressive view was that schools should fit the natural development and interests of children and should encourage self-expression through the arts—that children are "creative beings" who should be "nurtured, rather than disciplined, shaped, and controlled" (L. Olson, 1999, p. 26).

The next educational movement came into its own during the Great Depression and was called the social progressive, or social reconstructionist, movement. The educational reform agenda at this time included addressing the social ills created by laissez-faire capitalism and by the perceived inability of the family or community to provide for the basic needs of children. According to L. Olson, the legacy of this movement is manifested by professionals who bring health and other social services into the schools and in the move to involve schools in community issues (1999, p. 29).

The third strand in the progressive movement also has had long-reaching influence on education. Called the administrative progressive movement, this philosophy arose from the need to organize education to be more cost-effective in times of rapid growth in enrollment (L. Olson, 1999). It falls into the progressive philosophical camp because its proponents' rationale was the desire to help students adapt to society, rather than transforming society, by scientifically measuring students' abilities, grouping students based on ability, and then individualizing instruction by those groupings. Scientific testing and ability grouping (also known as *tracking*) were the legacies of this movement.

During the Korean War and the McCarthy era, progressive schools were criticized heavily for creating school environments without goals or educational standards, in which low performance was excused and from which students emerged without demonstrable social morals (L. Olson, 1999). Critics charged that without a solid academic foundation, students from disadvantaged backgrounds would remain disadvantaged and social inequities would be perpetuated. With the launch of Sputnik in 1957, progressive education was given less emphasis as the call arose for more math, science, and foreign-language education. Also known as academic rationalism (Eisner, 1985), this criticism evolved into the belief that the major purpose of schools is to "foster intellectual growth of the student in those subject matters most worthy of study" (p. 66).

In the 1960s and 1970s, the progressive movement enjoyed a temporary resurgence, with many notable contributions to the debate about pedagogy, including Bruner's article on discovery learning (Bruner, 1961). However, the pendulum swung back toward traditional educational approaches in the late 1970s with the back-to-basics movement, which brought minimum competency testing, increases in course requirements, and a reliance on standardized tests (O. S. Brown & Peterkin, 1999; L. Olson, 1999).

As you can see, the debate over educational reform has continued for over a century, with ongoing conversations about the best environments and pedagogy for educating young people. Current thinking about learning and the educational process has emerged from various disciplines. From psychology and counseling came Adlerian schools (Dubelle & Hoffman, 1984, 1986), the application of Reality Therapy to schools and adolescents (Glasser, 1965), and personality styles translated into education (Berens, 1988). The constructivist movement from psychology was brought into schools, holding that students need to construct meaning for themselves in order to learn. The implications of this educational strategy have been explored from kindergarten to college teaching (Palmer, 1998). From learning styles literature came various ways of conceptualizing learning: Gardner's eight intelligences (H. Gardner, 1983; Lazear, 1999), various models of learning preferences (Dunn & Griggs, 1988), and various ways of understanding thinking, including gender as a learning construct (Clinchy, 1989; Golderberger, Clinchy, Belenky, & Tarule, 1987).

Many educators have examined various pedagogical approaches espoused by different educational traditions and have opted to incorporate teaching methods that energize both teaching and learning. Cooperative learning, where students are encouraged to work together on projects (Gibbs, 1995; Slavin, 1994), and learning centers, where students move physically to a location in the room designed for group activities, have transformed many classrooms into highly mobile, interactive learning environments. New strategies for helping students acquire knowledge include manipulatives for math and abstract concepts, extensive creative writing strategies such as mind mapping and clustering (Rico, 1983), and socially reinforcing strategies such as Tribes (Gibbs, 1995), all of which are designed to assist students in the acquisition and retention of knowledge, skills, and attitudes.

Public schools of today, however varied they are in terms of philosophy, all answer to the federal and state governments in terms of accountability and funding. In 2001, the No Child Left Behind Act (NCLB) was passed, and the Elementary and Secondary Education (ESEA) Act was reauthorized (U.S. Department of Education, 2001). As we have already seen, the "primary purpose [is] the intent to close the achievement gap between disadvantaged students and their peers" (Dahir, 2004) through annual progress assessments in reading, math, and science (U.S. Department of Education, 2001). Information on the progress of individual students, plus information on the progress of the student body of the individual school, will go to parents to facilitate their decision making. Based on this progress, then, schools are evaluated and rated, and remediation efforts are outlined for schools that do not show satisfactory progress. This legislation has brought implications for the practice of comprehensive school counseling, as school counselors surveyed about their work with NCLB describe how it has created an impediment to their time with students (Dollarhide & Lemberger, 2006). For a full exploration of the issues of this legislation, visit the U.S. Department of Education's website at www.ed.gov/nclb and the National Education Association (NEA) website at www.nea.org/esea.

We will now leave our examination of philosophies of education, but we will see these philosophies reemerge in our next chapter, on schools.

REFLECTION MOMENT

Think back on the various classrooms you've been in. Have you ever been in a traditional classroom? How did it feel? Have you been in a more nontraditional, more informal classroom? How did that feel? In which class did you feel more motivated to learn?

Describe the purpose of education. What are schools supposed to do? What, exactly, is your philosophy of education? Based on that philosophy of education, describe what a school would look like that followed that philosophy. What would that school do? What would teachers do? What would counselors do?

PHILOSOPHIES OF SCHOOL COUNSELING

If you pick up a book, open it to the middle, and begin reading, you will get to the end of the book never truly understanding the relationships among the characters, the true depth of the story, or the journey of the main character. The drama and characters are seen in a smaller frame of time and understanding, becoming flattened and two-dimensional in the process. Without context, events, people, and places become oversimplified stereotypes, seen though a lens focused on current experience. However, if you read the entire book and spend time reflecting on the story, you would have the context within which to understand the ending, and you might better understand the insights within the story that could help you in your own life journey.

In the same way, it would be a mistake to attempt to understand school counseling as it is today in this country without also examining school counseling of yesterday. As you read these philosophies, think about how each is still evident in schools today, and how this "clash of the philosophies" can result in conflicting definitions of the job of the school counselor.

Guidance/Careers Emphasis

The development of school counseling is linked to the development of secondary education. Until the late 1800s in the United States, education was defined in terms of reading and writing, necessary to achieve pious living through reading the Bible. Education about life—learning about jobs, relationships, and duty to one's community—was seen primarily as the responsibility of the family (Hine, 1999). Organized education was more common at the elementary ages than in adolescence, because the work produced or wages earned by older children often was needed for family survival (Hine). However, with the advent of the Industrial Revolution, the nature of education changed.

The Industrial Revolution brought the need for higher-level skills. Awareness of these skills was articulated in the mission of the first high school in the country, Boston English High School, established in 1821 "to give a child an education that shall fit him [*sic*] for an active life, and shall serve as a foundation for eminence in his [*sic*] profession, whether Mercantile or Mechanic" (Hine, 1999, p. 144). But the social ills that came with the Industrial Revolution—poverty, ethnic slums, corruption, and moral decay—generated awareness of the power of the schools as a tool for social remedies (L. Olson, 1999; Schmidt, 1999) that fueled the birth of the school counseling profession in the early 1900s.

Two persons are primarily credited with the emergence of school counseling, then known as vocational guidance. Jesse B. Davis, principal of a high school in Grand Rapids, Michigan, in 1907, began a program in his school to include guidance lessons in English composition classes to "help students develop character, avoid problem behaviors, and relate vocational interests to curriculum subjects" (Schmidt, 1999, p. 7). A year later, Frank Parsons, who is credited as the "father of guidance," issued a report of his Vocational Bureau, in which the term "vocational guidance" first appeared. In this report, Parsons called for vocational guidance to be provided by "trained experts" and offered in all public schools (Gysbers & Henderson, 2000, p. 4). In response, Boston elementary and secondary schools hired vocational counselors from their teaching staff and charged them, in addition to their regular teaching duties, with the following partial list of responsibilities:

1. To gather and maintain occupational information, including making arrangements with local librarians for the shelving of books about vocations
2. To arrange and present lessons in occupations and encourage teachers to connect their curriculum to vocations
3. To interview pupils "who are failing, attempt to find the reason, and suggest a remedy"
4. To use cumulative records and intelligence tests when advising children
5. To encourage students to remain in school
6. To "recommend conferences with parents of children who are failing or leaving school" (Gysbers & Henderson, 2000, p. 5)

It is easy to see the connection between these duties and the duties of current professionals in school counseling. For the nascent profession, this was the genesis of professional identity, training, and definition. Vocational guidance in schools grew around the country (Gysbers & Henderson, 2000). The emphasis of the secondary school as preparation for vocations, college attendance, and productive citizenship emerged as the rallying point for the passage of compulsory attendance legislation. This served to maintain focus on careers as the outcome of schooling and directive guidance as the activity by which those outcomes were guaranteed (S. B. Baker, 2000). Many school administrators, teachers, and counselors still hold these beliefs.

Further reinforcing the directive guidance function of school counselors was the need to classify young men into various activities within the military during World Wars I and II. Educational and vocational psychometrics, or mental measurement, grew in importance with the development, widespread validation, and acceptance of group-administered intelligence tests (S. B. Baker, 2000). "Psychometrics offered school guidance not only the tools for assessment but also corresponding respectability because the tools seemed so precise and scientific" (p. 4). Bolstered by the administrative progressive movement (L. Olson, 1999) discussed earlier, advising students on ways to reach their potential by identifying their limitations became the cement that hard-set advisement and directive guidance as the role of counselors during the 1930s and 1940s. Called "trait and factor" guidance, this approach was characterized by testing students' intelligence, interests, and abilities, then using that information to advise them about vocational and adjustment issues (S. B. Baker, 2000).

Challenged as too narrow, too restrictive, and inadequate to address students' developmental issues, emphasis on test-and-tell, directive guidance waned in popularity during the late 1940s and 1950s as the mental health emphasis emerged.

Mental Health Emphasis

As criticism mounted concerning the emphasis on "guidance" and "advisement," conversations were occurring in the educational and psychological arenas that would culminate in the second direction of school counseling. The writings of John Dewey in the 1920s caused many education professionals to reexamine their philosophy based on a more student-centered, progressive view of the role of education (L. Olson, 1999), and the writings of Carl Rogers in the 1940s and 1950s caused many mental health professionals to reexamine their philosophy based on a more holistic view of the relationship between guidance counselors and students (Schmidt, 1999). According to Schmidt, "this focus moved the profession away from the counselor-centered perspectives of earlier times and emphasized a growth-oriented counseling relationship as opposed to an informational and problem-solving one" (p. 11). At this time, mental health services and counseling became "the central secondary school guidance function, with all other functions in supplementary roles" (S. B. Baker, 2000, p. 6). As you can see, school counseling was practiced only in high schools; it had not yet reached the middle school or elementary schools.

The agenda of the social progressive movement in education was welcome, because it gave counselors greater awareness of their role in facilitating the development of all students in terms of their social, emotional, educational, and vocational needs. The emphasis on the role of the counselor as the mental health provider of the school was incorporated into the training of many school counselors during the 1950s and 1960s—when the National Defense Education Act of 1958 was funding the training of record numbers of school counselors (S. B. Baker, 2000, p. 6). It is the legacy of the mental health emphasis of this era that many counselors still hold the view that their primary role is to be the mental health provider for the school (S. L. Smith & Archer, 2000). However, in the 1960s, conversations emerged in the professional counseling literature challenging the focus of counselors on the limited number of students who needed crisis counseling and therapeutic services (S. B. Baker, 2000; Schmidt, 1999). In this reevaluation of the profession, and in discussions about the emerging role of middle school and elementary school counselors, there was increased advocacy for "developmental rather than remedial goals for elementary and secondary school guidance" (S. B. Baker, 2000, p. 8), leading to the third wave in defining what school counselors do: developmental guidance.

Developmental Guidance

During the late 1960s and through the 1970s, school counselors became increasingly aware of the need to prevent problems by providing educational activities that promote healthy adjustment, social awareness, interpersonal problem solving, and vocational development (Wittmer, 2000), moving school counseling solidly into elementary and middle schools. And if the foundation unit of education is the classroom, what better venue to provide this preventative programming than in the classroom itself? As Wittmer stated, "The question becomes, who does the most good? The school counselor who works with 25 children (using a large group guidance approach) in a six-week, one hour per week unit on improving self-concept, or the school counselor who spends six hours with one child in crisis? Although the latter is important (and may even be more fun for some), it is obvious that the school counselor using the former approach meets the needs of more students and does much more good in the long run" (Wittmer, 2000, pp. 4–5).

While some authors use the term "developmental guidance" to refer to all activities of a school counselor (Gysbers & Henderson, 2000), other authors cite the terms "guidance" and "development" as archaic (S. B. Baker, 2000). According to Baker, the term "developmental guidance" is limited, denoting a focus on classroom interventions more often associated with elementary school counseling programs. Furthermore, the strong association between the term "guidance" and the role of the counselor (Schmidt, 1999) suggests that the responsibility for guiding young people is the sole purview of the counselor, a fallacy that continues to trap counselors in inappropriately directive relationships with students (such as overreliance on test results) and in inappropriate administrative tasks (such as enrollment management). Hoyt (1993) also found that, when surveyed, American School Counselors Association leaders expressed the preference for the term "counseling" rather than "guidance" when referring to the program offered by the school counselor.

> **REFLECTION MOMENT**
>
> Take a moment and reflect on your experience as a student interacting with your school counselor. Based on what that person did and said, can you identify her or his philosophy of school counseling? Did that person adopt an "expert" stance, provide directive guidance, and focus more on your career development than on your personal, social, or academic development? Or did that person assume a more therapeutic posture toward you, focusing more on your mental health? Did your school counselor(s) come to the classroom to present lessons and facilitate discussions about personal adjustment, academic success, or career development? Can you see a connection between when a counselor was trained in school counseling and his or her philosophy of school counseling?

Comprehensive School Counseling Programs (CSCP)

So, what's the correct way of defining school counseling? There is no one absolute way of defining school counseling. What we see in today's school counseling is a field manifesting a "number of themes, all having varying degrees of influence across training programs and among counselors. The newer activist, developmental, service-oriented, and eclectic themes mixed with remnants of the trait and factor, adjustment, administrative, and counseling themes that were [are] still very much alive" (S. B. Baker, 2000, p. 9).

However, in the mix of various philosophies, it is possible to articulate a path that outlines what school counselors need to be able to know, feel, and demonstrate. It is called "comprehensive school counseling" (or developmental school counseling) (Paisley & Hubbard, 1994; Paisley & Peace, 1995), and it brings together the various roles and responsibilities with which school counselors are charged. In this book, we will use the National Model from ASCA, the professional association of school counselors, as our template for examining comprehensive school counseling programs (CSCPs). Let's first explore the documents that ASCA developed to describe what school counselors do (Role Statement) and to describe appropriate outcomes of comprehensive school counseling programs (the National Standards). Next, we will examine the ASCA School Counselor Competencies, then we will look briefly at the ASCA National Model.

ASCA ROLE STATEMENT AND NATIONAL STANDARDS   School counselors have joined together in a national association, the American School Counselor Association (ASCA), which has defined the role of the professional school counselor:

> Professional school counselors are certified/licensed educators with a minimum of a master's degree in school counseling making them uniquely qualified to address all students' academic, personal/social and career development needs by designing, implementing, evaluating and enhancing a comprehensive school counseling program that promotes and enhances student success . . . Through leadership, advocacy and collaboration, professional school counselors promote equity and access to rigorous educational experiences for all students. Professional school counselors support a safe learning environment and work to safeguard the human rights of all members of the school community (Sandhu, 2000), and address the needs of all students through culturally relevant prevention and intervention programs that are a part of a comprehensive school counseling program (Lee, 2001). (American School Counselor Association, 2009; par. 1–2)

ASCA (2009) goes on to outline what the professional school counselor does in a comprehensive school counseling program that follows the ASCA National Model (2005). As you will see in Chapter 5, a professional school counselor articulates the philosophy and mission of the program and implements a comprehensive delivery system. This delivery system includes teaching life skills and prevention programming in classes, providing individual planning, and intervention counseling for individuals and groups. These activities are supported through management agreements and collaborative efforts, and then reflected in the outcomes reporting process. According to the ASCA Role Statements, "Professional school counselors develop and implement data/needs-driven, standards-based and research-supported programs, and engage in continuous program evaluation activities. They also create results reports that demonstrate immediate, intermediate, and long-range effectiveness of comprehensive school counseling programs. Professional school counselors analyze outcome data to guide future action and improve future results for all students" (ASCA, 2009, par. 8). Research has linked these "future results" with overall school success.

What is school success? The National Standards for Student Academic, Career, and Personal/Social Development present guidelines for school counseling programs across the country (ASCA, 2005; Campbell & Dahir, 1997). These standards outline goals for school counseling programs, establish school counseling as essential and integral to the educational mission of all schools, promote access by all students, and describe the key competencies all students should be able to demonstrate by the end of their K–12 experience.

As summarized in Figure 1.1, the National Standards highlight three content areas that summarize the developmental themes of schools. There are reasons behind the order in which these content areas are presented. Competencies in academic development, as the primary mission of education, confirm that school counselors are integral to the mission of the school and district in which the counselor functions. Competencies in career development, the transition from school to contributing member of society, represent outcomes of education as defined by society. Competencies in personal and social development answer the need for young people to function in an informed citizenry addressing the challenges of modern living. This holistic approach to students provides the caring environment critical for development and has been linked to academic and personal success of students.

I. Academic Development

Standard A: Students will acquire the attitudes, knowledge, and skills that contribute to effective learning in school and across the life span.

Standard B: Students will complete school with the academic preparation essential to choose from a wide range of substantial postsecondary options, including college.

Standard C: Students will understand the relationship of academics to the world of work, and to life at home and in the community.

II. Career Development

Standard A: Students will acquire the skills to investigate the world of work in relation to knowledge of self and to make informed career decisions.

Standard B: Students will employ strategies to achieve future career success and satisfaction.

Standard C: Students will understand the relationship among personal qualities, education and training, and the world of work.

III. Personal/Social Development

Standard A: Students will acquire the attitudes, knowledge, and interpersonal skills to help them understand and respect self and others.

Standard B: Students will make decisions, set goals, and take necessary action to achieve goals.

Standard C: Students will understand safety and survival skills.

FIGURE 1.1 Summary: National Standards for Student Academic, Career, and Personal/Social Development

Each standard is accompanied by student competencies that define the standard. For example, Standard A under Academic Development states that "students will acquire the attitudes, knowledge, and skills that contribute to effective learning in school and across the life span." This standard involves three global competencies: improve academic self-concept, acquire skills for improving learning, and achieve school success. Each global competency is then further specified in language that allows counselors to evaluate the success of their students and their program in terms of attaining that competency.

ASCA SCHOOL COUNSELOR COMPETENCIES   In 2008, ASCA outlined the competencies that school counselors are expected to demonstrate, delineated in terms of the Knowledge, Abilities and Skills, and Attitudes required for that competency. The competencies are:

1. Plan, organize, implement, and evaluate a comprehensive, developmental, results-based school counseling program that aligns with the ASCA National Model.
2. Establish the foundations of a school counseling program aligning with the ASCA National Model.
3. Deliver a school counseling program aligning with the ASCA National Model.
4. Manage a school counseling program aligning with the ASCA National Model.
5. Monitor and evaluate the processes and results of a school counseling program aligning with the ASCA National Model.

While the above list might appear simple to demonstrate, the knowledge, skills, and attitudes required for each competency are extensive. During your training, you may find yourself challenged to attain mastery in all competencies—but that is why professional school counselors have attained a master's degree. Take advantage of every opportunity to expand your skills.

ASCA NATIONAL MODEL   In 2003, ASCA published its National Model (American School Counselor Association, 2005) as a means of helping practicing school counselors design and implement a comprehensive school counseling program (CSCP). This model consists of four interrelated components: foundation, delivery systems, management systems, and accountability. Each of these activities requires leadership, advocacy and collaboration, which will lead to systemic change. A summary of each of these components follows; a complete description of the National Model is explored in Chapter 5.

1. The Foundation of the model consists of beliefs and philosophy, a mission statement, and a reminder that the ASCA National Standards are the competencies that all students should develop as a result of being in a school with a comprehensive school counseling program (CSCP).
2. The delivery system consists of (a) the guidance curriculum designed to provide developmentally appropriate lessons to help students achieve the competencies; (b) individual student planning for academic goals and future plans; (c) responsive services of counseling, consultation, referral, and peer helping; and (d) system support of program management and administration.
3. The management system consists of agreements between the principal and professional counselor outlining how the counselor's time will be allocated, an advisory council, the use of data, action plans, appropriate use of time, and the use of calendars to inform everyone of the program.
4. Accountability refers to results reporting, performance standards for the professional school counselor, and a program audit that collects information about the program to guide future action.

These documents—the Role Statement, the National Standards, the School Counselor Competencies, and the National Model—outline a system of program expectations, program delivery, student competencies, and counselor competencies by which school counselors can prioritize, design, and evaluate the counseling activities in the school. As a statement of national scope, it is important that every counselor become familiar with these documents, and it is for this reason that these documents form the foundation of this book. It is vital that school counselors are knowledgeable about how the profession defines its role and the standards of effective programs and then apply those standards to design, implement, and evaluate the CSCP in their schools and districts.

CASE STUDY REVISITED

Integration

Now that you have read this chapter, go back and reread the Case Study. Reflect on and answer the following questions:

1. What is Bobbi's perception of education? Of school counseling? If you were to assign her to a philosophy of school counseling, which one would it be?
2. Would you want to work with someone like Bobbi as a school counseling colleague? Why or why not?
3. What insights can you develop relative to the way that teachers might perceive the work of the school counselor? ■

Suggested Readings

American School Counselor Association (2009). *The role of the professional school counselor.* Alexandria, VA: Author. Retrieved November 26, 2010 from http://www.schoolcounselor .org/content.asp?pl=325&sl=133&contentid=240. This resource, provided by ASCA, outlines the role and expectations of professional school counselors.

American School Counselor Association (2005). *The ASCA National Model: A framework for school counseling programs* (2nd ed.). Alexandria, VA: Author. This resource outlines the National Model with performance expectations and electronic sample forms that will make the transition to the National Model feasible for every school. This is the seminal statement from the profession about the ideal structure of school counseling programs.

Campbell, C. A., & Dahir, C. A. (1997). *Sharing the vision: The national standards for school counseling programs.* Alexandria, VA: American School Counselor Association. Every school counselor must be aware of the national standards for counseling programs and should use these standards in designing their programs.

Dahir, C. A., Sheldon, C. B., & Valiga, M. J. (1998). *Vision into action: Implementing the national standards for school counseling programs.* Alexandria, VA: American School

Counselor Association. The companion resource for the implementation of the national standards.

Gysbers, N. C., & Henderson, P. (2000). *Developing and managing your school guidance program* (3rd ed.). Alexandria, VA: American Counseling Association. This resource addresses the programmatic concerns of initiating change in the school system to move toward coherent school counseling programs.

Hahn, T. N. (1991). *Peace is every step.* New York: Bantam; Hoff, B. (1982). *The Tao of Pooh.* New York: Penguin; Hoff, B. (1982). *The Te of Piglet.* New York: Penguin. These three resources are recommended to help the reader to think outside the box of linear, Western society, with the hope that reflection on these readings will increase flexibility, creativity, and access to intuition.

McWhirter, J. J., McWhirter, B. T., McWhirter, A. M., & McWhirter, E. H. (1998). *At-risk youth: A comprehensive response for counselors, teachers, psychologists, and human service professionals.* Pacific Grove, CA: Brooks/Cole. A must-read for school counselors, this book provides wonderful insights about risk factors, issues facing youth, and issues facing educational professionals who work with youth.

2

Schools: Social Institutions

LEARNING OBJECTIVES

By the end of this chapter, you will

1. Be able to define and describe an effective school

2. Be able to identify the qualities of effective schools

3. Be able to describe the qualities of ineffective schools and those conditions that lead to unhealthy environments

4. Be able to define and describe a developmentally appropriate school

5. Be able to identify the qualities of developmentally appropriate educational programs

6. Be able to identify healthy relationships with colleagues in a healthy school system, understanding the role of the school

counselor relative to other professional and support personnel in the school

7. Understand the rationale for leadership by the school counselor to address closing the achievement gap, promoting student success, and preventing dropout behaviors

8. Understand the terms "participatory leadership" and "distributed leadership" and how this relates to healthy relationships within schools

9. Understand the need to monitor achievement, equity, and access to resources using outcomes-research findings and best practices from professional literature

CASE STUDY

Bullied to Death?

Eleana Sobol was a high school counselor who was new to the field. She felt a calling to the school environment and wanted to be source of hope and inspiration to students. As she got to know the teachers and students in her new school, someone told her about a sophomore named Cody who was exhibiting all the behaviors of depression and was engaging in self-mutilation. At first, the sight of the scars on Cody's arms revolted Eleana, but as she got to know Cody, she saw a side of the school that she had not seen before.

Eleana invited Cody to share experiences from his day-to-day life in the school, and learned that Cody was the regular target of several school bullies—some of whom appeared to be teachers. An artistic and sensitive student,

Cody's primary source of pain was the isolation and ridicule he experienced every day in the classroom, from the derision of peers to abusive treatment from several teachers. When describing his interaction with fellow students, Cody reported being physically pushed and slapped in the halls between classes, being laughed at in class, and having his things stolen. He described teachers who used sarcasm, used him as an example of stupidity, and gave his work lower grades than comparable work of other students. Eleana was shocked to hear about how Cody's two years in high school had left him with emotional and physical scars.

Eleana followed all the reporting policies of the school in ensuring Cody was safe, and then decided to talk with the principal about her concerns about bullying in the school. The principal was not impressed with Cody's story, saying, "Ms. Sobol, you don't take his stories *seriously*, do you? It is true that not every teacher will like every student, but that's life. Cody's going to have to learn how to work with people who don't coddle him *someday*, and he might as well begin now. If you ask me, you need to treat *him*, because you can't change the school."

CHALLENGE QUESTIONS

How do you feel about the principal's comments to Eleana? Is it possible to change a school? If it is possible, would you want to? What would you do if you were Eleana? What would you do if you were the principal? What are some of the possible interventions that could help the student? If things do not change for this student, what do you see as some of the possible outcomes? ■

WHAT MAKES EFFECTIVE SCHOOLS?

In the previous chapter, you had a chance to think about your philosophy of education. What is the purpose of education, and how well do schools accomplish their purpose? The research into effective schools suggests some ways to think about how educational philosophy and implementation of education policies can help students learn content and acquire skills to become productive, contributing adults in this society.

Effective Schools

Occasionally, educators want to infuse contemporary learning strategies into their schools and classrooms, only to find that parents, caregivers, or school board members have different educational philosophies—different ideas of how learning experiences should be designed (A. C. Lewis, 1994). One of our responsibilities as counselors involves helping all stakeholders understand youth development, the complementary processes of learning and teaching, and the qualities of excellent schools. Understanding excellent schools can only come from understanding how schools function as organizational entities and understanding what qualities culminate in effective educational environments (Bluestein, 2001; Sullivan & Shulman, 2005).

Professionals in schools today face tremendous expectations as well as tremendous challenges. Usually, school districts are governed by an elected body from the community, which makes all policy, financial, and educational decisions (Simon, 1999). Funding for schools comes primarily from state and local taxes; taxes paid by the community or communities in the school district for school support must be approved by the voters in that community or communities (Newman, 1994). School district board members are accountable to the voters for expenditures and outcomes for all school programs.

Education professionals are accountable to the parents/guardians of students and to the school board. With certain variations, professionals in schools are expected to

- Interact positively with the community
- Maintain high educational expectations
- Maintain test scores in crucial academic areas
- Provide special assistance to students with special physical, academic, and emotional needs
- Provide early screening and intervention for young students entering kindergarten
- Provide transportation to and from the school to within a reasonable and safe distance from the student's residence

- Communicate with parents/guardians/caregivers regularly
- Respond to parents' and caregivers' concerns
- Provide a safe, exciting, fun, invigorating learning environment
- Provide language assistance as needed
- Provide limited health services and screening for problems
- Provide limited mental health services and screening for problems
- Instill respect for the traditions and symbols of the country, state, and/or community
- Instill core values that transcend cultures, such as honesty, caring, respect, responsibility, and justice
- Provide education in fundamental behaviors such as problem solving, friendship building, and decision making
- Other requirements as determined by local school boards, state law, federal mandate, the community, and society as a whole

If these expectations are not met, it is easy to blame others. Parents and caregivers blame teachers, teachers blame parents and schools, schools blame the school board, the school board blames the community and parents, and everyone blames society, movies, music, and the media. If it takes a village to raise a child, then we are all accountable for the education our young people receive in our schools. Communities must be willing to fund excellent schools; schools must be willing to listen to the needs of the students, families, and the community; and parents and caregivers must be willing to participate in the educational processes of all children. Counselors can be a crucial link in the chain of excellence and achievement, facilitating communication and understanding among all stakeholders in the process of educating young people.

A broad synthesis of research, incorporating ideas emerging from youth development and resiliency literature, protective factors research, and developmental assets literature, yields eight outcomes desired by society for young people. According to the Center for Mental Health in Schools at UCLA's School Mental Health Project (SMHP, 1999; p. 5), these eight outcomes are

1. Academics, which includes connection to and commitment to learning, motivation for learning and self-learning, and feelings of academic competence
2. Healthy and safe behavior, which includes the ability to make good decisions about how to establish and maintain good physical health and a healthy lifestyle, solve interpersonal conflicts and problems as a means of managing stress, delay gratification, and resist impulses and unhealthy peer/social pressures
3. Social-emotional functioning, which includes the ability to relate interpersonally in a culturally appropriate manner; understand, express, and manage emotions; experience generally positive feelings about oneself, others, and the world; experience a sense of social and emotional competence and connection with others; and experience a sense of hope for the future
4. Communication, which includes basic communication skills and the ability to understand social cues and the perspectives of others
5. Character/values, which includes personal, social, and civic responsibility, honesty and integrity, and the ability to monitor one's own choices to maintain congruence between values and behaviors
6. Self-direction, which describes the ability to evaluate life situations and make effective long-term decisions that are appropriately autonomous and self-responsible
7. Vocational and other adult roles, which include those skills and attitudes that facilitate locating, securing, and maintaining employment, community involvement, intimate adult relationships, and other adult roles
8. Recreational and enrichment pursuits, which include engaging in behaviors and activities that improve quality of life, permit expression of creativity, and reduce stress

Given these eight outcomes as desired for young people, an effective school would provide the environment in which progress toward these outcomes is evident. According to

Travers, Elliott, and Kratochwill (1993), effective schools are characterized by connections among staff, teachers, students, and caregivers; consistently fair decision making and discipline; an environment of encouragement for academic and personal achievement; teaching that blends both the basics and methods that facilitate discovery; realistic but high expectations for all; and high accountability for learning (p. 16). In examining learning, the role of stress and fear clearly alter the way the brain processes information (Bluestein, 2001; National Research Council, 2000) and the issues of academic safety, emotional safety, social safety, behavioral safety, and physical safety cannot be denied (Bluestein, 2001). In an effective school setting, two principles emerge of primary importance: *a caring environment* and an *emphasis on holistic development* (SMHP, 1999, p. 5).

These two conditions are the result of collaborative efforts among schools, communities, and caregivers to provide a school environment in which (1) young people feel welcome and respected; (2) there are opportunities to make connections with caring adults and peers; (3) information and counseling are provided to help them determine what it means to care for self and others; and (4) opportunities and expectations are present that encourage them to contribute to the community through service and advocacy (Pittman, n.d.). These caring conditions and holistic factors do not appear magically; they are the result of hard work, determination, and the focus of the school and community on those elements that nurture young people. Moreover, research is clear that when these *support* elements are in place, there are substantial gains in *academic* achievement (Bluestein, 2001; Lickona & Davidson, 2005; Starkman, Scales, & Roberts, 1999). Counselors are instrumental in advocating for environments of respect and caring, and counselors share enormous responsibility for the holistic development of students. How do they accomplish this? By understanding schools: what makes them work and ways they fail.

REFLECTION MOMENT

What was the educational environment in which you grew up? What was the purpose you ascribed to education when you were a K–12 student? Torture? Play? Can you separate out those elements of school that nurtured you and those that did not to help you?

How Do We Know That a School Is Effective?

Imagine that you are in a school. What do you see around you? What do you smell, hear, see? Take a moment to experience that school.

When people imagine an elementary school, the images typically include the sound of young people's voices, laughter, bright colors of clothes and bulletin boards, and the smell of peanut butter, apples, and crayons. The emotions generated by these images are usually positive. In contrast, when asked to imagine a high school, the images are darker, more somber, less vibrant. Typical responses include crowded hallways, darker colors, angry voices, slamming lockers, a dusty-smoky smell. Why? Secondary school students are no less vibrant, no less creative, no less happy than elementary students are—or are they?

To understand school counseling, we must understand both the promise of effective schools and the reality of dehumanizing schools. We must be able to understand what contributes to, and what impedes, the development of our students. Because counselors are charged with facilitating the academic, career, and personal/social development of students, it is essential that counselors be willing to confront, as appropriate, those elements that impede students' development. Conversely, counselors need to empower themselves to advocate for those elements that contribute to students' development. You will be able to understand why those images of high school darken in comparison to elementary school if you understand the extent to which schools respond to the developmental needs of students.

School counselors see the full spectrum of students, with a wide range of needs. Some students seem to sail through school. They love going to school, they love learning, and they feel energized by their teachers, their peers, the subjects they study. Their lives are blessed with strong families, strong career goals, and strong social skills. For these students, the school counselor may be the person who challenges them to stretch, encourages their potential, and cheerleads for them in academics and beyond. However, such students are rare.

Other students do not fare well, struggling with social skills, academic skills, or life challenges. Many young people's physical, social, or emotional needs may not always be met. Nevertheless, many education professionals still struggle with why students fail. Don't all schools meet the educational needs of students? Just as family systems research has found that the way you were parented can determine, largely, the way you will parent, so it is with education. The way we were schooled, if unquestioned, translates into the way we school our young people.

The problem is that not everyone learns the same way. If you are one of those unfortunate students whose learning needs do not match what the school can provide, school after school, teacher after teacher, year after year, failure after failure, you learn one thing. You might not learn math, or reading, or history, but you will learn one lesson very well—that you do not belong in school, that you are stupid, useless, worthless, a waste of time for everyone. So you find ways to avoid being there, or ways to avoid facing yet another failure, or ways to make everyone think you know when you do not. Then perhaps you will find ways to make other people pay for making you feel bad, ways to settle the score a little, ways to make others wish they were not there, either.

Does this sound familiar? It should. We read about these students in the newspapers every day. Their pain becomes more obvious as time passes, their spirits more subdued each year as their self-esteem wears down. The person who started out as an energetic, bubbly kindergartner has come to high school expecting to fail.

What can counselors do to help? The answer may be found in the literature about developmentally appropriate schools, but to understand what is developmentally appropriate, let us first look at what dehumanizing schools look like.

DEHUMANIZING SCHOOLS   Schools, as a reflection of the society in which they were created, evolved ways of dealing with children based on models used in other sectors of society—namely, business. The model of efficiency of the 1860s through the 1930s was the factory, and schools evolved classrooms where everyone did the same thing at the same time (sit in rows, no talking, eyes forward) (N. Perry, 1992; Sheldon & Biddle, 1998), and everyone was expected to progress at the same rate based on chronological age (Morrison, 1997). The expressed goals of schooling, as described in the Cardinal Principles of Secondary Education written in 1918, were to teach health, a command of fundamental processes, worthy home membership, citizenship, ethical character, vocational preparation, and worthy use of leisure time (as cited in Morrison, 1997). The unexpressed goal of schooling was to instill a common morality, which came to mean non-denominational Christian (Newman, 1994, p. 149).

The process of learning involved rote memorization (Newman, 1994) of information deemed appropriate by the social mores of the time (Morrison, 1997). The relevance of the data was unquestioned—it was in the book, so it must be learned. Recitation, drills, and evaluation of recall in the form of objective tests were the norm (Shaffer, 1999).

Classes were controlled by the adult, in what is known as "teacher-centered" instruction. Teachers were required to maintain order, cover a body of material, and demonstrate that students have learned (Newman, 1994). A significant advantage of teacher-centered instruction is control, and as class sizes got bigger in the post–World War II baby boom, control became more and more important. In the eyes of school boards, schools were measured by test scores and cost-effectiveness (Newman, 1994).

What drove the factory model was competition: to establish and maintain the United States as the industrial giant of the world, we needed to train factory workers. What drove the need to control was fear—fear of the sheer numbers of students, fear of losing our competitive edge, fear that young people could not be trusted to make sound decisions. What drove education-by-memorization and teacher-centered classrooms was the "banking" model of learning (Sheldon & Biddle, 1998); the learner was an empty vessel, passively awaiting wisdom from the all-knowing expert in the front of the classroom who was the exclusive source of knowledge. Knowledge could not be gained by discovery, self-teaching, or intuition, but only after such grace was earned by many hours of hard work, sacrifice, and discipline.

The implicit curriculum of the factory model of education, according to Eisner (1985), is compliance with authority rather than initiative, dependence on others to provide answers, extrinsic motivation, and competitiveness with classmates. The intellect is nurtured at the expense of the affect; learning about the arts is no more than play that one earns when the serious endeavor of schooling has been finished. Eisner likens the school to a hospital environment, stamped with routine, sameness, sterility, and lack of privacy. "Schools are educational churches, and our gods, judging from the altars we build, are economy and efficiency. Hardly a nod is given to the spirit" (Eisner, 1985, p. 97).

The spirit is nurtured when it is in contact with caring others, but as Lipsitz (1984) pointed out, "Schools are peculiar social agencies, charged by society with socializing youth into that society *while excluding them from it*" (p. 7; emphasis added). She goes on to add that teachers and administrators represent all adults to young people who act out their ambivalence about adults, one another, and themselves. Perhaps it is this acting out that causes schools to exclude young people from any meaningful involvement. The search for identity, the struggle between dependence and independence, the quest for a life vision—all these developmental tasks are painful to watch.

It is easy to see how the schools described above would create places where the spirit, if not outright crushed, is at least substantially bruised. These are dehumanizing institutions, and young people who have endured 12 (or more) years of such institutionalization do not usually emerge whole. The price they pay is their creativity, initiative, flexibility, autonomy, and trust in themselves as change agents for tomorrow's world.

Yet if we agree that schools are charged with helping students to become citizens of tomorrow's world, we need adults who possess those very characteristics that factory-model schools are designed to eradicate (Lickona & Davidson, 2005; Sheldon & Biddle, 1998). Recall that in the definition of effective schools, the two most salient features of effective schools are a caring environment and a holistic orientation to the development of students. It is from the synthesis of the needs of tomorrow's world with the research into effective schools that the concept of developmentally appropriate education has emerged.

REFLECTION MOMENT

If you are like most people, there were elements of your educational past that did not work well for you. What were those elements? School as a whole, one particular school, one teacher, one other student? What could have helped you deal with those negative elements?

DEVELOPMENTALLY APPROPRIATE SCHOOLS   It would be inaccurate and unfair to claim that there was nothing of educational value to be gained from traditional schools. Among some positive lessons that are learned in a structured setting are punctuality, persistence, delayed gratification (Eisner, 1985), and the need to obey the rules, respect authority, and become good citizens (Shaffer, 1999). It is also true that some lessons, such as abstract concepts, are easier to learn in a structured, lecture-oriented setting (Shaffer, 1999). As we shall see, developmentally appropriate education incorporates these benefits of structured education and extends the range of learning experiences to reduce structure, as determined by students' developmental needs.

First coined to describe educational strategies for use with preschool-age children (Travers et al., 1993), developmentally appropriate education (also known as open classrooms

[Eggen & Kauchak, 1994]) refers to educational experiences that are tailored to the developmental needs of students in terms of social skills, emotional maturation, and academic strengths and challenges. According to Eggen and Kauchak (1994), developmentally appropriate education provides balance among academic, social, and emotional goals, in a well-organized classroom that includes an emphasis on peer and teacher interaction, active learning strategies, and intrinsically interesting learning activities. They characterize developmentally appropriate methodology as utilizing discovery, group projects, independent thinking, and reflection; motivation is intrinsic and based on curiosity; classroom organization is designed for individualized instruction and small-group interaction; and the educator's role is perceived as that of director and facilitator, rather than exclusively that of presenter (p. 111).

The key to understanding what makes these educational strategies "developmentally appropriate" is that the entire learning environment and all learning activities within that environment are designed based on what is most conducive to the learning of those particular students. Balanced consideration is given to the students' social, emotional, and academic needs; cooperation, rather than competition, drives peer interactions, and initiative, rather than compliance, is fostered.

According to Eggen and Kauchak (1994), open classrooms were criticized when educators misunderstood how to apply these concepts and allowed students to do whatever they wanted in class. The quality of learning suffered in those classrooms. As school counselors, we must be concerned for the holistic development of the student, so we must know how well students learn in developmentally appropriate classrooms.

Research into the academic efficacy of various pedagogies suggests that students will actually learn *more* in a developmentally appropriate learning environment (Charlesworth, 1996; National Resource Council, 2000; Schickedanz, Schickedanz, Forsyth, & Forsyth, 1998; Travers et al., 1993). The reasons students learn better involve how and why students learn. Since developmentally appropriate education allows for natural curiosity and intrinsic motivation to be expressed, students may learn better because they enjoy what they are learning. Studies have shown that intrinsically motivated learners retain memorized material longer, demonstrate a stronger understanding of both memorized and more complex material, and demonstrate greater creativity and cognitive flexibility (Sheldon & Biddle, 1998, p. 166). Furthermore, open classrooms allow students to learn in the way that is most natural to them, as "active, autonomous agents who learn better by being actively involved in education" (Shaffer, 1999, p. 611).

There is evidence that developmentally appropriate education, or open classrooms, provide additional developmental benefits in the social and emotional domains (Shaffer, 1999). Students in such classrooms expressed more positive attitudes about school, they were more self-directed, they displayed greater ability to cooperate with their classmates, and they exhibited fewer behavioral problems (Bluestein, 2001).

Hence, in any well-functioning academic setting, academic expectations and accountability for learning are high, and this environment is characterized by a strong connection between educators and students, an environment of encouragement, and teaching that blends structure and discovery (Bluestein, 2001; Travers et al., 1993). It would appear that developmentally appropriate education fits these conditions for effective schools. Given the preponderance of evidence in support of developmentally appropriate educational strategies, it is hard to argue for a return to "factory model" schools.

While developmentally appropriate education is not a guaranteed panacea for all the ills of schools and society, it does hold the promise of helping young people find their way to functional adulthood (Paisley & Peace, 1995). Fay and Funk (1995) summarized the essence of developmentally appropriate education: "All effective systems allow people to learn from the results of their own decisions" (p. 26). It is only through making decisions, and learning from the results, that young people attain functional adulthood. Developmentally appropriate schools provide healthier systems for nurturing young people because the central premise of the system is profoundly simple: *respect*.

In their book about educational psychology, Travers et al. (1993) advise new teachers that, to help students attain psychosocial maturity, teachers should treat them as *almost adults* ; that is, providing them with independence, freedom, and respect" (p. 105; emphasis authors'). The *Grolier-Webster International Dictionary* defines "respect" as "to hold in high estimation or honor; to treat with consideration; to avoid interfering with or intruding upon" (1975, p. 817). As counselors, we respond to other people with unconditional positive regard and respect for their values, attitudes, and experiences. Is it possible to hope that an entire institution can view students with respect?

The answer is a resounding "yes." Students need community, an "ethos of caring" to feel safe academically, socially, emotionally (Bluestein, 2001, p. 110). The basis of community and care is respect. *Respect is the foundation of all healthy relationships*, and students need all professionals who work in our schools to view them with positive regard and respect. We may not accept individual behavior within the boundaries of responsibility, accountability, and mutually respectful choices in a community, but we value each young person as a human being, with all the creativity, potential, beauty, and hope that any human being possesses. We respect their potential and their reality, and, as counselors, we hold onto our belief in their potential in the face of sometimes very painful reality. Recall from Chapter 1 that the necessary personal qualities of school counselors were described as creativity and imagination, flexibility, courage, belief, and passion. Here is where your belief and courage will be called into play.

As professionals, school counselors must be able to maintain the belief that young people will rise to our high expectations, and if they do not, that it is their life path to learn their life lessons another way. In any case, we must respect them as having a right to their opinions, talents, interests, and feelings—and help them learn appropriate and responsible ways to express those opinions, talents, interests, and feelings (Fay & Funk, 1995) in the context of a learning community. This is how we educate our young people into responsible citizenry in our society.

If we do not respect young people, we fall back into the factory model of schools, back into teacher-centered education, and back into the trap of the banking model of learning. Without respect, we revert to the "adult control → student acting out → more control → more acting out" cycle of interaction. With respect for young people and their developmental needs, we break that cycle, and opt instead for a more responsible and responsive school environment. We build a more holistic system, teaching healthier values, attitudes, and ways of relating.

Research into the national epidemic of dropouts highlights the need for systemic review and renewal (Smink & Schargel, 2004) to identify how students learn in various educational contexts. Contemporary improvement efforts have variable success rates, depending on the extent of district support (Duttweiler, 2004), but "relationships, responsibility, and respect" proved effective for a large, urban school district (Cassellius, 2006). One model of how this looks in practice is found in the example of "learning communities" (Schmoker, 2004) in which educational professionals collaborate effectively to improve education. It is in this spirit that we turn now to introduce collaboration and leadership.

REFLECTION MOMENT

What experiences have you had in a developmentally appropriate environment? How did those experiences feel?

EFFECTIVE RELATIONSHIPS WITHIN EDUCATIONAL COMMUNITIES

When we examine the implications of various philosophies of education, we have some sense of why school professionals often disagree about how best to help kids. Because these philosophies of education translate directly into the relationships we develop and nurture in an attempt to help our students learn, we can see how a school professional's philosophy of education can lead to effective or ineffective working relationships. However, you may be asking yourself, "Aren't we all here to help kids?" Understanding how our partners interact will help you appreciate the school counselor's relationship with our partners in education.

School counselors, as we will see, are charged with a large task: the academic, social/emotional, and career development of students (ASCA, 2005; Dahir, Sheldon, & Valiga, 1998). While it is natural that new professionals will feel tremendous professional pride, when such pride results in the belief that "the counselor is the only one who works with kids" or "the counselor only conducts one-on-one counseling," the counselor is creating a situation that is fraught with problems.

The national average student-to-counselor ratio was 457 to 1 in the 2008–2009 school year (American School Counselor Association, 2010). With that ratio, no one person alone (emphasis on "alone") can attend to all the academic, career, and personal/social needs of all the students in a school, even a small school. Not only does it take an entire community to raise a child, it takes an entire community to educate a child.

Community, in this context, refers both to the community outside a school and to the community within a school. Essential elements of students' lives, including their primary support system—caregivers and family—exist outside of school. To be effective on behalf of students, school counselors must be able to engage caregivers and families—to develop rapport, develop trust, make referrals, educate, consult, and counsel, if need be. In many schools, school counselors provide direct services to caregivers, teaching parenting and communication skills, teaching economic survival skills (such as resume writing and interviewing), consulting on the needs of students, and providing direct counseling through one-on-one sessions and support groups.

In addition, counselors must be able to work effectively with other members of the outside community. For example, counselors must have effective working relationships with social agencies, health providers, and other mental health providers to facilitate referrals. Since counselors are also charged with the career development of students, effective relationships with employers will facilitate career exploration programming. Effective relationships with community leaders will enable the counselor to be an effective advocate for schools and for children and may facilitate the exploration of external funding for schools and for school counseling programs.

The school system itself is also a community, and within that community are professionals with whom partnerships are essential. Effective partnerships with school board and central administration members, as well as with building-level administrators such as principals and directors, result in an increased districtwide awareness of and appreciation for the school counseling program. These partnerships yield respect, trust, communication, resources, and services that are more effective for students.

Other pupil services professionals (or student services professionals, depending on local terminology) are also essential. Many authors have written extensively on the need for greater collaboration among pupil services professionals such as school psychologists, school social workers, school counselors, and school nurses. Together, the pupil services team of counselors, psychologists, social workers, and nurses represent the expertise and training needed to support the learning of young people, to ensure that good physical health, good psychological health, and solid support systems enable young people to be successful—to become healthy and resilient learners. The pupil services team facilitates the personal/social development of students.

Finally, no discussion of effective partnerships within schools would be complete without a discussion of the need to partner with teachers. Counselors are experts in both the change process and the learning process—these processes are the foundation of each theory of counseling. Using our expertise to help students learn can go only so far without the primary partner in the learning process: the teacher. Many teachers are already aware of and appreciate the role that counselors play in schools, but not all are. It is essential that counselors work with teachers to facilitate effective referrals, problem solving, and communication with students, families, and administrators about students, their lives, and their challenges.

> **REFLECTION MOMENT**
>
> What are your perceptions of the professions of school administrator, school psychologist, school social worker, and school nurse? Have you had any experience with members of these professions? Were those contacts positive or negative? What will you do to learn more about these professions to enable you to interact effectively with the professionals you will meet in the future?

Leadership Role to Close the Gap and Monitor Achievement, Equity, and Access

There is no doubt that professional school counselors in comprehensive school counseling programs need to be proactive in many schoolwide efforts. Monitoring the school climate for respect is one profound example of the effect of the school counselor in the affective reality of the school. Likewise, school counselors have systemic, wide-reaching leadership responsibilities in the academic reality of the school, as school counselors are charged with monitoring student achievement, ensuring equity across student groups, and promoting access to educational resources (see ASCA Ethical Standards [ASCA, 2004], and the ASCA National Model [ASCA, 2005]).

Multiple professionals in the school share this responsibility, but it is critical that the school counselor take leadership in these efforts, as established in the ASCA National Model (ASCA, 2005). School counselors are leaders of the heart of the school, and as such, are charged with monitoring the learning conditions of the school, most especially for those students who, by demographic, economic, or cultural characteristics, might be vulnerable in the school environment. Leadership activities with the student system (students, parents, families), the school system (teachers, administrators, staff, other student service professionals), and the community, ensure dialogue on multiple fronts about the conditions that could impede the students' achievement and the resources that could enhance access and achievement. School counselors have access to schoolwide information (i.e., grades, behavior statistics, test scores) and must monitor that data to alert school professionals and families of the progress of students. With multiple professionals watching out for students, and counselors leading and advocating for equity, the achievement gap will narrow. Without this leadership of systemic interventions for students, the achievement gap widens and students who may have limited access to resources fall further behind.

It is not that the school counselor, in some Lone Ranger fantasy, will ride in on his or her white horse and fix all the ills in the school for everyone. However, the school counselor will engage in data collection to document the need for attention to learning gaps and expectations, and then will use that data to recruit other school professionals and community professionals to work with families and schools to address those gaps.

Participatory Leadership, Distributed Leadership, and Collaboration

To recruit colleagues and school professionals to address gaps, school counselors will engage and motivate others to work together to help students. Unlike traditional models of leadership in which one individual takes ownership of and responsibility for initiating change or making things happen (DeVoss & Andrews, 2006; Dollarhide, 2003b), two new conceptual models of leadership have emerged. These new models are participatory leadership and distributed leadership, and both bring a paradigm shift in our thinking about school counselors as leaders.

Participatory leadership is the intentional inclusion of carefully chosen others in decision making, policy making, and program design. According to Torbert and Rook (2005), "the participatory leadership paradigm is based on respect and engagement. It constructively focuses energy in every human to human encounter. A more advanced, more democratic and more effective model of leadership, it harnesses diversity, builds community, and creates shared responsibility for action. It deepens individual and collective learning yielding real development and growth" (n.p.).

This leadership model represents a more collaborative approach to leadership, and is one that could have significant usefulness for professional school counselors. Taken from the above description, participatory leaders:

1. Mobilize and engage *all* of a community's assets,
2. Purposefully and constantly connect day-to-day action with vision and strategy,
3. Create a healthy, energetic culture of openness and participation,
4. Are objectives driven (and constantly evaluate achievement of objectives).

In addition, participatory leaders embed good processes to facilitate collaborative action to achieve objectives, harness diversity in service of innovation and good decision making, visibly improve communication and individual accountability, and seek constant, breakthrough learning and development of self and others (Torbert & Rook, 2005).

While all this may sound idealistic, it is within the school counselor's range of existing skills that participatory leadership can be engaged. Most often used to describe the leadership style of prinicipals (San Antonio & Gamage, 2007), this approach to "getting things done" enables school counselors to build collaborative relationships throughout the building and district as needed. As an overview of the process, the participatory leader would, in collaborative conversation with others:

- Recruit stakeholders to provide input into the decision or effort,
- Explore assumptions and values of all participants in order to secure participation,
- Establish goals of participants, roles each would like to play in the change effort, and the purpose of the project at hand,
- Remain inclusive and responsive to all persons in the effort,
- Establish benchmarks and collect data to document progress,
- Engage (act), reflect on progress and direction, then reengage in a cycle of continuous improvement.

In a similar vein, Janson, Stone, and Clark (2009) describe a model of leaderhips called "distributed leadership," in which leadership is shared among professionals in a school in both formal and informal contexts and roles. This leadership style can be seen "through the interaction of two or more school leaders within their school context" (p. 101) in situations that allow for innovation and collaboration. In this way, school counselors can avoid the myth of the lone "heroic leader" (p. 100) that may confine school counselors to the belief that their leadership behaviors will undermine the leadership of the school prinicipal.

Accountability Leadership and Closing the Gap

In a preview of upcoming content, school counselors must be able to monitor all students in the school for academic, career, and personal/social achievement and full access to all educational resources. Using outcomes research findings and best practices from professional literature, today's professional school counselors must also use "accountability leadership" (Sink, 2009) to assess their programs to determine if students are learning in all three domains and to improve their services to all students. They need to be able to document the ways in which their programs yield measurable results for all students and for subpopulations within the student body in order to ensure the best possible educational outcomes for all.

According to Sink (2009), school counselors must be able to weave literature-based best practices with qualitative and quantitative data in order to fully understand the impact of their programs on their schools. It is only with this information that all members of the school community will come to understand the role of the school counselor and the efficacy of our programs relative to school success. When we are able to document and demonstrate our value added to the school, then our collaborative and leadership efforts will meet with greater success on behalf of our students.

CASE STUDY REVISITED

Integration

Now that you have read the chapter, go back and reread Bullied to Death? Reflect on and answer the following questions:

1. Based on what Eleana learned about Cody, how would you describe the school environment in terms of this chapter?
2. Based on the principal's comment, what might you guess about the relationships among the staff of the school?
3. Considering the premise that respect is the foundation of all healthy relationships, in what way(s) is lack of respect evident in this case study?
4. Can you "change" a school? Why or why not? What are some ways that you might consider "changing" the school?
5. How would leadership activities with all the systems (family, school, and community) help resolve this situation? What are some leadership activities you might consider in this case? ■

Suggested Readings

Adelman, H. S., & Taylor, L. (1998). Reframing mental health in schools and expanding school reform. *Educational Psychologist, 33*(4), 135–152; and Taylor, L., & Adelman, H. S. (2000). Connecting schools, families, and communities. *Professional School Counseling, 3*, 298–307. These two resources outline Adelman and Taylor's model of school-community collaboration, and represent a vision of the next step in creating seamless systems of support for children.

*Bluestein, J. (2001). *Creating emotionally safe schools: A guide for educators and parents*. Deerfield Beach, FL: Health Communications.

*Smink, J. & Schargel, F. P. (2004). *Helping students graduate: A strategic approach to dropout prevention*. Larchmont, NY: Eye on Education.

*Starkman, N., Scales, P. C., & Roberts, C. (1999). *Great places to learn: How asset-building schools help students succeed*. Minneapolis, MN: Search Institute.

*These three books are a wealth of information about schools and healthy educational environments. While not written specifically for school counselors, each book addresses research that speaks directly to the work school counselors do on a daily basis.

Fay, J., & Funk, D. (1995). *Teaching with love and logic*. Golden, CO: Love & Logic Press. The Love and Logic resources are invaluable to those working with children and are highly recommended for school professionals.

Anyone working with young people must have a depth of understanding about child and adolescent development, so any of the references that address development and/or educational psychology are also highly recommended.

CHAPTER

3

Moral, Ethical, and Legal Issues in School Counseling

LEARNING OBJECTIVES

By the end of this chapter, you will

1. Understand the source of our moral standards for counseling

2. Understand the relationship between those moral standards and the ethical statements of counseling

3. Understand the importance of knowing the Code of Ethics and Standards of Practice of the American Counseling Association

4. Be able to identify the major components in the Ethical Standards for School Counselors of the American School Counselor Association

5. Understand the laws that pertain to school counseling

6. Understand and apply a model of ethical decision making

7. Be familiar with several common ethical dilemmas in school counseling

8. Understand the importance of professional insurance and certification

9. Be familiar with and able to implement a plan of action for responding to legal action

10. Be familiar with several resources from which to obtain information in the event of future ethical dilemmas

11. Know several strategies for practicing in the most ethical manner possible

CASE STUDY

Jason's Casual Comment

Jason was flying through his advising appointments, proud that he had been on schedule all day. His 305-student roster was almost done; the principal would be happy that the counselors had been able to schedule all 1,213 high school students in the three weeks they were given. The computer hadn't crashed once so far this year, and with luck, he was keeping to his 10-minute scheduling appointments like clockwork. He knew that the director of their counseling program was trying to move the scheduling part of this process to the secretaries in the office, but until then, he was content to do as he was asked. At least it gave him time every year to talk with every one of his assigned students.

30

Two o'clock, and he was almost done for the day. He'd been on a roll all day, his energy high. "OK, Kim, right? How are you? It's been a long time since we last talked. Do you have your schedule ready?"

Kim was a quiet, withdrawn girl, very petite for her age. She was a sophomore this year, making average grades. She was one of those students who faded into the background in class, in the hallways, in the lunchroom. Jason never saw her in the halls talking to anyone; she was always alone. He wondered why she worked so hard at being invisible. He looked at her file while she came in and sat down.

"I've got a problem, Mr. Whitney," she mumbled, "but I'm not sure who to talk to. I don't want this getting around school."

Jason was thinking about her schedule, and offhandedly said, "Well, you can tell me. You know I won't tell your friends."

"Ok, then. I've been doing some things with my boyfriend that I'm not really proud of, but I don't know how to make it stop without losing him."

Jason's head snapped out of the file when he realized what she had said. "Oh, Kim, I don't know that I can keep that a secret. There are laws about reporting the sexual activity of minors, and your parents should. . . . "

"No way! Forget it then! You said you wouldn't tell, just now, you said you wouldn't tell! You lied! I'm out of here."

"Don't go, we need to talk about this!"

"No, there's nothing to say. Nothing. I'll deny I said anything. I'll make another appointment to work on my schedule. I'm feeling sick and want to go home. Don't make me puke on your rug to prove it." She looked at him with contempt, grabbed her book bag, and left.

All he could do was watch her leave. It was going to take him hours to straighten out this mess, and he didn't know if he could ever make it right with Kim. If he reported as he was supposed to do, she would deny everything, she would never trust another counselor, and things could get much more difficult for her all around. If he honored her wishes and didn't report, he could get into legal trouble involving the school, her parents, and heaven knows what else. So much for being on time.

CHALLENGE QUESTIONS

There are a variety of internal and external factors that contributed to Jason's problem. Based on your best estimate, what were the internal factors—things about Jason's personality—that affected his actions? What were the external factors?

What is the ethical dilemma? What are Jason's competing concerns?

Reread the scenario. Did Jason jump to a conclusion about what is happening with the boyfriend? Are there other interpretations of her words? What if he reports she is sexually active, only to find out that she wasn't talking about sex at all?

Does Jason have options in ways to proceed? What are those options? Are there ways to address all his concerns? What are they?

What would you do? ■

SCHOOL COUNSELING AND ETHICS

Counseling graduate students often ask, "How will I know what to do in an ethical dilemma?" And the only answer is, "It depends on what's important to you." A dilemma exists only when there are two or more equally compelling priorities confronting you. You have to know your professional ethics, relevant federal, state, and local laws, and the policies of your district and building, but this is only part of the whole picture. The missing pieces of the puzzle involve obtaining current information, knowing your professional priorities, and knowing how to think through the dilemma. The puzzle, when assembled, reveals a holistic picture of ethical counseling:

1. You have to know ethics, laws, policies, and procedures that pertain to your students very well.
2. You have to know how to get more information about current issues, laws, and expert advice.
3. You have to know your own professional priorities.
4. You have to know a process by which you can factor these elements together.

In this chapter, we will address all these topics.

In terms of ethics, the school setting is unique in many ways. Because school counselors work with minors, they must be aware of the rights of parents and legal guardians. Furthermore, because schools are highly regulated and legislated, counselors must have a sharp awareness of federal, state, and local laws; court decisions; state regulations; and school board policies. (For a detailed discussion of the sources of laws relative to school counselors, see Schmidt, 2003, Chapter 11.) In addition, school counselors must continually update their knowledge about each of these topics, because ignorance of the law is no excuse. This is not to suggest that counselors must become lawyers in order to practice counseling. The point is to know where to go when you have questions about your practice.

This chapter could easily be a course by itself. It is important to note that the discussion in this chapter is not intended to be your only exposure to ethics; you should take additional course(s) in ethics, read in the professional literature about ethics, and attend professional development opportunities (workshops, conferences) that address contemporary issues and changes in ethics, because ethical statements are regularly revised by professional associations. In this chapter, we will focus on ethical issues that are most relevant to school counselors. Let's begin with a discussion of the source of our ethics: morals and values.

THE MORAL VISION OF COUNSELING: OUR VALUES

Counseling as a profession has evolved a set of moral guidelines that shape our ethics and, in some cases, has resulted in the passage of laws to protect clients and the public (Christopher, 1996). The moral guidelines come from a shared set of assumptions about the therapeutic conditions that facilitate human development—those underlying assumptions of human nature as articulated in theories of counseling.

It is accepted by many that human nature is understandable when we acknowledge that everything we do is predicated on the satisfaction of needs, as filtered through our values. These values are interlocking systems of meaning and of significance, providing us with the foundation of our choices; we value one thing more than another, so we choose actions that provide us with what we value. These values are interwoven with our views of the world and provide the structure for defining good, bad, healthy, and unhealthy. Counseling has been shaped by how counseling theorists define these terms.

Christopher (1996) argued that, in Western culture, "good" is defined as authenticity, autonomy, and individualism. Counseling as a whole emphasizes self-actualization, self-esteem, autonomy, assertiveness, internal locus of evaluation and control, self-acceptance, and individuation. From this tradition, it is possible to ascertain the source of the five primary counseling values: beneficence (doing good), nonmaleficence (doing no harm), justice (fairness), autonomy (independent decision making), and fidelity (being true to one's word) (Hall & Lin, 1995; Herlihy & Corey, 1996).

It is important to note, however, that not everyone subscribes to this Western values system (Cook & Houser, 2009). In many multicultural traditions, "good" is defined in terms of collectivism, in which the self is viewed in terms of the referent group (family, neighborhood, and culture). In this tradition, emotional maturity is defined in terms of one's ability to uphold one's duty to family, maintain harmony, and demonstrate sensitivity to others' feelings. A person's self-worth comes from the ability to excel in social roles (Christopher, 1996; Cook & Houser, 2009). From this tradition, counseling has now added a sixth value: context and systems awareness.

Since our values shape our choices, we must think about how our values shape our therapeutic choices. As counselors, we promote what we believe helps the client make healthy choices and we discourage what we believe to be unhealthy choices. If we believe that individuation helps clients to make healthy, independent choices, we will encourage clients to individuate, to make choices independent from the undue influence of others. However, if we are not sensitive to non-Western values systems, it would be easy to push a client to make independent choices that could ultimately alienate the client from his or her social and cultural support system, which may not be in the client's best interest overall. Examples of the subtle nuances of cultural issues can be found in Cook and Houser's (2009) discussion of the ASCA Ethical Standards relative to Taoist and Hindu traditions.

It is important to see that our personal value system and our professional value system will affect our choices as counselors. Students have said, "Then this means that I must not have any values when I'm counseling," as if they could become values-neutral, somehow negating all their values as they counsel. This is not possible, and if it were possible, it is not beneficial. Our values are the essence of our humanity, and we can't, nor would we ever want to, negate that which makes us most human. To do so would negate the very thing that makes us effective counselors. Consider this metaphor. Our values are like a hearing aid. We attend to the world better as a result of the hearing aid, because it gives us access to the messages that are important to us. But for many, this hearing aid is tuned to amplify only certain frequencies, allowing us to hear only some messages and not others. We don't want to take off the hearing aid altogether—we want to broaden the frequency setting so that we can hear all messages. Rather than strive to become values-neutral (taking off the hearing aid), counselors should examine their values and attempt to make them as broad as possible (tune it to hear as many frequencies as possible), to acknowledge the wide range of various value systems that exist in the world.

According to Christopher (1996), awareness of our personal and professional values and morals leads us to examine our assumptions. Because different moral visions and values exist, we must be able to see the common moral strands that bind us together, such as truth, honesty, and the Golden Rule ("Do unto others as you would have done unto you"). Counselors must acknowledge cultural embeddedness and must seek to clarify and question their moral vision. Furthermore, we must ascertain how our moral vision affects our work as counselors and engage in critical dialogue about moral visions and values.

When we examine our values, we become aware of how these values shape our work as counselors. It is only with this continual examination that we are able to truly help our clients to find their own life path, because we can see how our values might interfere with the values of the client. For example, rather than simply assume that individuation is the best way for clients to grow and develop, we must question that assumption and jointly explore the client's view of individuation and potential isolation from cultural supports. As we mature in our ability to see our value system and explore the value system of the client, we become more effective counselors. It is easy to see why we need a deep understanding of our professional ethics; this is the instrument by which we protect the client from harm.

REFLECTION MOMENT

How would you prioritize the six professional values just presented? Rank order them: beneficence, nonmaleficence, justice, fidelity, autonomy, and context and systems awareness. Now justify the rankings. Hard, isn't it?

THE ETHICS OF THE PROFESSION

In general, ethics statements are the codification of our shared professional values. They function like curbs on the road; they define the limits of our practice, but within these limits, there is room to express individual preferences in how we practice the art and science of counseling. Some ethical statements mandate those activities that the profession deems essential for every counseling relationship (respecting the dignity of the client, fostering the client's positive growth and development, involving the family when appropriate, etc.). Other ethical statements define those activities that the profession deems inappropriate for every counseling relationship (engaging in dual relationships, seeking to meet personal needs, sexual intimacies, etc.). Between the "right" and the "wrong" are immeasurable shades of ambiguous gray. There is no such thing as perfectly ethical practice, and school counselors will be challenged to deal with this ambiguity as will every other counselor.

The values of the counseling profession are made operational in the codes of ethics (the Code of Ethics of the American Counseling Association [ACA, 2005] is available at www. counseling.org). Several examples will help to illustrate this point. For example, the value of beneficence (do good) is found in the directive to foster the client's positive growth and development, and the value of nonmaleficence (do no harm) is seen in the directives prohibiting discrimination, meeting personal needs at the expense of the client, dual relationships, and sexual intimacies. Justice is addressed in the ethical provisions involving appropriate fees and advertising for clients. The value of autonomy is addressed in the ACA Code's provisions addressing freedom of choice, informed consent, respecting differences, personal values, and confidentiality. The profession's value of fidelity is manifest in the Code's provisions for disclosure to clients, clear communication with other therapists serving clients, and responsibilities to multiple clients. Finally, the newest value, that of context and systems awareness, is visible in the directive to involve the family as appropriate, the responsibility to provide socially beneficial pro bono services, and the responsibility to inform a third person about a contagious, fatal disease.

In general, clients have three rights: the right to information, the right to choose, and the right to privacy (Herlihy & Corey, 1996). Under the right to information, clients have the right to have information about what the counselor is going to do, how it will work, any limitations to the counseling approach, any risks inherent in counseling, and the limits of confidentiality. The second right is the right to choose (e.g., the right to engage in or terminate counseling and the right to make personal choices). The counselor will respect the dignity and autonomy of the client to choose what is in the client's best interest, free from the values of the counselor. The third right is the right to privacy, which involves two issues: privileged communication and confidentiality.

Privileged communication is a legal concept protecting the content of therapy sessions from compelled testimony in court that must be spelled out in state statute (Herlihy & Corey, 1996). Most states do *not* name counselors as under the protection of privileged communication. On the other hand, confidentiality is both an ethical and legal concept, addressing the commitment of the counselor to keep confidential what is shared in counseling within the prescribed limits. These limitations to confidentiality must be disclosed as part of informed consent and will be discussed in detail later in this chapter. It is important to note at this point that in all states school counselors are mandated reporters in cases of suspected child abuse and/or neglect. This mandate is a higher professional priority than confidentiality (Remley & Herman, 2000).

Codes of Ethics

Both the American Counseling Association (ACA) and the American School Counselor Association (ASCA) have codified standards of ethical practice. The ACA (2005) has defined a Code of Ethics document that outlines the guidelines of the counseling profession as a whole. This document spells out prescribed and prohibited behavior in terms of the general counseling profession. All counselors, regardless of the setting in which they work, must be familiar with the Code of Ethics. As noted, this is available online. The Ethical Standards for School Counselors authored by ASCA (2004) is not an optional set of standards; it is *required* of all school counselors. In addition, when you provide group counseling you must know and abide by the ethics of the Association for Specialists in Group Work (ASGW); you can find their Best Practices document (ASGW, 2007) on their website (www.asgw.org). And because you will be working with students in terms of their career development, you must also follow the code of ethics for the National Career Development Association (NCDA); you can obtain their Code of Ethics (2007) from their website at www.ncda.org (click on the Guidelines tab). If you are a National Certified Counselor (NCC) or a National Certified School Counselor (NCSC) you must also follow the National Board of Certified Counselors (NBCC) Code of Ethics (NBCC, 2005);

if you are involved with any form of distance counseling or electronic contact with students, the NBCC Practice of Internet Counseling (n.d.) would be an excellent ethical resource for any counselor.

As a professional school counselor, you must follow the ACA, ASCA, ASGW, and NCDA ethical codes, and other codes as applicable to your work. A process for working through dilemmas that arise due to conflicting directives in these documents will be addressed later in this chapter; however, for the purpose of this book we will focus on the ACA and ASCA codes.

The ASCA Ethical Standards for School Counselors (ASCA, 2004) begins with an important preamble that outlines fundamental beliefs and values of the American School Counselor Association (ASCA, 2004). In the first section, it addresses responsibilities to students in terms of priorities, confidentiality, counseling plans, dual relationships, referrals, group work, danger to self or others as a limitation of confidentiality, student records (counseling notes), issues of assessment, technology, and peer helper programs. The next section addresses responsibilities to parents/guardians, described in terms of parents' rights and confidentiality. The third section outlines the counselor's responsibilities to colleagues and professional associates, specifically addressing professional relationships and the appropriate sharing of information.

Next, the Ethical Standards address the counselor's responsibilities to the school and the community in terms of protecting the welfare of the school and the comprehensive school counseling program, addressing conditions that infringe on the effectiveness of the counselor, as well as providing a mandate to collaborate with agencies, organizations, and individuals to deliver a comprehensive school counseling program. In the section addressing responsibilities to self, the Standards discuss professional competence and mandatory multicultural skills. In the section addressing responsibilities to the profession, the Standards outline appropriate behavior in terms of adhering to the ASCA Ethical Standards and Position Statements, professionalism, and research. Furthermore, professional school counselors are expected to contribute to the profession through membership in professional associations, sharing expertise with others, and mentoring new counselors. Finally, procedures for addressing the unethical conduct of colleagues is outlined.

As mentioned, you need to know the ethical expectations of both ACA and ASCA, as well as those of ASGW and NCDA. As these documents are continually updated and revised, you would be wise to download and print all these ethical codes, keeping them close at hand for your personal review and reflection. It is easy to lose sight of the nuances of ethics in the busy crush of the day.

LEGAL ISSUES

Legal issues of school counselors become more involved as the student matures toward the age of majority. With attainment of the age of 18 years, the student becomes autonomous in the eyes of the law and is vested with adult status (Remley & Herman, 2000). This is an important milestone in terms of the legal relationships in general and in terms of relationships with the school in particular.

One of the most important laws is the Family Educational Rights and Privacy Act (FERPA) of 1974, also known as the Buckley Amendment (Remley & Herman, 2000) and its recent modifications in the Grassley Amendment (Sealander, Schwiebert, Oren, & Weekley, 1999). In this legislation, schools receiving federal funds must provide access to all school records to parents of minor students and to the students themselves after they reach the age of 18. Parents and adult students have the right to challenge information in the records (Schmidt, 1999). Schools are prohibited from releasing records to any third party without the parents' written consent (for a minor) or the adult student's written consent.

Confidentiality of the records and protection of the identity of any persons receiving drug or alcohol abuse treatment are guaranteed by the Drug Abuse Office and Treatment Act of 1976 (Sealander et al., 1999). In middle and high schools, this act is important to know because it applies to "all records relating to the identity, diagnosis, prognosis, or treatment of any student involved in any federally assisted substance abuse program" (Sealander et al., 1999, p. 124). This would suggest that the counseling records of any students participating in substance use programs maintained by *any* organization receiving federal funds would need to be given greater protection than other counseling records; the information is protected even from the student's parents (under applicable state law). According to Sealander and colleagues (1999), the Drug Abuse Office and Treatment Act

> protects any information about a youth if the youth has received alcohol and/or drug related services of any kind including school-based identification. . . . When a teacher, counselor, or other school professional identifies student behaviors that could indicate a drug and/or alcohol problem, they can discuss this with the student or other school personnel. However, from the time an evaluation is conducted and/or a student assistance program begins alcohol or drug related counseling, the federal regulations are in effect. (pp. 126–127)

Awareness of this law is essential because it raises issues related to the appropriate and legal release of records and information about whether the student is receiving services.

Another legal area with which you must be familiar is legislation pertaining to the reporting of suspected child abuse or neglect (Lambie, 2005; Remley & Herman, 2000; Schmidt, 2003). The definition of abuse or neglect generally includes physical and sexual abuse, psychological and emotional torment, abandonment, and inadequate supervision. School counselors are mandated reporters of suspected abuse, meaning that counselors are not responsible for investigating the allegations, but must report when there is reason to suspect abuse or neglect (Schmidt, 2003; Sealander et al., 1999). You must obtain a copy of your state legislation and become familiar with its provisions, because these will vary widely from state to state. Procedures for reporting, who must report, and when the report must be made are important variables you must know. In addition, there may be school or district procedures for reporting; for example, the district may require all reports to be made by one designated individual. Reporting to this individual, however, does not absolve you of your legal responsibility to act to protect a child (Tompkins & Mehring, 1993). You must follow up to ensure that the report has been made.

Special education legislation has been increasingly important as instances of lawsuits increase. The Americans with Disabilities Act, the Individuals with Disabilities Act (Public Law 101-476), the Education for All Handicapped Children Act (Public Law 94-142), and Section 504 of the Rehabilitation Act of 1973 all address the rights of children to free and appropriate education and services (Erk, 1999; Schmidt, 2003). Counselors must be informed about these laws, because educational services for students are often coordinated with counseling services. Furthermore, as advocates for all students, counselors can educate others (students, parents, colleagues) about rights and responsibilities under the law (Erk, 1999; Schmidt, 2003).

Finally, Title IX of the Education Amendments of 1972 protects students against discrimination on the basis of sex, marital status, or pregnancy (Schmidt, 2003). This legislation guarantees equal access to educational programs, extracurricular activities (such as sports), and occupational opportunities. This law is also the foundation of the sexual harassment guidelines making student-on-student cross-sex and same-sex harassment a violation of the victim's civil rights, and as such, mandates that harassment be reported to school officials who have the responsibility to take appropriate action (C. B. Stone, 2000). As advocates for students and monitors of school policies and programs, counselors are in a unique position to address conditions or situations in the school that are discriminatory.

MORAL/ETHICAL DECISION-MAKING PROCESS

Many day-to-day ethical decisions are easy. You perform your job duties in a manner that is consistent with the ethics of ACA and ASCA, with the laws of your state, and with the policies of your school and your district. But what if those directives conflict with each other? How do you choose which of those to follow?

Ethical dilemmas are never easy; that's why they are called dilemmas. However, with a decision-making model, you can structure this decision-making process in a way that is professionally accepted. This means that if you are ever required to explain your decision to parents, school administrators, or legal representatives, you have followed a procedure that is supported by others in your profession.

One model is adapted from Herlihy and Corey (1996). In this model, there are seven steps:

1. Identify the problem, obtaining as much information as possible. Do not look for a simplistic solution. If it concerns a legal issue, obtain legal advice.
2. Apply the ACA Code of Ethics as well as the ASCA Ethical Standards for School Counselors.
3. Determine the nature and dimensions of the dilemma, considering the moral principles, reviewing the professional literature, consulting with professional colleagues and supervisors, and contacting state and national professional associations to obtain other perspectives.
4. Generate potential courses of action.
5. Consider the potential consequences of all actions and determine a course of action. In this step, you are looking for a solution or combinations of actions that best fit the situation and accomplish the priorities you have established.
6. Evaluate the selected course of action to determine if it is fair, if it would be an action you would want reported in the press, and if you would recommend the same actions to another counselor.
7. Implement the course of action.

An alternative model is that adapted from Stadler (1985). Before applying this model, Stadler suggests that you think through the following questions:

- What is legal? Do laws address this situation? If so, what are they?
- What is the policy of my employer?
- What is balanced for everyone involved that will promote a win/win for everyone's needs?
- How will I feel about myself if this becomes public knowledge? How will I feel if my family finds out about my choice?

If the answer does not become clear in that analysis, you implement the following four-step process.

Step 1: Identify competing moral principles that apply to the dilemma. This grounds you in the values of the profession. For review, these values are

1. Nonmaleficence—do no harm
2. Beneficence—promote good
3. Autonomy—promote self-determination
4. Justice—be fair; promote fairness
5. Fidelity—be faithful; keep promises
6. Context and systems awareness—consider the support system of the client

Step 2: Implement moral reasoning strategy. This step consists of several substeps and directives.

1. Secure additional information about the situation, your professional standards related to the situation, any laws that pertain to this situation, and any special circumstances surrounding this situation.
2. Secure additional information about the situation. Determine who has the information and what the procedures and processes would be for obtaining that information. Is informed consent required? Is a court order required? Obtain all needed information.
3. Rank the moral principles you identified from Step 1. This involves the application of your own individual professional judgment. Expect that all ethical dilemmas involve

all of these values to some extent, so do not be alarmed when you discover that others would rank the principles differently.

4. Consult with colleagues to find out what they would do in your situation. Be sure to maintain confidentiality in this process.

Step 3: Prepare for action. This step also consists of several substeps.

1. Once you have ranked the moral principles and consulted with others, you have a direction from which you will further examine your decision. You will now identify hoped-for outcomes. What is the ideal situation for all parties involved?

2. Brainstorm actions that you believe will lead to these ideal outcomes. List all possibilities, no matter how remote.

3. Evaluate effects of all these possible actions on everyone involved. This means you must consider the student, other students, the student's family, the staff with whom you work, the profession of counseling in general and school counseling in particular, the school, the community as a whole, yourself, and your family.

4. Much as we would like to believe that these decisions are grounded in the noble ideals of the profession, often these decisions are influenced by other emotions and concerns, such as power, prestige, reputation, fear of being sued, time constraints, poor time management, revenge, need for love, sexual attraction, and so on. At this stage, identify these competing issues and concerns that will influence your decision. Be honest with yourself. Discard optional actions that are primarily grounded in these issues and concerns.

5. With your prioritized values, consultation, self-awareness, and evaluation of actions, you will now choose a course of action that allows you to maximize benefits and reduce risks to everyone involved.

6. Before you act, you must test the action by considering all possible outcomes (intended or not) and all the possible problems that might occur as a result of your choice. Obtain more consultation if needed.

Step 4: At this stage, you are ready to act. To do this, you will

1. Strengthen your willpower, knowing that taking the action you have chosen may not be easy. Not everyone will agree with your decision. Stadler (1985) suggests
   a. Maintain your focus on your higher purpose.
   b. Maintain pride in yourself and in your integrity.
   c. Have patience with the process and with the outcomes.
   d. Be persistent with your goals, confident that you are following the best course for all concerned.
   e. Maintain a balanced perspective in hearing feedback.

2. Identify concrete steps necessary to take action.

3. Act.

4. Evaluate the effects of your actions and adjust as needed.

5. Attend to the moral traces that come as a result of your actions. This refers to the residual feelings of regret or pride that you feel as the effects of your actions become manifest. Would you do the same thing again in the future or would you make a different choice? Sometimes the best we can do is resolve to make a better choice in future situations. (Butler, 1993)

You will undoubtedly notice many consistencies between the two models just presented. Both models emphasize consultation, fairness, and careful consideration of all consequences. However, while the Herlihy and Corey (1996) model provides a reminder to consult with state and national professional associations, the Stadler (1985) model makes self-examination and self-awareness an explicit part of the process. Both of these actions are vital to appropriate ethical decision making. Consulting with state and national associations provides you with a broad view of what other professionals would do in your situation, reducing skewed perspectives as a result of local biases. Conducting a thorough and honest self-evaluation highlights your professional priorities and prevents selfish or self-serving motives from influencing your decision. Both the macro and micro levels of examination will help you maintain balance within your choices. We now turn to an examination of the nature of many of these choices.

REFLECTION MOMENT

Think back to the last time you confronted an ethical choice. (Can't think of one? Think of a time when you had to resolve a conflict between two people you cared about: two children, two siblings, your parents, two friends in college. That is a similar situation.) What, specifically, did you do about it? How did you resolve it? How similar or dissimilar was your process from those outlined above?

COMMON LEGAL/ETHICAL PROBLEMS

Before you read this section of the chapter, reread the ACA Code of Ethics (available online as noted previously) and the ASCA Ethical Standards for School Counselors (also available online). This section addresses some problematic issues for school counselors, but you will note that no definitive conclusions can be drawn about any of them. What is most appropriate to do in the face of any of these dilemmas depends on the context and your own professional priorities.

Confidentiality

It would be safe to say that the majority of dilemmas faced by school counselors involve confidentiality (Herlihy & Corey, 1996; Huss, Bryant, & Mulet, 2008; Isaacs & Stone, 1999; Lazovsky, 2008; Ledyard, 1998; Tompkins & Mehring, 1993). When confidentiality should be maintained, when confidentiality must be limited, how to communicate the concept of confidentiality, and how to secure the student's permission to disclose information are all highly legalized and problematic concerns.

In general, it is most helpful to think of confidentiality as the need to keep private the details of a counseling session, unless a compelling reason exists to reveal those details. In balance, however, both the ACA and ASCA urge counselors to involve parents and families in the counseling of minor children when appropriate. In addition, the ASCA Ethical Standards has an entire section of the ethics (Section B) titled Responsibilities to Parents/Guardians. This provides an excellent reminder to involve parents as appropriate while concurrently respecting the rights of the counselee. Remley and Herman (2000) issue a reminder that until a student reaches the age of 18, he or she is legally a minor and that, although your professional responsibilities are to minor clients, legal obligations exist to the parents' rights (p. 314). To prevent misunderstanding of this complex issue, Huss et al. (2008) advocate for the use of agreements with parents and administrators to clarify the conditions of confidentiality with minor clients, and suggest that information about confidentiality be promulgated on webpages, via electronic and personal contact with parents, and through any printed material from the school to the parent.

If, in spite of efforts to clarify confidentiality with students, a parent does invoke his or her parental rights to know, this does not compel revealing the details of counseling conversations; rather, in the role as advocate and consultant, counselors can empower students to find ways to share their struggles with their parents. If the counselor needs to provide information to the parent, the counselor is advised to inform and consult with students before giving information to parents (ASCA Ethical Standards). It may also be possible to negotiate the request for information with the parent, so that the trust between the counselor and the student is preserved and the concerns of the parent are assuaged (L. S. Kaplan, 1996; Remley & Herman, 2000). Again, the general rule of thumb would be to share general information with parents rather than the details of your work with students. Only in the case of the Drug Abuse Office and Treatment Act of

1976 is information about the student not to be released, even to the parent (Sealander et al., 1999). This may be modified, however, by state statute.

As cautious as you must be with confidentiality, there are still various legally mandated situations that require breach of confidentiality and should be revealed as a part of informed consent. These situations involve:

1. When there is danger to self or others (disclosure is "required to protect clients or identified others from serious and foreseeable harm") (ACA, 2005, B.2.a)
2. When there are suspicions of child abuse or neglect (in other words, crimes against a child) (Remley & Herman, 2000; Sealander et al., 1999)
3. When there is an emergency that requires information to protect the safety of the student and others (Sealander et al., 1999)
4. When court ordered (Remley & Herman, 2000)
5. In cases of sexual harassment (C. B. Stone, 2000)
6. In some states, when there is sexual activity, discussions of abortion, or criminal activity on the part of the minor

State variations in these mandates provide another reminder that school counselors must know the laws of the state in which they are employed.

There are differences in the ways that school counselors perceive confidentiality, depending on the issue, the age of the student, and the amount of contact with concerned others in the school setting. In a study examining the differences among counselors in terms of confidentiality, Isaacs and Stone (1999) found that high school counselors would breach confidentiality less often than counselors at other levels, depending on the danger level of the student's activity and the age of the student. "Counselors tend to see serious drug use, abortion, use of crack cocaine, suicide intent, robbery, and sex with multiple partners as areas which are serious enough to warrant a breach of confidentiality, though less so at the high school level" (p. 265). The authors believe that high school counselors breach confidentiality less often from the view that as students mature, they develop the ability to make independent decisions and become "mature minors" (p. 265).

In more recent study, Lazovsky (2008) found little consensus for when and why to breach confidentiality, highlighting the struggle counselors face with this aspect of ethical decision making. They found that school counselors across all three levels were most likely to breach confidentiality in cases of dangerous behaviors, followed by cases of unlawful behavior, and finally, issues of personal and family information. When respondents were asked for the rationale for their decision to breach or not to breach, they most often cited ethics as the reason for their decision with both dangerous and family issues, while they cited legal and procedural reasons for their decisions relative to unlawful behaviors. The author's conclusion: "The lack of consensus that characterized the school counselors' decisions and the varied reasons they presented to support their decisions emphasize that where ethical dilemmas are concerned, particularly those involving confidentiality, school counselors need to exercise careful and well-informed judgment in making their decisions" (p. 343).

Furthermore, the issue of confidentiality becomes more diffuse the more contact the counselor has with concerned others. Specifically, school counselors work closely with teachers and administrators, many of whom are interested and concerned about the progress of students. Counselors are often tempted to share too much information in their desire to help students be successful; care must be taken to obtain the student's permission before revealing detailed information to school colleagues (T. Davis & Ritchie, 1993; Watson, 1990). In addition, school counselors need to function as a part of the school's multidisciplinary treatment team, often involving both in-district and nonschool personnel and specialists. In this setting also, confidentiality can be addressed by informing students in advance that information may be shared with the team on their behalf (Strein & Hershenson, 1991). To maintain the student's trust, however, it would be wise to secure the student's permission, and then to only share general information.

Rights of Parents and Informed Consent

Informed consent involves consent for counseling itself, as well as consent for services within the limits and conditions of counseling. Here again we see how parental rights influence the work counselors do with students. Even though parental permission for counseling is not required by law in most states, the legal ability of the student to consent for counseling itself might be an issue (Remley & Herman, 2000). While the law holds that the age of majority is 18, there have been indications that younger persons might be "capable of assuming responsibility for their rights" (Ledyard, 1998). This means that a *mature* minor might be able to give informed consent for counseling (Isaacs & Stone, 1999; Ledyard, 1998), but counselors should be aware that if parents insist that counseling be discontinued, they "*probably* have a legal right to have their wishes followed" (Remley & Herman, 2000, p. 315; emphasis authors'). Counselors are advised to follow their district's policy about obtaining parental consent for counseling; generally, the younger the client, the more careful schools are to obtain parental permission.

The second issue of informed consent involves the information that is shared with students about the limits of confidentiality. This issue involved two topics: the timing of the information about informed consent, and the ability of the student to understand these limitations due to developmental maturity. In terms of timing, Isaacs and Stone (1999) found that 98 percent of the high school counselors they studied responded that they inform students about the limits of confidentiality. What is troubling, however, is that they also found that 50 percent of these same counselors indicated they inform students of the limits of confidentiality *only at a time when the discussion turns to the topics that might have to be reported.* Both the ASCA Ethical Standards and the ACA Code of Ethics require that information relative to the limits of confidentiality be discussed as the counseling relationship is initiated and throughout the counseling process as needed.

This is a challenge for elementary counselors, who may, by virtue of being present in hallways and playgrounds, be informed of confidential and private information about the student or the family in rather public places. To prevent such public family and self-disclosures, elementary counselors often share the role of the counselor, limits to confidentiality, and the meaning of counseling during classroom developmental curriculum presentations. These classroom presentations also provide counselors with the ability to find developmentally appropriate language to help young students understand these mature concepts. Many elementary school counselors are reminded of stories in which primary grade students will go home and tell their parents that they and the school counselor share a "secret," which, as you might imagine, usually prompts a parental phone call requesting an explanation.

For counselors at all levels, being respectful of the student's right to informed consent means that the limits of confidentiality are clearly explained to the student early in the counseling relationship, in developmentally appropriate terms.

Defining the "Client": Conflict of Interest between Student and School

Is the counselor foremost a *counselor* or an *employee*? There may be situations in which responsibility to students will conflict with responsibility to the school. While the ASCA Ethical Standards state that the counselor must inform officials of conditions that may be disruptive or damaging, this is couched in terms of concurrently honoring the confidentiality between the counselee and counselor. ACA directs counselors to establish clear agreements with employers about the conditions of the work but then also indicates that accepting employment implies that counselors agree with the employer's general policies and principles. If a school policy requires disclosure of confidential information, such as mandating that all employees report all suspicions of intoxicated students, the counselor could be caught in a dilemma. Issues of trust (How will students get help if they are afraid of getting into trouble?) as well as credibility (What if all the counselor has is an unsubstantiated rumor?) arise in such situations. What if the person spreading the rumor later recants the story, claiming that the report of an intoxicated student was revenge after a quarrel? Does the counselor still have to report? What if all attempts to change the policy are unsuccessful?

D. Kaplan and Allison (1994) would suggest that confidentiality with the student should be maintained, especially if the limits of confidentiality were not disclosed before the student shared the confidential information with the counselor. However, Remley and Herman (2000) indicate that school counselors must follow the rules, regulations, or policies of the school and the district, even while they work to get them changed. These authors argue that dismissal for insubordination could give you a forum to confront the employer's policy, but the burden of proof would be on you to show that the employer's policy was in violation of the standards of the profession and therefore unreasonable. They propose that educating the employer through information and persuasion would be a more collegial way to approach the situation. Notice in this discussion that even the authors in the field may disagree about the appropriate action to take, reinforcing the need for you to have a process by which you think through professional dilemmas as they arise.

Counselor Competence

Competence refers to skill areas in which you must be competent and skill areas in which you are not considered competent without additional specialized training. Skills areas in which you must be competent include the foundation counseling skills, the ability to encourage client growth and development in ways that foster the client's interest and welfare, the ability to design collaborative counseling plans, and others. These are competencies implied in the Code of Ethics (ACA) and in the Ethical Standards (ASCA) in which the profession defines those minimum performance standards required of all counselors and all school counselors. In addition to these skills, there are specialized issues—such as gender and cultural identity development, psychosocial development, and family development—that are foundation competencies for counselors working with young people (Lawrence & Kurpius, 2000). Counselors not performing in a manner consistent with these minimum performance standards are considered impaired, are required to seek assistance, and, if necessary, must limit, suspend, or terminate their professional responsibilities.

Conversely, there will also be skill areas in which you will need additional training to be competent. In this book, we will define school counseling within the parameters of counseling, educating, consultation and collaboration, and leadership, coordination and advocacy. In each of these activities, there will be areas beyond which you might be in danger of practicing outside the scope of your skills. For example, if you do not have a teaching certificate in your state, you cannot call yourself a teacher; if you do not have the professional qualifications, even though some of your work involves social work–like activities, you cannot call yourself a social worker. This is logical. However, can school counselors work with students with mental health issues such as depression, self-mutilation, and eating disorders? If you have attended a one-hour workshop on the interpretation of the Myers-Briggs, are you "competent" in its administration and interpretation? These are gray areas in the concept of competence.

In general, there are established standards of proficiency within the counseling profession to help you answer these questions. For example, most graduate programs in counselor education require a class in appraisal procedures and techniques, assessment, tests and measurement, or some other term referring to training in the evaluation, selection, administration, and interpretation of formal and informal instruments used in counseling. Successful completion of this course in your graduate program qualifies you to administer and interpret master's-level assessment instruments. Instruments that are required to be administered by master's-plus-training or doctoral-level professionals would be beyond the scope of your competence without such training.

Procedures from other specialty areas, such as marriage and family therapy, may also be beyond the scope of the practice of most school counselors, unless they have additional training in that area (K. M. Davis, 2001; Magnuson & Norem, 1998). Family systems therapy is more in-depth than doing counseling with a parent and student to help them communicate more effectively, and family systems therapy does require additional training. But, if a student in your school is diagnosed as having Asperger's Syndrome, you could work with that student to facilitate his or her academic, career, and personal/social development, as long as you obtain additional education through coursework, the professional literature, and/or conferences, and as long as you obtain consultation from expert others while you deepen your own understanding of all issues involved with that diagnosis.

As you develop professionally, you would want to remain aware of the lifelong need for professional development, renewal, and training. What you are learning in your graduate program is not all you will ever need to know to be an effective professional counselor. Remaining competent means you must attend conferences, workshops, and classes; you must be up-to-date in the professional literature; and you must monitor your effectiveness at all times to ensure that you are providing the best possible service for all your partners in the comprehensive school counseling program.

Clinical Notes

Clinical records in the form of private notes kept in the sole possession of the counselor are not subject to the Family Educational Rights and Privacy Act (FERPA), even though administrative records are. According to Remley and Herman (2000), as long as the counselor does not show them to anyone else, these are considered the counselor's private notes. The only access anyone would have to them is through court order, subpoena, or other legal process. Remley and Herman further suggest that counselors document enough information to jog their memory, "to document events that . . . demonstrate [they] have performed [their] responsibilities in an appropriate and professional manner based on 'standards of practice,'" *written in a manner that would be appropriate to read in front of the student and his or her family* (p. 317; emphasis added). These authors suggest that all public and private clinical notes be put on a record destruction calendar consistent with the destruction schedule for all records held by the district; ASCA (2004) recommends that "sole possession records [be shredded] when the student transitions to the next level, transfers to another school, or graduates." However, ASCA also recommends "discretion and deliberation" before destroying records pertaining to notes on child abuse, suicide, sexual harassment, or violence.

Online Counseling and the Use of Technology

Technology and its effect on the world cannot be denied, and counseling is not immune to these changes. It is entirely possible that school counselors might be contacted by students, parents, and colleagues who need professional services, but their only or best access to their counselor is from the privacy of their homes. In the event that this occurs, you should be aware that there are specific ethical issues involved in online counseling. ACA addresses these issues in the Code of Ethics (ACA, 2005) in Section A.12, Technology Applications. In addition, the National Board of Certified Counselors (NBCC, n.d.) has defined the Practice of Internet Counseling (available from www.nbcc.org). In this document, NBCC details various modalities and forms of technology-assisted counseling, as well as important ethics of using these modalities; you will want to download and print the NBCC standards for your own reference.

While this is not a complete list of all of the standards, NBCC highlights the following issues:

1. Counselors should take steps to address impostor concerns by using code words, numbers, or graphics.
2. Counselors should verify the identity of the consenting adult when counseling minors.
3. Counselors should provide instructions for contacting the counselor when he or she is offline by explaining how often e-mail messages are to be checked by the counselor.
4. Counselors should explain to clients the possibility of technology failure and direct them to call if problems arise in sending and receiving e-mail messages.

5. Counselors should explain to clients how to cope with potential misunderstandings arising from the lack of visual or auditory cues from the counselor or the client by asking for clarification.
6. Counselors should provide information about local crisis on-call and emergency services to clients.
7. Counselors should be respectful of clients' values and be sensitive to the local conditions and customs that affect clients' values.
8. Counselors should inform clients about encryption methods being used to ensure the security of communications.
9. Counselors should inform clients if, how, and how long session data are being preserved.
10. Counselors should follow appropriate procedures regarding the release of information and should work to ensure the confidentiality of the Internet counseling relationship.
11. Counselors should facilitate consumer protection regarding certification and licensing by providing links on their webpages to the websites of all certification bodies and licensure boards.

While the technology exists to provide counseling online, there is no reason to believe that counseling must be delivered using the Internet. It may be an option for various students, parents, and counselors, but there is no mandate to make online counseling available to your students. Certainly, the younger the student/client, the more concerns arise about the appropriateness of contact via technology. If you choose to use this medium, be aware of the issues and questions surrounding its use and potential misuse by being aware of relevant ethics.

In addition, many school counselors will establish and maintain a webpage for the comprehensive school counseling program (CSCP). These are wonderful ways to inform all our partners about what we do and why we do it. Consider how invaluable that resource can be for students, parents, and teachers to access important information about student issues (confidentiality [Huss, Bryant, & Mulet, 2008], anger management, bullying, friendship, cutting, eating disorders, etc.), learning styles and study skills, and career information. The caveat with providing this information is that whereas most counselors will find it easier to provide a link to the source, they must be very careful to check the link regularly. Official sites for organizations such as ACA, the U.S. Department of Labor, or the U. S. Department of Education will remain relatively consistent, but organization websites owned by private web providers may change without notice. We know of a counselor who lost her job because the address of a private website that could be accessed via a link on her counseling webpage was sold to another organization—and this new organization changed the content of the site to pornography. In addition, any computer connected to the Internet must have firewalls to protect against hacker access to confidential school and counseling records.

One recent development concerning firewalls: one counselor reported recently that students had circumvented the school's firewall by using a foreign-language translation program. Consult regularly with your district's information technology (IT) professionals to maintain your site's integrity.

Diversity and Values

Although it is ethically mandated that counselors are competent in counseling persons of diversity, not all counselors are equally competent in this area. In terms of cultural diversity, recent studies suggest that school counselors still need additional understanding of racial identity development and multicultural within-group differences (Holcomb-McCoy, 2001), as well as a sense of competence to address cross-cultural issues (Constantine & Yeh, 2001). Many counselors do not attend to multiculturalism as an important part of their work, believing that "students of color would rather work with someone from their own culture, so why should I pursue training in their culture?" It is clear from recent research that ethnicity is not what helps to establish a strong therapeutic alliance; rather, it is the perceived similarity between the counselor's and student's attitudes, values, background, and socioeconomic status (Esters & Ledoux, 2001). "After all, a school counselor who shares a student's attitudes and values and a similar background and socioeconomic status will, by most definitions of culture, share more of the culture and will thus be more similar than a school counselor who is simply a member of the same race. This finding should be encouraging to school counselors who find themselves attempting to build a counseling relationship with a student or a group of students with whom they differ in either race, sex, or both" (p. 169).

However, as humans, our identity does provide greater comfort in dealing with some students and greater challenge when dealing with others. Understanding racial identity development and multicultural dynamics will help counselors understand more clearly those areas of congruence between their values and attitudes and those of their students. In a recent qualitative study exploring the comfort level of middle school counselors in terms of same-sex or cross-sex working relationships with students, all of the respondents indicated that they found same-sex working relationships "more comfortable and natural" (Rayle, 2005, p. 155). As Rayle stated, "It is possible that cross-gender relationships are a substantive cultural issue for middle school counselors due to young adolescents' emerging sexuality, relationship, and gender identity issues" (p. 155). Similarly, Thorn and Contreras (2005) describe one district's decision to hire a Latina counselor to address the needs of their growing Latino population, as students' and families' needs for support, free of a translator, became crucial to address.

The establishment of a nurturing counseling relationship is the counselor's responsibility under the moral imperative of beneficence, but there is also a moral imperative to protect from harm (nonmaleficence). Issues of diversity also extend to the rights of students to have a safe, harassment-free educational environment. Not only does this pertain to students of cultural diversity, it also extends to students of economic diversity, sexual diversity (gay, lesbian, bisexual, and questioning youth), and values diversity (religious choice, moral choice).

The first source of diversity we will discuss is economic diversity. One of the most critical source of values is socioeconomic status. As the gap widens between the richest and the poorest, and as more and more families fall below the poverty line, the gulf between the "haves" and the "have nots" also gets wider (Payne, 1996). School counselors at every level, as stewards of the climate of the school, must be alert to the school experience of those who are most impoverished, those who may well become the target of teasing or bullying because they don't have the latest clothes or shoes. It is easy to become complacent in our own affluence and not notice those who exclude and diminish others on the basis of income, or worse yet, join in when students victimize each other on that basis.

In terms of sexual diversity, schools have a legal obligation to address student-on-student sexual harassment, and schools that do not can be held liable for violating the federal civil rights law under Title IX of the Education Amendments of 1972 (McFarland & Dupuis, 2001). By extension, students who are harassed by virtue of their sexual orientation must be protected and nurtured (McFarland & Dupuis, 2001), and their educational experience must not be marred by sexual violence and harassment (C. B. Stone, 2000). Recall that school counselors must report instances of sexual harassment to administration under Title IX, but the identity of the victim may be protected by the student's request for confidentiality, even if it hampers the school's ability to respond to the report (C. B. Stone, 2000).

Finally, in the widest context, diversity really refers to differences in value systems. Counselors are enjoined from imposing their values on their clients, no matter what the age of the client. Both ACA and ASCA address this specifically in their respective ethical documents, mandating that counselors actively respect the dignity of the client and promote the welfare of the client. It is only through careful self-analysis and self-awareness that counselors can come to articulate their own value system and avoid imposing that value system on clients. (Recall the hearing aid metaphor earlier in the chapter?) To examine how challenging this can be for school counselors, consider the following questions:

1. Do you believe in abortion, the right to life, or does it depend on the situation?
2. Do you believe in corporal punishment? When does a spanking become a beating? When does striking a young person become child abuse?

3. Do you believe that a 16-year-old is old enough to consent to sexual relationships? How old is old enough to give consent for sex? How old is old enough to give consent for marriage? What is the difference between those concepts?

4. What are your attitudes regarding same-sex relationships? Do same-sex parents provide the same home environment that traditional parents provide?

5. What are your attitudes regarding mixed-race relationships?

6. What are your attitudes concerning nontraditional families? Is divorce acceptable? Is single parenting as good as having both parents in the home (even if the relationship between the parents is hateful and destructive)?

7. What are your assumptions about people who live in poverty? What about people who live in the wealthiest neighborhoods?

8. Hard work is a value also. How would you react to a student or parent who wants to go on welfare rather than work? How would you react to a student or parent who wants to contemplate nature rather than work? What if he or she wants to write a great novel, a great play, a symphony, rather than work? Do your answers differ depending on the situation? Why?

9. Your student and the student's parent define "fun" as drinking to inebriation. Your spouse "relaxes" the same way—sometimes, you do too. Is it OK for the adults and not for the student? Or is it OK for the student? If marijuana were not illegal, would that be OK? Why or why not?

These questions just scratch the surface of the values questions faced every day by school counselors. If you aren't careful, your values and your attitudes will be communicated in your work, and then you're in violation of the ethics. You have to begin to think of these issues now.

It is important to note that the intent is to advocate for respectful, inclusive, and safe schools because everyone has the right to be free from harassment and the inappropriate imposition of another's values, not just because the counselor or school wants to avoid being sued. The intent is to reinforce our belief that respect, inclusiveness, and safety are the right conditions under which to educate young people, no matter who they are. Our laws and ethics make it our moral imperative to protect all young people and to promote their healthy development.

PROFESSIONAL LIABILITY, INSURANCE, AND CERTIFICATION

Many school counseling students are surprised and alarmed when they learn that they may be sued in the course of their work as a school counselor. With the rise in student risk behaviors, suicides, and school violence, the duty to warn and protect takes on a much heavier burden than in previous years (Remley & Herman, 2000; Simpson, 1999). School counselors may be held liable for breach of confidentiality, negligence, or malpractice, for providing inadequate services, and for not protecting the student from suicide and/or threats of harm from others.

But aren't school counselors covered by the insurance of the school? Not if the interest of the school and the interest of the counselor are different (Remley & Herman, 2000). If the charges suggest that the counselor acted in contradiction to school policy, the counselor's interests and the district's interests may be very different. To distance itself from fiscal liability, the district may suspend or dismiss the counselor, claiming that the counselor was not acting on behalf of the district when the problem behavior occurred. For example, a counselor is charged with sexual harassment of students. The school has a policy against sexual harassment and will dismiss or suspend the counselor when the complaint is filed. In this way, the school minimizes its liability, and the defense used by the school's attorney will be to locate the blame on the accused, thereby distancing the school from responsibility and reducing the monetary judgment. The counselor must now obtain legal services, paying out-of-pocket for attorney's fees and any judgments against him or her.

It is for this reason that school counselors are urged to obtain their own professional liability insurance ("Personal Liability Insurance," 2000; Remley & Herman, 2000). Such insurance is available through membership in the national counseling professional associations: ACA and

ASCA. (Contact these organizations via the Internet to learn more about professional liability insurance.)

Factors that may mitigate the cost of such liability insurance are professional licenses and certifications. In addition to state certification and/or licensure for school counselors, school counselors may want to consider national certification as a counselor and/or school counselor through the NBCC. This additional level of professional recognition is obtained through successful completion of the National Counselor Exam (NCE), a comprehensive exam offered around the country, and documented postgraduate experience and supervision. This qualifies counselors to become National Certified Counselors, or NCCs. With additional documented hours of school counseling education and experience, counselors can qualify to become National Certified School Counselors, or NCSCs. Continued credentialing with these certifications require additional professional development and education. To obtain more information about these certifications at the national level, you can contact the NBCC through its website at www.nbcc.org, under the Certifications tab.

In addition, school counselors in some states are eligible for status as a Licensed Professional Counselor, or LPC (different states refer to this status by different names; consult your state for the appropriate designation). Since standards vary from state to state, you will want to obtain information from your state to explore this possibility. Furthermore, the National Board for Professional Teaching Standards (NBPTS) offers counselor certification, and many states will increase the salary of counselors who obtain this level of credentialing. (See their website for their requirements at www.nbpts.org.) The point is that school counselors who are willing to go the extra mile to document their professional expertise and commitment will benefit in terms of professional recognition, and possibly, remuneration.

RESPONDING TO LEGAL ACTION

The first thing most counselors do when they are served with legal papers is become very anxious. But it is important to not to panic. If you are served with a subpoena for records, information, and/or testimony, the following steps are recommended *before you comply with the court order*:

1. Consult with professional colleagues about the situation.
2. Consult with your administration about the situation.
3. Consult with the school's or the school district's attorney.
4. Consult with your state and/or national professional school counseling association.
5. Review your documents about the situation.
6. Be prepared to protest the subpoena in court, arguing that the information in your possession is not relevant or appropriate. This protects the confidential nature of the counseling relationship.
7. If necessary, obtain legal advice on your own.
8. If the subpoena is for testimony at a custody hearing, Remley and Herman recommend that you do not become voluntarily involved. If you are forced to testify, limit your testimony to only factual information, not your opinions on the competence of one parent over the other. (Remley & Herman, 2000)

RESOURCES AND RECOMMENDATIONS FOR SCHOOL COUNSELORS

There are a variety of resources pertaining to ethics, laws, policies, and other issues. As has been mentioned several times, you will want to invest the time and energy in obtaining information about the professional standards and expectations of the American Counseling Association (ACA), the American School Counselor Association (ASCA), the Association for Specialists in Group Work (ASGW), the National Career Development Association (NCDA), the National Board for Certified Counselors (NBCC), as well as the references for articles and books about ethics from leaders in the profession. In addition, membership in your national and state counseling and school counseling associations entitles you to professional consultation with peers, most often through an ethics committee. Listservs may also be a way of communicating with professional peers to obtain feed-back about ethical issues, but due to the public nature of the list discussions, caution would be necessary to protect confidentiality. Strategies for establishing and maintaining your work as an ethical school counselor include the following:

1. Obtain professional supervision periodically from a peer. This involves inviting feed-back from a colleague about your skills in educating, consultation and collaboration, and leadership, coordination and advocacy. Most supervision focuses on counseling skills, however. This could be done in a conversational format but is most effective when done with a video- or audio-tape of your counseling with a student client. Due to confidentiality issues, you would need to ensure that you have permission from the student and the student's parents or guardians to tape counseling for supervision purposes.

2. Read about ethics in the professional literature. Once a year, do an online search of the professional literature to obtain copies of new articles about ethics in counseling in general and school counseling in particular.

3. Take additional workshops, courses, and/or conference sessions on current issues in ethics.

4. Keep current on contemporary issues in counseling, such as counseling strategies, new theories and techniques, and client issues. All of these areas are constantly evolving, and you must remain informed about each of them.

5. Obtain professional consultation as needed with peers about national, state, and local issues in schools and in school counseling. Networking with colleagues is essential.

6. Do not limit yourself to contact with school counselors alone. You need a broader perspective, so become networked with clinical/mental health, college, rehabilitation, and other counselors in your area.

7. You must have an effective referral network in place, so you must know the resources in your community. Learn about these professionals in terms of who they help, how they help, where they are located, how much they cost, and other details.

8. To avoid working in a setting with whose leadership you have an ethical difference of opinion, inquire into administrative policy during the interview to determine if you can live with its administrative philosophy (Tompkins & Mehring, 1993). For example, you can ask the interviewer about his or her experiences, positive and negative, with school counseling. Listen for areas in the response that indicate a lack of awareness or appreciation for important counseling issues such as confidentiality, parental consent, and mandated reporting.

9. You must know the laws for your state (Tompkins & Mehring, 1993). This involves some digging on your part, but you have to know what your state requires you to know before you step into a school.

10. You must be able to work with persons who hold different values than you do. Research continues to show that the best way to understand diversity is to know diverse persons; get to know people from many walks of life on a personal level. It is only through being open to diversity that you can truly know and become comfortable with various value systems. It is then that you can see, underneath the diversity, those common threads that bind us all.

CASE STUDY REVISITED

Integration

Now that you've read the chapter, go back and reread Jason's Casual Comment.

1. What was the comment he made that created the situation?
2. If Kim's comment was related to sexual activity, what do you think Jason should do? What are the questions you would like to ask her? What else do you need to know before you can act?

3. Assume that Kim's comment was not related to sexual activity. Now what are the questions you would like to ask her?

4. What do you believe is the appropriate level of parental involvement in this situation? What is the appropriate level of school involvement? Under what conditions, specifically, would you be mandated to report? List all of them.

5. How have your values shaped the answers you gave to these questions? ■

Suggested Readings

American Counseling Association. (2005). *ACA code of ethics*. Alexandria, VA: Author. It is imperative that all counselors understand the Code of Ethics for the profession. This document is also available at www.counseling.org.

Herlihy, B., & Corey, G. (1996). *ACA ethical standards casebook* (5th ed.). Alexandria, VA: American Counseling Association. This book presents the ethics of the ACA with illustrative vignettes and discussion chapters written by experts in the field.

Isaacs, M. L., & Stone, C. (1999). School counselors and confidentiality: Factors affecting professional choices. *Professional School Counseling, 2*, 258– 266. This article presents a study in which school counselors at various levels respond to hypothetical situations, involving age- and situation-specific concerns, in which they would break confidentiality. The findings highlight the unique perspectives of high school counselors juxtaposed with those of middle and elementary schools.

Lambie, G. W. (2005). Child abuse and neglect: A practical guide for professional school counselors. *Professional School Counseling, 8*, 249–258. This is a very comprehensive resource for school counselors on the topic of child abuse and neglect.

Payne, R. K. (1996). *A framework for understanding poverty* (3rd ed.). Highlands, TX: aha! Process. This is an excellent book written for educators working with economically diverse students, even though it has generated some controversy over its scientific rigor. There are updated books by this organization that are more connected to research into economic diversity and related value systems. It is well advised for school counselors to understand the issues of generational poverty as discussed in these books.

Sealander, K. A., Schwiebert, V. L., Oren, T. A., & Weekley, J. L. (1999). Confidentiality and the law. *Professional School Counseling, 3*, 122–127. This article presents current information relative to the laws affecting confidentiality in schools.

Six Qualities
of Comprehensive School
Counseling Programs

LEARNING OBJECTIVES

By the end of this chapter, you will

1. Know the six qualities of a comprehensive school counseling program (CSCP)

2. Understand and be able to articulate the issues and prototypes in student development in a *holistic* CSCP

3. Understand and be able to articulate the issues and prototypes in student development in a *systemic* CSCP

4. Understand and be able to articulate the issues and prototypes to create a *balanced* CSCP

5. Understand and be able to articulate the issues and prototypes to create a *proactive* CSCP

6. Understand and be able to articulate the issues and prototypes in a CSCP that are *infused* into the academic agenda of the school

7. Understand and be able to articulate the issues and prototypes to create a *reflective* CSCP

8. Be able to demonstrate an understanding of how these prototypes apply in a case study

CASE STUDY

Mr. Paulson Counseling Ty

Mr. Paulson was finishing up some paperwork before the bell rang to start the day, when Ty came into the office. "Mr. Paulson, can I see you today?" he asked.

"Yeah, Ty. Sure. What's up? Do you want to meet now?" He gestured to the chair by his desk when he saw Ty's face. "Have a seat."

Paulson paused to keep himself from swearing. "What happened to your face? Who did this to you?" Instinctively he began to reach up to the young man's face, but withdrew his hand when Ty pulled away.

"You know, man. The streets are a bitch." Ty paused. "That's not why I'm here. I'm getting pressure at home to get another job to help out more with the bills. I hate working at the burger place, but I do it to help out my mom. Now how am I gonna get the grades to get into college if I'm working two jobs? I'm already struggling in my science class and Miss Epps tells me I'm barely pulling a C. Now this.

"Maybe I should just give up the college thing anyway. Everyone tells me that I won't make it, because I don't know what I want to study. They think it's a waste of time. But I wanted to go just to get the hell out of the city. I don't think I'll have any life at all if I stay here. There aren't any jobs here, the ones that are here don't pay anything, and I don't want to live with my mom the rest of my life.

"And then there's this," he says as he points to the cuts and bruises on his face. "I'm sick of being beat up because I'm not cool—I work and go to school and don't want to make trouble. I'm just not going to take it anymore. Mom wants me to turn the other cheek, but how can I ever call myself a man if I don't stand up for myself and what I believe in?"

"Ty, I'd like to spend some time talking about these questions. Can I talk to your mom about ways we can both help you? Is that ok with you?"

"Sure, Mr. Paulson. That's cool. See you during my study hall."

CHALLENGE QUESTIONS

What are your reactions as you picture Ty? What questions came to your mind? What would you like to say to Ty? Where would you begin in your conversation with him? What do you think Mr. Paulson should do?

What do you see as Ty's biggest challenges? What will be the most helpful for him right now? In the long run? Are those different issues or not?

If Mr. Paulson does nothing to help Ty, where do you see this young man's future path taking him? ∎

COMPREHENSIVE SCHOOL COUNSELING PROGRAMS

You now have some perspective in terms of the history and development of the fields of counseling, education, and school counseling. You have also had a chance to think about what works and what doesn't work in American schools, how a school climate of respect benefits students and staff, and some of the ethical issues that surround the work of the professional school counselor. Now we will turn our attention to what you need to know to design and implement a comprehensive school counseling program (CSCP). To be comprehensive, a school counseling program must be

- *Holistic*, addressing the question "What do school counselors focus on with students?" The answer: all aspects of the student's development.
- *Systemic*, addressing the question "Who do school counselors work with?" The answer: all persons with whom the student interacts and all systems of significance in the student's life.
- *Balanced*, addressing the question "How do school counselors do their work?" The answer: by balancing their time in the primary activities of the school counselor—namely, counseling, educating, consultation and collaboration, and leadership, coordination and advocacy.
- *Proactive*, addressing the question "Why do school counseling programs exist?" The answer: to mitigate the effects of any experiences that may compromise the development of the students through primary, secondary, and tertiary prevention.
- *Infused into the academic curriculum*, addressing the question "How will kids access the program?" The answer: by infusing the CSCP into all aspects of the school experience, including the classroom.
- *Reflective*, addressing the question "How do we know we make a difference?" The answer: by being accountable to our schools, our students, and ourselves for the information about the impact our work has on the lives of our students.

These six questions, and the six qualities for CSCPs that answer these questions, will be essential for implementing a program in the school that truly benefits all children. For each of these six qualities, we will examine the issues that school counselors address within that topic, then present a "prototype," or template that can be used to design the *content* of your CSCP. (In Chapters 5 and 6, we will present the *form* or structure of your program in terms of the ASCA National Model [ASCA, 2005] and the various models for delivery systems within the National Model.)

CSCPs ARE HOLISTIC

The overall development of young people depends on so many factors: biological, social, familial, and educational, to name a few. Because the school environment is the context in which school counselors work, we focus on those developmental domains in which we have influence. Those domains are academic development, career development, and personal/social development. Think of this chapter as a road map. In Chapters 1 and 2, we discussed the outcomes of excellent education: that is our destination. To get to that destination, our students must maximize their personal potential in each area: academic, career, and personal/social success. This part of the chapter is designed to help you understand where students are headed with their development and how to help your students achieve the most within each domain.

Academic Development

There is no doubt that the mission of the school is academic development—the lifelong ability to acquire and use new information, new insights, and new ways of seeing and interacting with the world. Addressing academic development as the first domain is a confirmation of the partnership between school counselors and the educational mission of the institution. Being an effective partner in the educational process means that counselors are able to help students with that mission. Academic issues are often why students come to the counselor: academic failure, educational planning, academic mediation, and academic impediments to learning. These are all issues that counselors attend to in this domain.

MULTIPLE INTELLIGENCES   The following prototype is presented to give you one model for thinking about the learning of young people. This is not the only way to conceptualize academic development, but could help you conceptualize challenges to learning.

The traditional definition of intelligence as a univariate construct, the "individual's capacity or innate potential for learning," has been challenged for a number of years (Travers et al., 1993, p. 231). What has replaced this elementary definition of a complex construct are various models, both psychometric and practical (Esters & Ittenbach, 1999).

Based on the work of Howard Gardner (H. Gardner, 1983; H. Gardner & Hatch, 1989; Lazear, 1999), one practical and useful model for understanding academic development involves understanding the concept of multiple intelligences. According to Gardner, an intelligence involves the ability to solve a problem or create something that has meaning in a particular context, and it is this view of intelligence as related to *context* that is unique and powerful. Gardner asserts that individuals possess the full spectrum of intelligences, but that we have natural strengths that bring one or more of these strengths into use more often than the others. Furthermore, the issue of context becomes important in that we choose to access certain intelligences based on context and situation.

This perspective on intelligence is particularly useful for understanding why a student learns (motivation and predilection for learning), how a student learns (acquisition and retention of information), as well as how a student manifests that learning has taken place (performance on academic tasks). In other words, when you understand an individual's unique constellation of intelligences, you can understand why that student is interested in certain subjects, how the student learns, and how the student might prefer to demonstrate her or his understanding of the subject learned.

The intelligences include verbal/linguistic intelligence, logical/mathematical intelligence, visual spatial intelligence, bodily/kinesthetic intelligence, musical/rhythmic intelligence, interpersonal intelligence, intrapersonal intelligence, and naturalist intelligence (Lazear, 1999). Information about the individual's unique intelligence constellation can be obtained through conversation with the student, through discussions of what the student finds interesting, how he or she learns things, and what he or she does for fun. You don't need a formal assessment to understand which intelligences the student possesses and uses.

REFLECTION MOMENT

What were your academic issues in school? What were your grades like? Did you study hard, or did you play hard? What were your life priorities? What were your "easy" subjects, and which ones really challenged you? Ask significant others what they remember from their school days. Compare your hardest and easiest courses with theirs. Talk about what made those courses seem hard or easy. See if you can identify their intelligence constellation. How would you have wanted to be treated if you went to someone for help with a hard course that he or she thought was easy? What are the implications for your counseling style?

Career Development

Career development is an important part of what school counselors do at every level. Some issues in this domain include fear of making a "mistake" in career selection and the effect of rapid world changes on confidence in career predictions. In addition, some parents and teachers are reluctant to begin career discussions early in a student's life; conversely, some adults pressure students to decide too early. Other students struggle with pressure from adults to be practical in their career decision making rather than following dreams, and sometimes parents and others push students into college as a means of "guaranteeing" success.

LIFELONG CAREER PROCESS   What does the career decision process look like, both in terms of the process itself and in terms of the outcomes? From a whole-life perspective (Dollarhide, 1997), the process of making viable career decisions involves seven steps (Dollarhide, 2000a):

Step 1: Understanding of self (knowledge of one's likes, dislikes, abilities, skills, gifts, challenges, values, needs, dreams, lifestyle goals, personality, interests)

Step 2: Understanding of the world of work (knowledge of career paths, job titles, salary levels, employers, employment environments, occupational projections, training requirements)

Step 3: Reality testing (firsthand experience through employment, volunteering, internships, cooperative education jobs, lab experiences, job shadowing)

Step 4: Commitment (making a decision, with relative confidence, in the face of uncertainty)

Step 5: Career preparation (accessing formal or informal training for the job or occupation)

Step 6: Placement/career entrance (using job-seeking skills, filling out applications, writing cover letters and resumes, participating in interviews, then accessing opportunities in the chosen occupation)

Step 7: Evaluation and renewal (as the individual matures throughout life, the core self changes in terms of likes, dislikes, values, and other variables outlined in Step 1. Concurrently, there are changes in the work world. Individuals continuously evaluate their level of career satisfaction, and will begin again at Step 1 when their level of career satisfaction reaches a low-point threshold of tolerance. If they still like the tasks of the occupation, they may decide to change employers. If they dislike the tasks, they may decide to change occupations entirely.)

In terms of outcomes, Henderson (2000) studied persons who were happy at work and found striking similarities among those studied. They were "notably similar in their particularly dogged commitment to follow their interests, their competencies, and what they enjoyed doing. Consequently, their careers tended to follow a *positive meandering path*" (p. 309; emphasis added). This metaphor feels particularly empowering, and will help students and families feel less pressure to make the right choice right now. Similarly, Gellatt (1991, 1996) presents one response to the dilemma of decision making in times of uncertainty and rapid change. Dubbed "positive uncertainty," he suggests a personal decision-making philosophy or paradigm to help people both "imagine and create possibilities" (1996, p. 391). In this paradigm, people are urged to balance two opposing perspectives simultaneously. To maximize adaptability and flexibility while maintaining focus on a desired life/career outcome, positive uncertainty would urge being "focused and flexible" about life and career goals (p. 391). To maximize learning while maintaining awareness of career information, this philosophy would maintain being "aware and wary" about what is known, since "facts" change all the time (p. 391). To maximize the power of dreams while remaining grounded, people are urged to "be objective and optimistic" about their beliefs (p. 391). Finally, to maximize the power of creativity while engaging in reality testing, Gellatt would suggest being "practical and magical" in one's career behavior (p. 391).

The implications for students? Keep dreaming those big dreams, and never eliminate the possible to settle for the probable.

THE CAREER PORTFOLIO   One tool for facilitating the career development process is the career portfolio, in which students systematically explore their career ideas and understanding of self. There are a variety of ways such portfolios can be constructed, from highly individualized to highly structured.

In this portfolio, students document their self-knowledge in terms of personal qualities, personal skills, decision-making processes, and various competencies. They document their educational development, including things they know about their own learning, their plans for after high school, and various competencies. Finally, they document the results of their career exploration and planning, including the results of any career assessments taken and various career competencies. The final document is a personal career plan, in which students synthesize their self-knowledge, awareness of the world of work, career assessment information, training options, and skills into a viable list of career and training options that seem workable. The emphasis is on the word "options." The goal isn't to force students to make a career choice; the goal is to empower students to identify options that will focus further exploration.

CAREER CLUSTERS   Frequently, these portfolios are focused on career clusters. Promulgated by the National Association of State Directors of Career Technical Education Consortium (2006, www.careerclusters.org/16clusters.htm), the 16 clusters are

1. Agriculture, Food, and Natural Resources
2. Architecture and Construction
3. Arts, AV Technology, and Communications
4. Business, Management, and Administration
5. Education and Training
6. Finance
7. Government and Public Administration
8. Health Science
9. Hospitality and Tourism
10. Human Services
11. Information Technology
12. Law, Public Safety, Corrections, and Security
13. Manufacturing

14. Marketing, Sales, and Service

15. Science, Technology, Engineering, and Mathematics

16. Transportation, Distribution, and Logistics

In some schools, the curriculum is organized around the career clusters, so that both college-bound and non-college-bound students will graduate ready for whatever their postgraduate plans may be.

REFLECTION MOMENT

Recall your career journey. Were you intentional, focused, and deliberate, or did your career follow a "positive meandering path"? Do you know, with certainty, how your career path will unfold? (What do you want to do when *you* grow up?) What is the most empowering thing anyone said to you about your career path? What is the most destructive thing anyone said to you about it? What can you do now to avoid ever inflicting that same disappointment and disillusionment on any of your students?

Personal/Social Development

The third domain that forms the foundation of holistic comprehensive school counseling programs is the development of personal and social skills. This is an area in which many counselors feel especially comfortable, because it is the domain in which counseling itself is focused. Some examples of issues in this domain include the search for identity, relationship development, development of acceptance of others, skills for coping with change and adversity, and the search for rites of passage into adulthood.

IDENTITY ACHIEVEMENT   Marcia (as cited in Craig, 1996) referred to the resolution of the adolescent identity crisis as "identity achievement" (p. 439). This was defined as people who have made commitments to their careers and their own "individually formulated moral code" (p. 439). It is easy to see how this development of personal identity, morality, and definition resonates with the concepts of intelligences and careers discussed in the previous sections. Working to help young people develop higher cognitive skills concurrently helps them to think critically about their choices and to reflect on their responsibility for choice. It also puts into perspective the risk taking and experimentation with expression that young people exhibit during identity exploration (Craig, 1996, p. 453). Since experimentation is an essential part of choice, it might behoove school counselors to discuss the concept of safe risk taking with families and school professionals. In this context, safe risk taking would involve allowing young people safe expression of individuality without adult boundaries. For example, what does it hurt to allow a young person to wear a dark-colored shirt in the summer sun, rather than a light-colored one? That young person will learn that dark shirts do indeed get hot in the summer sun and will choose the light one next time. If life lessons are really learned only the hard way (Fay & Funk, 1995), then allowing young people to experience the consequences of their choices is the best way we can help young people learn about choice.

However, identity development for students of diversity will be unique. Since identity development depends on how young people see themselves and how others see them, those qualities that cause them to see themselves as "less than" are intensely painful and embarrassing. Adults tell young people to be proud of their unique qualities; the reality is that such appreciation often comes much later in life. The journey toward accepting oneself and others can begin in school, and the struggles of young people to accept their own diversity (the full spectrum of uniquenesses: race, gender, religion, sexual orientation, ability status, culture, etc.) can be facilitated by the school counselor. Many authors have addressed the unique challenges of diverse persons, developing models to describe racial identity development (Atkinson, Morten, & Sue, 1989; Helms, 1994), disability identity development (Scheer, 1994), female identity development (Pipher, 1994), male identity development (Pollack, 1998) and gay and lesbian identity development (D'Augelli, 1994). Each of these perspectives has made a significant contribution to the understanding of the developmental journey of diverse persons.

School counselors who are aware of the diversity of their students and who understand the theories of diversity identity development can better understand the painful aspects of the process of identity development, such as rage, isolation, and the need to associate with those of their diversity. Furthermore, knowing about identity development can help counselors communicate with students, by knowing when to help students connect with positive role models of their own diverse culture. Finally, counselors who use the insights gained from knowing identity development theories can help students integrate the best of both perspectives, teaching tolerance toward others in the process.

There are other constructs that will be helpful to school counselors who work with students on the basis of personal/social issues, such as self-esteem, emotional intelligence, and hope/resiliency. Branden (1994) examined self-esteem, defining it as two interrelated concepts: "the disposition to experience oneself as competent to cope with the basic challenges of life and as worthy of happiness" (p. 27). In that definition, it is easy to see that the foundation of self-esteem is competence or self-efficacy, and this comes from experiences in which meaningful challenges are met and dealt with effectively (Travers et al., 1993). Branden also stresses that self-esteem is a process (meaning lifelong effort) and a practice (meaning that self-esteem must be actively earned). Similarly, the concept of emotional intelligence can be helpful to school counselors. Goleman (1995) described emotional intelligence in terms of five domains: (1) knowing one's emotions, (2) managing one's emotions, (3) motivating oneself, or "marshaling emotions in the service of a goal" (p. 43) to enable sustained attention, management of stress, and delayed gratification, (4) recognizing emotions in others primarily through empathy, and (5) understanding and managing relationships effectively, or understanding and managing the emotions of others. It is through these five elements of emotional intelligence that people learn about themselves, acquire goal-directed behaviors and attitudes, learn about others, and acquire leadership skills and interpersonal effectiveness. Finally, hope and resiliency are important concepts to note. C. R. Snyder (1994) defined hope as "the sum of the mental willpower and waypower that you have for your goals" (p. 5). In this context, goals are those objects or accomplishments that we desire that serve as "mental targets for our thoughts" (p. 5). In order to have hope, then, students would need (1) clearly articulated, meaningful goals, (2) a sense of willpower or energy to move them toward those goals, and (3) high waypower, or the mental flexibility needed to find alternative routes should the path be blocked. Together, hope, emotional intelligence, and self-esteem can help most students who are confronting barriers to learning.

REFLECTION MOMENT

Do you remember struggling with your identity? What sorts of things did you do to express your individuality? What was the reaction of adults to your forms of self-expression? Are you a person of diversity? In your youth, what was your level of self-esteem? What was your level of emotional intelligence? What was your level of hope? How did the events of your life affect your self-esteem, emotional intelligence, and hope? How did school impact your experience?

CASE STUDY REVISITED

Integration

Go back and reread Mr. Paulson's conversation with Ty.

1. There are examples in this conversation of Ty's struggle in all three domains. Find an example of each. ■

Mr. Paulson Meets Ty's Mother

Later that day, Mr. Paulson called Ty's house to make an appointment to meet with Ty's mother.

"Thank you for coming in, Mrs. Bonté. I'm Calvin Paulson, Ty's counselor. Please call me Calvin. Ty came in this morning with some bruises on his face and concerns about school. I'd like to see what we can do together to help Ty deal with things."

Mrs. Bonté nodded. "I've been concerned about him. He's not been himself lately, more moody and irritable with everyone. What do you think's going on?"

"Well, he seemed upset with his needing to work more to help out at home. He said his grades are slipping, and he's not sure he can get into college. What can you tell me about what you see at home?"

Mrs. Bonté's eyes grew moist as she thought about her son. "He's such a good boy, always helping out with everything. He's my oldest, and he took over after his daddy died three years ago, helping out with his two younger brothers. I'm working all I can at my job, but I don't earn a lot. Ty watches his brothers, and that's no easy task—they like to needle him and pick fights with each other. I do know that Ty has his hands full until I get home.

"Ty usually starts dinner, then when I get home, he goes to his job. When he gets home from his work, he does his homework and studies until all hours of the night, because he wanted to get into college. Now he doesn't know what he wants to do, go to college or stay home and take care of me and the boys.

"I was sick for a couple of weeks and lost some hours at work; now I owe the doctor some money and all the bills are late. Ty insisted that he could work more hours or get a second job to help pay those bills, even though I told him I didn't want him to. His dad and I put some money aside so that the boys could go to college if they wanted. If I save that money for his schooling, I need his help for the bills, which means he won't be able to study as much and may not even get into college. If I use that money now for the bills, there won't be anything for his tuition." She sighed, feeling the weight of her worries.

"He's really having a tough time in his science class," she continued. "I don't know what it is about that teacher, that Ms. Epps. She seems to ride Ty pretty hard. He said that she seems mad at him all the time, but he's not sure what he did to cause it. Then there are problems with some of the kids on the block—some name-calling and pushing. I'm not sure what that's about, because he won't talk about that, either.

"I see him sinking, Calvin, and I don't know what to do about it. Look at all the things he's having trouble with—his brothers, the money worries, his job, his grades, Ms. Epps, the kids on the street. I don't know what to do to help him. I don't even know where to begin." ■

REFLECTION QUESTIONS

Think about what you heard from Ty and now you've heard from his mother. Do you understand Ty better, now that you see the context of his life? When you first heard from Ty that he needed to work more to help his family with the bills, did you jump to any conclusions about his parents? (Be honest!) Now that you know more, do you feel more compassion for him and his family?

CSCPs ARE SYSTEMIC

Recall the story in Chapter 1 of the little girl who threw stranded starfish back into the sea. It is true that we can help individual starfish by putting them back in the ocean, but if the water is polluted or poisonous, the starfish won't survive, in spite of our best efforts. Our work with students has to incorporate the environment and context in which our students live; otherwise the poison from that context will render our best efforts moot. This section of the chapter addresses the ocean of the starfish, the context of our students' lives.

Undeniably, the systems that surround children as they grow exert dramatic influences on development (Saginak, 2003). All young people are shaped developmentally by their environmental systems or context. It is in these contexts that young people learn the rules of living; values are acquired and explored and attitudes are shaped. It is also in these contexts that young people learn the rules of relating: to themselves, each other, their families, and society as a whole. These systems include broad and diffuse relationship webs, such as communities and cultures, as well as intermediate relationship webs, such as schools, to the most intimate of relationships, those with families and peers. The developmental resilience of young people will reflect the extent to which the systems in which they matured were healthy, respectful, and nurturing. This is where school counselors come in; they help young people understand and cope with the reality of the systems in which they are embedded.

The skills each child develops in response to his or her own unique systems context are as unique as the context. From community, culture, school, family, and peers, young people learn about the world, their place in the world, and by extension, themselves, in the process of socialization. According to Craig (1996), "socialization is the lifelong process by which individuals learn to become members of a social group, whether a family, a community, or a tribe. Becoming a member of a group involves recognizing and dealing with the social expectations of others" (p. 95). Each of these relationships teaches important social skills, and because of the connection between emotional intelligence (Goleman, 1995), identity, and life success, it is no leap to state that systemic components in the CSCP are crucial to students' overall K–12 success. These systemic components are programmatic responses to the needs of communities, cultures, schools, families, and peer groups in which our students are embedded (Blustein & Noumair, 1996).

In a systemic view of development, it is essential that school counselors be mindful of two rules of systems:

1. All actions within a system affect all members of that system. Much like all elements of a mobile move when one element is touched, all parts of a system resonate if there is a disturbance anywhere in the system.
2. Young people can be profoundly affected by the values and attitudes that are directly or indirectly taught through that system.

Community, Culture, School, Family, Peers

COMMUNITY   From the broadest perspective, young people are a part of a community—both geographic and sociological. Our geographic boundaries shrink every day; young people with access to the media are bombarded daily with messages about the state of the world and their place in that world, often to the detriment of the child. Excessive violence, gratuitous sexuality, and rampant consumerism are plainly visible in the ethos of the United States. Violence and sexuality are part of young people's everyday lives—from newscasts, to video games, to movies, music, and television talk shows.

Rampant consumerism is a product of our capitalist society. Regardless of family income, in this competitive, capitalistic society, it's not enough. Our market-driven, advertisement-saturated culture makes everyone feel inadequate; the goal of the marketing profession is to make us want things we don't have (Fox, 1994). It's little wonder that young people, who are painfully status- and self-conscious, feel the effects of peer pressure to have bigger, more, better, newer, biggest, newest, best. It's a race with no winners (except in the corporate world), and young people are played for all they are worth, because marketing an image to young people is big business.

In addition to the reality of our sociological community, we now see how technology is reducing our geographic community. Computers are both a gift and a curse in modern society. We can communicate around the world, access information, transact holiday shopping, and produce volumes of work in a fraction of the time it took a short decade ago. However, it is also a dangerous toy in the family den; through it, pedophiles access new victims, threats of violence are delivered, young people withdraw further from meaningful human contact, and new addictions are fostered.

CULTURE   It would be a mistake to try to summarize all the multicultural literature in this book, and oversimplifying would be disrespectful of the members of those cultures. It would also be a mistake to assume that you, the reader, have not had any exposure to multicultural education.

Diversity can be experienced through cultural affiliation, gender, sexual orientation, socioeconomic class, being differently abled, or many other diversity constructs. Diversity is any aspect of our lives that makes us feel different from others; some experience this as negative, but others experience it as a positive influence. It is crucial that school counselors are aware of how cultural values and attitudes are learned from the cultural context(s) of our lives (Payne, 2003; Scheer, 1994; Schmidt, 2006; T. B. Smith, 2004). These cultural contexts can include but are not limited to attitudes of society in general (for example, magazine ads that communicate a Eurocentric vision of beauty), attitudes of significant adults (jokes and comments made by family, teachers, and other significant adults), and attitudes of peers (teasing, bullying, provocation or aggressive actions of peers).

SCHOOL   In Chapter 2, we discussed schools as social institutions, and you were invited to consider dehumanizing schools and developmentally appropriate, effective schools. As we contemplate the effect of systems on our students, we must be aware of the values, messages, attitudes, and rules that are taught in our schools. We must examine how young people are taught to relate to each other, themselves, and the world around them. If the messages taught are "Don't trust anyone; they will hurt you"; "Don't trust yourself; you're stupid (lazy, crazy, incompetent . . .)"; "Don't try; it won't do any good"; or "Don't care; no one cares for you," then the cycle of pain, fear, hatred, and self-loathing will be perpetuated.

FAMILY   School counselors must also be aware of the influence of families, students' primary social context, on students' social, emotional, and cognitive development (Craig, 1996). These influences are two-directional and mutually reciprocal, with complicated and unpredictable interrelationships conveying rules, expectations, and experiences between members and across generations (Craig, 1996). Even within the same family, each person experiences the family unit and family events in a unique and idiosyncratic way (see Dinkmeyer et al. [1987] for a discussion of this concept in Adlerian counseling; see S. M. Hanna & Brown [1999] for a discussion of this concept in family systems counseling).

One of the primary roles of the family is as a socializing agent, as the family "interprets for the child the outside society and its culture. . . . Parents express their cultural values to their children in their attitudes toward such daily choices as food, clothing, friends, education and play" (Craig, 1996, p. 94). The challenge, especially in the current social reality of the United States, is that "the more diverse the social fabric [of society], the more pressure exists on the family system" (p. 94) to teach and perpetuate the family's unique values. The struggle of the family to teach these values determines the influence of the family system on the children directly, and on their schools indirectly.

The influence of families can range from positive, nurturing, motivating, and empowering (Schickedanz, Schickedanz, Forsyth, & Forsyth, 2001, p. 467), through ambivalent, neglectful, to overtly hateful and destructive (McWhirter, McWhirter, McWhirter, & McWhirter, 2007). When this influence is positive, children learn positive social skills. Unfortunately, when positive learning is not possible, children are left with socially inadequate skills, or skills that foster domination and/or violence—a lesson many young people learn from their homes, where they witness violence daily (McWhirter et al, 2007; Tolan & Guerra, 1998). In fact, violence that is witnessed most often by young people is relationship violence, in which one family member or "loved" one assaults another. When family stability is missing, we have good documentation of the negative effects (McWhirter et al., 2007). Community-wide economic instability, stagnation, racial and social intolerance, poor health care (mental and physical), poor childcare, and a host of other problems can cause increased stress in the home. This stress often resonates with stress and vulnerability in the family system, increasing the risk for divorce, family violence, neglect, substance abuse and addiction, and mental health problems, which then resonate with increased stress on the children living in the home (McWhirter et al., 2007).

These problems have a direct correlation with academic achievement, career development, and personal/social life functioning. For example, Noble (2000) found that students whose parents earn less than $36,000 a year or who have experienced three or more major problems at home (e.g., parental unemployment, chronic health problems, death, separation or divorce, or the need to work to help support the family) are more than twice as likely to be low academic achievers as high academic achievers (p. 15). According to Schickedanz et al. (2001), "parents . . . can affect their children's cognitive performance by creating an environment that leads to positive emotions and mood states, [as] [r]esearch demonstrates that a sad or angry mood leads to poorer performance at cognitive tasks like those children perform in school" (p. 467). These family stressors also have a direct correlation with more serious behaviors, such as school dropout, substance abuse and addiction, teenage pregnancy and risky sexual behaviors, delinquency, violence, and suicide (McWhirter et al., 2007).

As families change, emotional support for children often becomes uncertain. Chaos in the family results in chaos in the student's life, and traditional support systems of extended family members are not always ready, willing, or available to pick up the slack. As a result, young people are often adrift emotionally, seeking significance and safety from others like themselves. The result is affiliation with other disenfranchised youth—a gang (McWhirter et al., 2007).

PEERS According to Saginak (2003), it is through interactions with peer groups in addition to the family system that students develop a sense of identity and learn how to function as independent adults in society. "Peer groups help adolescents resolve internal conflicts and reduce anxiety by serving as sounding boards without arousing guilt or anxiety, respecting competencies as seen in social and athletic skills, and providing honest and critical feedback about behaviors and personal attributes" (p. 57). Peers model behaviors, teach values, and promote select attitudes—some to the benefit and some to the detriment of the student. "Just as peer groups can exert positive peer pressure such as leadership skills, they can also exert negative peer pressure in the form of deviance and antisocial behavior" (p. 59). There are a variety of peer groupings.

Cliques are small, socially cohesive groups of friends who share similar ages, socioeconomic status, interests, attitudes, and preferences (Dunphy, as cited in Muuss, 1988). They have the ability to exert extreme pressure on their members to maintain structure and organization (Saginak, 2003).

Crowds are larger social groups, usually made up of several cliques. They "are not as cohesive as cliques, individuals are not necessarily friends, and their value structures tend to be more varied than those of cliques" (Saginak, 2003).

Peer clusters are youth who tend to engage in deviant, antisocial behavior; they have a tendency to gravitate toward each other, forming peer clusters. These are small subsystems that are highly organized, maintain rigid boundaries, and are highly resistant to change. These groupings often enforce compliance through physical intimidation, eventually developing into gangs (Saginak, 2003).

Gangs are organized structured groups that form for a common purpose, usually involving unlawful or criminal behavior. "It is the breakdown of homes, schools, and communities that has led to the prevalence of gangs in today's society. Many teens feel isolated in their families, misunderstood within their school buildings, and disengaged from their communities, and they are seeking connections elsewhere" (Saginak, 2003, p. 59).

REFLECTION MOMENT

Think about the effects your community, culture, family, and peers have had on your development. What did you learn from each system? Take a moment and list five of your deepest, most closely held values. Now, one by one, examine which system(s) taught you that value, which system(s) challenged those values, and, in the face of those challenges, how you felt about yourself as you battled that system.

Developmental Assets

In an attempt to understand resilience in young people, the Search Institute has examined and conducted research to determine those conditions that allow young people to thrive. "All children and youth need a stable, positive sense of self and an ability to increasingly regulate themselves, a belief in their overall competence and skills at social problem-solving, and a connection to caring adults" (Starkman Scales, & Roberts, 1999, p. 7). To accomplish these goals, the Institute has outlined 40 Developmental Assets, 20 "external" assets and 20 "internal" assets (see Table 4.1).

TABLE 4.1 **Forty Developmental Assets**

Category	Asset Name and Definition
	External Assets
Support	1. **Family support**—Family life provides high levels of love and support.
	2. **Positive family communication**—Young person and her or his parent(s) communicate positively, and young person is willing to seek advice and counsel from parent(s).
	3. **Other adult relationships**—Young person receives support from three or more nonparent adults.
	4. **Caring neighborhood**—Young person experiences caring neighbors.
	5. **Caring school climate**—School provides a caring, encouraging environment.
	6. **Parent involvement in schooling**—Parent(s) are actively involved in helping young person succeed in school.
Empowerment	7. **Community values youth**—Young person perceives that adults in the community value youth.
	8. **Youth as resources**—Young people are given useful roles in the community.
	9. **Service to others**—Young person serves in the community one hour or more per week.
	10. **Safety**—Young person feels safe at home, at school, and in the neighborhood.
Boundaries and Expectations	11. **Family boundaries**—Family has clear rules and consequences, and monitors the young person's whereabouts.
	12. **School boundaries**—School provides clear rules and consequences.
	13. **Neighborhood boundaries**—Neighbors take responsibility for monitoring young people's behavior.
	14. **Adult role models**—Parent(s) and other adults model positive, responsible behavior.
	15. **Positive peer influence**—Young person's best friends model responsible behavior.
	16. **High expectations**—Both parent(s) and teachers encourage the young person to do well.
Constructive Use of Time	17. **Creative activities**—Young person spends three or more hours per week in lessons or practice in music, theater, or other arts.
	18. **Youth programs**—Young person spends three or more hours per week in sports, clubs, or organizations at school and/or in the community.

(Continued)

Category	Asset Name and Definition
	TABLE 4.1 (Continued)
	19. **Religious community**—Young person spends one or more hours per week in activities in a religious institution.
	20. **Time at home**—Young person is out with friends "with nothing special to do" two or fewer nights per week.

Internal Assets

Category	Asset Name and Definition
Commitment to Learning	21. **Achievement motivation**—Young person is motivated to do well in school.
	22. **School engagement**—Young person is actively engaged in learning.
	23. **Homework**—Young person reports doing at least one hour of homework every school day.
	24. **Bonding to school**—Young person cares about her or his school.
	25. **Reading for pleasure**—Young person reads for pleasure three or more hours per week.
Positive Values	26. **Caring**—Young person places high value on helping other people.
	27. **Equality and social justice**—Young person places high value on promoting equality and reducing hunger and poverty.
	28. **Integrity**—Young person acts on convictions and stands up for her or his beliefs.
	29. **Honesty**—Young person "tells the truth even when it is not easy."
	30. **Responsibility**—Young person accepts and takes personal responsibility.
	31. **Restraint**—Young person believes it is important not to be sexually active or to use alcohol or other drugs.
Social Competencies	32. **Planning and decision making**—Young person knows how to plan ahead and make choices.
	33. **Interpersonal competence**—Young person has empathy, sensitivity, and friendship skills.
	34. **Cultural competence**—Young person has knowledge of and comfort with people of different cultural/racial/ethnic backgrounds.
	35. **Resistance skills**—Young person can resist negative peer pressure and dangerous situations.
	36. **Peaceful conflict resolution**—Young person seeks to resolve conflict nonviolently.
Positive Identity	37. **Personal power**—Young person feels he or she has control over "things that happen to me."
	38. **Self-esteem**—Young person reports having a high self-esteem.
	39. **Sense of purpose**—Young person reports that "my life has a purpose."
	40. **Positive view of personal future**—Young person is optimistic about her or his personal future.

The external assets consist of the relationships and opportunities that are provided to young people, including Support, Empowerment, Boundaries and Expectations, and Constructive Use of Time. The internal assets, those values and skills young people develop that are used for self-governance, include Commitment to Learning, Positive Values, Social Competencies, and Positive Identity.

The Developmental Assets weave all systems together to create the solid fabric of support for students. Family, peers, school, and community are all connected in ways to facilitate healthy development for each child. In fact, Starkman et al. (1999) report that the more assets a child experiences, the more likely it is that child will succeed in school and make healthy choices in terms of alcohol and drugs. Furthermore, "young people who are already vulnerable and at high risk of making poor health choices and being unsuccessful in school and other areas of life—because of abuse, violence, or other developmental deficits—experience an even greater positive impact from having developmental assets in their lives" (p. 13).

Because these assets can be directly correlated with academic success, schools have been very receptive to learning about the assets. The Search Institute has compiled these insights into numerous resources for schools (administrators, teachers, counselors, and other school professionals), parents, community leaders and churches, and students themselves, and has been actively promoting this message of hope and resilience.

Systemic Change and Multisystemic Interventions

To facilitate these assets, school counselors must expand their ways of thinking about their students' context. Writing from a school perspective, Keys and Lockhart (1999) applied multisystemic insights to working with families, peers, community, and the school. They focused on and described the role of the school counselor in multisystemic interventions: "School counselors who function within a multisystemic paradigm expand the traditional definition of consultant and coordinator to reflect an emphasis on systemic change and collaborative relationships with families and the broader community" (p. 104). With this redefined view of the student and school counseling, school counselors must adopt five new ways of working:

1. School counselors must be a liaison between the school and the community, facilitating and coordinating a school's efforts to contact and access community resources and services.
2. School counselors must function as a member of the team of school and community professionals dedicated to the delivery of "wraparound services" for students and their families. This means that services are designed around the needs of the family and are not agency- or school-driven and confined. Examples of the membership of such integrated service teams include representatives from social services, law enforcement, education, juvenile justice, welfare, mental and physical health, nutrition, and substance abuse programs.
3. School counselors have the group facilitation skills, consultation skills, and collaboration skills to function as the group process facilitator in a multisystemic service view, which would include establishing a warm environment, facilitating group norms, monitoring the group process to facilitate productive contributions by all members, building consensus, negotiating conflicts, and other tasks.
4. School counselors should empower themselves as social advocates who work "to effect changes in policy, organizational structure, and service delivery practices" within both the school building and the larger school system (p. 106).
5. Finally, school counselors should view themselves as family advocates, who can connect families with services in the school and in the community.

These interventions can have a profound effect on the systems in which our students live, and we can see the far-reaching and important effects we can have on the lives of students, their families, the entire school, and whole communities.

REFLECTION MOMENT

What are your reactions as you read about these new visions of schools, school counseling, and systemic change? Think about your feelings right now. Are you enthused? Overwhelmed? Are you able to visualize these new services? Many new counselors report that these ideas for multisystemic services are hard to conceptualize because they don't have a firm grasp on what comprehensive school counseling is, much less this expanded vision of service delivery. If this is the case for you, file this information away in the back of your mind and let it stay there until you've worked for a year or two in the field. Then you can revisit this chapter to see if any of them might work for your school.

CASE STUDY REVISITED

Integration

Now that you have both a developmental and systemic view of Ty's life, what ideas do you have for interventions to help with the situation? What are the systemic issues you see? What can Mr. Paulson do to help Ty with his grades; would a conversation with Mrs. Epps be helpful or harmful? What resources are available to help him from the prior list of social resources? Evaluate his situation in terms of the Developmental Assets. What interventions are suggested by that evaluation? ■

CASE STUDY CONTINUED

Mr. Paulson's Efforts

Mr. Paulson continued to think about Mrs. Bonté and Ty all day. This was his first year as a school counselor and he wanted to do the right thing, but wasn't sure what that was at this point. He figured that it was time to consult with his director of counseling.

The director of counseling for the high school, Bob Winters, had been with the school for over 25 years and had designed the program. Bob had seen many principals come and go, but the guidance service was still going strong. As a high school counselor, Bob learned that his job was primarily to schedule students, write the master schedule, coordinate the school-to-work program, coordinate the school's testing processes, secure information on scholarships and write recommendation letters, and help students get into college. When Calvin Paulson was hired, Bob finally had someone with whom he could share his burden, which he did gladly. Calvin and Bob shared the students evenly for scheduling, and Bob maintained much of the administrative work of which he was fond. Bob never really liked working with the students directly.

Knocking on Bob's door, Calvin asked for a couple of minutes of Bob's time. When he was invited in and seated, he gave a quick update. "I have this junior who is struggling in science, but wants to go to college. He's working hard to take care of his brothers and mom, to help pay bills when she got sick. He's a good kid, and I want to help. Mom is worried, too. The problem is that I'm not sure where to start. Do we have information on financial assistance for families? Or do you know of anyone I can call? Do you think I could meet with the family to. . . ."

Bob cut him off at that point. "Whoa! Sorry, bucko, but I don't think that's really our job. We're not social services here—we're a school. And in this guidance office that's what we do—*guide* kids to college. We're just an add-on here; we don't have the authority to work with kids in their academics—science especially! You're not this kid's parent or this kid's social worker. And we sure as heck don't have time to do family counseling—we barely have time to do the things we are supposed to do, important things like scheduling and testing. That reminds me, here are the test packets for next week. You need to label each one with the student's name, student ID number, and homeroom. . . ."

Whose position do you identify with? Given what you've read to this point in this book, what reactions do you have to Mr. Winters's comments? If you were Mr. Paulson, what would your response be to Mr. Winters? ▦

CSCPs ARE BALANCED

There are various ways to define "balance" in comprehensive school counseling programs, and each of these definitions helps us to understand how to conceptualize the work of the school counselor. In comprehensive school counseling programs, balance needs to be maintained:

1. In terms of balanced concern for academic, career, and personal/social issues (Campbell & Dahir, 1997), which are the domains we will see in the Domains/Activities/Partners (DAP) model for a delivery system presented in Chapter 6
2. In terms of balance within the activities of the school counselor—namely, counseling, educating, consultation and collaboration, and leadership, coordination and advocacy (Dollarhide & Saginak, 2003), which are the activities we will see in the DAP model presented in Chapter 6
3. In terms of balanced concern for all partners in the process—namely, students, parents, colleagues, and community (Dollarhide & Saginak, 2003; Keys & Lockhart, 1999), which are the partners we will see in the DAP model discussed in Chapter 6
4. In terms of balance between prevention goals (developmental goals) and intervention goals (also known as treatment or remediation) (Baker, 2000), which we will examine in terms of the need for proactive programs in a CSCP program

What happens when the school counseling program is not balanced in all these ways? Out-of-balance conditions in these four areas result in problems in the work of the counselor, which are easiest to identify in terms of out-of-balance activities. Numerous studies have been conducted into the work of the school counselor documenting the need for reevaluation of the priorities for various counselor activities. In their study, Burnham and Jackson (2000) examined how counselors allocated time within their programs. They found the majority of respondents (69 of 80) reported involvement with nonguidance activities. Of their 80 respondents, 65 percent reported being involved with student records, 56 percent with scheduling, 49 percent with transcripts, 44 percent with office sitting, 38 percent with bus duty, and 28 percent with attendance. Overall, their respondents reported time spent in nonguidance activities ranging from 1 percent to 88 percent of their time, with an average amount of time being 25 percent. This means that fully one-fourth of their respondents' time was spent on nonguidance work. Clearly, balance within the activities of the program will reduce the likelihood that time will be siphoned off for nonguidance activities.

Balanced Counselor Activities

Balanced concern for the domains and partners has been discussed in the previous chapter, as we examined the ways that CSCPs focus on the needs of individual students and on the needs of the systemic influences of community, peers, and family. Balanced concern for prevention and intervention, in terms of the content of programs offered in the CSCP, will be discussed in the next section of this chapter. This leaves the question of balance within the activities of the CSCP to discuss.

Let's focus on the activities of the school counselor, which have been described in the literature in very consistent terms. S. B. Baker (2000) describes appropriate activities as counseling, proactive developmental curriculum programming, consulting, referral and coordination, providing information, enhancing transitions, and assessment. Similarly, Schmidt (1999) defines a CSCP as consisting of "counseling, consulting, coordinating, and appraisal services offered in response to the identified needs, goals, and objectives . . . given priority as the result of adequate assessment and analysis of students', parents', and teachers' needs . . . as a series of processes that include planning, organizing, implementing, and evaluating" (p. 39).

In this book, we will use the Domains/Activities/Partners model (Dollarhide & Saginak, 2003) to highlight how services should be delivered (see Chapter 6 for a complete discussion of this and other models for the delivery system). The DAP model highlights the primary activities as *counseling, educating, consulting and collaboration, and leadership, coordination, and advocacy*. Counseling refers to individual and group counseling, as well as making referrals as a means of bringing closure to counseling relationships. It is the most essential activity that students indicate they want from the school counselor (Hutchinson & Bottorff, 1986; Wiggins & Moody, 1987). Educating refers to providing the developmental curriculum, facilitating transitions, advisement, placement, and assessment and appraisal. Consulting refers to problem solving, referring, enhancing communications, and mediation, while collaboration involves bringing all members of the educational endeavor into the conversation about what works for kids. Leadership involves developing and maintaining the vision of the CSCP and promoting the importance of a developmentally appropriate learning environment, including public relations, committee service, schoolwide programs, and accountability for the work of the professionals in the CSCP. Coordination refers to the management of logistics to bring programs to the partners of the school counselor. Finally, advocacy refers to leadership-related activities designed to educate with passion, those activities that enhance others' empathy for students, schools, families, the CSCP, and better human relationships.

It is important to know that balance among these activities does not mean "equal time." It refers to the need to balance activities based on the needs of the partner being helped.

REFLECTION MOMENT

Have you ever found yourself in a professional situation where your sense of balance was at odds with those of the leadership of the program? How did that feel? What did you do to address that out-of-balance situation?

CASE STUDY

Integration

Mr. Paulson is in a school guidance program (the term "guidance" is used very intentionally there). Based on what Mr. Winters said, what are the ways in which this program is out of balance? ■

CASE STUDY CONTINUED

Mr. Paulson wonders where the school system has failed Ty. Or has it? Ty stated that he is interested in college, but he is making choices under stress that are likely to limit his academic and vocational opportunities. Mr. Paulson wonders what he could do to be more helpful to Ty. Has Ty ever worked with a counselor on his choices? Has he ever had any classroom lessons on stress and stress management? And what did Ty mean when he said he "is just not going to take it anymore"? Is he headed for a violent confrontation with the people in the neighborhood? How can that be prevented? ■

CSCPs ARE PROACTIVE

Being "proactive" means the counselors in a CSCP work to prevent problems before they become serious impediments to the success of the student. But because school counselors do not control all aspects of the students' lives, being proactive also means working to mitigate challenges to the students' success; these efforts involve intervention and treatment, also known as secondary prevention and tertiary intervention.

To understand what is meant by the terms of prevention, intervention, and treatment, school counselors must understand the concept of being "at risk." McWhirter et al. (2007) define "at risk" in terms of risk from "dangerous future events" (substance use, abuse, and addiction; early sexual behavior and/or unplanned pregnancy; early departure from school; criminal and/or violent behaviors). They identify five categories on a continuum of risk status (p. 8):

Minimal Risk   Students with positive socioeconomic demographics; positive family, school, and interpersonal interaction; and limited psychosocial and environmental stressors (McWhirter et al., 2007, p. 8). These students would benefit from prevention programming to help them maintain healthy choices in case of future challenges.

Remote Risk   Students with negative socioeconomic demographics; less positive family, school, and peer interaction; and some psychosocial and environmental stressors (McWhirter et al., 2007, p. 8). These students also would benefit from prevention programming to help them maintain healthy choices in the face of their challenges.

High Risk   Students with negative socioeconomic demographics; negative interpersonal interaction; numerous psychosocial/environmental stressors; and development of personal at-risk markers: negative attitudes, emotions, and skills deficiencies (McWhirter et al., 2007, p. 8). These students would benefit from intervention programming to help them change their attitudes and to help them improve their coping skills.

Imminent Risk   Students with negative socioeconomic demographics; negative interaction with others; numerous psychosocial and environmental stressors; development of personal at-risk markers: negative attitudes, emotions, and skills deficiencies; and the development of dangerous unhealthy behaviors (McWhirter et al., 2007, p. 8). These students also would benefit from intervention programming to help them focus on their choices and their responsibility to change, and to help them improve their life skills.

At-Risk Activity   Students with negative socioeconomic demographics; overall negative interactions; numerous psychosocial and environmental stressors that escalate into more high-risk behaviors; development of personal at-risk markers, such as negative attitudes and skills deficiencies that place them solidly in the at-risk category (McWhirter et al., 2007, p. 8). This includes the development of gateway behaviors and activities that put them at risk for other categories of risk behaviors (McWhirter et al., 2007, p. 8). For these students, treatment would be warranted.

These authors caution that professionals working with adolescents not use the term "at risk" to denote students or families doomed to failure; rather, the term is to be used to describe students who are "at risk" in terms of their context. It is important to remember that risk status is usually related to poverty, racism, and the limited economic opportunities in impoverished communities. The term "at promise" suggests a more optimistic and empowering view of the stressors in the environment; the student is "at promise" for resilience and coping.

In terms of the search for identity, some students have relatively stable internal parameters, boundaries beyond which they will not go because they know at least that much about themselves. "Drugs are not me," or "Piercing that part of my body grosses me out." Proactive prevention programming can help these students to maintain healthy choices. These are students who are at minimal and remote risk.

Other students may be suffering from what Marcia (as cited in Craig, 1996) described as "identity diffusion," in which the young person lacks a sense of direction or motivation to determine a life direction. To avoid dealing with their identity crisis, these young people seek activities that provide immediate gratification, or they experiment "in a random fashion with all possibilities" (p. 439). These students don't know who they are, who they want to be, or where they belong. Counselors will see them as a result of their lack of motivation (excessive absenteeism or chronic truancy), as a result of their method(s) of immediate gratification (unwanted pregnancy, substance abuse and/or addiction, poor impulse control in the classroom, excessive risk taking), or as a result of their bizarre behaviors as they experiment with the style of the month. Intervention can help these students, who can be thought of as being at high risk and imminent risk.

Finally, for still others, the identity crisis has been resolved; the problem is that the student despises the self she or he has found. These students engage in seriously self-destructive behaviors, such as self-cutting, self-mutilation, eating disorders, suicidal behaviors and risk taking, and substance abuse. The differences between identity diffusion and identity loathing are the intensity of the self-inflicted damage and the intentionality of the act of self-destruction. Treatment is warranted for these students, who clearly are involved in at-risk activity.

Prevention, Intervention, and Treatment

School counselors must be able to see the connection between risk status, behavioral manifestations, and comprehensive counseling programmatic responses. These responses are categorized into three levels: prevention, intervention, and treatment (McWhirter et al., 2007).

PREVENTION   The prevention level includes programmatic responses that are designed to enhance resilience and prevent at-risk characteristics. Examples of prevention efforts are school-wide programs for excellence, character education, the developmental curriculum delivered in the classroom, and working toward an environment of respect and inclusion.

INTERVENTION   The intervention level includes programmatic responses that are designed to arrest the deterioration of existing at-risk characteristics, or to mitigate against the effects of psychosocial or educational stressors. Examples of these responses include individual counseling, group counseling, family interventions and home visits, consultation with teachers, consultation with parents, and conflict mediation between teachers and students.

TREATMENT   The treatment level includes programmatic responses that are designed to address fully developed at-risk behaviors. In some cases, counselors can adequately address the treatment needs of students though groups and one-on-one counseling, but often, students who need treatment are best served by mental health professionals in the community. Outside counseling for students who need treatment does not imply that counselors are not trained to provide such assistance to students. Rather, outside therapy for students who need treatment reflects the intensity of treatment (often students in treatment need several sessions each week), and the necessity of medications to assist with the therapeutic process (which counselors are not authorized to prescribe).

A close examination of the at-risk categories and the accompanying descriptions suggests there are specific connections between what students are experiencing and their danger for at-risk behaviors. Examining both resilience and risk can lead to important insights for counselors. According to McWhirter et al. (2007, p. 113), there are five characteristics—the "five Cs of competency"—that discriminate young people who are at high risk from those who are at low risk. The five characteristics are (1) critical school competencies (basic academic skills and academic survival skills), (2) a concept of self and self-esteem, (3) positive communication skills,

(4) effective coping abilities, and (5) control (decision-making skills, delay of gratification, and purpose in life). These five characteristics can serve as a template to understand the differences between prevention, intervention, and treatment. Prevention efforts would be undertaken to enhance or increase students' acquisition of the "five Cs of competency" (McWhirter et al., 2007, p. 113). Intervention efforts would begin as counselors notice students struggling in one or more competency, or if the counselor became aware that the student was moving from a lesser risk category into high or imminent risk. Finally, treatment efforts would begin as counselors notice students exhibiting serious struggles that indicate the student is in the at-risk activity category.

As you may have already noticed, the "five Cs of competency" (McWhirter et al., 2007, p. 113) resonate with the three developmental domains of academic, career, and personal/social development, as well as with the Developmental Assets discussed in the previous chapter. Now that you have had a chance to reflect on the levels of at-risk status and differences between prevention, intervention, and treatment, let's look at why CSCPs must be integrated into the academic curriculum, the fifth quality of a CSCP.

REFLECTION MOMENT

What was your risk status when you were young? Did that status change over time? If so, what caused it to change? How will these insights help you when you become a school counselor?

CASE STUDY REVISITED

Integration

Using the at-risk continuum, identify where Ty would be placed in terms of his risk status and explain your reasoning. What comprehensive counseling programmatic response—prevention, intervention, or treatment—would you recommend for Ty?

Assess Ty in terms of the five Cs of competency. With which competencies does Ty need help? What would you do to help him develop, refine, or enhance those competencies? ◼

CASE STUDY CONTINUED

Mr. Paulson thought about Ty's struggle in his science class. Since Mr. Paulson's arrival in this school, he had not really had the chance to meet the faculty. Perhaps he might go to Ms. Epps's office and introduce himself. Maybe it was time to become familiar with the academic side of the school, so that if Ty gave him permission to talk with Ms. Epps about his college plans, she might be open to talking about ways Ty could bring up his grade. It couldn't hurt to try, right? He decided to visit Ms. Epps in her office.

As he walked toward the science wing of the school, he tried to compose the best approach. The last thing he wanted was to come across as accusing Ms. Epps of anything, of being too hard or unfair. He'll just see how receptive she might be to the developmental agenda and to the expertise he has to offer in terms of student development.

After he introduced himself, she insisted that he come in and have a seat. Right away, he could tell she would become a strong ally to the school counseling office. "Tell me what I can do to help you teach your kids," he began.

She jumped right into that offer. "In my previous school, the counselors would come to our classes and teach various topics that met our standards and also met theirs," she offered. "They would present on healthy choices in terms of drugs or cigarettes, for example, when we talked about biology. I'd love to have you come to my classes so that they are getting more than just academics. Do you have any groups going for students? I have a couple of kids who I need to refer to you. . . ."

"This is wonderful!" thought Calvin. "Perhaps I will be able to help more kids than just Ty," and he smiled as Ms. Epps talked about her concerns for her kids. ◼

CSCPs ARE INTEGRATED WITH THE ACADEMIC AGENDA

ASCA (2003) enjoins all counselors to design programs that reach all students, yet it is clear that, in some schools, the school counseling program is considered an extra "service" or an "add-on." In this view, school counseling is not comprehensive; it does not reach all students. As you will recall from Chapter 1, there are multiple philosophies of school counseling, and each focuses on one or two functions of a school counselor. In the guidance/career emphasis, school counselors were administrators who provided career direction and college information; in the mental health emphasis, school counselors remain in their offices providing "therapy"; in the developmental guidance emphasis, school counselors worked hard to get into the classrooms. Now, in the comprehensive school counseling program movement as represented in the ASCA National Model (ASCA, 2003), school counselors are full partners in the educational activities of the entire school.

Curricular and Programmatic Integration

Derived from the National Standards for Student Academic, Career, and Personal/Social Development (guidelines for school counseling programs across the country [ASCA, 2003; Campbell & Dahir, 1997]) many states have developed their own state-level standards. These state-level standards comprise the developmental curriculum for which school counselors are responsible, just as teachers are responsible for the academic curriculum.

As a professional school counselor, you are responsible for delivering this curriculum, as will be discussed in detail in Chapter 9. In addition, infusion with the academic agenda means that school counselors are not penalized for asking to see students as appropriate; it means that the school counseling program is viewed as essential for students' development by our partners in the schools. So infusion is a broad concept, addressing the extent to which the CSCP is viewed as integral to the educational process by administrators and faculty; and it is specific to include the extent to which teachers allow students out of class to see the counselor and the extent to which counselors are allowed access to students during the course of the day to provide prevention and intervention programming.

Specific ways to infuse the CSCP prevention and intervention activities are as varied as the schools that are served. Based on the counselor's ability to communicate a vision of a CSCP, allies can be recruited from school boards, administration, other student support professionals, teachers, staff, janitors—and these allies can be integral to the counselor's efforts to reach out to all students.

REFLECTION MOMENT

What is your reaction when thinking about how to talk to teachers about the possibility of using classroom time to deliver the developmental curriculum? In Chapter 9, you will be challenged to think about how to integrate the developmental curriculum with the academic curriculum using multiple intelligences. Many states have developed a "crosswalk" that connects the developmental curriculum with the academic curriculum of the state. How would you use such a document to support your request for classroom time?

CASE STUDY REVISITED

Integration

What if Ms. Epps had not been receptive to Mr. Paulson? What could he have said that would not have violated Ty's confidentiality? ■

Later that day, Calvin was still pondering what else he could do to help Ty, while absently applying labels to the test packets, when Bob popped his head into Calvin's office. "By the way," he said casually, "don't forget that I will need your performance evaluation for this year on my desk by the end of the week. I will meet with the principal next week to discuss it; then we'll meet with you to give you our feedback on ways to improve for this next year."

Calvin shuddered involuntarily. He wondered how he would ever document his work with a student like Ty, a "work in progress." But then, aren't all students still "in progress"? Shaking off his worry about Ty, he said to Bob, "Do you have an example that I can use to look at while I write mine?"

Mr. Winters shook his head. "No, this is the first year we've had to do them. Just write up what you've done this year in a paragraph or two. Don't be real specific; keep it general. You don't want to make me look bad." ▪

CSCPs ARE REFLECTIVE

Reflection involves spending time thinking about the efficacy of your efforts as a school counselor and the efficacy of your CSCP. Evidence of this reflection, which is an ethical and moral mandate, comes in the form of examination and documentation of your work.

It has been a challenge for school counselors to document their work. After all, counseling is confidential, isn't it? How do you document that this student is passing third grade, that one is getting along better with her friends, that boy decided not to commit suicide, and a student you counseled two months ago is finally turning his attitude around and coming to school? Besides, where will you find the time to collect all that information? School counselors work very hard as it is, and now they have to count everything they do on top of it all? The problem is that for years, counselors have been stumped by these questions.

Professional reflection results in accountability. Many authors discuss the need to be accountable (S. B. Baker, 2000), and there is no question that school counselors must be accountable to their schools, to their communities, and to their students for their comprehensive school counseling programs and for their own contribution to the program. As we will see in Chapter 7, school counselors are accountable for their time, for the quality of their work, and for the quality of the program overall as evaluated on the basis of needs and outcomes (Hutchinson & Bottorff, 1986). For example, S. B. Baker (2000) indicated that school counselors are professionally and morally bound to evaluate (gather information about one's programs and services) and be accountable (report the results of the evaluation) (p. 300). Schmidt (1999) also called upon school counselors to "identify your role in the school, account for the time you allot to specific activities, and measure whether or not these services make a difference in the lives of students, parents, and teachers" (p. 275). In fact, it is so important that the American School Counselor Association has devoted one entire element of the National Model (ASCA, 2003, 2005) to the accountability system.

But accountability is often misunderstood to mean that school counselors must "bite the yearly bullet" to pull data together and write a self-evaluation, something to be avoided like the plague. The challenges of collecting meaningful data on the efficacy of school counseling interventions is significant, especially when youngsters' developmental progress is not easily attributable to anything done in the schools. Expand your definition of accountability so that you can envision a process of effective management, needs and outcomes assessment, reflection, and program improvement. Management of the program is more than being accountable for the results of the program—it is a continuous process. As a part of leadership and coordinating activities, counselors need to manage, evaluate, and improve their CSCP—in essence, effectively lead the program—and this starts with reflection.

Reflection on Quality of Program and Counselor Performance

Reflection is both an internal and external process. When counselors reflect on the quality of their work, and then take responsibility for that work through actions to improve their work, they effectively manage their program. What, exactly, does it mean to "manage" a program?

According to Hersey, Blanchard, and Johnson (1996) management consists of the functions of *planning, organizing, motivating,* and *controlling*—functions that are consistent across all types of organizations and all levels. Planning is defined as setting goals and objectives and developing "work maps" showing how goals and objectives are to be accomplished. Organizing involves bringing together resources to accomplish the goals and objectives derived from the planning process. Motivating involves working effectively with the human resources available to meet those goals and objectives, and controlling refers to the use of feedback and results "to compare accomplishments with plans and to make appropriate adjustments where outcomes have deviated from expectations" (p. 11).

Are these terms foreign or familiar to you? They are functions that may be contrary to the counselor's preference to work with people (not data) and in which counselors seldom receive training (S. B. Baker, 2000). The importance of personal, professional, and programmatic reflection is elaborated and explored in Chapter 5, in which the ASCA National Model will be discussed in terms of the management system, data collection and analysis, and accountability. This model contains explicit directions and formats for the collection and analysis of data for program evaluation and improvement and for counselor evaluation and improvement.

In spite of the fact that these terms may seem unfamiliar, you have done these activities. Unless you have a maid who does all your shopping and cooking for you, believe me, you have done each of these functions. When you made out your shopping list, you were planning. When you went to the store, bought your groceries, then brought them home and put them away, you were organizing. When you cooked the meal and thought about whether it tasted good to you, you were assessing. When you decided to cook it again next month or throw away that recipe, you were evaluating and using that information to engage in planning. When you bragged to your friends that you cooked beef Wellington and it was delicious, you were accounting for your time. Not so frightening now, is it? Reflection is the first step toward responsibility and accountability for the work of the counselor and the program.

Now that you have the foundation of a comprehensive school counseling program, it is time to examine what the national association, the American School Counselor Association (ASCA), has to say about comprehensive school counseling programs. The next chapter is devoted to the ASCA National Model for School Counseling Programs, in which we will look in detail at school counseling's foundation, management system, delivery system, and accountability as defined at the national level.

REFLECTION MOMENT

Some counselors believe their time is too precious to waste it on gathering data and information about the outcomes of their work and then don't understand how their programs get cut. Can you see how accountability and program survival are connected? How do you think school counselors can collect important outcomes information about the CSCP from the students, parents, school colleagues, and community colleagues with whom they work?

CASE STUDY REVISITED

Integration

If the program and the professionals are not adequately, fairly, and completely evaluated, what are the risks to the program and the professionals? Based on what Mr. Winters said, what concerns do you have about Calvin Paulson's evaluation? If you were to evaluate the program in that school, what grade would you give it for its programmatic responses to Ty's situation? ■

Suggested Readings

Brandan, N. (1994). *The six pillars of self-esteem.* New York: Bantam. This book defines self-esteem in terms of intentional practices that reinforce a healthy life direction. Many practical suggestions for developing self-esteem are provided that can help school counselors design counseling and curricular experiences to foster self-esteem in students.

Brookfield, S. D. (1987). *Developing critical thinkers: Challenging adults to explore alternative ways of thinking and acting.* San Francisco: Jossey-Bass. The book contains wonderful insights into ways to help young people develop their critical thinking skills. While not written as a counseling manual, this book has many implications, both for counseling and for the developmental curriculum.

Gellatt, H. B. (1991). *Creative decision making using positive uncertainty.* Los Angeles: Crisp. Many school counselors are faced with helping students make important decisions in the face of uncertainty, and Gellatt offers ideas for reframing this stressful situation into one that is intuitively engaging for both counselor and student.

Goleman, D. (1995). *Emotional intelligence: Why it can matter more than IQ.* New York: Bantam. This book helps counselors understand and articulate to faculty and staff why the developmental curriculum is important. It provides a holistic perspective of what constitutes a well-functioning person in this society.

Hanna, S. M., & Brown, J. H. (1999). *The practice of family therapy: Key elements across models* (2nd ed.). Belmont, CA: Brooks/Cole. This book is helpful for school counselors to understand the process of family counseling.

Hansen, L. S. (1997). *Integrative life planning: Critical tasks for career development and changing life patterns.* San Francisco: Jossey-Bass. This author writes about life-career planning from a holistic, existential view; this philosophy can help counselors to retain that holistic foundation while engaging students in discussions about their future.

Hersey, P., Blanchard, K. H., & Johnson, D. E. (1996). *Management of organizational behavior: Utilizing human resources* (7th ed.). Upper Saddle River, NJ: Prentice Hall. This book, written for business professionals, gives a wonderful overview of leadership and management practices.

King, P. M., & Kitchener, K. S. (1994). *Developing reflective judgment: Understanding and promoting intellectual growth and critical thinking in adolescents and adults.* San Francisco: Jossey-Bass. Since intellectual development and academic maturity are goals of the comprehensive school counseling program, counselors will benefit from an understanding of what their students are working to attain. This book provides many insights that can help counselors design counseling and curricular experiences to help students develop intellectually.

Lazear, D. (1999). *Eight ways of teaching: The artistry of teaching with multiple intelligences.* Arlington Heights, IL: SkyLight Training and Publishing. This book offers educators practical ideas for engaging students of all ages in the learning process, by designing learning experiences tailored to each student's individual intelligence constellation.

Payne, R. K. (2003). *A framework for understanding poverty* (3rd ed.). Highlands, TX: aha! Process. This invaluable resource helps counselors understand the dynamics of poverty, a community and cultural issue.

Pipher, M. (1994). *Reviving Ophelia: Saving the selves of adolescent girls.* New York: Ballantine. This book describes the challenges of growing up female in this culture.

Pollack, W. (1998). *Real boys: Rescuing our sons from the myths of boyhood.* New York: Holt. This book outlines the challenges of growing up male in this culture.

Snyder, C. R. (1994). *The psychology of hope.* New York: Free Press. Detailing research into the concept of "hope," this author provides a prototype of hope that is teachable to students. Each component is then discussed in detail, providing insights that can help counselors in counseling and educating students, faculty, and parents.

Starkman, N., Scales, P. C., & Roberts, C. (1999). *Great places to learn: How asset-building schools help students succeed.* Minneapolis, MN: Search Institute. Any of the resources of the Search Institute (www.search-institute.com) would be very helpful for counselors; this book provides direct insights for school professionals in the process of using Developmental Assets as an organizing foundation for educational programs and services.

5

The ASCA National Model

LEARNING OBJECTIVES

By the end of this chapter, you will

1. Understand the rationale for a National Model

2. Understand and be able to articulate the ASCA National Model in general

3. Understand and be able to articulate the National Model Themes of Advocacy, Leadership, Collaboration, and Systemic Change

4. Be able to discuss the Model Elements of Foundation, Delivery System, Management System, and Accountability

5. Be able to apply the National Model in theory and in practice

CASE STUDY

Cadence's Big Decision

Cadence was very excited that she had finally made a decision about what she wanted to do with her life. After completing her degree in elementary education, she realized that her passion was not in the classroom—it was working with the children to help them with problems. She had a chance to talk with the school counselor, Kayli, when she was doing her student teaching, and learned a lot about the counselor's job. Cadence then invited Kayli to do some classroom developmental guidance in her room and decided that the combination of classroom guidance and one-on-one and group counseling gave her the perfect opportunity to combine all the things she loved most into one profession.

The problem was that when she mentioned it to someone, she was often met with a negative reaction. These reactions were disheartening; after all, she was talking about starting a graduate program, in which the investment of time and resources would be substantial. She wanted to understand these reactions so that she could feel confident in her decision.

Her cooperating teacher said that counselors are just extra baggage to the school—what was needed were more teachers. One of her fellow students at the university said he thought counselors didn't contribute to the students' lives at all, that counseling was just "playing head games." A parent of one of her students said that she thought counselors shouldn't be allowed to work with kids, that all they did was interfere with the parents' rights to discipline their own children. And Cadence's own mother said that she had no idea what counselors did in schools except work with kids who were really sick. None of these comments were consistent with what Cadence had learned from the counselor at her school, so she went back to talk to Kayli about these reactions.

"It's not a well-understood profession," Kayli shared. "There are numerous ways to define the work a school counselor does, and it's hard to get consensus about what a counselor *should* do. Everyone wants to have a say in what school counselors should do—from teachers, to administrators, to parents, to the public."

"Isn't there anyone who speaks for the school counseling profession, who can make definitive statements about what school counselors are all about?"

"Yes, it's the professional association, and they have made such a definitive statement, called the ASCA National Model. But they face two challenges: how to inform teachers, administrators, and parents about this Model and how to reach those school counselors who aren't members of the professional association. We have a coherent forum to advocate for the profession, to help everyone understand what school counselors do and why they do it, but we need more people willing to get involved to spread the word."

"Sounds exciting!" Cadence said, wondering how political advocacy fit into the job of a school counselor. This was turning into a tougher decision than she thought.

CHALLENGE QUESTIONS

What are the images you have of the job of a school counselor? Given what you have read so far in this book, what do you know about what counselors do and why they do it? What do you believe they *should* do? ▪

THE PROFESSIONALIZATION OF SCHOOL COUNSELING

What is a "profession"? According to the *Grolier-Webster International Dictionary of the English Language* (1975), it is "a vocation requiring specialized training in a field of learning, art, or science; a body of persons engaged in a calling or vocation" (p. 761). With specialized training in a discipline, persons in that vocation define their work within a professional identity, and in the process, develop a commonly shared set of rules and norms for the profession. As we saw in Chapter 3, these rules and norms evolve into codified ethics and standards of practice by which persons in that profession are expected to abide and by which persons in the profession are held accountable. Sometimes these standards and expectations are translated into law (as in legislation protecting confidentiality between doctor and patient, lawyer and client, and priest and penitent); other times these standards and expectations are enforced by the profession alone in codes of ethics.

The process of professionalization for the counseling profession in general is not new, but for some counseling specialties, the process has been more recent. This latter description applies to school counseling. As we saw in Chapter 1, comprehensive school counseling evolved as recently as the 1980s (American School Counselor Association, 2005), and comprehensive school counseling programs (CSCPs) emerged in the literature in the late 1990s. The necessity of CSCPs is still being debated in many communities around the country. Just because the profession of school counseling recognizes their worth does not mean that the general public agrees.

The huge challenge posed for the profession of school counseling is how to promote consistent norms and expectations among those the profession serves. After all, as the job and definition of the school counselor changed over the years, so have the experiences of those being served by the school counselor. The parents of today's students were in school 20, 30, or more years ago, and all they know about the job of a school counselor is what they saw in those schools years ago. How will they know that the profession has evolved unless current school counselors educate them?

As a result, today's school counselors have challenges ahead of them. They must remain current with their profession, and this means being committed enough to the profession to be an active, involved member of the professional association. It is through active involvement that members remain true to their life vocation, the calling to work effectively with children and families in schools.

THE ASCA NATIONAL MODEL

As an extension of those professional rules and expectations, ASCA has published a number of documents. You will recall that we discussed those recent publications in Chapter 1, when we visited the ASCA Role Statement (ASCA, 2009), the ASCA School Counselor Competencies (ASCA, 2008), and National Standards for Student Academic, Career, and Personal/Social Development (ASCA, 2005; Campbell & Dahir, 1997). In these documents, the profession has attempted to define the job and competencies of the school counselor and the expected outcomes of a CSCP in terms of students' knowledge, skills, and abilities.

It is important to note that every school counselor should be knowledgeable about the National Model from the original source, not just from secondary sources like this one. Reading this chapter will not substitute for personal examination of and reflection on the original publication. (A copy of the Model can be ordered directly from ASCA at www.schoolcounselor.org.)

Overview of the Model

As you can see from Figure 5.1, the National Model reflects the Themes, Elements, and flow that are the essence of school counseling. The *Themes* are Leadership, Advocacy, Collaboration, and Systemic Change. As we will see in the next section, these themes constitute the environment in which school counselors conduct their work. The *Elements* of the Model include Foundation, Delivery System, Management System, and Accountability, which give structure to the day-to-day work of the school counselor. Finally, the *flow* of the Model indicates the directionality of the elements and the manner in which feedback moves through the program elements to ensure the highest efficacy of the school counselor's work.

The Themes: Leadership, Advocacy, Collaboration, and Systemic Change

The Themes of the Model are critical for understanding the context, or environment, of the school counselor's work. These themes highlight the systemic nature of the work and provide a template for understanding the importance of these four topics. They surround the diagram of the day-to-day

® The ASCA National Model graphic is a registered trademark of the American School Counselor Association.

FIGURE 5.1   ASCA Model

work of the school counselor, as they would in the field. A legacy of the Transforming School Counseling Initiative (The Education Trust, 2009), this systemic awareness has propelled school counselors into leadership positions in schools through the use of data, systemic advocacy, and new roles as change agents. Efforts in Leadership, Advocacy, and Collaboration result in Systemic Change, which then results in the need for new efforts in Leadership, Advocacy, and Collaboration to bring about more Systemic Change in a cycle of systemic institutional renewal.

LEADERSHIP Leadership will be discussed in greater detail in coming chapters, but we will examine it briefly here. The National Model states that "school counselors serve as leaders who are engaged in systemwide change to ensure student success" (ASCA, 2005, p. 24). According to Bolman and Deal (1997), leadership involves four "frames" or contexts for leadership: structural leadership (ensuring that the organization you lead is effective), human resource leadership (inspiring others to follow), political leadership (working with others who hold power in the setting you lead), and symbolic leadership (leading using a vision). Taking a chronological, prescriptive view, Kouzes and Posner (1995) describe leadership in a five-step template: challenge the process, inspire a shared vision, enable others to act, model the way, and encourage the heart. It is possible to create a template for leadership that combines the contexts in which leadership must take place (adapted from Bolman & Deal, 1997) with the chronological view of leadership proposed by Kouzes and Posner. This view of leadership captures many elements of vision, growth, and dynamic environmental interaction necessary for the evolution of the profession of school counseling and the improvement of schools for all children. Examples of leadership include chairing a committee on campus climate, serving as an advisor to a student group, and serving on a schoolwide student issues committee.

ADVOCACY The role of advocacy, the second theme, is described by ASCA: "School counselors advocate for students' educational needs and work to ensure these needs are addressed at every level of the school experience. . . . School counselors work as advocates to remove systemic barriers that impede the academic success of any student" (ASCA, 2005, p. 24). To "advocate," as defined by *Grolier-Webster International Dictionary of the English Language* (1975), is "to plead in favor of, as of a cause, policy, etc.; to defend by argument; to recommend publicly; to support or vindicate" (p. 17). When you advocate, you are attempting to persuade someone to embrace your point of view; you are teaching them about your perspective on a given subject. Because you are "pleading," "defending," "supporting," you are doing this educating with some emotion; advocacy is educating with passion. True leadership involves passion, enthusiasm, and advocacy, which means that leadership and advocacy are linked. School counselors are advocates for students, families, teachers, and schools; they use their pivotal position to enhance understanding of the issues involved in healthy development of both individuals and systems.

COLLABORATION The *Grolier-Webster International Dictionary of the English Language* (1975) defines "collaborate" as working together with others, cooperating. Drew (2004), in his discussion of conditions that help students graduate, elaborates further, defining collaboration as the building of interdependent systems to achieve a common goal that cannot be achieved by each entity working alone. ASCA (2005) highlights the role of collaboration in the Model, stating that "school counselors build effective teams by encouraging genuine collaboration among all school staff to work toward the common goals of equity, access, and academic success of every student" (p. 25). Examples of collaboration include serving on the administrative council for the school, working with teachers to develop and deliver the developmental curriculum, and working with parents on a fund-raising project for the parent-teacher association (PTA).

SYSTEMIC CHANGE Taken together, leadership, advocacy, and collaboration culminate in systemic change: "Collaborating as leaders within the school, counselors have access to quantitative and qualitative data from the school and relevant community sources. They use these data to advocate for every student, ensuring equity and access to a rigorous curriculum, which maximizes postsecondary options. Systemic change occurs when policies and procedures are examined and changed in light of new data" (ASCA, 2005, p. 25). Examples of systemic change are visible when efforts toward leadership, advocacy, and collaboration bear fruit—when more parents come to parent programs and classes and are more involved in the school, when school administration changes a policy because the counselor's efforts have shown it to be detrimental to the educational process.

REFLECTION MOMENT

Reflect on Richard Long Harkness's famous quote: "What is a committee? A group of the unwilling, picked from the unfit, to do the unnecessary." What is your reaction? What has been your experience with committees? Now reflect on what ASCA has presented in terms of the Themes of the Model. It is through the work of committees, task forces, and other work groups that school counselors accomplish systemic change. How does that affect the view of committees as seen by Harkness?

The Elements

The Elements of the Model, which constitute the body of the Model, outline the structures that school counselors must have in place to do their work. In order to accomplish this important work, school counselors must have a solid Foundation, they must have Management and Delivery Systems, and they must have Accountability. In this section, we will examine each of these elements, as ASCA has provided both descriptive (what could be) and prescriptive (what should be) information about each element.

THE FOUNDATION   The foundation of a solid CSCP includes beliefs and philosophies, a mission statement, and the ASCA National Standards for Student Academic, Career, and Personal/Social Development (ASCA, 2005). This foundation addresses our beliefs about the profession, the values embedded in our work, and our philosophy about who we are and what we contribute to the lives of the students and our partners in the educational process.

The Model highlights our collaborative role in the school by building the foundation on a collaborative process based within a school team, an advisory board or advisory council. These stakeholders are assembled from partners with whom the school counselors must collaborate (students, parents or guardians, colleagues in the school, and colleagues in the community). Once the partners have been assembled, school counselors lead discussions, as outlined below, to articulate beliefs, assumptions, values, and philosophy. In a systematic way, each topic is explored.

Beliefs   ASCA begins the process of building this foundation with a private exploration, on the part of each participant, of fundamental beliefs on a wide range of topics. General topics include student achievement, support for students, understanding of learning styles, and the importance of reaching every student. Specific to school counseling, topics include the role of the CSCP in supporting the mission of the school, educational reform and the counselor's role, and the role of all partners (students, parents and guardians, colleagues in the school, and colleagues outside of the school) in the CSCP (ASCA, 2005, p. 28). After this private reflection, a group discussion ensures to help all members of the advisory council understand each other.

Assumptions   When applied to the CSCP, these beliefs are the underlying basis for the assumptions about the CSCP. It is through the examination of assumptions that school counseling teams (the advisory council and the professional counselors) create a consensus that translates into the philosophy statement of the program. ASCA provides some example assumptions, including those that parallel Chapter 4 of this book:

- A CSCP reaches every student.
- It is comprehensive in scope.
- It is preventative in design.
- It is developmental in nature.
- It is integral to the educational process. (ASCA, 2005, p. 28)

Values   While not explicit in the Model, the discussion of values is also integral to the development of a philosophy statement. Values represent what we believe to be important, what we hold most dear. The difference between values and beliefs is that beliefs are cognitive; they are usually derived and experienced intellectually and are expressed as "I think." Values, on the other hand, are derived and experienced affectively and are usually expressed as "I feel." Values relative to this process could include for all advisory council members:

- What is most important: academic, career, or personal/social development?
- What is the second most important?
- Who is the most important partner: students, parents and caregivers, colleagues in the schools, or colleagues in the community?
- Who is the second? Third?

For the professional counselors:

- Why did I become a school counselor? What do I dream of accomplishing professionally? Personally?
- Where do I want to see my program go? What is my vision of the future of my CSCP? What is my ideal role in that ideal CSCP?

Although developed privately, discussions about these values, coupled with the discussion of assumptions, can help team members understand the unique perspectives of each member.

Philosophy   The philosophy statement is developed by consensus, and addresses six topics (ASCA, 2005, pp. 28–29):

1. A set of beliefs motivating program innovations
2. A set of values visible to all
3. A set of principles guiding professional contributions
4. Statement of professional conduct
5. Statement committing counselors to continuous professional growth
6. Source of collective power

Furthermore, ASCA (2005, p. 29) states that, at a minimum, the philosophy statement should

1. Indicate a shared belief system about the ability of all students to achieve
2. Address every student
3. Address student developmental needs and focus on primary prevention
4. Address the school counselor's role as an advocate for every student
5. Identify persons to be involved in the delivery of program activities
6. Specify who will plan and manage the program
7. Use data to drive program decisions
8. Define how the program will be evaluated and by whom
9. Include ethical guidelines or standards

From this point, the work team will develop a *mission statement*. The mission statement, the second part of the Foundation, is developed from the work done relative to beliefs, assumptions, values, and philosophy. This statement "describes the program's purpose and provides the vision of what is desired for every student," "aligns with and is a subset of the school or district's mission," and "should be clear, concise, and specific as to the program's intent and what the program will contribute" (ASCA, 2005, p. 30). Furthermore, the mission statement should

1. Be written with students as the primary clients
2. Advocate for the equity, access, and success of every student
3. Be written for every student
4. Indicate the content and competencies to be learned
5. Show linkages with the school, district, and state department of education mission statements
6. Indicate the long-range results desired for all students (ASCA, 2005, p. 30)

Finally, the ASCA National Standards for Student Academic, Career, and Personal/Social Development (ASCA, 2005; Campbell & Dahir, 1997) are included as part of the Foundation of the Model, as it outlines the competencies of knowledge, attitudes, and skills that students should attain as a result of being in a school with a CSCP. (The document, originally titled "National Standards for School Counseling Programs," has been renamed to more accurately reflect the content of the standards.) The domains of academic, career, and personal/social development remain the "broad developmental areas" (ASCA, 2005, p. 32) within which school counseling programs make their contribution to the success of each student. For each domain, measurable goals are to be defined for each school year to provide data for program and systemic improvement efforts. Just as each state has established academic competencies to determine academic success, these National Standards outline developmental competencies to assist school counselors in determining the developmental success of students. It is this data that inform the school counselor's leadership, advocacy, and collaboration efforts to bring about program improvement and systemic change. Just as philosophy statements need to be linked from schools, districts, and states to the philosophy of the CSCP, so too will counselors work to link the National Standards with existing school, district, and state competencies.

THE DELIVERY SYSTEM   The delivery system is the template that is used to define what school counselors actually do. The delivery system described by ASCA in the National Model is based on Gysbers and Henderson (2000); however, as we will see in Chapter 6, there are other templates to consider. In this chapter, however, we will examine the Gysbers and Henderson template as presented in the National Model.

There are four parts to the Gysbers and Henderson (2000) model as it is presented in the National Model: the school guidance curriculum, individual student planning, responsive services, and system support. Each of these parts is further broken down to provide direction to the delivery of the CSCP to students.

School Guidance Curriculum   The "guidance" curriculum identifies the responsibility of the counselors to provide a "written instructional program that is comprehensive in scope, preventative and proactive, developmental in design, coordinated by school counselors, and delivered, as appropriate, by school counselors and other educators" (ASCA, 2005, p. 40). This curriculum consists of learning opportunities, designed for the development of knowledge, skills, and attitudes, that are derived from the National Standards and district standards. Since counselors are responsible for the planning, designing, implementing, and evaluation of this curriculum, their responsibilities make them accountable for documenting the learning that results. According to the National Model, the guidance curriculum may be delivered in any of the following venues: classroom instruction, small-group discussions, presentations to parents and guardians, large-group assemblies, and collaborative planning and coordinating of instruction with other school personnel.

Individual Student Planning   In these activities, school counselors work to ensure that all students have future plans and make progress toward attainment of personal, educational, and postsecondary and occupational goals. In this area of service delivery, counselors help students to define their academic, career, and personal goals; make plans on the basis of those goals; and transition to the next phase of their development in the attainment of those goals. Activities through which counselors provide these services include individual or small-group appraisal and individual or small-group advisement. Topics addressed in these settings could include financial aid, graduation requirements, course selection information, and test score interpretation and analysis addressing abilities, interests, skills, and achievement.

Responsive Services   Even in the best school imaginable, students will still need counselors to respond to immediate needs that arise. These needs include academic issues such as academic failure or retention; career issues such as career counseling for postsecondary life; and personal/social issues such as crisis counseling and suicide prevention, support during painful or difficult personal transitions (death of family member, divorce of parents), or unhealthy choices (sexual activity, substance use/abuse/addiction). These responsive services are provided through such strategies as individual and small-group counseling, consultation, peer facilitation, and referrals to community resources (ASCA, 2005, p. 42).

System Support   School counselors, as members of the school community, contribute in important ways to support the school's educational mission. Through professional development, school counselors provide in-service training to colleagues and keep their own professional development current through membership in professional associations and contributions to the literature about school counseling. Through consultation, collaboration, and teaming, school counselors consult with parents and school colleagues, provide community relations support and outreach, and serve on advisory councils and district committees. Through program management and operations, school counselors maintain the management system for the program, analyze data needed for planning, and engage in "fair share" (ASCA, 2005, p. 44) activities commensurate with other professionals in the school.

THE MANAGEMENT SYSTEM   The Management System includes information school counselors need in order to effectively manage a comprehensive school counseling program. Topics covered by this section of the Model include Management Agreements, Advisory Council, Use of Data, Action Plans, Use of Time (for CSCP activities and non-CSCP activities), and Calendars.

Management Agreements   A vital part of the effective functioning of any organization is the structure that supports program efforts—the invisible "skeleton" of the program. For a program to be effective, everyone involved in the program must understand the roles, expectations, and priorities of all activities in the program. It is through management agreements that these are articulated and disseminated, that assignments are made through careful analysis of the data and a carefully designed action plan. The document must be negotiated with and supported by administration from both the building and the district to be considered viable. Topics that should be included in these agreements would include

- Assignment of students to counselors to ensure access to the CSCP
- The person(s) who will provide each program activity within the CSCP and a schedule for those activities
- The amount of time to be devoted to each aspect of the delivery system
- How counselors will be compensated for work beyond the regular workday
- The budget available for materials and supplies to implement the program
- The need for professional development to ensure the best possible CSCP
- The structure for the support services for the CSCP

Advisory Council   The advisory council "reviews the program goals, competencies, and results, and participates in making recommendations to the school counseling department, principal, and superintendent," providing critical "support, input and recommendations for program development and improvement" (ASCA, 2005, p. 47). Introduced as a part of the process for establishing the Foundation of the CSCP, an "advisory council is a representative group of persons appointed to both advise and assist the school counseling program" (ASCA, 2005, p. 47). ASCA advises members from all constituency groups: students, parents, teachers, counselors, administrators, school board members, and business and community representatives. This group will be configured and charged with duties to support the CSCP's efforts.

Use of Data   ASCA maintains that a CSCP is data-driven, and as such, derives from the "careful analysis of student needs, achievement, and related data" (ASCA, 2005, p. 49; C. B. Stone & Dahir, 2007). The types of data school counselors collect include

- Student progress data:
  - Student achievement data, defined as data that measure students' academic progress, such as standardized test data, grade point averages (GPAs), Scholastic Assessment Test (SAT) or American College Test (ACT) scores, promotion and retention rates, and so on
  - Achievement-related data, defined as data derived from behavior correlated with academic achievement, such as discipline referral patterns, suspension rates, attendance rates, homework completion rates, and so on.
  - Standards- and competency-related data, defined as data measuring student mastery of the ASCA's National Standards, such as percentage of students with four-year plans on file, percentage of students who apply conflict resolution skills, and so on.
- Disaggregate data, separated by demographic variables such as gender, ethnicity, socioeconomic status, vocation, language spoken at home, special education, grade level, and teachers.
- Program evaluation data, or data collected to document the impact of the CSCP, would include:
  - Process data, documenting how a program is conducted, including statements like "I provided group counseling to five groups from grade 5, totaling 45 students, in which I addressed anger management."
  - Perception data, answering the question "What do people think they know, believe, or can do?" and measured through pre-post surveys, documentation, skill demonstrations, or evaluation forms. An example of perception data from the personal/social domain could include a statement such as "Ninety-eight percent (44 of 45) of students in an anger management group reported that they learned how to recognize anger triggers."
  - Results data, documenting the impact of an activity or program through results, including statements such as "As a result of the group counseling, none of those students has been referred for fighting, resulting in a 25 percent reduction in discipline referrals for fighting in the school."

The Model highlights the need for data to be collected and analyzed over time, documenting the change for students over one semester, one year, and over a number of years, to identify and understand trends. Analysis of data need not be complicated; rather, statistics that are understandable and measurable repeatedly are most useful for planning and evaluation (C. B. Stone & Dahir, 2007). Furthermore, most of the data needed for understanding trends within the school are already compiled in the data system for the school and/or the district, so the management of the data need not be an impediment to this process. As highlighted in the Model (ASCA, 2005, p. 52), activities that document how all students, regardless of income, gender, or ethnicity, are assisted through the CSCP will close the educational gap for students and emphasize the vital nature of the work of school counselors.

Action Plans   Each CSCP must have a time line for the provision of two specific components of the program: the developmental curriculum and the activities for closing the achievement gap in the school. These Action Plans are designed by the counselors, then are negotiated with and approved by the administration of the school. The first document, the Action Plan for the Developmental Curriculum, is based on the ASCA National Standards (Competencies and Indicators). For these Action Plans, a chart is developed that details the topic, the domain and standard related to that topic, the curriculum materials to be used, the dates of delivery of the curriculum, the number of students to be impacted, the class or subject in which the curriculum will be provided, an overview of the evaluation method(s), and the contact counselor (ASCA, 2005, p. 54). For the Action Plans that detail the Closing-the-Gap activities, the Plan contains everything listed above, with the addition of the disaggregated data relative to achievement of various populations that justify the programmatic interventions listed.

Use of Time   Through the careful documentation of counselor time, it is possible to identify activities that do not contribute directly to the goals of the CSCP. ASCA recommends that school counselors spend a majority of their time providing direct services to students; and although everyone contributes to activities required to maintain an institution (such as serving on committees or providing lunchroom supervision), it is crucial that counselors maintain their responsibilities in such a way that their primary focus is always on the goals of the CSCP.

Calendars   ASCA further highlights the appropriate use of time through the Model's inclusion of calendars as a means of maintaining focus on program goals as well as a means of communication and accountability. A three-tiered approach to scheduling can assist CSCPs to maximize each counselor's time and efforts: an annual calendar highlights activities for yearlong planning of presentations, collaboration and services for parents, and the delivery of the developmental curriculum; a monthly calendar serves as a reminder for upcoming events and themes; and a weekly calendar provides flexibility and accountability. Together, these tools define how services within the program will be delivered.

THE ACCOUNTABILITY SYSTEM   In this section of the National Model, data collected as a part of the Management System are compiled, evaluated for program improvement, and prepared for dissemination. With this part of the process, accountability is ensured, the program improves, and the value of the CSCP is communicated to building and district administration. Several processes highlight fully accountable programs: results reports, school counselor performance standards, and the program audit.

Results Report   As data are collected relative to program efficacy, they are compiled and maintained for dissemination to administration, parents, and teachers, as well as for program evaluation and improvement. One forum for this compilation is the Results Report (ASCA, 2005, p. 60), in which the following is included:

- Grade level
- Lesson content area, located by ASCA Domain/Standard
- Curriculum or materials used
- Process data, such as methods of delivery (small-group topics and number offered, classroom subjects and number of presentations), dates, and number of students
- Short-term perception data, such as pre-post tests of knowledge
- Intermediate and long-term results data, such as attendance, test scores, graduation rates, or other measures of behaviors
- The implications of the results on the school and the counseling program

In addition, the impact of the results of such efforts will be tracked over time and compiled for presentation to administration. In this report, demographics, graduation rates, discipline and attendance data, test scores, and other data are used to document progress of students in each of the domains of school counseling and are "analyzed in relation to progress made toward school-wide mission and achievement goals" (ASCA, 2005, p. 62). As a summary document, the Impact-Over-Time Report contains

- Student demographics, such as enrollment data, gender, ethnicity, grade levels, languages, students on free and reduced lunch
- Academic achievement data, such as test scores, grade point averages, and dropout and graduation rates
- Career development data, such as numbers in career programs of work exploration, job shadowing, and job mentoring, or number of students who have identified a career direction or career cluster
- Personal/social development data, such as climate survey results, substance use data, and school crime/violence data
- Parent and guardian involvement: number of parents at conferences, workshops, and events

The goal of the Impact-Over-Time Report is to put the Results Report within the context of the entire school, to highlight the growth of students in each domain over time. As each year passes, the same data is collected to allow administration and the CSCP staff to understand the changing nature of students and their challenges in education. As the Results Report for the year highlights the school counselor's efforts of that year, the Impact-Over-Time report serves as accountability for the past year and a planning tool for the coming year.

School Counselor Performance Standards   The Performance Standards (ASCA, 2005, p. 62) for school counselors outline the professional activities and expectations as defined by the profession; these standards are the basis of the much-expanded School Counselor Competencies released in 2008. It is recommended that the Standards and Competencies be used in the yearly evaluation process, both for counselor self-evaluation and for administrative counselor evaluations. Professional development and learning opportunities result from careful analysis and reflection on skills and conceptual deficits.

The Program Audit   The National Model document provides counselors with the audit format and process to be used in the design and continuous improvement evaluation of the comprehensive school counseling program. In summary, the Audit document provides a definition of each component of the National Model and then provides a template for determining the extent to which the program meets each component (ASCA, 2005, pp. 131–141). The intended use of the tool is to document four critical areas for program evaluation and improvement:

- The major strengths of the program
- The areas in need of improvement
- Short-range goals for improvement
- Long-range goals for improvement

The results of the Program Audit, along with the counselor evaluations and the Results Reports, all provide administrators with information to assess the health and viability of the CSCP. Furthermore, accountable programs subject to active evaluation and continuous improvement are more likely to engender parent and teacher support, which is more likely to result in administrative support. Positive growth and effective public relations are the outcomes.

REFLECTION MOMENT

What concerns do you have as you look at the National Model? Is it comforting to know that there is an outline of the professional expectations, or is it intimidating to think about all the expectations placed on you as you enter your new profession? Recall the daunting process of applying for graduate school, and reflect on what you heard were the expectations of graduate students. How did you manage your anxiety around that process? What did you learn from that experience that you can use now?

The Flow

Look again at the National Model on page 76. The black-and-white graphics were carefully chosen to communicate the flow of information and data through the four elements of the CSCP. As you can see, the Foundation, comprising beliefs and philosophy, mission statement, and ASCA National Standards for Students, feeds into the Management System (the nuts and bolts of managing the CSCP) and the Delivery System (the day-to-day activities of the CSCP). In turn, both the Management System and the Delivery System feed into Accountability process, as data collected from program management duties and from the delivery of the CSCP flow together for evaluation, program improvement, and dissemination. Finally, you will notice that the white arrows into the Accountability block create a black arrow pointing from Accountability to Foundation, as the results of the reports and the evaluation process are used to further refine the mission statement and assess progress toward the students' attainment of the ASCA National Standards for Students. The border around the Model that contains the words "Systemic Change–Advocacy–Leadership–Collaboration" reflects the environment of the work school counselors do in terms of the Themes discussed earlier in this chapter.

CASE STUDY REVISITED

Integration

Go back and reread the opening case study, then answer the following questions:

1. When you read the discussion between Cadence and Kayli, what would you say in response to each of the following arguments?
   a. Counselors are just extra baggage to the school—what is needed are more teachers.
   b. Counselors don't contribute to the students' lives at all; counseling is just "playing head games."
   c. All counselors do is interfere with the parents' rights to discipline their own children.
   d. Counselors work only with kids who are really sick.
2. Would the National Model help Cadence with her decision? How would you use the National Model to help Cadence decide whether to become a school counselor?
3. How will the Themes of the Model (namely, Leadership, Advocacy, Collaboration, and Systemic Change) relate to Kayli's conversation with Cadence? ▪

Suggested Readings

Every professional school counselor must be familiar with the standards and expectations of the profession as articulated by the American School Counselor Association. The most important resources follow. Contact ASCA via the Internet to obtain a copy of each of the documents.

American School Counselor Association. (July/August 2008). School counselor competencies. *ASCA School Counselor, 45*(6), 64–73.

American School Counselor Association. (1999). *The role of the professional school counselor.* Alexandria, VA: Author.

American School Counselor Association. (2005). *The ASCA national model: A framework for school counseling programs* (2nd ed.). Alexandria, VA: Author.

Stone, C. B., & Dahir, C. A. (2007). *School counselor accountability: A MEASURE of student success* (2nd ed.). Upper Saddle River, NJ: Pearson.

6

Models of Delivery Systems

LEARNING OBJECTIVES

By the end of this chapter, you will

1. Understand the difference between prescriptive and nonprescriptive school counseling delivery models

2. Recognize current models of school counseling programs (e.g., American School Counseling Association [ASCA] National Model) and their integral relationship to the total educational program

3. Appreciate contemporary frameworks and guiding principles that supplement the development and implementation of effective school counseling programs

CASE STUDY

School Counseling For All

The Forall School District is new to comprehensive school counseling and struggles with ways to utilize school counseling services in a comprehensive districtwide program. The district's current school counseling program lacks a clear philosophical basis, mission, and organizational structure. What implementation does exist is inconsistent across schools. Some schools have programs that appear developmental in nature. For example, the school counselor visits classrooms and presents guidance lessons, yet the lessons are fragmented and disconnected from the school's curriculum and overall mission of the school, or the district for that matter. The lessons are more like the topic of the week. Others schools rely on more of a responsive services approach and are continually putting out fires and responding to crises. Moreover, the district's test scores, graduation rates, and overall academic achievement results are decreasing and parents are beginning to complain. To add to the district's overall discontent, the student population is evolving and changing, which is influencing school climates. The district knew that changes were in order and began to consider ways that the school counselors could lead a districtwide initiative. Thus, the district administration provided funding for the school counselors to attend training in comprehensive school counseling and ways to implement comprehensive school counseling. The training focused on creating a districtwide comprehensive school counseling program that would support students' academic achievement, career exploration, and development, and enhance their personal and social development as they learn and grow. Likewise, such a program would target specific areas that needed addressing such as attendance rates, grades, discipline referrals, graduation rates, and so on, depending on the unique needs of a particular school and community within the district. The ways in which the program was structured and implemented depended on the nature of the school, its vision and mission, and the needs of the students; meaning that no one program model would fit every school. The training introduced the school counselors to a variety of delivery models for implementing comprehensive school counseling, each of which seemed likely candidates for their district. The counselors' initial task after the training was to determine the delivery model most appropriate and fitting for their school.

The counselors reconvened to begin the process of sorting through the pieces of their programs by conducting a districtwide school counseling audit. This process would involve an assessment of the program pieces in place, those that were "under construction," and those program components that either were in need of redesign or did not exist. The administration and school board supported comprehensive school counseling yet struggled with a district description and overall guiding mission statement. The school counselors were involved in a variety of activities across buildings and concentrated most of their efforts on assisting students with personal issues and providing services. They were aware of the need to involve students in more career exploration activities and lacked the means to implement such activities. Overall, how the counselors were using their time in relation to a district mission and rationale for school counseling was unknown. The individual schools were able to produce some data and evaluation outcomes; however, the information they provided did not connect to any specific program goals and objectives. Most of the evaluation data was subjective and anecdotal, coming from parents, teachers, and students who voiced their appreciation and respect for the school counselors in such remarks as, "Our school counselors are wonderful! They help us feel good about ourselves, encourage our children, and assist the schools in many ways."

The challenge facing the counselors was how to pull all of these pieces together and decide on a delivery model that would best suit the needs and goals of the district's school counseling programs. Would it be one delivery system model? Would it require more than one model, a combination perhaps, to fit with the district's definition, mission, and rationale for school counseling? How would it vary from building to building? Would one delivery system work best in one building and another in another building? What are the district's philosophy, rationale and mission of school counseling? The counselors would definitely need to review the delivery models the learned at they training to make an informed decision for their district. This was going to be a lengthy, time-consuming process.

CHALLENGE QUESTIONS

If you were one of the school counselors in the Forall School District, how would you go about selecting a particular delivery model for implementing a comprehensive school counseling program? What would you need to know about the delivery models, frameworks, and guiding principles in order to make an informed decision? What might you look for in a delivery model, framework, and/or guiding principles to fit the needs of your community, school, and students? ▪

DELIVERY MODELS

Schools are vast with challenges, responsibilities, and needs. The daily operation of a school entails tremendous planning, preparation, structure, and accountability. Introducing a comprehensive school counseling program into the mix could feel quite overwhelming. We expect that what, when, where, how, and who questions saturate the minds of those contemplating such a feat. Likewise, we anticipate the challenges these types of questions will produce.

Developing a comprehensive school counseling program begins with identifying the delivery model that best suits the mission of your school counseling program, your school, the students, and the community. You might ask yourself, "What is a delivery model and why do we need one?" Alternatively, you might wonder, "We currently have a fully implemented program, yet our data reveal that we are missing some underlying assumptions and principles. Do we have to toss out our program and start over from scratch?"

We believe many school counselors and districts struggle with these and other questions as they grapple with how to implement or expand a comprehensive school counseling program. The emphasis on academic achievement has propelled school counselors and their programs into the forefront of school reform efforts. Whereas we view school counselors as professional counselors and educational specialists who hold a pupil services license, the ASCA role statement (2009) defines school counselors as licensed educators who specialize in counseling and foster students' success in school through programming efforts that target academic, career, and personal/social development. Programming initiatives, interventions, strategies, and more, all reside within a comprehensive school counseling program. A first step in implementing a program relies on a selecting delivery system that fits the philosophical vision of the district, the school, the students, and the community it serves. Whether you choose the ASCA National Model, one of the additional models we will present in this chapter, or a combination of models and frameworks, the choice is up to you and the stakeholders involved. What is important is that you develop a structure for delivering your program effectively by meeting the needs of your students, school, and community.

CHALLENGE QUESTIONS

What is your definition of the role of a professional school counselor? How will you go about integrating your definition into your professional identity development? ▪

Think of a comprehensive school counseling delivery model as the vehicle for driving your program, a mode of transportation, so to speak. Various models exist, all of which can transport your program. Each model differs in unique and individual ways; however, all can support, or drive, a comprehensive school counseling program effectively. You could view the contemporary frameworks and guiding principles as vehicle accessories, or means of enhancing or expanding your comprehensive program in specific areas such as social justice or strengths-based counseling.

We encourage school counselors to research and learn as much as possible about the various delivery models, frameworks, and supporting principles available in order to guide your decision making and choice accordingly. Ultimately, you and your stakeholders will choose the model, and perhaps add-ons or extensions, that will best transport your program across your school toward school success for all students. The model of delivery you choose will structure the ways in which you implement, manage, and evaluate your school counseling program. The frameworks and supporting principles you might add on to enhance and supplement your program will address specific values and beliefs that support ways in which you promote the development of young people.

The various models of delivery assume specific "philosophical assumptions," essential program components, and specific goals and objectives that make them unique (D. Brown & Trusty, 2005, p. 80). We will present a variety of delivery models, some of which were in existence before the ASCA National Model and include contemporary frameworks and guiding principles that align with the ASCA National Standards for School Counseling (ASCA, 2005) and support the mission of the Education Trust (2003). The differences among these models are how each one articulates their specific goals and objectives around the three domains of academic, career, and personal/social development (D. Brown & Trusty, 2005). In most cases, the goals and objectives of the delivery models focus on all of three of these areas. The selection of which model to choose comes down to which will best meet the needs of your program's goal and objectives.

The delivery models for school counseling date back to the 1950s and nationwide school reform efforts. These efforts thrust school counselors into initiatives designed to promote math and science, workforce preparation, and vocational guidance and counseling. In the 1970s counseling services evolved into comprehensive results-based programming focused on student success and academic achievement. The nation's focus on academic achievement continued with "add-on" initiatives and guaranteed guidance services (R. White, 1981), based on national trends and societal needs, all in the name of helping students succeed in school and beyond.

Delivery models generally fall into one of two categories: *prescriptive* or *nonprescriptive*. Prescriptive models tend to rest on clear assumptions as to the role and function of school counselors and school counseling programs. Based on specific guidelines, prescriptive models detail "do's and don'ts" for school counselors, which may include the use of a calendar, what percentage of a school counselors' time should be spent in specific areas, and what activities school counselors should be engaging in. The ASCA National Model and perhaps your state's model are prescriptive. For example, the ASCA National Model presents a specific counselor-to-student ratio and percentage of time given to counseling services and responsibilities.

Nonprescriptive models rely more on aligning the role and function of school counselors and school counseling programs with the needs of the school and the student body. Specific assumptions and "do's and don'ts" are not characteristic of nonprescriptive models, meaning school counselors are freer to use their time and delivery strategies as deemed appropriate (D. Brown & Trusty, 2005). For example, the Essential Services model frames comprehensive school counseling around four components of counseling, consulting, coordinating, and appraising; however, the school counselor is free to schedule and adjust his or her times according to the needs of the program.

Specifically the ways in which you lead and support your program goals and objectives rest on a continuum of implementation strategies. For example, a school counselor may rely mainly on classroom and large-group guidance, whereas another school counselor may devote a majority of his or her time to individual and small-group counseling programs. Still another school counselor may implement more schoolwide counseling programs such as teacher-advisor, peer facilitation, and mediation programs to meet the specific goals and objectives of the school counseling program. Choice of delivery models and strategies for implementation generally emerge from district or building philosophies and missions, needs assessments, and ongoing program evaluation.

REFLECTION MOMENT

Reflect on the two categories of delivery model. Identify strengths and weaknesses of each category. Next, consider your personality style as a developing school counselor. Do you prefer a more detailed and specific organizational structure, or do you prefer to have more freedom and flexibility within your organizational structure?

Let us say that your style and preference of a delivery model is different from the needs of your school and students. Reflect on the differences and conflicts you discover and ways in which you might proceed in your development.

The Developmental Guidance and Counseling Model

Developmental Guidance and Counseling (Myrick, 1993, 2003) is a long-established model for delivering school counseling programs. In fact, Florida relies on Myrick's model as a foundation of its school counseling program guidelines (Holcomb-McCoy & Mitchell, 2005). Developmental guidance focuses on developmental learning behaviors, tasks, skills, and experiences necessary for children and adolescents to be successful in school and in life. Grounded in developmental theory (Erikson, 1963; Ivey, 1986);, the model assumes that "human nature moves individuals sequentially and positively toward self-enhancement" (Myrick, 1987, p. 31). As individuals move through each consecutive stage of development, they acquire certain skills, behaviors, and attitudes that support them through each transition from one stage to the next. However, as individuals transition from one stage to another, they naturally encounter discomfort, confusion, and sometimes difficulties. The intent of a developmental guidance program is to promote awareness and learning about development and transition, provide support and skill development, and prevent problem situations from occurring in advance (Myrick, 1987).

Six counselor interventions or functions frame the role of the school counselor, which are individual counseling, small-group counseling, classroom or large-group guidance, consultation, coordination, and peer facilitation. Myrick's intent was that school counselors spend the bulk of their time engaged in individual, small-group counseling, and classroom/large-group guidance, which aligns with the preventative focus of the model. Counselors could then divide their remaining time between consultation, coordination, and peer facilitation services. This type of time allotment supports prevention efforts, which Myrick believed would transform school counselors' role from a "crisis-based orientation to a planned orientation" (Holcomb-McCoy & Mitchell, 2005, p. 2).

Individual counseling, according to Myrick's model (Myrick, 1993), "is a primary counselor intervention in the schools" (p. 142). He proposed that school counselors maintain an active caseload of students (six to eight) with whom they meet twice a week for up to 10 to 12 weeks (Holcomb-McCoy & Mitchell, 2005). This is an advantage and highlight of Myrick's model because of the appreciation and importance given to individual counseling as a prevention strategy.

REFLECTION MOMENT

Explore the priority given to individual counseling in this model. What is your position on individual counseling as a component of school counseling programs? Discuss your rationale in class and debate the pros, cons, and challenges.

Developmental guidance curriculum is sequential, and is integrated easily into the existing academic curriculum. Teachers and school counselors collaboratively and cooperatively incorporate the curriculum into the regular academic curriculum, which includes specific life skills to prepare students for adulthood. Eight specific objectives generally frame the curriculum. They are: (1) understanding the social environment, (2) understanding self and others, (3) understanding attitudes and behavior, (4) decision making and problem solving, (5) interpersonal and communication skills, (6) school success skills, (7) career awareness and educational planning, and (8) community pride (Myrick, 1993).

In addition to these eight program objectives, seven principles of developmental guidance provide direction to program implementation and evaluation. Developmental guidance (1) is for all students; (2) has an organized and planned curriculum; (3) is sequential and flexible; (4) is an integrated part of the total educational process; (5) involves all school personnel; (6) helps students learn more effectively and efficiently; and (7) includes counselors who provide specialized counseling services and interventions (Myrick, 1993).

Developmental guidance programs depend on the collaboration and participation of everyone working together to promote students' personal, academic, and social growth (Myrick, 1987, 1993). Teachers especially play a vital role in developmental guidance and student success. One of the most successful approaches to directly involving teachers in the personal development of students places the teacher as an advisor to a group of 15 to 20 students who become his or her advisees (Myrick & Myrick, 1990). In this role, teachers interact with students on a more personal level, build closer relationships, and serve as "everyday advocates" for their students (Gonzalez & Myrick, 2000, p. 243). You might see this type of program often referred to as an advisory program, a mentoring program, or a teacher-advisor program (TAP).

Modeled after elementary schools, TAPs organize students under a team of teachers, then assigns a homeroom teacher who meets with the students regularly and serves as advisor to the students (Alexander & George, 1981). Homeroom provides a time for teachers to facilitate and process developmental guidance lessons and units with their students. Guidance units generally focus on getting acquainted, study skills and habits, self-assessment, communication skills, decision making and problem solving, peer relationships, motivation, conflict resolution, wellness, career development, educational planning, and community involvement (Myrick, 1993).

Collaborative counselor-teacher relationships describe developmental guidance programs. A school counseling advisory committee solidifies the counselor-teacher relationship and provides a practical solution for creating a collaborative, team environment between counselors and teachers. The committee meets regularly to identify students' needs and concerns, brainstorm ideas, review curriculum, design prevention programs, explore strategies for specific interventions, and examine data and evaluation measures (Myrick, 1993).

Counseling interventions in developmental school counseling programs consist of the six basic counseling strategies: individual counseling, small-group counseling, large-group guidance, peer facilitator training and projects, consultation, and coordination of guidance services. These interventions are the general recommendations for the role and function of school counselors in developmental school counselor programs (Myrick, 1993).

Small-group counseling is an additional school counseling intervention and highly valued in developmental guidance programs. Whereas individual counseling might be more appropriate for students who are uncomfortable sharing in groups, small-group counseling works well with students who are willing to connect with others in a small-group experience. Myrick (1993) delineates three small-group counseling approaches to meet the needs of students in schools. They are: (1) crisis centered, (2) problem centered, and (3) growth centered. Most of the groups that school counselors develop based on the needs of students fall into one of these three categories of groups. Crisis-centered groups target current and urgent issues that students experience, such as sudden loss, death, violence, environmental catastrophes, and other immediate tragedies that students need to process and/or explore. Problem-centered groups take the shape of study skills, time management, coping with stress, effective communication and social skills, conflicts and peer relationships, and avoiding alcohol and drugs. Growth-centered groups focus on personal and social development, which is a key component within comprehensive school counseling (Myrick, 1993).

Large-group counseling according to Myrick (1993) involves a larger number of students and the topics are less personal in nature. The school counselors serves as more of an information provider and teacher, which equates to more structure and less individual attention. Large-group counseling or classroom guidance is the key means to integrating school counseling into the academic curriculum. Elementary school counselors are experts at classroom guidance and use it as an effective intervention for delivering developmental guidance to all students. Teachers often collaborate with the school counselor in the guidance lesson and connect it to the academic lesson. We encourage this type of teacher-counselor collaboration as a means of integrating the guidance lesson into the overall scope and sequence of the schoolwide curriculum. We also believe that when teachers and counselors co-facilitate guidance lessons in the classroom, their relationship models the importance of the school counseling curriculum in their learning. Examples of classroom guidance include resolving conflicts with people, communicating effectively, choosing a career, celebrating differences, making healthy decisions, effective ways to problem solve, and human sexuality. Large-group guidance may also take the form of teaching students a career development software and ways to access and create their career portfolios, or teaching students peer mediation skills as part of a schoolwide peer mediation program. Historically, the Florida Classroom Guidance Project, implemented in Orange County, Florida (Myrick, Merhill, & Swanson, 1986), proved effective with fourth-graders. Elementary and middle schools across the nation have replicated and advanced this model as an effective means of meeting the developmental needs of students.

Peer facilitator programs as a counseling intervention are unique to developmental guidance. This popular intervention trains selected peer facilitators in basic helping skills, which enable them to assist and support other students. Although parents and other adults have great influences on children, peers are most influential during the school years. Most youngsters would rather turn to a peer/friend than a parent, teacher, or other adult when encountering a problem (Myrick, 1993). Some examples of peer facilitator programs include peer tutoring, peer mentoring, and peers working alongside in-school suspension programs; tutoring students who have missed extended amounts of school due to special circumstances; tutoring students in specific subjects; and peer mediation. Extensive training and supervision are absolute necessities when students are assisting other students. School counselors serve as process monitors, consultants, and supervisors in peer programs. The National Association of Peer Program Professionals (NAPPP) is a nonprofit corporation whose mission is to help adults establish, train, supervise, maintain, and evaluate peer programs. We encourage school counselors to refer to NAPPP for suggestions, guidelines, and resources for developing and implementing peer facilitator projects and programs.

Consultation as a school counselor intervention is dynamic, systemic and an integral role within developmental guidance programs. Myrick (1993) asserts that school counselors cannot intervene directly with every persons' crisis or need. Consultation is an indirect approach to supporting the development and academic achievement of students. In a consulting role, school counselors work with individuals and systems on matters that involve, most often, students. Instead of the school counselor working directly with the student, the consultation process assists in empowering others (e.g., parents, teachers) to work with the student. What the authors favor about consultation is the learning and empowerment that takes place, especially for the person working directly with the student(s). They learn from working with the counselor, which empowers them should similar situations arise in the future.

Coordination (Myrick, 1993) as a counselor intervention entails the management of the developmental guidance program and all of the guidance services provided to students. The function of coordination involves planning and programming, gathering and informing, allocating and resourcing, arranging and organizing, development and operations, and supervision and leadership. School counselors can lead by coordinating the total guidance program, the guidance committee, student appraisal or testing, child study teams, behavioral interventions, crisis intervention, referrals, peer facilitator and TAP programs, special events, and curriculum committees.

Envisioning this role, you can see that coordination can easily absorb a counselor's calendar and time. Myrick (1993) noted the importance of protecting the other five counselor interventions from coordination overload. Building an effective working relationship with administration and maintaining a calendar are essential means to preventing intervention imbalance. All six of the counselor interventions are vital to the success of a developmental guidance program, thus it is imperative that school counselors schedule their time in the best interest of the students they serve. School counselors can often find themselves merged into duties that are not counselor related yet important to the functioning of the school. Beginning counselors often take on more coordination efforts than necessary because of their need to please, fit in, and maintain a job. Likewise, we urge school counselors to reflect regularly on ways they are using their time. Are there specific interventions you avoid or shy away from due to a lack of confidence or training? Myrick notes that counselors can sometimes grow quite comfortable in the coordination role when they feel less effective or competent in running small groups or conducting classroom guidance.

Implementing a developmental school counseling program relies on a series of implementation strategies. They are: (1) administrative understanding and support; (2) selecting a school guidance advisory committee; (3) developing and writing a philosophy statement; (4) needs survey; (5) developing and writing a program rationale; (6) setting goals, objectives, and developing strategies for implementation; and (7) accountability (Wittmer, 1993). Our belief is that most of these strategies are clear and straightforward. We suggest referring to Myrick (1993) for detailed systematic ways to progress through the implementation process. However, we do want to give attention to the school counselor and accountability in developmental guidance and counseling.

Accountability encompasses the process of being responsible for one's actions and the outcomes of those actions. It is ongoing and provides continual feedback, data, and results to questions such as, "What's working?" "What's working and needs improving?" and "What is not working and needs revising?" School counselors and the program they deliver are accountable for the services they provide and the effectiveness of those services, and should ask questions such as, "What are the needs of our students? Based on the needs, what are my goals and objectives? Were the strategies and interventions I employed to meet my goals and objectives effective? Am I effective in my role and function as a school counselor?" An accountability system of checks and balances enables school counselors to have a clear understanding about their programs and the services they are providing.

Developmental guidance and counseling is a comprehensive preventative delivery model grounded in a well-planned, developmentally appropriate guidance curriculum that is integrated with the existing academic curriculum for all. A majority of the program goals and objectives depend on classroom guidance; however, developmental guidance programs also include specialized counseling services and interventions. The challenge with implementing a program using this model is the lack of structure it provides for designing, organizing, implementing, and evaluating a program (Schmidt, 2008). The importance of coordination, time management, managing program priorities, and schoolwide collaboration in the total education process of helping students learn more effectively and efficiently is essential (Myrick, 1993; Schmidt, 2008).

A key highlight of developmental guidance programs are TAPs and the time they free up for counselors to meet with students on an individual basis or in small groups without interrupting the regular academic schedule (Myrick, 1993). This equates to more *counseling* time! A second highlight is that the school counseling curriculum is integrated K–12, which means that all students receive developmental guidance throughout their school experience. Florida, Missouri, and Wisconsin have well-respected TAP programs. Examples are the program in Green Bay, Wisconsin, entitled "Our Time"; Mehlville High School's Teacher Advisor Program in Missouri; and in Florida, Hillsborough County's "Quality Time", Orlando's "IMPACT," and Sarasota's "Prime Time" programs (Gonzalez & Myrick, 2000).

REFLECTION MOMENT

Discuss the Developmental Guidance and Counseling model. Envision yourself implementing Myrick's model. Which components will you keep and which components might you revise or not use? What added components might you need? Reflect on your reasons.

The Essential Services Model

The Essential Services model has been a method of delivery for decades. Based on the *trait-and-factor approach* (D. Brown & Trusty, 2005), the Essential Services model, a nonprescriptive model, evolved out of differential psychology and studies concerned with the "measurement of human traits and environments" (p. 82). Recall the traditional career-planning process of assessing students' values, interests, skills, and abilities and using the results to assist students in locating an occupation that matched their assessment (D. Brown & Trusty, 2005). The original components of the Essential Services model included counseling, educational and occupational information, student appraisal, and placement (D. Brown & Trusty, 2005; R. I. Gibson, Mitchell, & Higgins, 1983; Williamson, 1939). Schmidt (2003) updated the Essential Services model to reflect the components of *counseling*, *consulting*, *coordinating*, and *appraising*. These four broad categories make up the current components of the Essential Services model and provide a structure for school counselors to design their roles and functions within their programs (D. Brown & Trusty, 2005).

The counseling component includes individual counseling, group counseling, student counseling, and parent and teacher counseling (Schmidt, 2003). Individual counseling is likely to be developmental in nature and focus on problem solving, decision making, "relationships, and self-development" through a variety of modalities such as play therapy, "nonverbal interactions, and modeling techniques" (p. 80). Group counseling, which reaches a larger number of students, might focus on developmental issues such as transitions, peer and family relationships, and other personal/social issues. The component of parent and teacher counseling recognizes that parents and teachers often approach school counselors for assistance with personal problems and concerns. Realistically, the adults that surround, teach, support, and raise today's students will find themselves in need of a genuine, caring, and unconditional active listener from time to time. Whereas school counselors, by nature, listen fully and empathize with individuals' troubles, we encourage you to make every effort to refer parents, teachers, and other adults to the appropriate community services. Schmidt (2003) views this type of service to parents and teachers as a "combination of counseling and consulting processes" (p. 83).

ROLE-PLAYING MOMENT

Set up a role play involving a school counselor and a teacher. The teacher comes to you seeking counsel concerning her feelings of frustration, hopelessness, and sadness. She shares that her feelings are getting in the way of her relationships with her students and her teaching. Some of her students' parents are beginning to complain to the principal, and she fears losing her job. However, she needs her job because of her partner's recent layoff. Role-play this scenario for about 10 minutes. After the role play, process the school counselor's role. What did you notice? What fears emerged? Challenges? Process the school counselor's role and ways in which you might handle this as a future school counselor.

Consulting activities in the Essential Services model might include a variety of consulting services for administration, staff, teachers, parents, and students (Schmidt, 2003). In this role, school counselors might serve as a resource for school and community information, career opportunities, educational opportunities, and financial assistance. Instructional consulting services describe activities such as classroom guidance, parent education, and teacher in-services. Interestingly, Schmidt (2003) places classroom guidance under the component of consulting suggesting that school counselors do not play a *direct* role in the delivery of classroom guidance.

REFLECTION MOMENT

I (Kelli) often wonder about school counselors being the only providers of classroom guidance. Within our school counseling program, we devote a lot of time to training our school counseling students in classroom management and ways to "teach" or present classroom guidance effectively. Teachers are experts in teaching and school counselors are experts in processing; thus, would it not make sense that teachers and school counselors collaborate or co-deliver classroom guidance? What are your thoughts?

Problem-solving consulting activities involve parent-teacher conferences, administrative conferences, and student services team conferences. Other consulting services might include developing guidance curriculum, individual student planning, school climate initiatives, and special events and projects. The key to deciphering a school counselor's role in providing consulting services is to determine whether the role requires the school counselor to assume a direct or indirect role.

The essential services component of coordination focuses a school counselor's time on data collection and sharing, referrals and follow-up, and schoolwide events (Schmidt, 2003). Data collection equates to test administration, test results, and student records. Referrals and follow-up include activities that require school counselors to network and connect with community agencies and private practitioners. Schoolwide events could be activities such as student recognition assemblies, career awareness campaigns, teacher-advisor programs, and peer-helper programs.

Appraising emphasizes assessment and evaluation of students and the overall school environment (Schmidt, 2003). Student evaluation activities are concerned with tests, inventories, observations and interviews, and group assessment. Environmental evaluation activities involve assessment of school climate, families, and peer groups. Schmidt (2003) suggests that assessment activities be priority in the planning process "because assessment is the fuel for counseling and consultation" (D. Brown & Trusty, 2005, p. 82). In other words, if I do not know where I am going, how will I know when I get there? Assessment activities include assessing the current program to determine what is working, what needs revising or adjusting, what needs implementing, and what needs tossing. Assessing the needs of students, parents, and teachers, and determining resources to meet needs are also a component of assessment activities. We feel it is important that school counselors view assessment as an ongoing process and embrace the wealth of objective information assessment can provide.

A disadvantage of the Essential Services model is that is does not account for all of the activities of a school counselor; the list of services school counselors provide is merely too extensive and might lack alignment with the services intended. This could create a problem when attempting to educate stakeholders about the program and the services it provides. However, the four components of counseling, consulting, coordinating, and appraising, generally considered as interdependent activities, target all students' personal/social, educational, and career development needs (D. Brown & Trusty, 2005). The challenge lies in the way school counselors delineate their role and function in such a way as to avoid falling prey to an abundance of duties not related to being a school counselor. Detailed planning, role delineation, and advocacy would be essential. On the other hand, the Essential Services model has the advantage of prioritizing assessment, which is a key component of counseling and consulting services.

REFLECTION MOMENT

Consider the Essential Services model and ways you see it supporting comprehensive school counseling. Explore ways you might expand or revise the Essential Services model that would address the disadvantages mentioned.

The Results-Based Program Delivery Model

The Results-Based Student Support Program model (C. Johnson & Johnson, 1998) targets the academic, career, and personal/social domains, and "integrates the program into the educational experience of each student" (p. 7). A nonprescriptive delivery model, results-based school counseling focuses on *all* students achieving identified educational, career, and personal/social competencies to be successful in school and beyond high school. Results-based models ask, "How are students different as a result of the school counseling program?" (S. Johnson & Johnson, 2003, p. 2). Accountability practices in this context ask, "To what extent are *all* students achieving the identified needs?"

Counselors, students, parents, school personnel, social workers, psychologists, nurses, and specialists collaborate in the organization, planning, and implementation of programs, strategies, and interventions designed to meet the identified needs of students (S. Johnson & Johnson, 2003), especially those students traditionally "left behind." Otherwise known as teaming, school counselors lead in the development of support teams that aid students in achieving the desired outcomes. The Education Trust (2003) promotes this acute focus on students who are underserved by our education system. According to Reese House, former director of the new National Center for Transforming School Counseling, we must focus on efforts to ensure that school counselors have the data and knowledge they need to lead schools' efforts at increasing academic achievement for all students and closing the gap between groups.

Within a results-based program, counselors use assessment and evaluation data of student needs to select, design, and implement results-driven programs that achieve results. Regular and ongoing program evaluation reveals students' abilities to demonstrate the desired competencies and outcomes (S. Johnson & Johnson, 2003). For example, as part of a program evaluation, one might ask, "How many high school juniors achieved proficiency in postsecondary planning strategies as a result of tenth-grade career-planning workshops?" The data gathered from this type of question can uncover a wealth of information that could inform program efforts. Likewise, by disaggregating the data, school counselors can uncover the needs of student populations that current efforts are not meeting. School counselors also participate in an evaluation of their abilities to lead and manage the school counseling program. Continuous and ongoing evaluation, combined with constant analysis of disaggregated data, provide systemic management to the school counseling program and accountability for the progress of all students (S. Johnson & Johnson, 2003).

The program elements of a results-based school counseling program are congruent with the school district's philosophy, curriculum, and other educational programs, which provides organizational structure and gives school counselors flexibility to use their time in ways best suited to meet the needs of their school counseling program and the students (S. Johnson & Johnson, 2003). Each element serves an individual purpose, and when combined, creates a school counseling program focused on achieving results. Schools and districts are free to design and deliver curriculum, manage and implement programs, and use their resources and allocations to achieve the results that best meet the needs and desired results for their students (S. Johnson, Johnson, & Downs, 2006).

A results-based program is a systems-oriented delivery model that is proactive, preventive, and designed to reach all students as an integral part of the academic curriculum. School counselors who lead and manage results-based programs will often experience an expansion of their knowledge and skills beyond traditional counseling and crisis interventions to that of curriculum, program, and research specialist. Developmentally age-appropriate programming as part of the educational component assists students with acquiring lifelong problem-solving and decision-making skills (S. Johnson & Johnson, 2003), and leaves time allocations, scheduling, and process decisions up to the school counselor. School counselors structure their schedules and time based on the goals of the program as defined by the assessed needs.

The program and system elements within a results-based school counseling program interact systemically to create a framework "within which counselors administrators, parents, community members, and students collaborate to ensure that students receive the knowledge, attitudes, and skills they need to become successful, contributing adults" (S. Johnson & Johnson, 2003, p. 4). The elements are interrelated, interdependent, and correspond well with school district philosophies, curricula, and other educational programming efforts. Results-based program elements are (1) mission, (2) philosophy, (3) conceptual model of guidance, (4) goals, (5) competencies, (6) management system, (7) results agreements, (8) needs assessments, (9) results plans, (10) monitoring system, (11) advisory council, (12) master calendar of events, and (13) glossary.

The mission statement for your results-based school counseling program is the foundation that provides the context for the entire program. Most important, a well-defined mission statement "identifies the same targets for everyone" (S. Johnson et al., 2006, p. 28) and links with the subsequent mission statements. For example, the mission statement for your school counseling program links to the mission of your school, which links to the mission of the school district, which links to the mission of the state department of education. Mission statements generally include all students, primary competencies, hierarchy of linkages, and long-range results and desires for all students.

Establishing the philosophy follows an accepted mission statement. Your program philosophy is the set of guiding principles that everyone agrees on for implementing the school counseling program. Guiding principles generally evolve in part from personal and professional expectations, or principles, which are also included in the program philosophy. Philosophy statements often begin with a sentence stem such as "The counselors in Forall School District believe that . . ." Another example might change the wording somewhat to "The school counselors in Forall School District agree that . . ."

Conceptual models are the framework, which rests on the mission, the foundation of the program. The program philosophy guides the implementation process. The glossary defines all the terms, concepts, and phrases in the school program document and ensures understanding and clarity. Wellman (1962) proposed the original conceptual model for guidance programs that the profession as adapted for framing today's school counseling programs. The model includes the four categories of goals—educational, career, personal, and social—and their interaction with the competencies: knowledge, skills, and attitudes. These dimensions interact across specific populations within a school to create a comprehensive school counseling program.

Delineating the goals, standards, and competencies for a results-based program is important because "they define how the program prepares students for future success" (S. Johnson et al., 2006, p. 57). Goals and standards are what your program intends to provide. Standards, or benchmarks, are generally state or nationally defined. Goals tend to originate at the school level. It is essential that program goals maintain a hierarchy linkage. For example, there must be a direct connection between the goals, content guidelines or standards of your school counseling program, your building and district, and your state. Competencies are often referred to as indicators, formative data, or "the age- or grade-specific knowledge, skills, and attitudes" that gauge whether students are moving toward proposed goals and the mission of the program (p. 58). We encourage you to refer to S. Johnson and Johnson (2003) and S. Johnson et al. (2006) for an in-depth explanation and discussions of these elements.

REFLECTION MOMENT

Reflect on a Results-Based Student Support Program model. Envision using this model to deliver your school counseling program. What fears do you have about developing beyond a counselor to a curriculum and research specialist? What will you need in order to achieve success in these roles?

The Strategic Comprehensive Model

D. Brown and Trusty (2005) developed the Strategic Comprehensive Model for School Counseling Program out of their desire to advance comprehensive school counseling. With respect to the popular models and the growth in comprehensive school counseling, Brown and Trusty were concerned with the notion of counseling programs implementing preconceived competencies instead of assessing for specific student needs. We assume that professionally developed competencies are focusing on students' needs; however, the strategic model suggests that counselors strategically assess for students' needs, which assures that students are receiving the most appropriate program interventions and counseling strategies. Likewise, the lack of alignment between interventions, outcomes, and the evaluation of outcomes influenced the development of the strategic model. The question posed relates to how school counselors will improve or expand their programs if they lack specific data as to what works and what does not. Closely aligned needs, interventions, outcomes, and outcome evaluations are key characteristics of strategic school counseling programs.

Strategic school counseling programs (D. Brown & Trust, 2005) are nonprescriptive, which gives school counselors the flexibility to deliver their programs "based on factors such as their level of expertise, the availability of resources to support the program, the characteristics of the student body and the community, and a number of other factors that are out of school counselors' control" (p. 89). Brown and Trusty assert that school counselors incorporate efficient management and accountability systems (e.g., ASCA National Model), and align the goals of the school program with the goal of education, yet encourage school counselors to avoid limiting their mission statement to a narrow or single focus. Programs designed "for all" can often fall short of providing the specific interventions and services needed by student populations such special education, gifted and talented, at-risk, and various diverse student populations. Strategic school counseling prioritizes assessing student needs in a strategic way that decreases the chance of marginalizing student populations by creating an inclusive school counseling program that meets the diverse needs of *all* students.

Strategic school counseling programs are developmental, preventive, remedial, and emphasizes academic achievement and closing achievement gaps (D. Brown & Trusty, 2005). The components and subcomponents of the model are "1) facilitating normal development (prevention and development; 2) serving at-risk students (remedial services and referral; 3) life skills development (goal setting/planning, educational development, and career development; and 4) leadership and program management (leadership, program and personnel evaluation, public relationship, resource development, planning, management/coordination; and 5) school citizenship, which varies across schools" (p. 91).

REFLECTION MOMENT

Reflect on the Strategic School Counseling model. Envision using this model to deliver your school counseling program.

The Domains/Activities/Partners Model

We developed the Domains/Activities/Partners (DAP) model (Dollarhide & Saginak, 2003), which provides school counselors with both a systemic model for organizing a comprehensive school counseling program (CSCP) and a systematic way of thinking about their role and function as a school counselor. The DAP model emphasizes student-focused activities that result in student competencies and success through collaborative partnerships with counselors, students, parents, colleagues in the schools, and colleagues in the community (Dollarhide, 2003a). Collaboration between all partners in the education process is crucial "to the success of our students, our programs, and our schools" (Dollarhide, 2003a, p. 93).

To ensure the success of a DAP comprehensive school counseling program, school counselors must have a systematic way of conceptualizing their work in order to design programmatic interventions, prioritize conflicting demands on time, and evaluate both their effectiveness and that of their program (ASCA, 2003; Baker, 2000; Gysbers & Henderson, 2000; Schmidt, 1999). With these assumptions in mind, we designed a model that serves a variety of purposes. It increases the emphasis on student achievement and development while concurrently reducing the emphasis on non-student-focused activities and provides a systematic way of thinking about the work of the school counselor that fits with the ASCA National Model. As you can see from Figure 6.1, the DAP model could serve as a framework for delivering the National Model.

The DAP model outlines the *domains* of student competencies that focus the work of the counselor and the program, the *activities* in which school counselors engage to facilitate the students' success in those competencies, and the *partnerships* that are crucial to the success of our students, our programs, and our schools. As you can see from Figure 6.1, the shading indicates the primary activity with that partner. While the domains define our work with students, each activity is nonetheless applicable to each partner in the model. Figure 6.2 gives a description of each square in the model to help you conceptualize how each activity with each partner in the model would appear in practice.

DOMAINS/ACTIVITIES/PARTNERS MODEL

FIGURE 6.1 Domains/Activities/Partners Model (shading indicates primary activities with that partner)

Block	Description	Example
1a	Individual or group counseling with students about academic issues	Providing a group counseling experience in test anxiety
1b	Individual or group counseling with students about career issues	Providing individual counseling in career exploration
1c	Individual or group counseling with students about personal/social issues	Providing a group counseling experience for students who struggle with substance abuse
2a	Educating students in academic success issues	Providing a developmental curriculum lesson in study skills
2b	Educating students in career issues	Providing a developmental curriculum lesson in resume writing
2c	Educating students in personal/social issues	Providing a developmental curriculum lesson in healthy choices
3a	Consulting and collaborating with students about academic issues	Providing consultation to students who are working to establish a new award for academic excellence and collaborating with administration for the award
3b	Consulting and collaborating with students about career issues	Providing consultation to students who want to make application to specific colleges and collaborating with college counselors to provide information
3c	Consulting and collaborating with students about personal/social issues	Providing consultation to students about school policy on bullying and collaborating with teachers to promote a bully-free playground
4a	Leadership with students and advocacy on academic issues; coordinating academic events with/for students	Advocacy with students to encourage all students to consider college and coordinating students in building a college file on the counseling website
4b	Leadership and advocacy with students on career issues, and coordinating career events with/for students	Leadership of students who want to petition the school board for more funds for technical education courses and coordinating a career fair for students
4c	Leadership with students and advocacy on personal/social issues; coordinating personal/social events with/for students	Leadership of students who are organizing a fund-raising event for suicide awareness; coordinating the work of students to build a resource library on bullying
5	Counseling parents and caregivers	Short-term counseling with a grieving parent who has lost a child
6	Counseling with colleagues in the school	Short-term counseling with a colleague who has lost her teaching job
7	Counseling with colleagues in the community	Short-term counseling with a community colleague who is frustrated over budget cuts
8	Educating parents and caregivers	Providing a parent workshop on positive discipline
9	Educating colleagues in the school	Providing a workshop for school colleagues on psychopharmacology

FIGURE 6.2   Domains/Activities/Partners Model, Detail

Block	Description	Example
10	Educating colleagues in the community	Providing a workshop for community counselors who work with your students on the school staffing process
11	Consulting and collaborating with parents and caregivers	Consulting with parents about student's academic progress
12	Consulting and collaborating with colleagues in the school	Consulting with teachers about classroom discipline issues with ADHD students
13	Consulting and collaborating with colleagues in the community	Consulting with college admissions counselors on current graduation requirements
14	Leadership and advocacy with parents and caregivers; Coordinating events for parents and caregivers	Leadership of a group of parents who are organizing a parent-teacher organization (PTO), or organizing a health fair for families of low-income kindergartners
15	Leadership, advocacy and coordinating events with colleagues in the school	Leadership and advocacy for kids with teachers on issues of inclusion and bridging the achievement gap; coordinating a tour of a new college for the teachers in your school
16	Leadership and advocacy with colleagues in the community; collaborating with or coordinating events for colleagues in the community	Advocacy for your students with college admissions counselors in the area or coordinating a campus visit for students who are interested in a certain college or university

FIGURE 6.2   (Continued)

THE DOMAINS: ACADEMIC, CAREER, AND PERSONAL/SOCIAL DEVELOPMENT   The three domains of the DAP model align with the ASCA National Standards domains—academic, career, and personal/social development (ASCA, 2003). These three domains and associated student competencies, combined with those competencies outlined by the school/district, define a school counselor's work. Consistent with the ASCA National Standards for Student Academic, Career, and Personal/Social Development (ASCA, 2003; Campbell & Dahir, 1997), the domains of the model consist of the student competencies promulgated in that document. Counselors designing programs for their school and district would insert those competencies (see Figure 1.1) and those prioritized within their district to define the primary focus of their comprehensive school counseling program. Even though the National Standards for Student Academic, Career, and Personal/Social Development address only the Domains within the Student Partner column, they are the most important priority of the comprehensive school counseling program.

THE ACTIVITIES: COUNSELING; EDUCATING; CONSULTING AND COLLABORATING; LEADING, ADVOCACY, AND COORDINATING   The four activities most appropriate for school counselors, as advocated by ASCA, are counseling; educating; consulting and collaboration; and leadership, advocacy, and coordination (ASCA, 2003; Dollarhide, 2003a). Figure 6.1 describes each unit of the model and ways in which the model might appear in practice (Dollarhide, 2003a). The DAP model, more so than other delivery models, aligns completely with the ASCA National Standards and the National Model. Over the last 20 years, appropriate school counselor activities have been described as counseling, developmental curriculum programming, consulting, referral, coordinating, providing information (advising), enhancing transitions, assessment/appraisal, and system support of public relations, committee service, and community outreach (ASCA,

1999; Baker, 2000; Gysbers & Henderson, 2000; Schmidt, 1999). We have synthesized these insights into four major activities: counseling; educating; consulting and collaborating; and leadership, advocacy, and coordinating. We believe that these terms incorporate the activities of the other models, in that

1. *Counseling* refers to individual and group counseling, peer facilitators, the use of assessment in the counseling process, as well as making referrals as a means of bringing closure to counseling relationships. We list counseling first as the foundation of the comprehensive school counseling philosophy and as the most essential activity that students indicate they want from the school counselor (Hutchinson & Bottorff, 1986; Wiggins & Moody, 1987). Chapter 8 discusses this activity.

2. *Educating* refers to the delivery of the developmental curriculum, facilitating academic transitions, advisement, placement, and assessment and appraisal. In addition, this term, more than the term "guidance," accurately describes what counselors do in the schools, and clearly describes how comprehensive school counseling attunes with the mission of the school. This activity is described in detail in Chapter 9.

3. *Consulting* refers to problem solving, referring, enhancing communications, and mediation. We feel this activity is a hybrid between counseling and educating, requiring specialized and unique skills. In addition, *collaboration* is addressed as a partner activity to enable consulting to take place, and often these activities merge and flow in everyday application. Furthermore, making consultation and collaboration distinct parts of the Delivery System provide for both the Themes of the ASCA National Model (Collaboration and Systemic Change) and the Management System and Accountability to be explicit in the activities of the school counselor. Chapter 10 discusses these partner activities.

4. *Leadership, Advocacy, and Coordination* involve several areas: developing and maintaining the vision of the comprehensive school counseling program, promoting the importance of a developmentally appropriate learning environment, and then taking steps to ensure that the vision is brought to life. In addition, *Leadership* is one of the Themes of the ASCA National Model (ASCA, 2003). *Advocating* refers to activities that educate with passion, those activities that enhance others' affective understanding of and empathy for students, schools, families, the comprehensive school counseling program, and better human relationships. It includes, as ASCA (1999, 2003) points out, championing what is best for students, their families, schools, and the community, and is also one of the Themes of the ASCA National Model. *Coordination* refers to the logistics associated with bridging programs and partners. All of these activities provide information to the school and the district about the program, general outreach and public relations, school/professional/community committee service, and programs that reach a large audience of students.

THE PARTNERS It is vital that you understand why we use the concept of "partnership" when discussing the people involved in the comprehensive school counseling program. First, it is important to reinforce the collegial, collaborative, and egalitarian nature of the relationships counselors must develop with everyone in the school setting. Second, it serves to reinforce the active nature of the participation in school counseling programs as counseling, educating, consulting/collaboration, and leading/advocacy/coordinating are all active, intentional behaviors, both for the counselor and for others in the process. Third, it is important for counselors to remember that it takes a whole community to raise a child. Similarly, it takes an entire community to educate healthy and resilient young people; no one person can do it alone. Therefore, no one school counselor, no matter how talented and dedicated that person may be, can be the only helping professional for our students. We must reach out and establish these broad, inclusive partnerships for the students' benefit. The work of the school counselor could not happen without our partners in the process. In addition, the National Model includes Systemic Change as one of the themes, and the Management System and Accountability both incorporate the work counselors do with colleagues in the schools. By considering all these individuals our partners, we explicitly include these individuals as part of our work.

Similarly, school counselors have responsibilities to all of partners. Just as the profession has articulated the National Standards for Student Academic, Career, and Personal/Social Development, there is also the need to understand our program goals with our adult partners. We propose these goals in Appendix A to stimulate conversations about our work with adult partners.

Our primary partner is the student. At its most fundamental level, school counseling would not occur without students; their development is the very essence of the comprehensive school counseling program. By calling them partners in the process, we hope to convey that they, too, are stakeholders in the program; their involvement in the program, in many cases, is voluntary, and so we cannot take for granted that they will avail themselves of the services we have to offer. We must actively solicit their continued involvement.

Our second partners are parents, guardians, and caregivers. They, too, have a stake in the school counseling program (Schmidt, 1999). Involvement of the student is contingent on parental approval (depending on the age and circumstance), so we cannot forget that, by extension, parents influence whether we have students with whom to work. Their involvement is essential (Colbert, 1996).

Our third partners are our colleagues in the schools. Teachers, administrators, school social workers, school psychologists, school nurses, and the administrative staff are very involved with how our program functions and how effective we can be. By extension, this includes professionals from other schools, at the district level, and in the school counseling profession as a whole.

Finally, we have partners in the community. From the mental health professional who provides therapy, to the physician who provides medication, to the local businessperson who provides jobs, these stakeholders need to be included in the school counseling program as their work may have implications for individual students and/or the school.

THE ADVISORY BOARD Vital to the success of a comprehensive school counseling program delivered using the DAP model is the existence and functioning of an effective advisory board. A supportive, objective, active advisory board is a key component to an effective comprehensive school counseling program and requires specific attention when creating it. We strongly encourage school counselors to give priority to creating a dynamic and diverse advisory board that will guide program efforts, advocate for change, and be a voice for school counseling in the district.

As outlined in the National Model, the process of building a comprehensive program begins with building the foundation of an agreed-upon philosophy and mission statement. Concurrent with the discussion of partners, it is important to determine how to operationalize the concept of "partner" into the building of the advisory board. Ultimately, the advisory committee should consist of representatives of each group of partners; however, the members you invite to sit on the advisory board will depend on the demographics and makeup of your local community, district, and school. Carefully consider the size of the group in order to maximize the ability for members to meet as a group over several sessions.

1. *Students.* Select student representatives from all areas, including marginalized and diverse groups. Include students from across the spectrum in terms of academic ability, family income, language in the home, grade level, and school involvement. Strive to select student representatives that reflect the overall demographic makeup of your building.

2. *Parents, guardians, and caregivers.* Select parents and caregivers from all economic levels of your attendance area, including those who reside in shelters and/or who are homeless (Strawser, Markos, Yamaguchi, & Higgins, 2000), and reside in a variety of neighborhoods.

3. *Colleagues in the schools.* Select representatives from teachers, aides, administrators, and other student services professionals. Go outside your school building to invite counselors from other schools, including your feeder schools (if any) and counselors from the schools to which your students transition. In addition, invite representatives from the district level of administration, perhaps including the director of pupil services and even a representative from the school board itself.

4. *Colleagues in the community.* Invite representatives from a variety of employers, the business community, mental health providers, medical professionals, and organizations who have a stake in young people's academic success and school achievement. In addition, you may wish to invite colleagues from other social service agencies with whom you interact and refer to for services.

The advisory board has several purposes. First, the members will assist you with designing the comprehensive school counseling program. Because of the variety of partners and voices represented on the board, an array of perceptions and perspectives on school counseling will emerge and converge. The potential is invigorating and exciting, and instrumental in the development of an effective comprehensive program.

Second, the board will support and guide you as you implement the program. Implementing a comprehensive school counseling program is a monumental, long-term effort. It is not a something we throw together in a couple of meetings, then sit back and enjoy. Implementing a CSCP *is* one of the key roles and functions of a school counselor, and is probably one of the more challenging roles. Your goal is to develop a working advisory board that will be behind you 100 percent, as you maneuver through the growing pains, politics, and realities of getting the program off the ground.

Third, the advisory board will assist you in the assessment and evaluation of your program. Because of the importance of accountability and evidence-based practice, it is imperative that your advisory board consists of people who are committed to and understand developmentally appropriate schools, the development of young people, and comprehensive school counseling. The result of assessment and evaluation is data, and with data comes dissemination and decision making. Members of the board will need to be able to assist you with sorting through the data, making sense of it, and determining ways to best use the data to improve programming and student services.

REFLECTION MOMENT

Consider the Domains/Activities/Partners (DAP) model and envision using this model to organize a comprehensive school counseling program. What components of the model are appealing to you? Which components might you revise or alter?

CONTEMPORARY FRAMEWORKS AND GUIDING PRINCIPLES

Strengths-Based School Counseling

Strengths-Based School Counseling (SBSC) is a set of guiding principles that evolved out of empirical evidence supporting a shift from deficit-oriented means of working with young people to empowering and positive orientations. Developed by Galassi and Akos (2007), SBSC grew out of contemporary studies of developmental psychology, education, positive psychology, resiliency, school counseling, and social work into an evidence-based framework for delivering comprehensive school counseling. Focusing less on reduction of barriers, strengths-based school counseling programs give great attention to increasing development assets and promoting strengths and resiliency.

The principles attune to and augment the ASCA National Model with its specific focus on supporting students' development of particular strengths and abilities, which the research directly links to positive youth development. The authors of SBSC did not intend for it to serve as a model of delivery for comprehensive school counseling. Rather, Galassi and Akos (2007) created SBSC to serve as a "framework for deciding what should be emphasized" in comprehensive school counseling programs (p. 28). Likewise, SBSC complements many of the objectives within the Transforming School Counseling Initiative (TSCI).

The foundation of SBSC rests on six guiding principles, which are (1) Promote Evidence-Based Student Strengths; (2) Promote Evidence-Based, Strengths-Enhancing Education Environments; (3) Promote Context-Based Development for All Students; (4) Emphasize Promotion over Remediation and Prevention; (5) Emphasize Evidence-Based Interventions and Practice; and (6) Emphasize Promotion-Oriented Developmental Advocacy at the School-Building Level (Galassi & Akos, 2007). These guiding principles emphasize the importance of holistic development and evidence-based practices across all three domains of academic, career, and personal/social.

Outcomes and direct and systemic services are unique to SBSC programs. Developmental outcomes become the driving force of the school counseling program from which evidence-based interventions and strategies emerge. Services generally include direct services in the form of counseling and assessment, or systemic, which includes consulting and advocacy. Most notable is SBSC's attention to the school and community environment, creating effective educational and developmental environments for students. Galassi and Akos (2007) clearly illustrate the importance of creating strength-enhancing environments for promoting evidence-based student development. Furthermore, SBSC programs promote ethnic and racial identity development for all students and seek to increase academic achievement and decrease achievement gaps. SBSC programs are flexible, adaptable, and respond effectively to changes and revisions in educational efforts and society. Counselor educators will appreciate SBSC's alignment with accreditation standards and school counselor preparation. Disadvantages seem to mostly point toward the time and money necessary to implement evidence-based practices, interventions, and strategies.

REFLECTION MOMENT

Reflect on a Results-Based Student Support Program model. Envision using this model to augment a comprehensive school counseling program. Process your thoughts around deficit models of working with students versus a strengths-based model.

A Social Justice Approach to Comprehensive School Counseling

The Social Justice Approach to school counseling is a response to the specific needs within today's schools that potentially go unnoticed unless consciously and clearly delineated within the framework of a comprehensives school counseling program. Whereas the ASCA National Model catapulted national school counseling efforts and provided a solid framework from which to develop comprehensive school counseling programs, inequity, oppression, and sociocultural barriers continue to create achievement gaps for students in diverse groups. Within a social just approach, six key elements or functions (the six C's) of school counseling target closing achievement gaps and confronting inequities in schools. They are: (1) counseling and intervention planning; (2) consultation; (3) connecting schools, families, and communities; (4) collecting and utilizing data; (5) challenging bias; and (6) coordinating student services and support (Holcomb-McCoy, 2007).

Counseling and intervention planning from a social justice framework (Holcomb-McCoy, 2007) takes into account the student's family, culture, and environment. By using a "person-in-environment" approach, counseling and intervention planning acknowledges students' "background experiences, their interactions with others in their families and immediate community, the resources in their environment, and most important their adaptive and maladaptive interactions with other people in their environment" (pp. 23–24). Counseling from a sociocultural and ecological perspective insists that school counselors be culturally competent and experienced in cross-cultural practices.

Consultants from a social justice perspective assume the role of advocate for students who are underachieving, at risk, or are members of diverse groups (Holcomb-McCoy, 2007). In the role of consultant, school counselors can advocate for students and families who do not receive equitable services, treatment, accommodations, and education. Many times students who feel oppressed and disregarded by the educational system feel afraid to use their voices or they have no voice within privileged systems and institutions. School counselors who ground themselves in a social justice approach use their voices and are the voices for those students who are passed over and get lost in the educational system.

School counseling programs that model a social justice approach create strong partnerships between the school, family, and community. Knowing that school counselors have limited time and resources, connections with families and the community are vital to the success and achievement of students, especially culturally diverse and at-risk students. The partnerships between social justice schools, families, and the community promote educational opportunities for families with limited access that address oppression, cultural diversity, and social justice (Holcomb-McCoy, 2007). School counselors who connect beyond the school walls and who build authentic relationships with families and communities chip away at the mortar in the wall that divides schools from the very communities they are attempting to serve.

Collecting and using data is critical in all models of comprehensive school counseling; however, a social justice school counseling program relies on data to reveal achievement gaps and student groups that are not achieving or receiving equitable services and educational opportunities. Holcomb-McCoy's (2007) emphasis on collecting and using data brings up the importance of consistently desegregating data as part of the analysis process. For example, a school counselor gathers data indicating that 13 percent of high school juniors drop out prior to graduation. It is imperative that the school counselor take the next step and disaggregate the data to determine the makeup of the 13 percent. Is the 13 percent mostly at-risk students, males, diverse groups, or low-income groups? Disaggregating the data is the only means of identifying where to target best practice interventions and strategies toward precisely the students or group of students we are hoping to impact.

Bias and prejudice exist throughout our schools and communities. Challenging bias is an integral and integrated disposition and characteristic of social justice school counselors. Though not comfortable and often wrought with fear, we must remain dedicated to confronting biases and prejudices – both ours and others (Holcomb-McCoy, 2007). Our voices are essential in opposing bias, prejudice, oppression, marginalization, and inequity in our schools and communities to help students attain their educational aspirations.

All too often, low-income, at-risk, and culturally diverse students do not gain access to the more rigorous or advanced curriculum. Social justice school counselors are instrumental in building a support services structure to ensure that students receive academic services and support. Coordinating student support services involves developing partnerships with local universities, civic groups, and community businesses to enhance students' success and provide support for low-income, at-risk, and culturally and ethnically diverse students (Holcomb-McCoy, 2007).

REFLECTION MOMENT

Reflect on a Social Justice Approach to school counseling. Envision using this model to deliver your school counseling program. What additional personal and professional development might you need in order to implement an effective social just school counseling program?

Integration

Now that you have read the chapter, answer the following questions:

1. What are the school counselor's greatest challenges?
2. What three questions could you pose to the school counselors to encourage their thinking about the delivery model(s) most appropriate for the district's school counseling program?
3. Which model or combination of delivery approaches would you choose for delivering comprehensive school counseling? Provide your rationale. ▬

Suggested Readings

School counselors are encouraged to be knowledgeable about current delivery models for implementing comprehensive school counseling programs. The following recommended readings will provide important resources for deciding which delivery model(s) are most appropriate for attaining the goals of your building's school counseling programs.

American School Counselor Association. (2003). *The ASCA National Model: A framework for school counseling programs.* Alexandria, VA: Author.

Baker, S. B. (2000). *School counseling for the twenty-first century* (3rd ed.). Upper Saddle River, NJ: Merrill.

Brown, D., & Trusty, J. (2005). *Designing and leading comprehensive school counseling programs: Promoting student competence and meeting student needs.* Belmont, CA: Brooks/Cole.

Galassi, J. P, & Akos, P. (2007). *Strengths-based school counseling: Promoting student development and achievement.* Mahwah, NJ: Lawrence Erlbaum Associates.

Gysbers, N. C., & Henderson, P. (2000). *Developing and managing your school guidance program* (3rd ed.). Alexandria, VA: American Counseling Association.

Holcomb-McCoy, C. (2007). *School counseling to close the achievement gap: A social justice framework for success.* Thousand Oaks, CA: Corwin Press.

Johnson, S., Johnson, C., & Downs, L. (2006). *Building a results-based student support program.* Boston: Lahaska Press.

Myrick, R. D. (1993). *Developmental guidance and counseling: A practical approach* (2nd ed). Minneapolis, MN: Educational Media Corp.

Paisley, P. O., & Hubbard, G. T. (1994). *Developmental school counseling programs: From theory to practice.* Alexandria, VA: American Counseling Association.

Schmidt, J. J. (2003). *Counseling in the schools: Essential services and comprehensive programs* (4th ed.). Boston: Allyn and Bacon.

Sink, C. (2005). *Contemporary school counseling: Theory, research, and practice.* Boston: Lahaska Press.

CHAPTER

7

Accountability, Action Research, and Data-Driven Outcomes

LEARNING OBJECTIVES

By the end of this chapter, you will

1. Understand the urgency of integrating effective accountability practices across school counseling programs and counseling interventions

2. Value the importance of using data to address achievement gaps

3. Have grasped the importance of using data to evaluate program effectiveness and to determine program needs

4. Understand the use of formal and informal methods of evaluation including quantitative and qualitative data to evaluate their school counseling program and to demonstrate program results

5. Recognize ways to use student data to support program and intervention decision making

6. Embrace the importance of collaborating with stakeholders and partners regarding evaluation and the dissemination of results

7. Appreciate the importance of sharing school counseling program results to professional school counseling community

8. Be able to differentiate between process, perception, and results data and the importance of using all three types of data in accountability practices

9. Identify the use of technology in conducting research and program evaluation

10. Recognize the importance of using data to demonstrate the ways in which the school counseling program affects student achievement

11. Understand and be able to advocate for appropriate school counselor performance appraisal process based on school counselors' competencies and completion of the guidance curriculum and agreed-upon action plans

12. Comprehend the necessity of using self-appraisal related to school counseling skills and performance and working with administrators to use performance appraisal instruments that reflect appropriate responsibilities for school counselors

13. Have gained an understanding of the importance of conducting a program audit in the planning and evaluation of school counseling programs

"Mt. Data's Dilemma!"

The Mt. Data school district's counselors are in a quandary. At a recent districtwide school counselor meeting, the administration informed everyone that the district's assessment and evaluation practices had to be revised and updated to reflect the growing national school reform movement. The administration shared that because of national and state budget cuts, state departments of education were now going to hold school districts accountable for the education and services they provide to students. No longer could school counselors submit annual reports that included only process, anecdotal, and qualitative data. School counselors were now going to have to demonstrate using hard data that their school counseling program and the interventions they were implementing were having a positive impact on students' academic achievement and school success. Likewise, school counselors were now going to have to rely on evidence-based and outcome-driven practices, which meant that the services and programs they were providing had to be based on student needs and proven effective. In addition, the data gathered and analyzed would have to inform their school counseling program and the interventions they were offering.

The school counselors responded with heavy sighs, confused glances around the room, and whispers about how they could possibly accomplish what sounded like a very daunting task. One counselor raised his hand and said, "We already have maxed-out schedules and calendars. How can we now be expected to gather and track data?" Another school counselor expressed, "We all know that we do good work. Some of what we do simply cannot be measured." Additional counselors shared, "The students enjoy our programs, lessons, and groups. You mean we'll now have to start using what the research says is effective?" A final group of frustrated counselors cried, "We never trained in how to gather and use data. We have no idea where to begin!"

The administration echoed the counselors' concerns and went on to say that the state department of education expected all educators and professionals in the school, including them, to demonstrate ways in which their efforts link directly to academic achievement and school success. As one administrator commented, "Young people attend school for one reason, which is to learn. If we are unable to demonstrate that our teaching, programming, and interventions enhance learning, then the state assumes we are not needed." The director of school counseling expanded, "It is no longer enough for a school counselor to report that he or she met with 500 students, ran 10 small groups, facilitated 200 conferences, or taught 300 classroom guidance lessons in a year." The director took a deep breath and concluded, "Just because we think it works or because we've always done it this way will no longer be good enough reasons to continue any educational or counseling intervention. We *must* have to have the data to prove it."

The room grew very quiet and the school counselors simply stared. Their thoughts were spinning with such questions as, "Where do we begin?" "How will we ever be able to demonstrate that what we do enhances students' learning?" "What data do we gather?" "What do we do with the data once we have it?"

CHALLENGE QUESTIONS

If you were a school counselor in the Mt. Data School District, where might you begin in the process of becoming a more accountable school counselor and district? What initial steps might you take? What process might you use to demonstrate that you and your school counseling program positively affect students' learning and academic achievement? ◼

For years, school counselors have attended to the development of young people and provided valuable and essential counseling services to students throughout their school experience. For the most part, school counselors generally kept track of the services they offered by collecting the number of students served and the array of services provided in an academic year, such as orientations, IEP (Individualized Education Plan) meetings, classroom guidance lessons presented, and small groups offered. The school counselors' calendars also publicized ways in which school counselors used their time. Overall, the public seemed satisfied with the ways in which schools were operating, that students were achieving, and the role of school counselors in the lives of students. However, after the release of *A Nation at Risk* (D. Gardner, 1983), which revealed to the nation the catastrophic state of public education, educational reform efforts took shape and the face of schools and education, including school counseling, changed. Consequently, school districts across the nation were being held accountable for the academic achievement of the students they served (Loesch & Ritchie, 2005), and this new accountability included the work of school counselors.

School counseling accountability, or providing evidence that what school counselors do makes a measurable difference in students' academic achievement and success in school (Cobia & Henderson, 2007), is an essential component of school counseling programs and has been since the 1920s (Gysbers, 2004). The ASCA National Model and the Transforming School Counseling Initiative (TSCI) were instrumental in jump-starting conversations aimed at accountability practices that target measurable results and outcomes. Indeed, the ASCA National Model details the importance of accountability by demonstrating and documenting ways in which students change as a result of the school counseling program (C. B. Stone & Dahir, 2006). However, the data that school counselors have been gathering and reporting over time has not generally demonstrated effectively that what they do affects students' learning and attainment. The data that school counselors have been collecting has amounted to numbers of contacts and services, which does not reveal effectiveness and accounts only for the school counselor's time. Likewise, school counselors have not received adequate training in methods of demonstrating accountability (Kaffenberger & Davis, 2009) and evaluating their school counseling programs. Given the lack of preparation in accountability strategies, school counselors have not felt competent or confident integrating accountability into their school counseling programs, and in many instances have avoided it. Kaffenberger and Davis (2009) noted that unless school counselors know *why* collecting data and using it is important, and *how* to gather and make sense of the data, school counselors and the schools they serve will continue to flounder with how to influence students' educational success most effectively. Dimmitt (2009) emphasized that "because we think it works or because it's always been done this way are no longer legitimate reasons to continue any educational or mental health intervention" (p. 395). Furthermore, Dimmitt stresses that school counselors are under an ethical obligation to guarantee that their programs and interventions assist all students in succeeding in school. Sink (2009) echoed that school counselors *must* lead accountability efforts and demonstrate accountability leadership in order to inform and sustain their school counseling programs.

Articulating the value of accountability and integrating it clearly and consistently into school counseling programs and interventions is essential to closing achievement gaps, implementing school reform efforts, and creating systemic change. Professional school counselors, more than ever, are charged with developing, managing, and utilizing accountability strategies that monitor student achievement and appraise the school counseling program. School counselors must demonstrate that their role and function in the school affect academic achievement and school success directly and positively. Our hope is that after reading this chapter and completing some of the activities and exercises, you will embrace using data to drive your school counseling program and interventions. This chapter is written to foster the value of accountability in school counseling and present ways to use evaluation, evidence-based practice, and action research that will increase your confidence, competence, and *accountability* as a professional school counselor.

REFLECTION MOMENT

Process your thoughts and feelings toward integrating accountability into your school counseling program. What thoughts and feelings arose? What will you need in order to feel competent and confident integrating accountability into your school counseling program?

USING DATA TO DEMONSTRATE ACCOUNTABILITY

Data is raw (Ackoff, 1989); it generally results from measurement and provides evidence in the form of process data, perception data, and results data. *Process data* documents "who, what, where, when, and how long" (Dimmitt, Carey, & Hatch, 2007, p. 41) students receive services or interventions. For example, 135 students received special education services during the

2009–2010 academic year at XYZ Middle School. *Perception data* provides evidence of what students learned, which usually connects to standards and competencies. For instance, students who participated in a large-group guidance lesson on school success and postsecondary planning learned to create academic goals, identify and explore postsecondary options, and recognize the ways in which school success and academic achievement relate to postsecondary and career aspirations (C. B. Stone & Dahir, 2006). Lastly, *results data*, which will be most of our focus in this chapter, is the missing piece in current accountability efforts. Results data demonstrate whether the program services and implemented program services and interventions are having a positive effect on their "ability to use attitudes, skills, and knowledge to change their behavior" (Dimmitt et al., 2007, p. 44) measured by "achievement or achievement-related data" (p. 44). The ASCA National Model encourages school counselors to integrate the use of all three forms of data into their accountability plans and practices.

School districts maintain a vast array of data that school counselors can access before launching into their own data-gathering practices. District offices generally house data management departments as do state departments of education. Generally, data tracked most often comprise (1) *achievement data*, (2) *attainment or access data*, and (3) *school culture and climate data* (Holcomb-McCoy, 2007). Achievement data generally target learning outcomes, such as grades and performance and standardized test scores. Attainment or access data take in students' movement through the educational system, such as enrollment, retention, promotion, postsecondary and transitional patterns, and special programming for special education, gifted, and talented students. School culture and climate data consist of data that reveal information about thoughts, feelings, behaviors, and attitudes such as attendance rates, suspensions and expulsions, staff relations, campus morale, embracing diversity, and campus safety. Data can be quantitative or qualitative in nature. *Quantitative* data describe frequency, percentages, and ratios presented in number form. *Qualitative* data illustrate meaning and experience, and can be portrayed using narratives, interviews, observations, objects, or other visual forms. Quantitative data might be the easiest to work with when using such statistical programs such as Excel, SPSS, or EZAnalyze; however, qualitative data can add depth and richness to quantitative data by revealing individual experiences in relation to the quantitative data gathered. However and important to note, *data by itself is generally useless unless compared with or viewed in relation to other data*. Thus, we need to analyze data, examine, and interpret the data in ways that generate meaning and inform us.

Here is an example: Mt. Data's senior class of 2010 graduated 472 students or 92 percent of the senior class. This data, a number or a percentage, has little meaning except to provide us with a measurement. However, when we analyze and interpret the data, it transforms into useful information, which takes on meaning, arouses conversations, and informs decision making. For example, if we compare the number of Mt. Data's seniors that graduated in 2010 (472, or 92 percent) to the number that graduated in 2009 (492, or 94 percent), we establish a relational connection that gives meaning to the data (Ackoff, 1989). Thus, conversations might emerge around the two sets of data that perhaps will lead to additional conversations, decisions, and/or more data analysis.

Wait! Don't stop there! Probably the most important step in analyzing data involves disaggregating data. Go back to our example. The graduation rate of the graduating class of 2010 is *aggregate data*, which describes the entire data set. *Disaggregate data* is broken down by specific demographics of interest, which presents patterns, themes, and trends within the aggregate data. For example, say that the graduation rate of the class of 2010 is 88 percent. To gain a clearer picture of the makeup of the 88 percent, we disaggregate the data by gender, ethnicity, free and reduced lunch, and special education. Knowing ways in which the data breaks down into these particular subgroups gives meaning to the data. Without disaggregating the data we will not have a clear picture of the demographics of percentage that graduated. Likewise, and probably even more important, we want to disaggregate the 12 percent that did not graduate in order to gain an even clearer picture of the demographics of the number of students graduating compared to the number of students not graduating. Vitally important to remember is that disaggregated data can reveal achievement gaps and inequities in schools (Holcomb-McCoy, 2007). Observing the ways in which aggregate data breaks down can stimulate important conversations about the implications of the data and ways we might want to proceed or intervene. Conversations and questions that disaggregated data can prompt include:

1. There appears to be an achievement gap in reading, math, or science among different groups of students. Is the gap growing larger, smaller, or staying the same?
2. In math, our Hmong male students seem to be achieving at a lower rate than White male students are. Why are the Hmong students struggling, and how will we increase their performance?
3. There are more students who live in poverty and minority students in special education classes than there are in advanced placement classes. What are the reasons behind the difference and what will we do about it?

Be aware that having conversations about data is not for the faint of heart. Often discussion regarding data can provoke a range of feelings that might uncover biases, racial attitudes, and even denial about what the data are suggesting (Holcomb-McCoy, 2007). We urge school counselors to rely on their active listening and process skills when facilitating discussions concerning data and the significance of the data.

Lastly, disaggregated data can also inform school counselors about professional development needs for teachers, and if there is a relationship between parental involvement and student success in school. We can also look at the data across classrooms, subjects, grade levels, schools, districts, or states. A wealth of information about student achievement and barriers to student achievement can be uncovered through the process of disaggregating data. Once you have the disaggregated data, the next step is to look for larger trends and patterns in the data that informs your school counseling program and the interventions within the program.

REFLECTION MOMENT

Consider additional ways that you might choose to use disaggregated data in your school counseling program. Traditional ways include gender, racial/ethnic descriptors, economic indicators (those on free and reduced lunch programs) and special education designation. Now think about your high school experience; are there de-facto trends you recall about which students were successful and which ones were not? How would you use data to document those trends, and what interventions might you implement in response?

Disseminating Data

After analyzing the data, the next step is to organize the data in ways that you can easily share with stakeholders or partners. A variety of graphs, charts, and pictographs are available for user-friendly data reporting. Some data, such as qualitative data, might be easier to share through video, narratives, or in their original form such as calendars, schedules, or syllabi (Holcomb-McCoy, 2007). Most important is to ensure that the ways in which you report the data will accurately and clearly convey the results or outcomes you most want your stakeholder or partners to grasp from the data. Figure 7.1 reports the change in the number of in-school suspensions after the implementation of a behavioral intervention program. After collecting data for four consecutive quarters, the data was analyzed and reported using a bar graph. The bar graph clearly and concisely demonstrates a change in the aggregate data from the first quarter to the fourth quarter. Figure 7.2 reports the same data; however, the data was desegregated by ethnicity in order to uncover additional information about the data set that the aggregate data does not reveal. The school counselor could also disaggregate the same data according to gender, grade, special

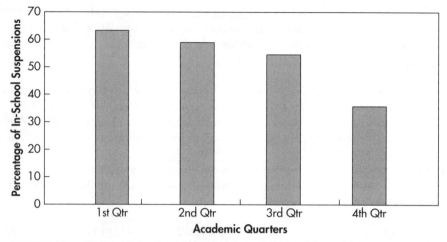

FIGURE 7.1 Effects of Behavioral Intervention on In-School Suspension

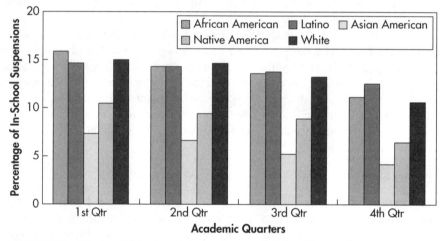

FIGURE 7.2 Effects of Behavioral Intervention on In-School Suspension

education programming, and free and reduced lunch to gain additional information for stakeholders or partners to consider.

The ASCA National Model outlines a structure for organizing and planning accountability practices. To be accountable for the program, school counselors must present the findings of the results reports, program audit, and other assessment and evaluation processes to the building administrator (or the professional responsible for evaluating the counselor). (We encourage you to obtain a copy of the National Model from ASCA to view the Program Audit documents.) Various information will be appropriate to share with a range of partners. All the information is presented to the administrator, including the results of the assessment process (the report card of the program and the counselor) and the results of the evaluation process (plans for professional development and program improvement determined on the basis of the assessment results that will feed back into the planning process).

Information shared with partners and stakeholders usually consists of how well the program is functioning and plans for improvement. One idea for disseminating the information could be a newsletter sent to students, parents, teachers, colleagues in the schools, and colleagues in the community. Other ideas include columns in the school and community newspapers, a webpage, articles in counselor journals, and reports for the local school board (Schmidt, 2003).

A note of caution: it might be advisable to consult with the advisory committee, your administrator, and other counselors in the district to determine how much information to disseminate. In the early years of the program, while you are still building rapport and creating respect for your program and your professionalism, you might want to be selective in how much you share. Too much "negative press," or public discussion of your struggles to launch your program, might damage your attempts to establish your credibility with your partners. Be judicious with the negative information you send out so that you do not end up compromising your program. Additional ways to disseminate results data is through presentations at local school board meetings, PTO/PTA meetings, staff and faculty meetings, and professional conferences, workshops, and seminars.

In addition to the information to be disseminated to stakeholders and partners, your advisory council is also a means of accountability (See Chapter 6 for a discussion of the advisory council). First, it is important to recognize that your council is a political body, representing your partners—students, parents, teachers, staff, administration, and community. Your leadership of this council will be crucial in your planning, design, evaluation, and growth of your school counseling program. Topics to present to the advisory council include closing-the-achievement-gap efforts and results, programwide results reports, and the result of the program audit. The point is to inform stakeholders and partners as to ways in which the school counseling program is supporting student achievement and success in school. Having your program visible and recognized across groups and disciplines informs, promotes, and substantiates you as an accountable school counselor and a professional leader in the field.

REFLECTION MOMENT

Using data might bring up competence and confidence issues for school counselors in training. What fears do you have about using data in accountability practices? What additional awareness, knowledge, and skills do you need in order to address your fears and embrace working with data in your school counseling practice?

Evaluation

Evaluation has a goal of revealing information about a specific population in a specific context, which for our purposes, is schools. Essentially, evaluation asks, "Did this program or intervention make a difference for these students, in this setting?" (Dimmitt, 2009, p. 395). For example, the Second Step Violence Prevention Program developed by the Committee for Children is a nationally recognized and researched violence prevention curriculum. Research on Second Step has demonstrated that the program may reduce aggressive behavior and increase prosocial behavior in school (Carey, Carey, Hatch, Lapan, & Whiston, 2008; Frey & Sylvester, 1997; Holsen, Iverson, & Smith, 2009; Holsen, Smith, & Frey, 2008). However, will Second Step have an effect with a specific group of students in a particular school? We cannot say with confidence unless we undergo evaluation. As an example, ABC Elementary School implements Second Step across grade levels to increase student's sense of safety while in school and reduce school disorder and violent behavior. It is the process of evaluation that will determine if the program was effective and inform the school and stakeholders or partners of the results of implementing the program.

For sake of creating a teachable moment, let us say that the data reveals that Second Step was effective at increasing students' sense of safety and reducing school disorder and violent behavior. What does that have to do with academic achievement? Research has suggested (Chen & Weikhart, 2008) that positive school climate and peer relations increases students' ability to learn through various means. If students feel safer in school, they will attend school, which has a direct effect on attendance. Students who feel safer in school will give more attention to learning and less attention to worrying about the consequences of being at school such as being hurt or bullied.

Attendance (Roby, 2004) and school climate (Brand, Felner, Seitsinger, Burns, & Bolton, 2008) are two factors linked to academic achievement and school success. Thus, school counselors who closely monitor, through evaluation, the effects that programs and interventions are having on factors that directly associate with learning and attainment are providing invaluable information for sustaining their role within schools.

Essentially, five types of evaluations aid school counselors with accountability efforts. The five types are: (1) *needs assessments*, (2) *outcome research*, (3) *formative evaluation*, (4) *implementation evaluations*, and (5) *outcomes evaluations* (Dimmitt, 2009). Needs assessments are important in the early planning processes of a school counseling program. School counselors use data from needs assessment to inform their selection of interventions, such as small groups, presentations/workshops, classroom guidance lessons, schoolwide initiatives and programs, and professional development initiatives. The most common means of initiating a needs assessment is through observations and conversations with teachers, parents, administration, and students. The information from these observations and conversations can be used to generate the questions used in an actual "systematic" needs assessment (D. Brown & Trusty, 2005, p. 128). Generally, needs assessments are conducted through a survey format that can simply be distributed across partners and stakeholders, and scored with ease. In the age of technology, it is common for school counselors to send needs assessment surveys out via the Internet using such programs as Survey Monkey, Zoomerang, or Survey Gizmo. Large-scale needs assessments can generate a wealth of data; however, with any data collection process, school counselors must disaggregate the data by groups in order to identify the specific needs of these groups. It is important to note that not all demographic variables will be noted on a survey instrument, causing a group with specific needs to be overlooked. For example, sexual orientation is generally not a demographic noted on a survey instrument. For this reason, it is imperative that school counselors create informal ways, such as focus groups and individual interviews, to assess the needs of hidden demographic groups like LGBTQ (lesbian, gay, bisexual, transgendered, questioning) students (D. Brown & Trusty, 2005).

Once you identify the specific needs of your school and students, published outcome research can be useful in locating interventions. For example, perhaps through a large-scale systemic needs assessment you discover a high need to address peer relationships, school climate issues, and attitudes concerning violence, harassment, and bullying behaviors. The school counseling advisory council and you through investigation decide to consider the Second Step Violence Prevention Curriculum (Committee for Children, 2002). Through the process of exploring published *outcome research*, the council and you can determine, in a general sense, if the Second Step program is effective with students. Dimmitt (2009) suggested that selecting interventions that have already been proven effective makes it "easier to know what student outcomes to measure, information about the intended results, and what behaviors, knowledge, or skills have typically been impacted" (p. 397). Whether Second Step will work effectively in your building and with your students depends on a number of factors that can be determined only through additional evaluations. However, using outcome research to support your choice in interventions definitely increases the likelihood of the intervention being successful and meeting students' needs.

Formative evaluation occurs during the implementation process to assess whether the program component or intervention is having the effect(s) you intended (Dimmitt, 2009). Consistent and ongoing monitoring is essential to making adjustments, revisions, or alterations to ensure a sound and quality implementation. Dimmitt et al. (2007) recommended monitoring two facets of the formative evaluation throughout the implementation process. The two facets are: (1) making sure students are receiving enough exposure to the intervention and (2) monitoring the way in which the intervention is being implemented and how the intervention was designed to be implemented. Using Second Step as our example, conducting formative evaluation strengthens the implementation process and increases the likelihood of the intervention meeting the desired outcomes. First, we want to ensure that students were receiving ample exposure to the violence prevention curriculum. If not, the data will reveal where we are lacking coverage so that we could make the necessary adjustments to the curriculum delivery process. Second, we want to evaluate whether we are implementing the violence prevention program as the Committee for Children intended and as noted in the published outcome research.

"When people think of evaluation, outcome evaluation is typically what they have in mind" (Dimmitt, 2009, p. 398). Outcome or results evaluation measures "the extent to which the desired changes are occurring, what is and is not working, how student outcomes are being improved, and so on" (p. 398). Developmental classroom activities and school counseling services that address specific student outcomes or results must be evaluated in order to determine if the activity or services is meeting the specified benchmarks, competencies, or standards. Gysbers (2008) recommended that a results-based evaluation plan be an integral and ongoing part of school counseling programs. Without an evaluation plan in place, school counselors have no way of providing hard evidence that what they are implementing is meeting students' needs. In this regard, it will be essential to conduct outcome evaluations over time to determine if the Second Step Violence Prevention program was effective at changing the school climate, violence, and bullying behaviors. Effectiveness is determined by gathering data or evidence. In this case, evidence of the effectiveness of the program might be gathered through incident reports, discipline referrals, and school climate surveys. As we learned previously, it will be important to disaggregate the data to determine the effectiveness of the program across groups and demographics.

REFLECTION MOMENT

Consider the five types of evaluations. Envision ways in which you could utilize the five types of evaluation to inform and strengthen a school counseling program.

DATA-DRIVEN EVALUATION

Data supports, or drives, the ongoing improvement and sustainability of school counseling program. Data-driven school counseling programs are *programs driven or informed by the data they generate*. Results from data provoke conversations and inform decision making for moving the school counseling program forward in the name of student achievement and educational attainment. Isaacs (2003) conveyed the following passionately:

> Measurement in education is meant to communicate information about problems or their solutions, about making consistent decisions about student performance and learning, about what discrepant performance or problems might be, about which problems to solve when faced with many, about how to solve them, and about how to allocate fiscal and human resources. These decisions affect the professional life of all educators and the lives of the children and families counselors serve. Thus, if these critical decisions are being made based on data, it is in every school counselor's interest to have an arsenal of skills in collecting, manipulating, analyzing, presenting, and evaluating data. Counselors must become data-driven decision-makers and thus transform school counseling programs into responsive interventions based on information. (p. 288)

For example, the ASCA National Model anticipates that students will achieve competencies in three developmental domains (academic, career, and personal/social). Students' progress over time in achieving the competencies is the "results" that create the "data" in a data-driven school counseling program.

There are several models available that provide structures and frameworks for evaluating school counseling programs (Dahir & Stone, 2003; Dimmitt et al., 2007; Gilchrist, 2006; Issacs, 2003; R. S. Johnson, 2002; Lapan, 2001; Love, 2002; Poynton & Carey, 2006; Reynolds & Hines, 2001; Rowell, 2006; Uellendahl, Stephens, Buono, & Lewis, 2009). Some of the models are whole-school systemic change models (R. S. Johnson, 2002; Love, 2002). Other models focus on school counseling programs (Dahir & Stone, 2003; Issacs, 2003; Uellendahl et al., 2009) and educational reform efforts (Reynolds & Hines, 2001). Furthermore, some of the models target results-based interventions (Lapan, 2001; Rowell, 2006), which are based on identified student standards, competencies, and benchmarks and rely on data to determine if they are meeting the vision and mission of the desired program. One model integrates the important domains of all the models into an evidence-based model to data-driven practices (Dimmitt et al., 2007). Although additional differences exist between the models, each tends to follow a general model for data-based decision making. The seven-step chronological process is: (1) describing the problem, (2) generating vision data, (3) committing to benchmarks, (4) identifying where and how to intervene, (5) selecting interventions, (6) evaluating interventions, and (7) monitoring problem data (Dimmitt et al., 2007). Table 7.1 presents the data-driven accountability models visible in the literature and school counseling research.

REFLECTION MOMENT

Review Table 7.1. As you review the models, what thoughts and feelings do you have? Which of the data-driven accountability model(s) would you feel most comfortable using? Why?

TABLE 7.1 Data-Driven Accountability Models

Model	Steps
SOARING (Gilchrist, 2006)	S – Standards O – Objectives A – Assessment R – Results I – Impact N – Network G – Guide
M.E.A.S.U.R.E. (Stone & Dahir, 2003)	M – Mission E – Elements A – Analyze S – Stakeholders-Unite R – Reanalyze, Reflect, Refine Results E – Educate
EBD (Dimmitt, Carey, & Hatch, 2007)	1. Problem Description: Knowing what needs to be addressed 2. Outcome Research Use: Knowing what is likely to work 3. Intervention Evaluation: Knowing if the intervention made a difference
(Issac, 2003)	• Identifying a problem and goal for improvement. • Developing a vision and goal for how you would like to see it change. • Identify measurable changes that you would like to see. • Develop a research plan and blueprint in the context of counselor activities and appropriate student development elements. • Implement the plan with periodic measurement of change of effect. • Collect and analyze data using simple statistics and use information to determine if desired change occurred or if a program reached desired goals. • Report results in simple terms using graphic representations; share with colleagues for feedback and reflection. Use the results in adjusting the program or intervention.

TABLE 7.1 (Continued)

Model	Steps
SPARC (2001)	• Principal's Message • Student Support Personnel Team • School Climate and Safety • Student Results • Community Partnerships/Resources • Content
(Johnson, 2003)	1. Getting started: Building the leadership and data teams 2. Killing the myth: Building dissatisfaction 3. Creating a cultural of inquiry: Assessing where you are, why you are there, and what needs to change 4. Creating a vision plan for your school 5. Monitoring progress
(Love, 2002)	1. Commit to student learning vision and standards 2. Collect and analyze student learning and other data 3. Formulate learner-centered problem 4. Set measurable student learning goals 5. Develop learner-centered systemic action plan 6. Take action 7. Monitor results
(Reynolds & Hines, 2001)	1. Vision data 2. Current data 3. Data target 4. Force field analysis 5. Strategy development 6. Planning 7. Action
IDEAS Model (Poynton & Carey, 2006)	Step 1: Identify a question Step 2: Develop a plan Step 3: Execute plan Step 4: Answer the question Step 5: Share results
(Lapan, 2001)	Program Planning P1 Define the direct relationship between student outcomes and comprehensive programs. P2 Define the direct relationship between student outcomes and characteristics of effective school environments. P3 Define the indirect ways in which student outcomes are realized because the comprehensive program helps to create a more effective school environment. Evaluation E1 Measure outcomes for students directly related to the comprehensive program. E2 Measure aspects of the school environment improved by the comprehensive program. E3 Measure the impact of changes in the school environment on student outcomes.

ACTION RESEARCH

Creswell (as cited in Dimmitt et al., 2007) considered *action research* "the study of one's own work, with a focus on practical issues" (p. 99). In terms of school counseling, action research seeks to answer questions and provide answers that inform and strengthen our work as school counselors. Rowell (2006) viewed action research as an "action-reflection-action" process whereby "initial thoughts about change are followed by concrete action to make change, which then are followed by further observation and analysis of what has taken place to prepare for the next action steps, and so on" (p. 379–380). In other words, action research is a continual cycle of action and research as a means of uncovering problems within the school and determining if what was used to address the problem worked (Rowell & Carey, 2009).

Let us return to the implementation and evaluation of the Second Step Violence Prevention Program. Analysis of the data revealed that, overall, the program was effective at addressing school climate issues, reducing incident reports of bullying behavior and violence in school, and decreasing behavioral referrals. However, disaggregated data revealed that special education students were continuing to report a substantial amount of bullying and violence behavior while attending school. In this case, the outcome evaluation provokes questions that might be addressed best through action research.

A vital necessity to action research is collaboration. Because action research goes beyond the practice of evaluation, school counselors may need additional support and expertise to entertain the notion of conducting action research. For example, university faculties are generally experts in research design, methods, and analysis (Maliszewski & Mackiel, 2002). Their input can provide an objective voice in methodology decisions and decrease the possibility of errors that could confound the research. Likewise, collaborating with university faculty might diminish the fears that school counselors often experience when considering conducting research. Dimmitt et al. (2007) described the importance of "creating an environment that encourages questioning and active engagement in intentional education practices" (p. 99). Stakeholders and partners across groups are valuable assets to action research because of the wealth of perspectives that individuals bring to the table when collaborating on action research. Likewise, collaboration involving individuals with multiple roles and functions encourages new ideas, shared perspectives, and discourse, which ultimately leads to stronger research outcomes. In our example, school counselors might involve special education teachers, school psychologists, and university professors to collaborate on action research to address the question "Why are special education students continuing to feel bullied, harassed, and violated in school?"

REFLECTION MOMENT

Consider ways in which counselor educators and school counselors might collaborate on action research. What about school counseling interns and school counselors? What might get in the way of counselor educators, interns, and school counselors in the field working together on action research? Reflect on ways you will integrate action research as a professional school counselor and approach opportunities to work with counselor educators.

SCHOOL COUNSELOR ACCOUNTABILITY

Evaluating the school counseling program is one means to demonstrate accountability. School counselors themselves are also evaluated based on specific criteria related to the role and function of a school counselor. Sounds easy enough, right? However, evaluating school counselors continues to engender uncertainty and confusion because, generally speaking, we are still not quite sure about what it is that school counselors do. Schmidt (2008) outlined a process for evaluating school counselors to aid administrators in answering the question

"What are school counselors suppose to accomplish and what practices illustrate effective functioning?" (p. 272):

1. Determine the school counselor's major functions and identify specific activities that define these functions. This step depends on the delivery model that frames the school counseling program and the delineated roles and functions of the school counselor within the delivery model. For example, the ASCA National Model provides a structure for school counseling programs *and* school counselor roles, function, and competencies. The identified school counselor practices and competencies outlined in the National Model can be integrated easily into an effective evaluation tool. Likewise, the Domains/Activities/Partners model provides activities; highlights outcomes in terms of ASCA Student Competencies (ASCA, 2005), adult competencies (Appendix A), and the ASCA School Counselor Competencies (Appendix B); and identifies partners whose input would be valuable to measure the effectiveness of the school counselor.

2. Determine the nature of measurement to be used to assess school counselor performance. This can be accomplished one of three ways:

   a. Assess the outcomes or results of particular activities or interventions selected by the school counselor that address identified concerns.

   b. Assess school counselor performance by examining the implementation of program services and intervention in relation to an agreed-upon standard.

   c. Combine Items a and b by stating what outcomes or results should be observed and at what level of implementation these outcomes are expected.

3. Design and create ways to gather data in order to evaluate whether school counseling services have been provided and that the services have been provided the level of implementation that meets the intended outcomes (pp. 272–273).

The evaluation process of school counselors is generally conducted by building principals and district-level counselor supervisors. The ASCA School Counselor Competencies (Appendix B) provide a meaningful context for these evaluations and may be used in the design of school counselor evaluation instruments. The gathering of information for the evaluation can take place through observations, audio- and videotaping, interviews, self-assessments and portfolios, and products, such as reports, audits, and instructional or informational materials. Likewise, school counselors can be evaluated by way of feedback from stakeholders and partners, personnel memos, and schedules and records (Schmidt, 2008).

To account for their time, school counselors are highly encouraged to utilize a master calendar to plan activities throughout the year, highlighting events and programs with schoolwide themes, and reflecting the reality of the ebb and flow of the academic year. A well-planned master calendar can often go awry due to unplanned events that arise throughout the school year, such as crises and other undetermined emergencies or needs. Maintaining a calendar can reveal a school counselor's true use of time and whether she or he is using school time to support the vision and mission of the school counseling program. We recommend that school counselors distribute their master calendars to all stakeholders or partners as needed and post a weekly and/or monthly calendar in a visible location in the building to increase access and reduce the likelihood of someone saying, "I can never find the counselor. She/He is never in the office!"

Generally, the school counselor's calendar reflects the needs of the students throughout the year. For example, programs that target orientation for new students are more common during the fall, whereas programs to assist students with testing strategies and the management of test anxiety might be more common around the testing cycle for the school. Likewise, transition programming and preparing students for summer and the next school year are more visible in the spring. Classroom guidance and small-group counseling are noted on the calendar consistently throughout the school year. The use of action plans (to deliver the developmental curriculum and address closing-the-gap activities) serve as important information in the design of the calendar. As part of the evaluation process, it is important to analyze time spent providing direct service to students in order to determine if future adjustments are needed.

CASE STUDY REVISITED

Integration

Taking what you learned from this chapter about accountability, let's revisit our original questions: After reading the chapter, where might you begin in the process of becoming a more accountable school counselor with the Mt. Data School District? What initial steps might you take? Who might you involve? What process might you use to demonstrate that you and your school counseling program positively affect students' learning and academic achievement? ∎

Suggested Reading

American School Counselor Association. (2006). Research methods in school counseling [Special issue]. *Professional School Counseling, 12*(6).

American School Counselor Association. (2009). Action research in school counseling [Special issue]. *Professional School Counseling, 9*(5).

Corbin, J., & Strauss, A. (2008). *Basics of qualitative research* (3rd ed.). Thousand Oaks, CA: Sage.

Dimmitt, C., Carey, J. C., & Hatch, T. (2007). *Evidence-based school counseling: Making a difference with data-driven practices.* Thousand Oaks, CA: Corwin Press.

Loesch, L. C., & Ritchie, M. H. (2005). *The accountable school counselor.* Pro-ed.

8

Counseling

LEARNING OBJECTIVES

By the end of this chapter, you will

1. Understand how counseling may be perceived by colleagues in the school setting and be able to design ways to communicate with them about the nature of counseling and how important it is for students

2. Be able to articulate when individual and group counseling may be appropriate as prevention and intervention, and when to refer to community counselors for treatment

3. Understand how school counselors function in crisis intervention and suicide prevention

4. Understand how to provide multiculturally and developmentally appropriate individual and group counseling

5. Be able to conduct needs assessments and outcomes assessments for individual and group counseling

6. Be able to discuss the ethical issues of using assessment instruments in counseling

and identify various assessment instruments for counseling in each domain

7. Understand school-appropriate theoretical options for counseling and how to use multiple intelligences when developing theoretically congruent counseling interventions

8. Be able to evaluate the advantages and disadvantages of group counseling

9. Be able to articulate the difference between structured/psychoeducational and process groups in the schools

10. Understand and articulate the issues involved with peer facilitators

11. Understand systems perspectives and be able to articulate why school counselors need to work with adult partners

12. Be able to apply systems thinking when analyzing counseling as an appropriate intervention with an adult partner

PHILLIPE AND THE ANGER MONSTER

Case Study

Dovey read the note from the second-grade teacher, Ms. Miller, without surprise. For the third time this month, one of her students was acting aggressively on the playground, resulting in another fight. Ms. Miller, who had witnessed the confrontation, described the student, Phillipe, as bossing other students, refusing to play cooperatively, and finally, as the one to hit first when the other children refused to comply with his demands for the basketball. As an elementary school counselor for 12 years, Dovey had worked with many students who seemed unable to control anger, just like Phillipe. Knowing there were only so many of these episodes the principal would tolerate before asking the family to find another school for the boy, Dovey wanted to help this child find some way to channel his anger besides bullying and fighting.

Dovey called Phillipe into her office at the next recess. Because of Phillipe's age, Dovey used play materials to allow him to "play out" some of his issues, rather than attempt to engage him in traditional counseling. She used reflection to track his play scenarios and found his affect expressed through play to be profoundly aggressive, angry, and violent, after which he would become tearful and sad. After meeting with him almost daily for two weeks, she decided that his anger was not abating after play-counseling sessions, which she found to be unusual. There did not seem to be consistent themes when she asked him who the "bad guys" were in his play, but the "victims" of his play violence were always "little boys." Her attempts to explore real events behind the play were unproductive, as Phillipe would always state at the end of a session that he was "OK" and wanted to go back to class. Meanwhile, the fighting on the playground continued.

Not surprisingly (as people who have been in schools would attest), there were several second- and third-grade boys this year who had been involved in fighting, and Dovey decided that Phillipe and some of these other boys might benefit from a group counseling experience. This would give them all a chance to learn about anger management skills and to explore some of the sources of their anger. She obtained permissions from the parents, and started a group to help these youngsters learn about the "anger monster" and how to make the "anger monster" smaller.

CHALLENGE QUESTIONS

1. What are your reactions to Phillipe's playground behavior? Consider that all anger comes from *fear* and *pain*. Reflecting on this, what changes in your reaction? Does that help you to reframe his behavior in more compassionate terms?

2. What experiences do you have with alternative methods of counseling? Where can you go to learn more about counseling methods with young children? With middle school students? With high school students?

3. How do you think the group experience will work for Phillipe?

4. How might you use older peers to help him?

5. What questions do you wish to answer about Phillipe's life situation? What are your tentative hypotheses about the systems of his life—his classroom, his home, his neighborhood? ■

THE SCHOOL COUNSELOR AS COUNSELOR

The work we do with students is a partnership—a symbiotic relationship that exists because our work helps students to achieve the outcomes of education, and their full cooperation gives our profession its unique position as a member of the education team. Our partnership with students begins with the foundation of our profession: counseling. Whether we are conducting individual counseling or group counseling, we are school counselors, not registrars, not bus monitors, not vice principals.

Nor is it correct to assume that we are mental health counselors. Our colleagues in the community who specialize in clinical or mental health counseling have unique skills and abilities (for example, extended training in substance abuse, depression, or other diagnoses that involve long-term treatment). Recent statistics would suggest that 1 in 5 children has a diagnosed mental or affective disorder, and 1 in 10 has an emotional disturbance (Mellin, 2009). In fact, there are groups that promote the closer alliance of school counselors with the mental health agenda for children and youth; many school districts contract with state or local mental health entities to provide clinical mental health professionals in the schools. The time of these school-based mental health counselors is often devoted to students who have mental health diagnoses, while the professional school counselor's time must also be allotted for the activities identified in the DAP model: the developmental curriculum, group counseling, working with administration in leadership and consultative roles, and working with other partners such as teachers and parents.

As the basis of everything we do, the profession of counseling provides guiding philosophies, ways of viewing students, and ways of helping students. The importance of counseling as an essential part of a counselor's job is reinforced when examining student needs. When students were surveyed to measure how they perceived school counselors, the counselors in schools with the highest ratings reported that they devoted 71 to 72 percent of their time in individual and group counseling (Wiggins & Moody, 1987). Furthermore, when students were asked what services they needed in high school, 89 percent responded that they needed career counseling, and 60 percent indicated that they needed personal counseling (Hutchinson & Bottorff, 1986). Sadly, only 40 percent said they received career counseling, and only 21 percent said they received any personal counseling. These studies serve as reminders that students value counseling. The value of this activity is indicated in the DAP model, as this activity is considered one of the primary activities.

Counseling is not just for students who are "troubled," as counseling enhances a student's academic, career, *and* personal/social functioning. According to ACT, "students who see themselves as competent and effective, with a realistic view of themselves and their abilities, are more than three times more likely to be high achievers as low achievers. . . . Students who have a low level of motivation to succeed, or who have a high level of anxiety about their schoolwork or home environment are five to six times as likely to be low achievers as high achievers" (Noble, 2000, p. 15). The domains of academic development, career development, and personal/social development resonate with each other; counseling for concerns in one area can improve a student's functioning in all areas. But there are many misconceptions about counseling, and this is where we will begin in our discussion of counseling.

Misconceptions of Counseling

It is easy to see how misconceptions about counseling could exist; for many adults, their only experiences with counselors were the career guidance counselors or the mental health counselors they knew in their high school days. (Recall the historical context of school counseling.) Because of that training in either the career guidance or mental health models of school counseling, school counselors functioned very differently than counselors of today—but our colleagues and the parents of our students don't know that. Adding to this misunderstanding are movies and public events that portray counselors in general as charlatans (or worse, criminals), and counseling as ineffective or manipulative, or even as brainwashing. It is important that counselors are sensitive to the questions and concerns that arise about individual and group counseling and are proactive in helping others understand the nature of counseling.

Letters to parents and teachers at the beginning of each year help to introduce the nature and scope of the comprehensive school counseling program in general and school counseling activities specifically, both individual and group counseling. Follow-up communication reminds them of the work you do with students, parents, colleagues in the school, and colleagues in the community. Furthermore, professional accountability as outlined in the National Model demands that school counselors communicate regularly with administrators, at both the building and the district levels, about the activities of the counselors and of the CSCP as a whole. This can help alleviate misunderstandings.

Prevention, Intervention, and Treatment: When to Counsel and When to Refer

As you will recall, prevention efforts are often associated with classroom developmental curriculum and schoolwide efforts to improve the school environment. Intervention efforts are often associated with individual counseling, group counseling, and parent-student-teacher-administration consultation and mediation. Treatment is called for when the student's issues are chronic, deeply traumatic, or deeply seated in the personality, such as issues of chronic depression, survival of abuse or violence, or severe anger management (Mellin, 2009). In terms of this chapter, we are focused on counseling, which is usually classified as prevention and/or intervention.

In general, counselors try to enhance the positive elements of a student's life (known as strengths-based counseling [Masten, Herbers, Cutuli, & Lafavor, 2008; Park & Peterson, 2008], positive psychology [Pedrotti, Edwards, & Lopez, 2008; C. R. Snyder & Lopez, 2007] or developmental assets [Search Institute, 2010]) and mitigate the effect of negative elements through prevention efforts. Counseling is preventive in the attempt to mitigate the negative effects of some aspect of the student's life, usually in terms of one or two meetings. If the issues are more troublesome, counselors work primarily with short-term and medium-term issues that arise for students through intervention, referring for treatment outside the school as needed. Intervention involving short-term issues may be addressed in four to eight counseling meetings (which could last from 10 to 30 minutes, depending on the situation) and usually involve predictable developmental issues (such as relationship issues, transition issues). Intervention involving medium-term issues could require a counselor's involvement (counseling, consulting with teachers, acknowledging the student with an encouraging smile) for a semester and involve issues that often resolve themselves as the student matures and as time passes (such as relationships or grief). Deep-level issues are those for which the student may require lifelong recovery work and for which the counselor would provide immediate intervention and support, with referral to community mental health counselors for treatment (such as substance addition, suicidal behaviors, depression).

Treatment consisting of in-depth, intensive, or medication-assisted therapy is most often not conducted in schools. When students are in need of treatment, most school counselors refer those students to mental health therapists in the community (S. L. Smith & Archer, 2000). For example, if it is discovered that a student is severely depressed due to years of sexual abuse, that student may need medications, frequent sessions, and intensive recuperative therapy to address the depression and begin healing old scars from the abuse. The community therapist and the school counselor would collaborate so that the school counselor:

1. Knows what medication(s) the student is taking
2. Would be available if the student experienced a crisis during school
3. Would assist in the coordination of IEP (Individualized Education Plan) meetings or other efforts aimed at ensuring academic, career, and personal/social success
4. Would provide individual counseling for academic, career, and personal/social issues
5. Includes the student in any groups currently meeting for students with similar issues

Crisis Intervention and Suicide Prevention

Trauma does not stop at the school property; crisis from the home and community follows students into the school, and crisis in the school comes into the home. The term "crisis," an event that exceeds the organism's ability to cope, is used to refer to two contexts: one in the school community and one in the individual lives of students. Crisis in the school community could include a death of a member of the school community, a school shooting, an accident, an intruder—any number of unexpected and/or traumatic events (Kerr, 2009). A crisis in an individual student's life prompts concern about suicide. For both these events, school counselors have a duty to respond appropriately.

Building crisis response involves appropriate channels for communication and information, both inside and outside the school community (this latter communication chain is determined by the school district). These internal channels are often established by a school crisis committee; the school counselor should at least be a member of this committee, and in the best possible scenario, the school counselor should provide leadership of this committee. The committee will establish predefined levels of crisis and appropriate levels of response for each, including information chains and protocols to provide information to students, faculty, families, and the outside community (Kerr, 2009). Once established, these crisis protocols are evaluated during debriefing after each crisis, or at minimum on a yearly basis.

Individual crisis intervention is also known as suicide prevention, intervention, and postvention. Excellent resources are found in Capuzzi (2009), Granello and Granello (2007), and McGlothlin (2008); all are worthy of being on any school counselor's library shelf. According to Granello and Granello, many school counselors struggle to implement suicide prevention programs because some school professionals believe the following myths:

1. Suicide prevention does not have any place in schools.
2. Talking about suicide will cause suicide.
3. Schools can be sued if they have a suicide prevention program.
4. Suicide prevention programs lead to contagion and copycat suicides.

Prevention efforts involve informing all members of the school community (students, teachers, parents, administrators, student support professionals) about suicide and the warning signs of suicidal ideation. In addition, the school counselor teaches basic assessment strategies so that everyone can help in intervention efforts, and promotes referral to the school counselor if there are any concerns about potential suicide. It is important to remind those being trained that they should err on the side of caution and not be afraid to ask tough questions (Granello & Granello, 2007, p. 184).

For the counselor, it is critical to take every threat seriously, ensure the safety of the student, consult with colleagues, inform and involve caregivers, and follow district and building protocol (Capuzzi, 2009; Granello & Granello, 2007; Muro & Kottman, 1995). There are several acronyms that are helpful in remembering the topics for suicide assessment. The first acronym is comprised of the warning signs of suicidal ideation and potentiality; the second is a means by which to assess the level of immediacy and lethality of the suicide plan.

IS PATH WARM? (American Association of Suicidology, n.d.)

I	Ideation
S	Substance Abuse
P	Purposelessness
A	Anxiety
T	Trapped
H	Hopelessness
W	Withdrawal
A	Anger
R	Recklessness
M	Mood Changes

SLAP (Granello & Granello, 2007, p. 196)

S *Specificity* of the suicide plan. The more specific and detailed the plan is, the greater the concern and need for action. Ask when, where, and how the student plans to kill him or herself, and probe for details that will tell you how much thought the student has put into this plan.

L *Lethality* of the means for carrying out the suicide plan. Means of self-injury that are immediate (i.e., guns, driving head-on into a truck) are deemed more lethal than means that take time to enact (i.e., overdose) that may also allow for discovery and rescue.

A *Availability* of the means for carrying out the suicide plan. If the suicide plan calls for shooting him or herself, but the student has no access to guns or plan to acquire the needed gun, then the level of overall immediacy of the plan is low. If, however, the student states that the gun is under the parent's bed in an unlocked box, then the level is very high because the student (1) knows exactly where the gun is and (2) is able to get to the gun with little trouble.

P   *Proximity* to help is the final lethality and immediacy criterion. Will there be time for discovery and rescue? If the suicide plan involves an overdose when the student is home alone while the parents are out of the country on a month-long vacation that generates more concern than a plan to overdose at a party.

Based on the level of assessed risk, the most appropriate intervention strategies can be determined. Intervention strategies for suicidal young people are both immediate and long-term. Immediate interventions involve what the counselor says to the student in the course of the suicide assessment, in which a list of things to do would include (K. A. King, 2006, p. 10; see also Granello & Granello, 2007; Muro & Kottman, 1995):

Remain with the student.

Ask direct questions for clarity and assessment of risk.

Encourage the student to express feelings.

Focus on the present, not the past or future.

Express sincere concern about the student.

Encourage the student to broaden his or her awareness of alternatives to suicide without minimizing the seriousness of the student's concerns.

Listen actively, calmly, and without judgment or criticism.

Follow your school's intervention plan and alert the crisis team in the building/district.

Contact the student's caregivers.

Refer the student to a community-based counselor or therapist.

The most effective interventions are those in which the student is enfolded in wraparound care, which includes family and parental support, community resources, and school monitoring for safety and support (Capuzzi, 2009; Granello & Granello, 2007). In this system of wraparound care, long-term interventions involve referrals to outside treatment for the underlying cause(s) of the crisis, medical support if needed, and the acquisition and ongoing practice of effective coping skills. Research supports the effectiveness of therapy for suicidal students and their families (Kalafat, 2006), and school counselors should have information available on the mental health resources in the community to provide to families. School counselors should be involved with students who are currently in treatment and/or recently returned from treatment in the community in order to (1) provide support and care when the student returns from hospitalization, (2) help the student acclimate to a postcrisis, more functional state in the school, (3) reinforce effective coping skills, (4) monitor stress levels, and (5) provide a safety net if the crisis state returns (Capuzzi, 2009; Granello & Granello, 2007).

Multiculturally Appropriate Counseling

In your development as a professional school counselor, you must develop the insight needed to be sensitive to multicultural and diversity issues. These issues transcend traditional definitions of "culture" to include gender, age, sexual orientation, religion, region, immigration status, home language, economic environment, physical ability and health, mental ability and health—any characteristic that could conceivably alter a person's value system, perspectives, and self-perception. Wittmer (2000a) points out that culturally skilled counselors know how crucial culture is to a student's identity development and know how to preserve the dignity of both the student and his or her culture. Since most counselors are trained in the middle-class, Christian, Euro-American worldview, there are often large gaps in understanding different cultures that need to be identified and addressed. To improve your understanding of other cultures and other perspectives, you will want to broaden your connections with persons of diversity, pursue multicultural professional development and training, and address multicultural differences explicitly with the student

("I don't know what it has been like to grow up in your culture. Tell me what growing up has been like for you."). Even what we think we know about another culture must be respectfully explored with each student of that culture.

Suffice it to say that the first steps to becoming a multicultural counselor involve an understanding of the Multicultural Counseling Competencies (Arredondo et al., 1996), which require counselors to first know their internalized societal messages about those who are "different" from themselves. We are challenged to examine the source and validity of these internalized messages, and to redecide from a holistic perspective about what we value and embrace in the human spirit. "Culturally skilled counselors have specific knowledge about their own racial and cultural heritage and how it personally and professionally affects their definitions and biases of normality/abnormality and the process of counseling" (Arredondo et al., 1996). They reflect on their "knowledge and understanding about how oppression, racism, discrimination, and stereotyping affect them personally and in their work" (Arredondo et al., 1996).

They then pursue "specific knowledge and information about the particular group with which they are working. They are aware of the life experiences, cultural heritage, and historical background of their culturally different clients . . . [They] understand how race, culture, ethnicity, and so forth may affect personality formation, vocational choices, manifestation of psychological disorders, help seeking behavior, and the appropriateness or inappropriateness of counseling approaches" (Arredondo et al., 1996).

Finally, the multiculturally sensitive counselor is able to weave these insights into self and culturally unique others into healing strategies.

> Culturally skilled counselors are able to engage in a variety of verbal and nonverbal helping responses. They are able to send and receive both verbal and nonverbal messages accurately and appropriately. They are not tied down to only one method or approach to helping, but recognize that helping styles and approaches may be culture bound. When they sense that their helping style is limited and potentially inappropriate, they can anticipate and modify it . . . Culturally skilled counselors are able to exercise institutional intervention skills on behalf of their clients. They can help clients determine whether a 'problem' stems from racism or bias in others (the concept of healthy paranoia) so that clients do not inappropriately personalize problems. (Arredondo et al., 1996)

This means that professional school counselors value diversity and are aware of their own internalized messages that may result in bias. They seek information about diverse others and then design interventions that honor the diversity of the student and that may include advocacy to address systemic bias that results in inequitable treatment of diverse students. They are agents of social justice in the schools, helping students both individually and systemically.

REFLECTION MOMENT

Can you recall a time that you felt misunderstood and treated unfairly because of some characteristic or group you represented? How did that feel? What did you do? Did you empower yourself to address the inequity, or did you feel powerless? What does that mean for students, who are regularly dismissed when they try to voice an opinion?

Developmentally Appropriate Counseling

Most counseling training programs teach basic counseling skills using the template of adults to help counselors-in-training learn about empathy, unconditional positive regard, active listening, and other counseling competencies. It is up to counselor trainees to generalize those skills to the unique populations with whom they will practice those skills in a professional counseling context. This means that now is your opportunity to take the foundation counseling skills you know and modify those skills to counsel young people in both individual counseling and group counseling settings.

Children and adolescents have unique developmental and contextual realities, which will influence how they respond to counseling. To practice effective counseling with K–12 students, we should be mindful of the following guidelines:

1. Young people need to be active because they possess a shorter attention span than adults.
2. Young people are still developing their own moral compass and intellectual, critical thinking skills. This means they are still developing their ability to tap their inner reality or insight.
3. Young people may not have the emotional intelligence to be able to identify their emotions, the source of their emotions, or words to describe their experience of their emotions.
4. Young people need to feel free to choose, while concurrently needing help articulating their framework (value system) by which to evaluate alternatives.
5. Young people need help developing strategies for generating and evaluating alternatives, making a commitment to an identifiable alternative, and then understanding the consequences of the choices they make. They are still refining their ability to draw cause-and-effect connections.

These important insights into the developmental realities and needs of students yield implications for both the manner in which we counsel young people and the content of our counseling. In terms of the *manner* in which we counsel students, we need to be aware of their activity level and attention span. We also need to be aware that they may have limited ability to understand themselves—limited insight. They may not be able to identify their feelings, or they may not have language to describe what they are experiencing. Most importantly, students must feel that their counselors trust them to make good decisions and believe in them.

In terms of the *content* of counseling, counselors must be aware that young people may need help articulating their own value system (the framework for evaluating alternatives) before conversations can take place about the alternatives themselves. The autonomy this dialogue teaches, and the respect this conveys, goes far in developing trust between the counselor and the student.

In addition, young students are still learning how to make decisions, practicing the process of identifying goals, articulating alternatives, evaluating alternatives, making a choice, and then designing a plan to implement that choice. Developing a counseling approach that emphasizes and teaches the process of decision making, in addition to the focus on the product of the decision making, helps students develop an important competency. Furthermore, it is very important that counselors understand that young people need help evaluating the consequences of their choices. Young students are still developing their abilities to understand cause and effect, so evaluating alternatives in terms of possible consequences is particularly challenging. For example, many researchers believe that adolescents engage in high-risk behavior because they see themselves as invulnerable, living the myth of "It won't happen to me" (Craig, 1996, p. 453). Helping young students understand that it can happen to them may be a hard sell, but without addressing this, young people are not effectively or realistically assessing the consequences of their choices (Ponton, 1997). Although some choices have nonlethal consequences (i.e., Should I go out for the soccer team?), the consequences of others are life and death or are life altering (i.e., Should I drink alcohol?). This means that school counselors need to be able to assess

- The student's attention span
- The student's level of insight
- The student's level of emotional intelligence (ability to identify emotions, the source of emotions, or his or her experience of emotions)
- The student's clarity of values
- The student's level of decision-making strategies
- The student's ability to understand cause and effect relative to his or her choices

> **REFLECTION MOMENT**
>
> Recall a time when you needed help making a decision. If the alternatives were clear, how did it feel if the person you asked for help doubted your ability to evaluate your alternatives? Conversely, if your alternatives weren't clear, how did it feel to have a helper who assumed it was all so clear and so simple? These are common experiences. The point is to become more sensitive to how you help young people in terms of their decision making.

Legal and Ethical Considerations

For both individual and group counseling, legal and ethical concerns are important to consider. Often students will use minor friendship concerns, scheduling, careers, or minor academic concerns to mask their real reason to talk to the counselor. As an ethical professional counselor, you must be aware of this and be prepared to work with students on a deeper level if their issues warrant it. The general rule is to be open to all issues, be sensitive to nonverbal cues, and be constantly assessing all areas of the student's functioning for those times the student needs more attention than the presenting issue might warrant. It is crucial that counselors give the time and attention needed to students who come to see them; not providing adequate care is unethical and unprofessional. Furthermore, not devoting adequate time and attention to students will damage the trust needed to make effective use of the counselor's time and expertise. Students of diversity, in particular, might find the counselor's office to be a threatening place, especially if the counselor represents a different culture or socioeconomic background than the student (Wittmer, 2000a). As the student establishes trust in both the person of the counselor and the process of counseling, the real reasons for the visit will be revealed.

Students also need to know that the counselor has a breadth of knowledge about student issues and what it means to be a young person, called "withitness" (Gordon, 1997). Students need to know that you're not going to "freak out" when you hear their problems. No counselor can know everything there is to know about every issue of every student, but counselors need to be knowledgeable enough about most issues to listen effectively for underlying themes and concerns, facilitate effective assessment and intervention, and help put the student at ease that help is possible. The case of an unplanned pregnancy can illustrate the embarrassment of sharing the "secret," the need for the counselor to be able to deal rationally with the "emergency," the need for the counselor to understand his or her own personal perspectives on the issue of teenage sexuality and parenting, and the need to be informed about options available in the community (Kiselica & Pfaller, 1993).

To be effective, you need to understand both the process of helping your students (your theoretical orientation and strategies) and the product of healing that you hope for your students (your insights into the student's issues). All of this is interrelated; how issues relate to each other and how you address various issues are shaped by your theoretical orientation. Let this serve as another reminder that you must, as an ethical counselor, be able to articulate and practice within your theoretical orientation.

Assessment within the Counseling Process

Assessment carries a variety of meanings in the counseling process—the first use of "assessment" refers to the compilation of needs and outcomes for program planning and evaluation, and the second use of "assessment" refers to use of formal and informal data collection during counseling for academic, career, and personal/social functioning.

As discussed in Chapter 7, needs assessment is essential for successful program planning and implementation, and outcomes assessment is essential for program improvement. Needs are usually assessed using surveys of students, teachers, and parents, and then individual and/or group counseling activities are planned in response to those surveys. Outcomes are assessed for individual and group counseling in terms of the numbers of participants, their evaluation of how helpful the counseling was, what they learned from the counseling experience, and then how their school-related functioning has changed as a result of counseling. As you will recall from the discussion of the National Model in Chapter 5 and the discussion of accountability in Chapter 7, the measures of functioning are frequently compiled in terms of grades, scores, discipline referrals, attendance, and other observable behaviors.

The second discussion of "assessment" will focus on counseling-related data collection. Many authors agree that assessment and appraisal of students are important counselor functions (S. B. Baker, 2000; Gysbers & Henderson, 2000; Loesch & Goodman, 2000; Schmidt, 1999). But the extent of the counselor's involvement with student assessment and appraisal is a subject of debate in the profession. Some authors would consider assessment and appraisal to be major activities in the comprehensive school counseling program (Loesch & Goodman, 2000; Schmidt, 1999), whereas other authors argue that school counselors use assessment and appraisal as components of other, more important activities, such as counseling (S. B. Baker, 2000) and individual planning (Gysbers & Henderson, 2000).

First, it is essential that you obtain an in-depth understanding of assessment instruments and concepts; this is usually accomplished by the completion of a discrete course in assessment or appraisal in the graduate program. As you will note in the ethics statements of both the American Counseling Association and the American School Counseling Association, you are required to know the purposes, nature, results, reliability, validity, limitations, and appropriateness of any instrument you administer, and you must be able to communicate those clearly to students and parents. Furthermore, you must be able to understand the differences between formal and informal assessment strategies, so that you are able to use informal assessment strategies, such as card sorts, case histories, and behavioral observation checklists, as professionally as the formal assessment instruments. A comprehensive discussion of these important concepts will not be attempted here; rather, the purpose of this discussion is to help you integrate information from that appraisal course with the comprehensive school counseling program as outlined in this text.

Second, it is important that school counselors are aware of the criticisms of certain instruments that are often used in the schools. For example, instruments that are not presented in a student's native language will yield results that are highly suspect. Similarly, instruments that are administered in adverse conditions, such as overcrowded, noisy rooms, or under conditions contrary to those of the norming population are suspect. The use of assessment instruments in ways for which they are not designed (such as confusing aptitude tests for achievement tests) will invalidate the results. And counselors must maintain a healthy skepticism about some dear and long-held myths of education, such as the concept of intelligence as a hard-and-fast, measurable characteristic (when, in fact, the concept of intelligence should be viewed as very plastic and fluid and might better be understood in terms of multiple intelligences).

School counselors most often use assessments in the counseling function within the three domains. Within the academic domain, assessments can help students to know their learning styles and strengths, which can then be helpful in academic planning, such as the Learning Styles Inventory (Dunn, Dunn, & Price, 1996). Aptitude tests, purportedly measuring a student's ability to achieve in certain areas, might also be helpful in a student's academic development. Such instruments would include the General Vocational Aptitude Battery (available from the U.S. Employment Service), the Armed Services Vocational Aptitude Battery or ASVAB (available from the U.S. Department of Defense), the Differential Aptitude Test or DAT (available from The Psychological Corporation), and the Scholastic Assessment Test or SAT. Tests that can be used to help assess a student's verbal and nonverbal functioning include the Peabody Picture Vocabulary Test and the Slosson Intelligence Test (these instruments must be carefully considered in terms of appropriateness for different ages of students).

Within the domain of career development, there are many instruments and computer programs that can help students further their self-knowledge and match that self-exploration with information about the world of work. These instruments include the Self Directed Search (available from Psychological Assessment Resources), the Strong Interest Inventory (available from

Consulting Psychologists Press), and the Kuder General Interest Survey (available from Science Research Associates). Computer programs such as BRIDGES, DISCOVER, and SIGI are also designed to help students evaluate and understand their interests, lifestyle choices, and possible career options.

In the personal/social domain of development, counselors often use assessments to help students understand themselves better, such as the Myers-Briggs Type Indicator (MBTI, available from Consulting Psychologists Press). This instrument comes with a high school form and is often used to help students with career decision making.

INDIVIDUAL COUNSELING

Every counselor will select the theoretical orientation that works for him or her, and you will want to focus on those theories that lend themselves well to the school environment. Given that students don't often have much time for one-on-one sessions and that schools are not perceived to be the best setting for intensive psychotherapy, school counselors usually adopt a theoretical orientation that works well within time constraints (S. L. Smith & Archer, 2000). Three counseling approaches that are often practiced by school counselors are Adlerian therapy, solutions-focused or brief therapy, and reality therapy.

In brief, Adlerian counseling (also called Individual Psychology) can provide insights into the student's family dynamics (Carlson, Watts, & Maniacci, 2006). Addressing family value systems, birth order, goals of behavior, and self-defined inferiority, Adlerian insights can prove very useful in understanding how a student uses behavior to gain significance in his or her social setting: family, friends, and class. Helping strategies involve facilitating students' understanding of how their behavior reflects choices that were developmentally appropriate for the family context, but are not appropriate for the school context. This theory lends itself well to counseling infusing play, art, music, or other creative applications.

Solutions-focused brief counseling (Metcalf, 1995) engages students in considerations of when the problem is not such a big problem, then assists them in applying "what was working then" to now. This structured approach to counseling provides counselors with a series of questions and prompts that maximize impact and minimize students' storytelling. Direct and empowering, this approach gives students choice and control over the situation, and lends itself well to the developmentally triggered issues of friendships, stress, anger, and academic competencies.

Reality therapy is also a structured approach to counseling K–12 students, as it was originally developed for use in a school for delinquent girls (Glasser, 1965). The acronym WDEP prompts exploration of the *wants* of the student (phrased in therapeutically meaningful ways), the *direction* of the student (What is he or she doing to get what he or she wants?), *evaluation* of the direction (Is doing what the student is doing getting him or her what she or he wants?), and *planning* for change if the evaluation reveals that the actions of the student are not getting him or her what he or she wants.

Using Creative Strategies and Multiple Intelligences in Counseling

Using creative strategies such as play, music, and art can greatly facilitate the connection and communication between the counselor and student. These insights are not age-bound; high school students "play" just as elementary students "play," but the form of the play is different. Learning what students in your school define as play can help you connect with them and can add valuable tools to your counseling repertoire.

Additional insights into how to work effectively with school students can be found in the concept of multiple intelligences (Lazear, 1999). These intelligences, as listed in Chapter 4, include verbal, mathematic/logical, artistic, musical, naturalist, interpersonal, intrapersonal, and kinesthetic strengths. If you know a student's strengths, you have important information that can be very useful in designing counseling interventions. For example, journaling, art, music, and poetry have been advocated for years as effective ways to counsel students, regardless of theoretical orientation

(Cormier & Hackney, 1999; Hutchins & Vaught, 1997). Effective counselors would naturally look for counseling methods that fit with the strengths of the student. Using Lazear (1999, pp. 142–145) and Corey (2004) as a springboard, the following list suggests some counseling strategies based on multiple intelligences and theoretical foundations:

1. *Verbal/linguistic intelligence:* Journaling, making up jokes, poetry, storytelling (Adlerian, person-centered)
2. *Logical/mathematical intelligence:* Creating formulas to show relationships between events (such as A ➜ B ➜ C from Rational Emotive Behavior Therapy, or REBT), creating logic/pattern games, syllogisms (Harrison, 2000a)
3. *Visual/spatial intelligence:* Guided imagery (Image Psychology [Parker, 1998]), art (Kahn, 1999)
4. *Bodily/kinesthetic intelligence:* Situation sculpting (psychodrama, family sculpting), sports, role playing, ropes courses and outdoor challenge experiences
5. *Musical/rhythmic intelligence:* Music or sounds, rapping, singing new words to an existing song (REBT)
6. *Interpersonal intelligence:* Insight counseling, group counseling
7. *Intrapersonal intelligence:* Insight counseling, metacognition techniques, emotional awareness
8. *Naturalist intelligence:* Archetypal pattern recognition of human nature, caring for plants and animals, natural world insights (e.g., social animals, pack behavior, insect colonies, flocking of birds and schooling of fish; rock formations and geologic forces; plants; weather phenomena), counseling outdoors while taking a walk with the student

This list is by no means exhaustive. As a counselor, you will develop your own ideas of counseling strategies that will be helpful with your students, but these ideas might help you identify strategies that will engage the student more fully in the counseling process.

REFLECTION MOMENT

What is your theoretical orientation? What theory and strategies would you use for Phillipe in the chapter Case Study? Did Dovey counsel Phillipe using one of the multiple intelligences outlined in this section? Which one?

GROUP COUNSELING

Research into the efficacy of group counseling indicates recent changes in the ways counselors perceive group counseling in the schools. In 1993, Carroll found that elementary school counselors did not feel that they had adequate skills in group counseling; they would have liked more training in groups in their graduate programs. By 1996, Dansby found that counselors generally felt "that small group work should be a vital part of any counseling program, that their programs would be more effective if they led more groups, and that they felt adequately trained to implement group counseling" (pp. 233–234).

Group counseling involves primary intervention (Dansby, 1996; D. W. Johnson & Johnson, 2000), and for some students, it may be the most therapeutic intervention they will experience. The intent of conducting group counseling is that participants will be able to learn about themselves, other people, life tasks, and authentic ways of relating in a safe, confidential setting. While there are similarities between group counseling and group educating, we will emphasize that group counseling, as we mean it in this chapter, has a therapeutic and intervention focus. Educating a large group (15+) of students will be considered in the next chapter on educating and curriculum delivery.

The importance of group counseling in schools cannot be overemphasized (Fleming, 1999). In fact, Keys, Bemak, and Lockhart (1998) suggested that group counseling is more effective than individual counseling to address the needs of students, most especially at-risk students. This contention is supported through research into violent youths, which suggests that peer-group interventions are effective in redirecting peer values, confronting antisocial behaviors, teaching problem-solving skills, and encouraging prosocial behaviors (Bemak & Keys, 2000; Tolan & Guerra, 1994).

Almost any topic a student will bring you could constitute a meaningful group experience. These topics can be addressed in either structured or process group formats.

Structured (Psychoeducational) versus Process Groups

To understand group counseling, it is important to understand that there is a difference between structured or psychoeducational groups and process groups. Structured/psychoeducational groups refer to group experiences in which the counselor takes direct leadership of the group, including identifying goals, presenting material with an assumed values orientation, selecting activities, and directing interaction. Often, structured group exercises (i.e., role playing, behavior rehearsal, didactic experiences) and curricular materials are used to move the group intentionally toward certain conclusions and insights involving a psychoeducational goal (Goldstein, 1999). For this reason, structured groups are often criticized for being too prescriptive (Keys, Bemak, & Lockhart, 1998). In spite of this criticism, structured psychoeducational groups continue to yield excellent results for students. Examples of structured group topics include decision making; friendship skills; stress and anger management; drugs, tobacco, and alcohol resistance; metacognitive skills (Brigman & Goodman, 2001); study skills; planning for college; and career exploration. As you can see from each of these topics, the outcome of the group is predetermined; each topic has a clear learning goal.

In contrast, process groups rely on the learning that emerges from the group interaction and spontaneous experiences that occur as the members learn to negotiate the natural progression of all relationships: forming (working through trust issues), storming (working through authenticity issues and interpersonal dissonance), norming (creating shared norms and rules for the group), performing (addressing the therapeutic topic or issue that brings members to the group), and adjourning (saying goodbye at the end of the experience) (Tuckman & Jensen, as cited in Kline, 2003). Furthermore, process groups do not have a clearly predetermined goal; each member comes to the group to explore her or his own choices, and there is often a greater emphasis on the support that groups can provide. In fact, what are commonly referred to as "support groups" are process groups. Examples of such process groups in schools would include groups for sexual orientation (Street, 1994); career counseling; learning issues such as attention-deficit disorder, self-concept, or self-esteem; changing families (divorce, blended families, nontraditional families); loss and grief; self-discipline; fears; support for addiction recovery; diversity support (Malott, Paone, Humphreys, & Martinez, 2010); and support for students who are being treated in the community for suicide risk and depression.

The extent of structure or the extent of process within the group is best conceptualized as a continuum, with highly structured on one end and highly process focused on the other. In the middle are groups that are blended. Perhaps the counselor has structure in the overall view of the group, but allows processing to be the main vehicle for change within each meeting. An excellent example of a blended group is presented by Muller (2000), in which she describes a group counseling experience for African American high school females to foster positive identity development. For each meeting, the facilitators have a stimulus experience or question to start the session, but then allow group interaction to guide the processing of that experience. It is always advisable that group leaders have activities planned for each meeting, in case the members are uncomfortable with sharing feelings or ideas (Posthuma, 1999). While silence is not a problem *per se*, some students might find extensive silence disconcerting, and chances of acting up increase as dissonance increases.

It is hoped that you will be able to see that many topics could be presented as either a structured group or a process group. For example, a topic like truancy could be a process group if the group is designed to allow members to clarify their values relative to attendance, explore their own attendance challenges, make choices about future behavior, and support each other in continuing those new behaviors. The same topic could be presented as a structured group if the intent is to teach the importance of regular attendance, emphasize strategies for reducing truancy, and then support members in truancy-reducing behaviors.

Implications and Considerations of Group Counseling

There are numerous advantages to providing services to students through a group counseling format. The first advantage involves developmental appropriateness; as young people develop, they become more peer oriented. It makes sense that counseling formats involving peers will meet with success (Ball & Meck, 1979). Group counseling harnesses that natural peer orientation to interest students in becoming involved in a group, engages them in values exploration and clarification, motivates them to attend, empowers them in the change process, and supports them while they try new behaviors.

A second advantage of group counseling involves efficiency. Conducting group counseling allows counselors to reach more students than is possible through one-on-one counseling. Students with similar issues will learn together, brainstorm ideas for growth for each other, and support each other as they struggle together. Furthermore, it connects students who may otherwise have little contact with each other and assures students who feel isolated by their problems that they are not alone in their suffering, providing significant therapeutic benefits; studies into the efficacy of groups have documented significant benefits for members (LaFountain & Garner, 1996; Nassar-McMillan & Cashwell, 1997; Zinck & Littrell, 2000).

Finally, there is a call in the literature for more systems awareness in our work in schools (Bilynsky & Vernaglia, 1999; Dansby, 1996; Fontes, 2000; Geroski & Knauss, 2000; Keys, Bemak, & Lockhart, 1998; Taylor & Adelman, 2000). Students come to schools as both products of, and producers of, change within the multiple systems of their existence. Working with students in group counseling allows counselors to expand their awareness of each student; what better way to see how students interact in their systems than to witness it firsthand?

However, group counseling is not for all students, nor is it for all issues. One of the most important limitations of group counseling is the issue of confidentiality. No matter how emphatically the counselor insists that all members respect confidentiality, some breaches will occur. Additional concerns involve the special relationship between schools, parents and other caregivers, and the school counselor in terms of the limits of confidentiality for health, safety, and legal reasons. In some cases, mandated reporting and/or informing parents of problems could result in serious trust issues with group members if those situations are not addressed in advance.

Furthermore, scheduling difficulties can seriously interfere with a counselor's ability to schedule groups, especially if there is no schoolwide study hall or period for such student-driven activities. Dansby (1996) found that lack of time and scheduling problems as well as difficulty getting students out of class were the top two sources of interference that hindered group counseling efforts. Clear communication about group counseling is a necessity for successful group counseling activities.

REFLECTION MOMENT

Have you ever had a group counseling experience as a member? As a facilitator? As a leader? Most counselors have had a course in group counseling in their graduate program, but one course may not give you a chance to fully explore your group leadership/facilitation skills. How comfortable are you with groups? With which ages and which issues would you be comfortable leading a group? How can you expand your comfort zone? Would Phillipe and other students like him be good candidates for a group for anger management? Why or why not?

PEER FACILITATORS

We must not neglect the powerful benefits that result when young people are actively involved in the counseling program. By this, we do not mean involvement as a student—we mean involvement as a peer helper (Foster-Harrison, 1995). In this program, older students would be selected and trained to act as peer facilitators, assisting the counselor in the logistics and management of a variety of services, including peer tutoring, peer mediation, peer helping, peer programs to help orient new students to the school, and peer facilitation of groups. Peer facilitators would need to be carefully screened for appropriateness with the counseling program (but those students with the best academic records are not always the most appropriate for peer training), persons to be helped, the specific counseling topic (academic subject, careers, adjustment issues for new students), and other factors. Special training would be provided in the helping process, listening, the basics of confidentiality, and facilitation of interaction. Most importantly, special attention would be paid to teaching peer helpers about the limits of their competence, so that the professional counselor would be involved immediately if there were any problems. It is crucial that these peer helpers are carefully supervised and monitored; even a well-trained peer facilitator is not qualified to conduct a group alone (Fleming, 1999).

A program of peer facilitation, with carefully selected, trained, and screened peer facilitators, can provide benefits for the counselor, the peer facilitator, and other students. For the counselor, the benefits of having peer facilitators are numerous; the peer facilitator can provide feedback about the progress of students being helped, serve as a role model to other students, and assist with some of the logistics of running the program, such as helping with scheduling and publicity. For the peer facilitator, this provides an opportunity to develop helping and leadership skills—a powerful way for the young person to "try on" roles connected with school-related and helping professions. One of the important ways that young people can develop and extend their "social interest" (to use an Adlerian term) is to help others, a powerful intrinsic motivator. Finally, there are benefits to the student population as a whole; peer helpers provide a safe method of connecting with the counselor in cases where trust is an issue, and it empowers students to see themselves, like the peer facilitator, as capable. In a 2000 study, students who had worked with a peer counselor were found to have a decrease in discipline referrals, improved attitudes toward school, improved school attendance, and improved grades ("Peer Counselors Help Kids," 2000).

CASE STUDY CONTINUED

Phillipe and the Anger Monster

As the group progressed, Dovey continued to meet with Phillipe. Dovey observed him in the classroom to see how he interacted with his peers and to see how the classroom environment "fed" his anger monster. There did not seem to be anyone in the class who picked on him or bullied him, but Dovey knew it was important to understand all the systems in which Phillipe interacted, so she knew these observations were not wasted.

As the group drew to a close, she continued to meet with him one-on-one. As he played out his anger, he often was able to talk a little more in the sad period after the angry play. About a month after their first meeting, he finally shared that his family was "full of anger monsters" and that he had trouble sleeping at night. Dovey called his home and asked for a meeting with his mother.

Phillipe's mother arrived in the school and sat down to talk to Dovey. "I know he's an angry little guy, but I don't know how to help him."

"Is there anything going on at home that might cause him to be angry?" Dovey gently asked.

Tears welled in her eyes. "Phillipe's dad moved out last week. We're getting a divorce," and she cried quietly. ∎

COUNSELING WITH ADULT PARTNERS

Systems Thinking: Families, Schools, and Communities

As a whole, educational professionals know the environmental factors needed for healthy development. We touched on these in Chapter 2, in which we discussed schools as systems, and again in Chapter 4, in which we outlined the systems in which students live. We looked at the developmental assets as conditions that support students in their development (Search Institute, 2010). The top six support assets are identified as family support, positive family communication, supportive adult relationships, a caring neighborhood, a caring school climate, and parental involvement in schooling.

When those developmental assets are missing, we have good documentation of the negative effects (McWhirter et al., 2007). Community-wide economic instability, stagnation, intolerance, poor health care (mental and physical), poor childcare, and a host of other problems can cause increased stress in the home. This stress often resonates with stress and vulnerability in the family system, increasing the risk for divorce, family violence, neglect, substance abuse and addiction, and mental health problems, which then resonate with increased stress on the children living in the home. All these problems can erode students' efforts to learn, grow, and prosper (McWhirter et al., 2007).

As you will recall from Chapter 4, systems thinking is a way of seeing and addressing these problems from a holistic, naturalistic perspective. It views all students as members of interlocking and dynamic systems of social interactions, which then informs intervention efforts aimed at those systems. You will recall from Chapter 5 that the National Model does indeed compel counselors to attend to systemic issues.

Does this mean that school counselors provide counseling for anyone who walks through the door? Most emphatically, no. Does this mean that school counselors provide family systems counseling? No, family systems counseling is a therapeutic treatment approach that requires specialized training. But we cannot ignore the pain of our families, schools, or communities. There are ways we can help, and problem-solving, intervention-level counseling for families, school colleagues, and community colleagues might be appropriate, depending on the situation.

Selection of Counseling as an Intervention

How might such systemic problems come to the school counselor's attention? Problems in the student's family might come to your attention in a case of child abuse, with an irate parent, or with a parent's request for assistance, for example. Problems in the school with colleagues might come to your attention when a teacher needs to process his or her frustration about students in the class, or when a colleague shares some personal issues with you. Problems in the community might come to your attention when an employer complains about your students in a work program, when the community identifies a problem with your students, or when a community colleague shares some personal issues with you. These experiences suggest that the adult partner is struggling with our students and may need help meeting the competencies for adult partners (Appendix A), and therefore deserves our attention.

The full range of actions available to school counselors vary from counseling, to educating, to consulting, to leadership, and advocacy. Although educating, consulting, leadership, and advocacy are the primary ways that counselors work with adult partners, counseling is always an option if warranted. In deciding whether to provide counseling as an intervention, these are the most essential issues:

1. **A student-focused problem.** The time and effort of counseling is justified if you believe that the problem is directly related to the development of your student(s).
2. **Time considerations.** Although there are scheduling implications for working with adult partners, there is also support for the efficacy and timeliness of family counseling in the resolution of school problems (Hinkle, 1993; G. Stone & Peeks, 1986; Wells & Hinkle, 1990).

3. Training in family systems counseling if you are providing family systems counseling. This is an ethical issue (Hinkle, 1993; Magnuson & Norem, 1998). It is important, however, to distinguish family systems counseling (systemic counseling approach with unique training requirements) from counseling with an individual parent, spouse, teacher, or other adult (individual counseling approach consistent with school counselor training). You do not need specialized training to provide counseling for a family member, parent, colleague in your school, or colleague in your community.

4. Administrative support. There are many studies that document the need, efficacy, and processes of systemic interventions. For administrators, the frame in which you present this part of your comprehensive school counseling program must include
   a. Needs assessment data that document the importance of this part of the program for your students
   b. Program evaluation data that support the effectiveness of this intervention as a contributor to student success
   c. Processes that highlight problem solving rather than treatment

5. Availability of referral support. In some isolated communities, there may be very limited mental health services available. The school counselor may represent the only option for help and may need to expand interventions accordingly (Cowie & Quinn, 1997).

6. The location of the problem on the prevention-intervention-treatment continuum. As with our discussion in Chapter 4 about the prevention-intervention-treatment continuum, there are some issues that are best addressed by community mental health treatment professionals. However, issues such as parenting skills or the renegotiation of family relationships to reflect healthy development are very appropriate for school counselor intervention.

What such counseling with our adult partners would look like depends on the situation, but the most common scenario involves defusing or stabilizing the situation, brief counseling toward solutions, and then referral to community mental health professionals if warranted. It is not our intent to suggest that school counselors are responsible for providing long-term treatment to all persons who interact with our students. But a few minutes with a caring listener can make all the difference for an adult partner who is at the end of his or her proverbial rope.

COUNSELING IN ACTION

The ways that individual and group counseling are implemented will vary from level to level, as the needs of elementary, middle, and high school students will vary widely. For example, at Ford Elementary School in Tucson, Arizona (a 2004–2005 Recognized ASCA Model Program [RAMP program]), the counselor maintains a consistent classroom curriculum schedule, so her frequent visits to classrooms for prevention programs reduce the need for individual or group counseling in the schools. She stated that although she does not see a large number of students for individual counseling, she will build time into her schedule for personal counseling as needed. In addition, she is available if the need for crisis counseling surfaces and will make referrals to community services when warranted, often consulting with other elementary school counselors or the district counseling office to assess appropriate referrals. She further reports that small-group work has decreased significantly due to the frequency with which she is delivering classroom guidance lessons. In many cases, counseling takes place in short conversations, over lunch, and during recess.

In middle schools, the counseling activities are more challenging due to scheduling. The Sequoia Middle School is located in Southern California in Fontana, a suburban area of Los Angeles, and is a 2005 RAMP school. This counseling program has adopted the logo of the Eyrie—Where Eaglets Fledge. Like eagles caring for eaglets in a nest, the counseling team wants their students to be nurtured, secure, and respected, and given a safe place to spread their wings while learning the skills needed to succeed in life. The concept of the Eyrie supports the understanding of the middle school years as times of rapid growth and development in cognitive, emotional, and physical characteristics for students and the necessity for gentle support and guidance by knowledgeable and caring adults. While one counselor is delivering classroom guidance activities, the other is available for individual and small-group counseling. During lunchtime students can drop by the counseling offices for brief chats and schedule appointments. Scheduled small-group sessions include TEMP sessions (Together Everyone Makes Progress), which are offered each trimester for students who are experiencing some type of turmoil in their life. Such experiences can include divorce or separation, approaching death of a loved one, and domestic violence. The counselors also implement Youth Connections, which is a privately developed program adopted and required by the school district for small-group counseling. The curriculum for the program was created by Rainbow Days Youth Connection and has tested reliability. Seven groups of 8 to 14 students meet for 6 to 10 sessions each year. These students participate in sessions addressing identity development, handling anger, goal setting, decision making, dealing with peer pressure, and drug and alcohol prevention. In addition, each counselor participates in crisis intervention training designed and provided by the school district, allowing for uniformity of the delivery of services throughout the district.

There is an extensive peer mediation program at Sequoia Middle School, where peer mediation is available daily for students. Peer leaders are trained in mediation and communication skills to encourage their peers to make positive choices when dealing with everyday conflict. A peer teacher meets with the students one class period per day to train them as peer helpers using the Peer Assistance Leadership (PAL) program and Schrumpf, Crawford, and Usadel's (1997) peer mediation book. In the classes, seventh- and eighth-graders learn listening and attending skills, problem-solving strategies, and the mediation process, culminating in peer mediation certification. After one year of class work, students who have excelled are chosen to become peer leaders who are then assigned to the counselor one class period per day for the purpose of providing mediation, personal support, and educational programs for students. These students conduct these programs within the counseling program offices where they receive supervision by a counselor. Peer leaders use PowerPoint presentations to work with small groups of eighth-grade students to explain the high school registration process, graduation requirements, and college entrance requirements. These small-group meetings are held prior to the high school counselors' involvement in registering the students for high school courses. Another service the peer leaders give is a meet-and-greet experience for new students by providing a welcome and tour of the campus on their first day.

At the high school level, individual and group counseling looks different. At Wakefield High School in Raleigh, North Carolina, (a RAMP school) the caseload per counselor is approximately 450 students, so individual planning is an area of challenge for the counselors—usually handled during classroom presentations. There is one counselor at Wakefield High School who is assigned to work with ninth-grade students in the Ninth-Grade Academy. The other counselors split up the remaining grades alphabetically. The counselors provide individual counseling to students on an as-needed basis. In addition, there are school-based mental health professionals who can provide services to qualifying students with Medicaid or Health Choice if the students do not have insurance coverage for private therapists. At times depending on a student's individual needs, the school-based mental health professional may obtain a release so that the school counselor can work with the student as well. The Student Assistance Program (SAP) counselor administers a needs assessment to students at Wakefield High School and then runs small groups to help meet identified needs. Target groups have included students who were newcomers to the area, children of divorce, substance abusers and their families, students interested in increased racial and ethnic understanding, gay and lesbian supporters, and retained ninth-graders.

CASE STUDY REVISITED

Integration

As you return to the Case Studies of this chapter, picture yourself as the counselor.

1. What new insights do you have into possible ways to work with Phillipe?
2. What are the issues you identified for Phillipe and his mother?
3. Where would you place your work with Phillipe in the prevention-intervention-treatment continuum? More importantly, where does each issue fall on that continuum?
4. What are the systemic issues here? Just because the classroom is not an angry place, does that mean the playground isn't either? What can you do to check that out?
5. What are your options with Phillipe's home situation? Would you counsel Phillipe's mother? Why or why not? ■

Suggested Readings

Bilynsky, N. S., & Vernaglia, E. R. (1999). Identifying and working with dysfunctional families. *Professional School Counseling, 2,* 305–313. This article presents a practical and user-friendly model of problem solving with families that can assist every counselor to feel comfortable with this process.

Dansby, V. S. (1996). Group work within the school system: Survey of implementation and leadership role issues. *The Journal for Specialists in Group Work, 21,* 232–242. This article provides an excellent overview of how counselors view the challenges and benefits of group counseling.

Harrison, T. (2000). Brief counseling in the K–12 developmental counseling program. In J. Wittmer (Ed.), *Managing your school counseling program: K–12 developmental strategies* (2nd ed., pp. 85–94). Minneapolis, MN: Educational Media. An excellent overview of several models of brief counseling in the schools.

Keys, S. G., Bemak, F., & Lockhart, E. J. (1998). Transforming school counseling to serve the mental health needs of at-risk youth. *Journal of Counseling & Development, 76,* 381–388. This article challenges many traditional assumptions of the school counseling field, a refreshingly holistic view of what school counselors can do to help all students.

Lewis, W. (1996). A proposal for initiating family counseling interventions by school counselors. *The School Counselor, 44,* 93–99. This article provides two practical approaches to conducting brief family problem-solving counseling that, should a referral for long-term family therapy be necessary, would provide the counselor with insight into the family's problems.

McWhirter, J. J., McWhirter, B. T., McWhirter, E. H., & McWhirter, R. J. (2007). *At-risk youth: A comprehensive response for counselors, teachers, psychologists, and human service professionals* (4th ed.). Pacific Grove, CA: Brooks/Cole. This book is a must-read for anyone working with youth and their families.

Nicoll, W. G. (1992). A family counseling and consultation model for school counselors. *The School Counselor, 39,* 351–361. The model presented in this article provides a strategy that allows the counselor to move between counseling and consultation as needed to address the family's problems.

Ponton, L. E. (1997). *The romance of risk: Why teenagers do the things they do.* New York: Basic Books. This author's mental health experience provides a frame for understanding why teens often engage in "crazy" risk taking.

Pryor, D. B., & Tollerud, T. R. (1999). Applications of Adlerian principles in school settings. *Professional School Counseling, 2,* 299–304. For the Adlerian counselor, a wonderful primer of how Adlerian counseling works in the school setting.

Sklare, G. B. (1997). *Brief counseling that works: A solutions-focused approach for school counselors.* Thousand Oaks, CA: Corwin. For the solutions-focused counselor, a wonderful primer of how brief counseling works in a school setting.

CHAPTER

9

Educating and Curriculum Delivery

LEARNING OBJECTIVES

By the end of this chapter, you will

1. Be able to define educating all partners, and discuss the importance of student competencies in terms of educating others

2. Be able to identify the source of the comprehensive developmental curriculum

3. Be able to describe the process of writing a lesson for the developmental curriculum

4. Be able to write a developmental curriculum lesson that employs multiple intelligence strategies

5. Be able to identify curricular areas within which developmental curriculum could be delivered

6. Be able to outline effective teaching strategies, including how to demonstrate respect for students' personal and intellectual integrity

7. Be able to outline a strategy of classroom management that is respectful and developmentally appropriate, including positive behavior support

8. Be able to identify reasons for educating our adult partners

9. Be able to describe appropriate considerations when educating adults

CASE STUDY

Donna's Lunchroom Duty

Donna had been at the high school for several years, and in that time, she found that eating her lunch in the faculty lounge provided her with valuable contact with the teachers. She made it a point to eat there at least twice a week and would use that time to talk to teachers about students, listen to their issues, and consult as needed about student issues. She knew that part of her job was to monitor the emotional climate of the school; time in the teacher's lounge was as important as time in the students' lunchroom for taking the emotional "pulse" of the school.

January was the month for midyear parent conferences, and everyone had been on edge since a car accident in late December in which several students had been injured. The police found marijuana and alcohol in the car. Since the driver and all the passengers were students at Donna's school, she had increased her visibility in classrooms providing developmental curriculum about healthy choices. She had communicated with all the teachers her concerns about the availability of alcohol and drugs in the school, but found that numerous teachers were still reluctant to give up classroom time for her to present her curriculum.

As she entered the lunchroom, several teachers invited her to sit with them, since they were in a debate about something. "We need you to settle this argument."

"Here's the thing, Donna. I say that the parents of the students in that wreck were at fault for not supervising them better. Where did they get the drugs and booze?" one teacher stated.

Another said, "No, you're wrong there. I've had a number of conversations with parents during conferences, and they all blame the school and the school counselor. They say the kids got the stuff here, and that it's the school's fault that they are experimenting with this stuff. They say that the school counselor isn't doing her job because no one is keeping the kids from using drugs. They think no one is addressing this. Sorry, Donna, but that's what I hear from the parents."

"What's wrong with these parents anyway?" interjected a third. "Now we have to parent these kids too? Aren't they supposed to monitor their kids' behavior, teach them about right and wrong? I didn't buy the booze those kids had, so why should the school be responsible?"

"Our standards are too slack," posed a fourth teacher. "If we went back to stricter standards, we wouldn't have these problems. They wouldn't have time to mess around with alcohol or drugs—they'd be too busy studying and worrying about exams to get away with partying!"

"So, Donna, what do you think?"

"Yeah, Donna, you're the expert, tell us who's right! Is it our fault, your fault, or the parents' fault?"

"I wish there was an easy answer! The problem is that we all play a part in helping students make good choices. We *all* need to be educated—kids, teachers, and parents—about deadly issues like teenage drinking and drug use," she replied.

"But we already know all that stuff," sniffed one of the teachers. "You need to educate the parents. . . ."

Donna sighed.

CHALLENGE QUESTIONS

1. What do you think about the opinions expressed around the table? Do parents need to be better educated about the realities of alcohol and marijuana? Do teachers need to be educated about parents? Do parents need to be educated about the school and the role of the school counselor? Do teachers need to be educated about the role of academics in the lives of high school students?

2. Who is responsible for educating students, parents, teachers, and the general public about young people, families, schools, and the role of the school counselor? If you were Donna, what would you say next? ▪

SCHOOL COUNSELOR AS EDUCATOR AND CURRICULUM SPECIALIST

Professional school counselors educate students in new ways of dealing with relationships with self, others, and the world, either by direct instruction or by allowing clients to discover and evaluate their life lessons. In addition, school counselors educate other adults about several issues: student development, equity in education so that no child is "left behind," educational strategies for students, healthy families and parenting strategies, paying for college—the list goes on (see Program Goals for the Adult Partners of the DAP Model, Appendix A). In this chapter, we will consider when school counselors are intentional about that instruction, in the second most essential function of school counselors—that of educating others.

The word "educate" has been carefully chosen over "teach." According to the *Grolier-Webster International Dictionary of the English Language* (1975), "teach" means "to give instruction to, to guide the studies of" (p. 1007), while "educate" means "to advance the mental, aesthetic, physical or moral development of; to qualify by instruction for the business and duties of life" (p. 313). The difference is subtle, but important. *Teaching* implies the traditional model of instruction, complete with all the connotations of the factory model of schools as described in Chapter 2. On the other hand, *educating* implies development, discovery, relatedness—all the qualities of developmentally appropriate education that was also discussed in Chapter 2. We believe that school counselors should not view themselves as master's-level teachers, because this implies competition. However, school counselors should view themselves as counselors *and* educators, roles that have been clearly articulated in the National Model and that cement our connection and vitality within the school system (Coy & Sears, 2000; Cuthbert, 2000; Gysbers & Henderson, 2000; Wittmer, 2000b).

As we will see in this chapter, school counselors are a source of information, inspiration, and consolation to many people—our students, the families of our students, our school colleagues, and our community colleagues—educating others about healthy development.

EDUCATING STUDENTS FOR HEALTHY DEVELOPMENT

The emphasis on educating students about healthy development has increased with discussions about character education, humanistic education, and values clarification (Charney, 2002; Kirschenbaum, 2000; Robinson, Jones, & Hayes, 2000; Williams, 2000), violence prevention (Elliott, 1998; Guerra & Williams, 1996; Sherman et al., 1998; Tolan & Guerra, 1994; 1998) metacognitive skills and academic success (Brigman & Campbell, 2003; Sink, 2005), and helping all youth function more effectively in today's world (Bluestein, 2001; Goldstein, 1999; Goleman, 1995; McWhirter et al., 2007; Rak & Patterson, 1996). These discussions have emphasized that school counselors must employ strategies to reach every student in the school, and the classroom has been the primary venue for that outreach effort. It is clear that counselors can no longer afford to be reactive, waiting for students to come to them with their concerns (Gysbers & Henderson, 2000; Wittmer, 2000b). These perspectives have been clearly articulated in the ASCA National Standards for Student Academic, Career, and Personal/Social Development (ASCA, 2005). The learning objectives derived from these Standards will be referred to as the developmental curriculum (not "classroom guidance").

Furthermore, the discussions of character education, violence prevention, risk reduction, and resiliency enhancement have also sensitized counselors to their crucial role in prevention and early intervention efforts. Recall from Chapter 4 that prevention activities are designed to mitigate the effect of internal and external realities that can cause students problems as they mature, whereas early intervention efforts are designed to help curb current unhealthy risk factors (McWhirter et al., 2007). As we encounter young people who struggle with self-esteem, family problems, abuse issues, learning problems, low impulse and emotional control, poor social skills, and a host of other concerns, we must be aware that developmental curriculum delivered in the classroom provides students with critical survival skills that are the essence of prevention and early intervention (Goldstein, 1999; Goleman, 1995; McWhirter et al., 2007; Rak & Patterson, 1996). In fact, research suggests that these classroom interventions can be as meaningful, and can provide intervention as powerfully, as small-group counseling (Nassar-McMillan & Cashwell, 1997; Shechtman & Bar-El, 1994; Shechtman, Bar-El, & Hadar, 1997). To ensure that these skills are being addressed, counselors must carefully develop and evaluate the content of their developmental curricula to meet the student competencies defined by the American School Counselor Association (ASCA) and by state or district mandates.

Student Competencies

As indicated in the DAP model as presented in Chapter 6, educating students is considered one of the primary activities with students. Furthermore, as you will recall from Chapter 5, comprehensive school counseling programs are designed to meet the standards for school counseling programs in terms of the National Standards promoted by ASCA (2005). To accomplish the goal of helping all students to maximize their academic, career, and personal/social development, school counselors structure their comprehensive program around the student competencies articulated in the National Standards. (Recall from the Foundation of the National Model discussed in Chapter 5 that the National Standards are the foundation of the CSCP.)

Moreover, many state departments of education and school districts have used the National Standards to refine their school counseling programs by articulating specific grade-level competencies, as recommended by Gysbers and Henderson (2000). Counselors need to know national, state, district, and local standards to understand which competencies to address in what order.

For the purpose of this chapter, we will continue to use the National Standards as the template of our discussion of the developmental curriculum and the process of educating our student partners. In these standards, students need specific knowledge, skills, and attitudes to be successful in their academic, career, and personal/social development. To help students to develop these competencies, it is easy to see that a comprehensive developmental curriculum addresses a wide range of developmental topics. This chapter is designed to help you understand, develop, and present developmental lessons to students on these areas. (In addition, see Paisley and Hubbard [1994] for examples of lessons.)

Assessing for Barriers to Learning

Students do not learn well when they are not able to focus—when events from their community, families, school, or classroom interfere with their ability to attend to learning. Recall Maslow's Hierarchy of Needs, which progress from survival needs (food, water, shelter, clothing), to safety needs (knowing your survival items will be where you left them), to social needs (knowing there are others who care about you), to higher-level needs such as self-actualization (Maslow, 1970). Using this simple structure, it is possible to see how barriers to learning can be sociological (e.g., poverty, racism), familial (stressed, fractured, or uncertain family interactions), psychological/biological (e.g., depression, health problem such as diabetes, asthma, or obesity), educational (e.g., poor academic self-esteem, academic disengagement, dyslexia, school phobia), or interactional (e.g., target of bullying, difficulty making friends)—or can be an aggregate of numerous issues (Bluestein, 2001; McWhiter et al., 2007). When there are learning challenges, it is critical that the school counselor assess all possible sources of the student's challenges—and not resort to blaming. A multifaceted assessment can assist in this wide-angle lens approach to viewing the student and his or her context.

With this wide understanding of the student, school counselors can then build effective educational experiences to help boost students' resilience. Efforts to teach coping strategies, appreciation for diversity, conflict resolution, healthy choices, and similar topics can increase learning (Bluestein, 2001; National Research Council, 2000).

Educating Using Multicultural Insights

To create schools in which students can learn, we must attend to conditions in the school that enhance learning. In what Bluestein (2001) termed "safe" schools, school counselors strive to facilitate school conditions that facilitate academic, emotional, social, behavioral, and physical safety. Academic safety involves giving students the room for imperfection; emotional safety is caring and cooperation; social safety involves fostering inclusion and valuing diversity; behavioral safety involves respectful discipline; and physical safety is self-explanatory. For the professional school counselor, these five aspects of safety are the foundation for fostering multiculturally meaningful education.

One suggestion is found in Goodman and West-Olatunji's (2010) examination of educational hegemony and traumatic stress in African American and Latino American students. They present the compelling argument that what have traditionally been viewed as the academic "deficits" of students of color such as academic disengagement, learning deficits, and other learning problems, such as attention-deficit hyperactivity disorder (ADHD) may be evidence of traumatic stress resulting from systemic oppression. Their suggestion is that counselors should engage in empowering school experiences, in which counselors:

1. Identify the impact of systemic oppression and traumatic stress in the school,
2. Deconstruct the oppression by examining other settings in which the student is valued and supported to find more affirming self-definitions,

3. Reintegrate the new meanings of self as empowered and valuable with the educational environment, and

4. Transform the experience into one that affirms resilience and coping, further empowering the student to address systemic oppression in affirming ways (p. 180).

In these interactions, the counselor must be willing to examine and discuss issues of power, privilege, and oppression in self and in the school; they must be willing to advocate for the end of educational hegemony and oppression. Goodman and West-Olatunji (2010) enjoin counselors to find ways to bring affirming and inclusive images, stories, and materials into the school so that diverse students can find a narrative in which they can derive cultural inclusion, empowerment, and success. In this context, school counselors are educating not only students but colleagues in the schools as well.

REFLECTION MOMENT

We are all diverse, yet those whose with visible diversity are most likely to face oppression, discrimination, and hegemony. What experiences have you had when your diversity was not accepted? How can you use those insights when thinking of ways to educate students and colleagues about systemic oppression that exists in the school?

DESIGNING LEARNING EXPERIENCES

Intent

Where does change begin—with change in thoughts, feelings, or behavior? Think about a significant change you made in your life, such as stopping smoking, starting exercise, or starting graduate school. What process did you go through before you actually made the change in your behavior?

The answers to these questions aren't just mental gymnastics; they are designed to help you think about where to begin when designing learning experiences. This insight is useful for you and your students, because most people know what they need to do to make their lives better. The reason people don't act on this knowledge is that something needs to happen to move that knowledge from their intellect (cognition) into the external world (behavior). What is that something? The answer to that question is the key to help young people move from "Yeah, yeah. I've heard this all before. I can spout all the conflict resolution/drug resistance/delay-of-gratification nonsense. . . ." to "OK. I can do that. I will do that." Here's a clue: that missing link between cognition and behavior is feeling, or affect.

This is where the passion of the counselor will be tapped. To be effective with our students, we have to know, deep in our souls, that what we teach has value, has meaning, and has the ring of human truth to it. Without that conviction from our "bones," we will teach from the intellect only, distancing ourselves from our feelings and the knowing of that truth. Palmer (1998) accurately captures what occurs in the classroom when that artificial rift between intellect and intuition is reinforced in the classroom.

> What we teach will never "take" unless it connects with the inward, living core of our students' lives, with our students' inward teachers. . . . We can speak to the teacher within our students only when we are on speaking terms with the teacher within ourselves. . . . Deep speaks to deep, and when we have not sounded our own depths, we cannot sound the depths of our students' lives. (p. 31)

What happens when intellect and intuition are joined, when the teacher's inner core speaks to the students' inner core, is the creation of a community of truth, where students and teacher alike are able to examine the subject as both knowers and learners (Palmer, 1998). The implications for pedagogy, for designing and presenting topics in the developmental curriculum, are consistent with the core concepts of developmentally appropriate classrooms—respect, conversation, discovery, and inclusion (D'Andrea & Daniels, 1996). Within this context, developmental curriculum is carefully planned and thoughtfully executed to establish and enhance the learning community of the classroom.

This does not prevent the counselor from presenting material to students for their consideration, nor does it mean that the class becomes free-for-all, 35-people-all-talking-at-once bedlam. To design developmentally appropriate learning experiences that invite students into the conversation (with you, with each other, with the subject), you begin with the intent to create a developmentally appropriate lesson. This is the first step: look for ways to engage students in experiences that facilitate discovery and in conversations that allow them to process their existing and emerging truths.

Instructional Purpose

Next, you will articulate your overall purpose within the framework of the student competencies of academic, career, or personal/social development. You will answer two questions: (1) What do you want them to know, to do, and/or to feel by the end of the instructional time? and (2) Is your goal prevention or intervention? The answers to these questions will help you allocate adequate time to delivering the topic.

Instructional time is usually defined in terms of lessons (defined as a single classroom visit, usually one instructional hour or "period") or units (defined as several lessons). Depending on the topic (what you want them to know, do, or feel) and the goal (prevention or intervention), you will extend or shorten the amount of time needed to accomplish your purpose.

For example, if your overall purpose is to help students who fight to learn anger management techniques, you will design a unit consisting of several lessons, each one addressing one topic. In this example, one topic would consist of learning anger triggers; the next would be relaxation techniques; the next would be options to anger; and the last would be role playing and practice. The reason you would want to allot adequate time for each of the four topics is that your goal is an early intervention, because these students are already choosing unhealthy behaviors. These behaviors must be unlearned before new behaviors are learned. However, if your students are not already engaged in physical fighting, your goal is prevention, and you might decide that one lesson would enable you to remind students of these anger management skills to prevent future problems. Generally, the less time you spend on a topic, the less "deep" the learning will go.

Learning Objectives

The next step is to create learning objectives for the student, which can be configured for each lesson or for the entire unit. These objectives should be related to outcomes for the student (not the process of presenting the material), specific, and measurable (Mager, 1997). From these objectives, you will have a basis for selecting the materials and instructional strategies for the lesson; you will have structure within which to be flexible and creative; you will have measurable results of your instruction; and you will have a basis for understanding and evaluating your instructional efficiency (Mager, 1997, p. 19). Your goals must also be developmentally appropriate for the age group you are teaching. Examples of learning objectives might include:

- Students will be able to identify at least three healthy responses when someone challenges them to a fight (all age groups).
- After watching a professional sporting event, students will write down at least 10 jobs related to sports, excluding the job of professional athlete (middle or high school).

Instructional Methods and Multiple Intelligences

Once you have identified the overall purpose and objectives of the lesson or unit, you are now free to design the instructional methods that will best meet those objectives within a developmentally appropriate context. It is important to remember that students need to be actively involved, both mentally and physically. Consider how to incorporate the insights gained from the concept of multiple intelligences: how can you address students with a variety of different intelligence strengths?

Too often, lessons within the developmental curriculum are targeted to students who think like we do—in other words, for students who are verbal, interpersonally intelligent, and intrapersonally intelligent. This means that those from the other five intelligence orientations are less able to benefit from the insights we hope to offer—left in their confusion, frustration, and perhaps, rejection of the developmental curriculum. There are a variety of instructional strategies that tap each intelligence area, and we should expand our instructional methodology to include all students in the class (Lazear, 1999, pp. 142–145). As you will recall, these include verbal/linguistic, logical/mathematical, visual/spatial, bodily/kinesthetic, musical/rhythmic, interpersonal, intrapersonal, and naturalist intelligences.

Common developmental curriculum delivery methods include presenting information, discussions, debates, quiet reflection and writing, artwork, journaling, role playing, demonstrations, experiments, and field trips. But don't let this list confine you—be innovative! As you can see from the next section (Integrating the Curriculum Using Multiple Intelligences) and from Tables 9.1, 9.2, and 9.3, the list of ideas is endless. Include discussions about what is important to the students, to their lives and their culture. Consider bringing contemporary music, movies, cultural events, and current events into the classroom. Go where the students are—to the movies they watch, the TV shows they enjoy, the music they listen to, the stores they frequent, the events they attend. Who are their heroes and stars? Pull insights from their lives for the students to consider.

Materials Needed

Based on your instructional methods, identify the materials you will need for each lesson. For example, books, paper, overheads, worksheets, permission slips for the field trip, predesigned roles for role playing, films, music, and art materials would appear on this list. Again, be creative in selecting your materials, looking for contemporary resources. The importance of timeliness cannot be overemphasized. Imagine you are designing a developmental curriculum lesson on marijuana. You may remember a movie made in the 1950s called *Reefer Madness*, in which the evils of marijuana are presented. If you used that movie today, students would laugh. Of course, if your intent in the lesson is to provide them with a juxtaposition of "old" ideas of drugs with "new" ideas of drugs, this movie would provide a humorous way to accomplish that goal.

Procedure

In this phase of building your lesson or unit, you will identify the specific activities for each lesson. It is helpful to know how each topic will be presented in terms of introduction, activity, processing, and closure (Cuthbert, 2000). Remember that each topic needs to be presented or experienced, processed in terms of how each student will apply the learning or insights gained from the lesson, and closed in terms of what new choices the student will make as a result of the learning. To neglect any of these phases will cause the lesson to be incomplete and fragmented. In the section of this chapter on Delivering the Curriculum, you will see detailed suggestions about how to structure the delivery of each lesson.

Evaluation: Outcomes Measures

Recall that the National Model mandates that counselors collect both perception data (what students think they know, believe, or can do in terms of competencies learned through the developmental curriculum) and results data (how that learning is translated into behaviors in the school). It is very important that you have a means of evaluating both the effect of the lesson or unit as well as your effectiveness in the presentation of that lesson or unit. To evaluate the effect of the lesson, use the student objectives to assess the extent of their learning. If your lesson involves homework, this provides you with tangible evidence of learning (in theory). (*Remember*: If you ask for homework from your students, always give feedback on those efforts. It isn't respectful to drop the "conversation" without follow-up.) Or, if you chose not to collect homework, you can design a pre- and posttest of the concepts or terms you will be discussing in the lesson. This way, you can collect pre- and postlesson insights to inform future classes you present on this topic.

In terms of evaluating your effectiveness in the design and/or presentation of the learning experience, solicit student feedback with an anonymous survey at the end of the class. This process can be informal, such as distributing note cards at the end of the class and asking students to tell you what they liked most and liked least about the lesson they just experienced. This way you will know what to adjust in future lessons.

INTEGRATING THE CURRICULUM USING MULTIPLE INTELLIGENCES

One of the biggest challenges to school counselors involves how to schedule the developmental curriculum. School counselors feel they are not able to deliver a developmental curriculum because of increasing pressure on teachers from high-stakes testing, meaning more reluctance to surrender precious classroom time (Dollarhide & Lemberger, 2006). In a study done in 2000, 78 of 80 K–12 counselors were able to deliver group/classroom guidance from once or twice a week, to monthly, to variable scheduling (Burnham & Jackson, 2000). The key to access to the classroom is *curricular integration*, meaning that the developmental curriculum supports the academic standards and benchmarks of learning. To accomplish this integration, counselors need to think about how their lessons dovetail with academic subjects.

Curricular integration involves two levels of effort: practical and conceptual. The practical efforts involve developing and maintaining an advisory cadre of teachers who will assist in the articulation, refinement, and implementation of your comprehensive school counseling program. This might be one use of the Advisory Council mentioned in the ASCA National Model, or a more informal group might consist of teachers only to support your integration efforts. This ongoing support and advisory cadre should consist of teachers who believe in the CSCP and who are willing to meet regularly to facilitate the holistic development of students through promotion of the program. Through their insights, you can survey other teachers to determine who is already presenting topics that satisfy the developmental curriculum and who is open to your presenting these topics. It is also with the input of this cadre that you can address the conceptual considerations of curricular integration.

The conceptual aspects of integrating the developmental and academic curricula are, once again, facilitated by the concept of multiple intelligences. Many lessons about human nature, relationships, human challenges, and other topics within the developmental curriculum can be explored through experiences associated with other intelligences. As previously mentioned, counseling is a highly verbal, interpersonal, and intrapersonal activity, but five other intelligence strengths are not tapped if all developmental curriculum lessons are focused on the first three. So if you are able to develop a lesson using the naturalist intelligence, it makes sense that you could approach science teachers to see if the developmental curriculum might be integrated there. For example, a science class might be exploring chemicals in the body. What better place to conduct a discussion of the effect of toxic chemicals from drugs, especially contaminated street drugs? The lessons relative to the alcohol, tobacco, and other drugs (ATOD) curriculum would be integrated into the science class, rather than presented as a separate lesson that they have heard over and over again.

Table 9.1 presents ideas of curricular integration for elementary school; Table 9.2 is for middle schools; and Table 9.3 is for high schools. Each one represents a different starting point in the crosswalk process between academic and developmental curricula. Expand this list to consider other teachable moments that exist in extracurricular activities, such as student government, dances, the school newspaper, the yearbook, athletics, and school clubs. What about integration with the school-to-work curriculum? With community service? With service-learning or volunteerism? The possibilities are endless, and you are bound only by the limits of your imagination.

TABLE 9.1 Curricular Integration, Elementary School, Grades 3–4

Student Competency/ indicator	Multiple Intelligences	Academic Subject	Lesson Idea
Cooperation/Work and play cooperatively/Describe differences between cooperative and competitive behaviors	Interpersonal using Musical	Music	In groups, students will write and perform music they created from objects in the class
Healthy ways to express needs, wants, feelings/ Learn acceptable ways of dealing with anger/Express feelings with "I" messages in timely, assertive, nonthreatening manner/Communicate with care and respect for self and others	Intrapersonal and Interpersonal	Writing	Students will reflect on the last time they got into a fight and write about what they would say now to that person about the fight.
Describe various occupations/ Understand wide variety of jobs	Visual/Spatial	Art	Students will create a collage of jobs they like cut from magazines
Listening and speaking to obtain information	Verbal/linguistic	Physical Education	Cooperative game
Locate health resources	Naturalistic	Science, History	Students take a field trip to a forest to learn about survival of the early settlers; relate that to how we survive in a modern medical world
Use adult role models to learn more about occupations	Kinesthetic	Social Studies	Dress up as your parents at work
Identify family and cultural background	Interpersonal and intrapersonal	Music History	Students will find out what music represents their family culture
Sense of interconnectedness and co-responsibility/Describe how people work together and depend on each other	Interpersonal	Social Studies	Design a city in the classroom
Identify personal indicators of mental, emotional, social and physical health	Naturalistic and Intrapersonal	Writing	Write a story about a time you were happy (e.g., fun vacation or holiday)
Describe own behaviors, accomplishments and how these influence career choices	Intrapersonal using Bodily/ Kinesthetic	Art, Writing	Students write a play about how someone with their experiences becomes a hero
Anticipate how their lives will be in the future	Verbal/linguistic	Writing	Write about a day in the student's life at the age of 30

REFLECTION MOMENT

What are your intelligence strengths? Think about your favorite classes in high school. Now imagine your least favorite classes. If you could take the excitement of learning through your intelligence strengths into those least favorite classes, what would your learning have been like?

TABLE 9.2   Curricular Integration, Middle School

Developmental Curriculum	Academic Curriculum	Examples of How to Teach Developmental Curriculum in Academic Classroom
Careers	Physical education	Students will discuss the various careers of the personnel needed to produce a professional football game on TV
Solving problems	Math	Students will take word problems and solve them. In groups, they will then relate those skills to daily problems.
Respecting and appreciating diversity	English	Students will read folk stories and superstitions from various parts of the world and discuss how different experiences lead to unique perspectives. They will write about what they found interesting in each story.
Communication	History	Students will learn about the communication between countries before they went to war with each other and talk about how the communication between them contributed to the choice to go to war. They will relate this to communication that leads to fights.
Cooperation	Science	Students will build a model of a structure from materials given in class, but they will do it without instructions. They will then talk about how they cooperated in the assignment—roles and so on.
Conflict resolution	Biology	Students will study social animals versus solitary animals, and relate what they learn to the "human animal" and human conflicts. What can they learn from the animals that live together?
Setting goals	Science	Students will design their own experiments and will learn how to set up their experiments by establishing goals for each stage of the experiment.
Making decisions	English	Students will watch a popular movie, discussing how the decisions made by the characters resulted in the events of the story. What decisions would they make that differ from those in the movie?
Self-knowledge	Art	Students will be placed in pairs. They will interview each other and create a collage of their partner's best qualities. Students will then discuss how they feel about the collage made about them, exploring discoveries of their good qualities. Were these known or hidden aspects of their persona?
Living drug-free	Social studies	Students will study the social fallout of drug use, focusing on the social problems that addiction creates, such as street people, crime, prostitution, and violence of the drug trade. What conclusions do they come to about drugs?
Making healthy choices about sex	Music	Students will evaluate the lyrics of different types of music in terms of messages about sexual choices. All types of music will be included. They will discuss how they feel about the music and these messages.
Understanding families	History	Students will study a famous family, such as a royal family or a prominent U.S. family for a particular historical period. Various situations within families will be explored, past and present. The student will then research the historical origins of their own family (past three generations) and then will be encouraged to share one interesting thing about their family tree.

(Continued)

TABLE 9.2 (Continued)

Developmental Curriculum	Academic Curriculum	Examples of How to Teach Developmental Curriculum in Academic Classroom
Understanding friends	Physical education	Students will be placed in small teams for safe trust-building experiences. Students will then discuss what allowed them to trust their teammates, relating that to qualities of healthy friendships.
Understanding stress	English/Business	Students will study the effect of advertising on their stress. What are the images and/or messages that increase stress? Decrease stress? Why?
Understanding life changes	Science	Students will study geological change in terms of the rise and erosion of mountains. Each phase of the birth to demise of mountains will be related to the life cycle of humans.
Understanding emotions	Music	Students will evaluate the effect of music on their mood and emotional state. They will relate those discoveries to their everyday lives.
Effective study skills	Math	Students will be given a pretest on a math skill, such as adding fractions. Then students will be allowed to review this skill by several different processes—reading, practice, talking to each other in groups, tutoring each other, and so on. They will then be given a posttest. Was their performance what they expected? Why or why not? What method of studying would work better for them?

TABLE 9.3 Curricular Integration: Secondary School

Intelligence	Academic Curriculum	Developmental Curriculum	Instructional Method
Verbal/Linguistic	English composition	Self-knowledge Self-understanding Self-acceptance Career dreams Job search skills	Journaling Poetry Concept papers Humor Creative writing Resume writing
	Literature	Relationships Character flaws: Addiction Obsession Insanity	Study of characters Storytelling Debate of characters
Logical/Mathematical	Mathematics	Decision making Problem solving Pro-con graphing Generation and evaluation of alternatives Calculating lifestyles	Syllogisms Outlining Logic/pattern games Calculating the cost of various lifestyles

TABLE 9.3 (Continued)

Intelligence	Academic Curriculum	Developmental Curriculum	Instructional Method
Visual/Spatial	Art Drawing Sculpture Photography	Career dreams Future family Lifestyle Self-concept Current family Emotional insight Emotion/behavior connections	Painting Drawing Imagery Mind mapping Collage Sculpture

Bodily/Kinesthetic	Physical education	ATODA resistance
		Relaxation training
		Health awareness
		Trust
		Self-protection
		Nonaggressive, self-
		  assertive training
			Exercise
			Physical experiences
			Ropes or challenge
			  experiences
			Martial arts

	Mechanical arts
	Home economics
		Career decision
		  making
		Goal setting
		Planning
			Working through a
			  problem
			Career experience

	Theater	Emotional expression Seeing emotions	Acting Role playing
Musical/Rhythmic	Music Band	Career imagery Stress management Relationships	Evaluating songs for 1. Career messages 2. Emotional messages Relaxation sounds

Interpersonal	Psychology
	Sociology
	Social studies
	History
	Political science
		Social skills
		Cooperation
		Relationships
		Trust
		Self-esteem
		Diversity
		  appreciation
		Social implications of
		  poverty
		Compassion
		Social responsibility
		Emotional communication
			Group experiences
			Conversation
			Empathy
			World court
			Jury duty
			Role playing
			Motivation exercises
			Trust exercises

Intrapersonal	Psychology	Knowing emotions Critical thinking skills Career decisions Personal values Relaxation	Self-reflection Emotional processing Metacognition techniques Personal application Meditation Journaling

Naturalist	Earth science
	Chemistry
	Biology, Botany
	Astronomy
	Health education
		ATODA resistance
		Healthy choices and
		  disease
		Social responsibility
		Family planning
		  choices
			Effects of toxins on
			  the human body
			Diseases (HIV, AIDS)
			Pollution
			Resource depletion

REFLECTION MOMENT

What experiences do you have in designing learning experiences? Are there steps you have found to be important to include in this process? For example, would you feel it necessary to practice the presentation of material before you take it into the classroom with real students? Rewrite the steps listed above, including any steps you feel would be helpful for you in the design and presentation of the developmental curriculum.

DELIVERING THE CURRICULUM

Exactly who delivers the developmental curriculum is an important question. In keeping with the concept that colleagues in the schools are our partners in the education of all students, it would be entirely appropriate that teachers would be as involved in the delivery of the developmental curriculum as they would be of the academic curriculum (Myrick, 1993). In many cases, teachers are already presenting topics from the developmental curriculum, but they may not recognize it as such. Meeting with the teacher advisory cadre will help you to determine where students are already learning the developmental curriculum and where additional efforts are needed to reach all students. Whether presented by the teacher alone, a teacher-counselor team, or the counselor alone, the developmental curriculum must be provided to all students.

Teaching Strategies and Lesson Planning

Effective classrooms are founded on respect, both personal and intellectual. Personal respect has been presented in terms of respect for each person and his or her perspective. Let's turn our attention to intellectual respect. What does this mean? You respect someone intellectually when you take the time to understand that person's level of intellectual functioning and then address him or her in terms that effectively match that level. Unfortunately, this is a common problem area for persons who are new to the classroom. Adults often talk down to young people, an error that will cause the adult to lose credibility in the eyes of the student (Valde, 2000).

Furthermore, intellectual respect also involves informing people about what is going to happen and inviting their consent, either tacit or explicit. For example, a physician who does not inform the patient that an injection will be administered, but administers it anyway, is not respecting the patient's right to choose or consent to the treatment. (Imagine how you would feel to be suddenly jabbed with a needle without consenting!) In the same way, a presenter in a classroom who does not inform students what the class entails is not respecting the student's right to choose whether to pay attention and thus, with that assumption, increases the likelihood that the student will choose to "check out." In the classroom, this means informing students the major areas of learning they will experience and asking them to join in the conversation. Getting their agreement up front that what you're presenting is meaningful, interesting, or important will increase their attention and decrease distracting classroom behavior.

There are a variety of models that address effective teaching and classroom management, but they all start from the same premise: when students are engaged in learning because you have structured the learning experience in a developmentally appropriate way, you will have a minimum of interruptions (Travers et al., 1993). In general, the qualities that define a well-structured learning experience include

- Having a meaningful, interesting lesson
- Getting the lesson started on time
- Having a clear idea of what you're doing from moment to moment
- Knowing what you want students to do and how they are to do it
- Establishing a respectful relationship with students

- Being aware of what students are doing
- Keeping the group focused on the topic
- Being able to design and manage transitions from topic to topic
- Being able to communicate expectations for appropriate behavior and consequences for inappropriate behavior
- Classroom rules that are clear, explicit, concrete, basic but global (Example: We will respect all opinions in here. We will communicate that respect by not using any put-downs.)
- Rules that are enforced fairly
- Addressing inappropriate behavior immediately
- Making corrections of behavior incrementally: proximity (getting closer to the unfocused student), subtle reminders (looking directly at the student, pointing at the work), verbal reminders (saying the student's name, asking him or her to focus), directions (telling the student to stop what he or she is doing and return to work), removal for a private conversation (asking the student to step into the hall where you can ask if he or she can work or if he or she needs to go somewhere for time out), to direct removal (depending on school procedure, sending the student or taking the student to the person or office responsible for discipline) (Eggen & Kauchak, 1994; Geltner & Clark, 2005; Goetz, Alexander, & Ash, 1992; Travers et al., 1993).

Since prevention of behavioral distractions is more effective than remediation, useful strategies that are consistent with developmentally appropriate classrooms include those proposed by Cuthbert (2000, pp. 128–129):

- Cohesion should be enhanced within the class, reminding everyone that we are all working together toward the same goal.
- Cooperation should be explained and modeled by the counselor, including taking turns, listening to others, respecting each other, and working together.
- Communication should be emphasized as the key to success for students. Allow students to express their feelings; use active listening, responding, and linking strategies to allow each student to feel heard and respected.
- Coaching allows you to help students learn new behavior by direct instruction and practice. Encouragement will help students feel safe taking risks as they practice.
- Contribution focus allows each student to feel that he or she has helped the group to reach its goals, through ideas, respectful quiet listening, or volunteering.
- Control issues are important to manage so that you lead the group without dominating it, yet maintain your role as the person responsible for content and delivery.
- Configuration refers to how the physical arrangement of the classroom is managed. Varying the layout of the room can add interest to the lesson and can help students break out of more passive learning modes.
- Closure, a summary of what is to be learned in the lesson, is important to remember. This allows the group to feel that the topic is finished and that it now "belongs" to them.
- Confidentiality, as the hallmark of the counseling profession, is important to address in large groups. Establishing a safe, inviting environment for conversation and learning could inspire students to share more than they intended. You need to remind the group that as listeners, everyone should be respectful of maintaining confidentiality; as speakers, everyone should carefully choose what they share with the group since confidentiality cannot be guaranteed.

Translating these insights into effective instruction involves knowing something about how to deliver instruction to a group of students. Hunter and Russell (1981) describe the seven steps of effective instruction, to which the insights of this chapter have been added. This constitutes what is known as a lesson plan.

1. Review previous learning and focus students' attention on what is to be learned. The example that will be used is from high school: "You already know that some relationships work over years and others do not last. Do you ever wonder why some marriages last and other don't? What are some of the reasons you've seen or heard that describe why relationships fail? What are the effects on people—adults and kids—when a marriage fails?"

2. Inform students about what they should be able to do at the end of the lesson and why it is important that they learn the material. *Example*: "Well, I don't want to see any of you live with those effects (insert class answers to the last question in the previous example: loss of income, loss of home, loss of children, loss of self-esteem). So let's talk today about relationships, what makes them healthy, what helps them last, so that you can think about the relationships that you choose. By the end of today's time, I'd like you to know what makes a healthy relationship and how to evaluate your relationships in terms of whether they are healthy."

3. Provide the lesson, using multiple intelligences and strategies for creative thinking. *Example*: Counselor talks about the qualities of healthy relationships and how to evaluate relationships, showing a clip from a popular movie that depicts a couple in a healthy exchange of ideas, agreement and disagreement, and compromise. The counselor asks "What qualities did these people show that illustrate healthy relationships?"

4. Model what you want the students to know. *Example*: "Here is a description of a relationship. Let's evaluate what is healthy and unhealthy about it. What do you notice about communication style?"

5. Throughout the lesson, check that students understand what you're presenting. *Example*: "How are we doing? Everyone understand?" If there are questions, address them.

6. Provide time for guided practice. *Example*: "Here's another description of a relationship. You can work independently or quietly with one other person" (for insights into providing choices, see Fay and Funk's [1995] *Teaching with Love and Logic*), "and we'll talk about it in ten minutes. Answer each question about the healthy and unhealthy aspects you notice. I'll walk around and answer any questions you have."

7. Review the major concepts of the lesson; then provide independent practice in the form of homework or a paper. *Example*: "OK, today we talked about healthy and unhealthy relationships in terms of . . . We took a look at some examples of each and applied those to evaluations of some relationships. Now I want you to go home and think of a relationship—either one you have been in or one that someone else (a friend, a relative) has been in. Don't tell me whose relationship it is, because that's not what's important. I want you to do two things. I want you to write out a description of that relationship, and then I want you to evaluate that relationship, using the questions on the case studies we talked about here in class today. Any questions? Then I'll see you tomorrow."

Finally, there is one important personal quality that comes from the literature for beginning teachers: the concept of "withitness." According to Gordon (1997), "beginning teachers need more than knowledge of content and teaching strategies. Insight into [student] culture is critical to success in managing a classroom" (p. 56). Withitness involves social insight, or knowing what is going on with students in the classroom. Effective educators understand how students communicate, both verbally and nonverbally; they know what students value and why; they know how students identify with others, whom they identify with, and why. Gordon proposes five strategies for developing and maintaining this connection with students (p. 58). First, become familiar with student/adolescent culture. Second, affirm the reality of students' concerns. If there is a prom coming up, their attention will be focused on that event. Use the event in your lesson. Third, relate content to students' outside interests: games, music, sports, fashions, trends. Fourth, know your students—their names, their interests, their social connections. And finally, share your humanity with students as appropriate. Let them get to know you as a human being and they will be more open to those times when your humanity shows. This includes some self-disclosure, humor, and your own emotional reality, or "weather."

Learning Communities and Classroom Management

As you may have surmised from prior chapters, respect is the hallmark of a learning community: respect for diversity, respect for the power of learning, respect for others, and respect for self. When students are engaged as collaborators and co-creators of their own learning, they are more likely to attend to the task of learning. When they are collaborators, they are invited into conversation within a learning community (Palmer, 1998), where educator and student work together for learning.

But what if the student does not want to join the conversation? *Teaching with love and logic* is derived from a system developed by Foster Cline (Fay & Cline, 1986), in which student misbehavior in the classroom is viewed as ways to avoid the pain of loss of self-esteem and autonomy (Fay & Funk, 1995). An artful blend of Adlerian natural and logical consequences with Control Theory/Reality Therapy's focus on choices (Glasser & Wubbolding, 1997), this approach highlights how young people test the limits of their environment. When this testing is brought into the classroom, an adult's natural reaction is to try to assert control. This sets up a cycle of testing, reacting, punishing, more testing, more extreme reacting, more rigorous punishing, and so on. Rather than perpetuate this system of control and punishment, Fay and Funk believe that people learn best from their own decisions and their own mistakes (p. 26).

The love and logic system consists of six steps. First, you build a relationship with students by noticing the students' likes and dislikes and quietly commenting on them to the students. These comments would not be judgmental or manipulative (not "I like the way you're doing that," but "I see you like skateboards"). Once these positive relationships are built, you set enforceable limits through enforceable statements of what you are willing to do. (Not "I will deduct ten points for each day late," but "I give full credit for papers turned in on time"). Third, you share control with students in terms of "small" decisions (not "I have to have all these papers in today," but "You can turn these in now or after lunch"). Fourth, if there are discipline problems, you implement disciplinary interventions that stop the undesirable behaviors, utilizing empathy and sorrow to connect with the student and to allow them to focus on the consequences ("Janet, I'm sorry that you are unable to work without talking. You can finish your work sitting over here or you can finish your work quietly at your desk. You decide."). Fifth, you would delay consequences to allow the student to think about her or his choices and to decide what he or she can do about the situation, such as in the following scenario:

TEACHER: "Tom, it seems hard for you to concentrate on your work today. What do you think might happen if you keep talking instead of working?"

STUDENT: "I might get a low grade."

TEACHER: "That's a possibility. What else?"

STUDENT: "I might have to stay after school."

TEACHER: "That's another possibility. Anything else?"

STUDENT: "You might not let me sit next to my friends."

TEACHER: "That's another possibility. Tell you what. I'll come back in a couple of minutes. If it seems you're still having trouble concentrating, I'll pick one of those suggestions." (Fay & Funk, 1995, p. 166)

Finally, as you can see in the above example, you give the same assignment the student initially had, underscoring your belief that he or she will learn from the consequence and make a better decision in the future.

This approach takes practice, since it takes unlearning the test-reaction-punishment cycle and replacing that with the connection-choice-empathic consequence cycle. For counselors who are delivering the developmental curriculum, the principles of this approach are intuitively engaging, since counseling involves the same choices—empathy and working through consequences. The practice and reflection involved in becoming comfortable with this approach are well worth it; becoming comfortable in the classroom determines how successful your teaching will be. And being an educator is an essential part of every school counselor's job.

Positive Behavior Support (PBS)

Positive Behavior Support (Sugai, n.d.) is a strategy from special education for schoolwide behavior management. Taken from strategies that have proven successful for students in special education, there is strong support for using these approaches in all schools. The Office of Special Education Programs in the U.S. Department of Education has a dedicated website at www.pbis.org that disseminates information on this approach.

Positive Behavior Support is a "major advance in schoolwide discipline" that emphasizes "schoolwide systems of support that include proactive strategies for defining, teaching, and supporting appropriate student behaviors to create positive school environments" (www.pbis.org). "Attention is focused on creating and sustaining primary (schoolwide), secondary (classroom), and tertiary (individual) systems of support that improve lifestyle results (personal, health, social, family, work, recreation) for all children and youth by making problem behavior less effective, efficient, and relevant, and desired behavior more functional" (www.pbis.org). This systemwide approach teaches and reinforces positive behavior while concurrently addressing negative behaviors. Insights are applied first in classroom and nonclassroom contexts, as teachers are advised:

1. Classroom positive expectations are taught to students and encouraged.
2. Classroom routines and cues are taught and encouraged.
3. Teachers are to engage in six to eight positive interactions with students to everyone negative interaction.
4. Teachers use active supervision and redirection for minor infrequent behavior errors.
5. Teachers use frequent precorrections for chronic errors.
6. Students with behavior challenges will have targeted social skill training and self-management instruction.
7. As needed, individualized instructional and curricular accommodations will be made to help each student learn in the least restrictive environment.
8. In nonclassroom settings, active supervision means scan for behavior, move close to precorrect for problems, and interact in positive ways.

Schoolwide Positive Behavior Support means that there is a common approach to discipline that all personnel endorse, with a clear set of positive expectations for behavior. There is a schoolwide continuum of procedures both for encouraging expected behaviors and for discouraging inappropriate behaviors; there are procedures for monitoring and evaluating both individual student behaviors and schoolwide responses to determine if adjustments are needed. As a research-based and evidence-based approach, Positive Behavior Support combines insights from special education, effective classroom instruction, learning theory, and educational psychology to create an effective strategy for behavior management in schools.

REFLECTION MOMENT

Think about your own school years. Can you remember being in trouble? Was that experience handled in a way to allow you to learn, or were you yelled at? Imagine that situation again, recalling as many details as possible. Knowing what you know now, what should have been done to make that a learning experience? Imagine yourself as the person who imposed the punishment; what do you think he or she was feeling as the situation unfolded? If you could go back to that moment and take all these wonderful ideas of classroom management with you, what would you do to enhance the learning of that young person?

EDUCATING ADULT STAKEHOLDERS

To foster the development of healthy systems, school counselors should also consider themselves educators of families, schools, and communities. There are many references in the literature to support the need for counselors to educate parents, school colleagues, and community colleagues. And as you can see from Appendix A, Program Goals for Adult Partners in the DAP Model, there is no shortage of ways to help our adult partners develop a greater understanding and appreciation of young people, schools, and the educational process. As the counselor of a CSCP, you are aware of systemic issues that impede our students' potential for success; as an educator, you can see that many of these issues can be addressed through educating our adult partners.

There are calls to provide parent education in almost every issue of professional journals related to school counseling and counseling. Educating parents has been called an essential part of every school counselor's training program (Crespi & Howe, 2000; Ritchie & Partin, 1994) to help counselors address parents' rationalization and learned helplessness (A. J. Clark, 1995) and to address systemic problems both within the family and between the family and school (K. M. Davis & Lambie, 2005; Evans & Carter, 1997). Furthermore, counselors should provide programs to inform parents about the school and to promote parent involvement in the student's education, which can help students feel more connected with the school, address problems with communication, and support at-risk students (Christiansen, 1997; A. J. Clark, 1995; Guiffrida & Douthit, 2010; Jackson & White, 2000; Peeks, 1993). In addition, educating parents and families about the issues or potential issues of their students can provide more systemic interventions (Talleyrand, 2010), in keeping with the ASCA National Model. Finally, it is essential that parents understand the counselor's role in the school so that parental insights can be tapped and parents will support the value of the CSCP (R. L. Gibson, 1990; L. S. Kaplan, 1997).

The task of educating our adult partners continues with the need to educate our colleagues in the schools. Teachers can benefit from better knowledge about current issues, including family issues such as homelessness, divorce, and custody (Evans & Carter, 1997; Strawser et al., 2000; Wilcoxon & Magnuson, 1999), and student issues such as ADHD, being an ESL (English as a second language) student, being at risk, sexuality and sexual abuse, diversity and systemic oppression, and sexual harassment (Christiansen, 1997; Erk, 1999; Goodman & West-Olatunji, 2010; James & Burch, 1999; McCall-Perez, 2000; C. B. Stone, 2000). Teachers can also benefit from training in interpersonal communication skills (Rice & Smith, 1993), dealing with their personal issues (A. J. Clark, 1995), and better understanding the role of the school counselor (R. L. Gibson, 1990; Jackson & White, 2000). Furthermore, principals can also benefit from a better understanding of the role of the counselor (Burnham & Jackson, 2000; Crespi & Howe, 2000; R. L. Gibson, 1990; L. S. Kaplan, 1997; Ponec & Brock, 2000) and from better appreciation of school systemic issues (C. B. Stone, 2000).

Finally, our colleagues in the community, including school boards, colleges and universities, community mental health providers, employers, and the community at large, could benefit from a better understanding of our students, our schools, and our role in the school (Bemak, 2000; R. L. Gibson, 1990; Gysbers, Lapan, & Jones, 2000; L. S. Kaplan, 1997; Luongo, 2000; McCall-Perez, 2000; Taylor & Adelman, 2000).

REFLECTION MOMENT

Imagine yourself in the role of educating other adults on these subjects. Which of these can you see yourself talking about with parents? With teachers? With administrators? With the public? Which of these topics would you present with the most passion and enthusiasm?

Educating Adult Partners: Considerations

It is important in this discussion that we briefly touch on the concept of "readiness to learn." This concept is as applicable to adults as it is to young students, and the essence is this: You can lead a horse to water but you can't make it drink. You can, however, make it thirsty in the hopes that it will drink because it *wants* the water. Strong (1968) found that clients evaluated counselors on the basis of their expertness, perceived interpersonal attractiveness (similarities), and trustworthiness; when the counselor was found to be sufficiently expert, similar, and trustworthy, the client felt greater investment in the counseling process. These same variables also influence the investment learners have in the learning process when persuading adults that change (in their opinions of students, families, schools, or the counseling profession) is appropriate.

Translated into concrete suggestions, your expertise in academic, career, and personal/social development should be introduced. Your graduate education in school counseling has provided you with unique training and insights into young people, schools, and the processes of education and growth. You will also want to highlight your similarities to those in your audience, since this tends to increase others' perceptions of you as a role model. Furthermore, your trustworthiness needs to be established; your goal is to foster those conditions that have been proven to be the most conducive to the education, growth, and development of your students. Assuring your audience that you have no ulterior motive, by either example or direct statement of the ethics of the profession, standards of confidentiality, or professional associations, helps them to know that you are not "selling them a bill of goods."

Sometimes, however, in spite of your best efforts, some of your adult partners will not want to learn anything new. They believe that nothing anyone can say is going to change their thinking on a subject. Your approach to these persons would be to assure them that you respect their right to their opinions (as long as those opinions and resulting behaviors fall within the limits of the law) and that, should they ever need to discuss this further, you would be happy to discuss it. At this point, all you can do is hope that they will come to you with questions about students, schools, families, teachers, or the counseling profession, if such questions ever arise.

Putting all these suggestions together for use in educating our adult partners would yield the following suggestions:

1. Know your audience. It is helpful to understand the extent of formal education of the people in the audience so that you can target their vocabulary. For example, when educating teachers, you can use the jargon and terminology of the educational environment, but with parents, avoid the use of jargon.

2. Remember your training in multiple intelligences and present information in multiple formats: words, examples, graphs, exercises, art, music, or examples from sports, science, food, architecture, television, movies, or other venues.

3. Be informed, but do not try to "fake it." If you don't know something, admit it, promise to find out, and arrange to get back to the questioner. Adults are insulted by know-it-alls who are not respectful of the audience's ability to detect false statements. Just one attempt to disguise a guess as a fact will destroy your credibility, trustworthiness, and expertise.

4. Be enthusiastic and passionate. As we will see in the chapter on leadership and advocacy, your passion can convince others to consider what you're presenting. Your enthusiasm creates an emotional bond with the audience that enables the learning to have more meaning and long-term impact. Your role as advocate means that you must have a greater sense of social justice and be willing to challenge others in the name of that greater justice.

5. In the presentation, begin with high levels of structure and expertise, then move to an awareness and appreciation of all perspectives on this topic, and then ask them to think of situations in which they found this to be true for themselves. Finish with an affirmation of their right as adults to make their own decisions, but indicate the problems that can arise if they do not apply the insights you are offering (but don't be an alarmist). Remind them that you are happy to consult with them in the future on this topic.

6. Do not lecture *at* your audience. Your audience is comprised of adults, and adults feel insulted when someone scolds them for incorrect behavior and feel patronized when someone talks at them in a lecture-hall format. Parents, teachers, administrators, and community colleagues do the best they can with students, based on what they believe students need. Your job is to help them to better understand what students need and to help them design strategies to best meet those student needs—not to shame or embarrass them.

7. Remember that the audience's perceptions of your expertise, similarity to them, and trustworthiness are important. Establish your expertise by sharing your professional training and experience (as appropriate). Establish your similarity to the audience by sharing relevant personal experiences or personal struggles with this topic (as appropriate). Establish your trustworthiness by assuring them that your sole intention is to help them function better in their lives (as appropriate).

8. Do not be surprised or frustrated with resistance to your topic. In every group, there will be those who will not accept what you have to say. Do not dismiss them, but encounter their resistance with calm equanimity. Find value in their contribution and, if you have time, explore those situational variables that made their experience an exception to your point. In this way, their objection becomes additional support for your topic.

REFLECTION MOMENT

What have been your experiences persuading or educating adults? Have those experiences been positive or negative for you? What skills would you like to improve to make those experiences more successful? What can you do now to develop or refine those skills?

EDUCATING AND CURRICULUM DELIVERY IN ACTION

As with all counselor activities, there is variation when looking at the way that educating looks at each educational level. At Ford Elementary School in Tucson, Arizona, the counselor reports that she uses educating as one of her primary ways to provide a CSCP to her students: she is a leader for the school's use of the program "Bully-proofing Your School," and she uses the ASCA National Standards for the elementary levels. She delivers the developmental curriculum to all her students, devoting 40 to 50 percent of her time to the guidance (developmental) curriculum. The topics of her curriculum derive from her work with teachers, and she uses the large number of online counseling-based lessons available from her district. In addition, she typically enters several different classrooms on a daily basis from 8 A.M. to 10 A.M., what is called a "literacy block" period to provide lessons or individual/group counseling.

At the middle school level, the counselors at Sequoia Middle School in Fontana, California, use character education as the foundation of the guidance (developmental) curriculum, and report spending 35 percent of their time delivering the curriculum. With the increased focus on classroom accountability in California, it was initially determined that counselors would provide curriculum through the elective and physical education classes. These classes combined seventh- and eighth-grade students, which did not allow for grade-level division of classroom guidance topics. To accommodate this blending of students, the guidance curriculum focuses on seventh-grade competencies and indicators for all students one year, and eighth-grade competencies and indicators for all students the next year. Seventh-grade competencies/indicators focus on study skills and eighth grade focuses on decision-making skills. The same class and topic configuration is maintained so that all students enrolled for two consecutive years will receive all of the lessons.

Initially, the Character Education lessons were delivered by PE teachers, who were assigned to provide lessons to all students at the beginning of the school year. The leadership team at Sequoia determined that ongoing lessons were needed throughout the year, which has led to all teachers providing Character Education sessions within their curriculum to promote positive behaviors and relationships on campus. The Sequoia school faculty and staff have "embraced the fact that in order for children to learn with their heads, they have to feel with their heart" (personal communication, N. Jarman-Dunn, 2005). This change has led to 90 percent of the school faculty, staff, and students participating in the Character Education program.

Character Education lessons are only part of the faculty and staff involvement in implementation of the guidance curriculum. Examples of faculty and staff helping students (beyond their "regular academic responsibilities") include teaching Life Laws lessons, participating in College Day and Red Ribbon Week, club advising, mentoring, Career Plan integration, Mix It Up Day interaction with students, and supporting counselor-led guidance lessons.

In addition, parent workshops have been offered on the topics of bullying, academic improvement, and high school graduation requirements. Work and family demands placed on parents have led to low turnout for some evening workshops, so the counselors have now prepared a series of workshops that are held once a month on multiple topics at different times of day. This strategy allows for flexibility in the parents' work schedule and parents have direct input into topic choice for any of the sessions on the given day.

In addition, the website for the school counseling program provides parenting tips addressing such areas as drug and alcohol prevention, college information, community and national services for adolescents, information on teen health issues, and discipline and communication styles. The website includes a link to a parent conflict survey created by Positive Parenting for Teens on the University of Minnesota's Extension Service website. This survey is straightforward and convenient for parents to use in gaining understanding of their child(ren) and themselves by interpreting responses to communication and discipline conflicts.

Finally, at the secondary level, Wakefield High School in Raleigh, North Carolina, infuses the developmental curriculum into the academic experience. Reporting that the counselors devote 15 percent of their time to delivering the guidance (development) curriculum, the school counselors do classroom guidance by grade level, generally beginning in November of the school year. By this time the counselors have already met individually with all seniors for senior interviews. As the school utilizes 4 × 4 block scheduling, the counselors meet for classroom guidance with half of all freshmen, sophomores, and juniors during the first semester and half during the second semester. Academic-related guidance is done through the English classes. Half of the students in the class are taken to the media center while the other half remain in the classroom focusing on their academic studies. During classroom guidance, the counselors focus on high school graduation requirements and the importance of academic success. These sessions are done in conjunction with the career development coordinator to make the idea of success more meaningful for the students. During the classroom guidance sessions, the students complete graduation plans and select their course of study. The counselors also provide copies and explain student transcripts in terms of college admissions. The counselors may also do some need-based lessons depending on teacher requests in certain classes. Examples include lessons on study skills, time management, PSAT interpretations, and college admissions.

Part of the classroom guidance includes career development activities. All students complete career interest inventories. The freshmen participate in a program called Futures for Kids. The juniors go to the College Foundation website where, in addition to completing interest inventories, they establish accounts at no charge with the College Foundation. This gives them access to information on careers, links to colleges and universities, and a universal college application. The counselors have the students take interest inventories online to infuse technology with the lessons.

CASE STUDY REVISITED

Integration

Go back and reread Donna's lunchroom conversation. Now that you have read the chapter, consider the following questions:

1. What messages are embedded in the statements made by the teachers? What insights can you draw about the constraints placed on the CSCP in that school?
2. What ideas do you have for classroom presentations on the subject of alcohol and substance abuse?
3. What ideas do you have for parent programs? For teacher programs? ■

Suggested Readings

Cline, F., & Fay, J. (1990). *Parenting with love and logic: Teaching children responsibility*. Colorado Springs, CO: Pinon Press. This book is the foundation of the Parenting with Love and Logic program, a very successful and valuable parent program.

Dinkmeyer, D., Sr., McKay, G. D., & Dinkmeyer, D., Jr. (1997*). The parent's handbook: Systematic Training for Effective Parenting (STEP)*. Circle Pines, MN: American Guidance Service. This book is the foundation of the STEP program, also a very successful and valuable parent program.

Fay, J., & Funk, D. (1995). *Teaching with love and logic*. Golden, CO: Love and Logic Press. An extensive look at the effective use of choice in a school and classroom setting, this book provides useful strategies for working with students. The key to these strategies is that students learn to want to act better, reducing the need for adults to force them to behave.

Goldstein, A. P. (1999). *The Prepare curriculum: Teaching prosocial competencies*. Champaign, IL: Research Press. Based on Social Learning Theory, this book is the result of the author's training experiences with youth who needed retraining in aggression reduction, stress reduction, and prejudice reduction. Structured small- and large-group experiences are outlined to enable the reader to use these lessons with prevention and intervention developmental curricula.

King, P. M., & Kitchener, K. S. (1994). *Developing reflective judgment: Understanding and promoting intellectual growth and critical thinking in adolescents and adults*. San Francisco: Jossey-Bass. This book gives the reader a full discussion of learning issues for adults, providing insights for promoting learning.

MacKinnon-Slaney, F. (1994). The adult persistence in learning model: A road map to counseling services for adult learners. *Journal of Counseling and Development, 72*, 268–275. This article is extremely helpful in articulating the relationship between learning and counseling in adults.

Mager, R. F. (1997). *Preparing instructional objectives: A critical tool in the development of effective instruction* (3rd ed.). Atlanta, GA: The Center for Effective Performance. A comprehensive discussion of how to establish the foundation of any well-developed learning experience.

O'Connor, K. (2001). The principal's role in report card grading. *NASSP Bulletin, 85* (621), 37–46. Although intended for a high school principal, this article outlines strategies for grading that could be very useful for counselors who must grade the work of students in the developmental curriculum.

Paisley, P. O., & Hubbard, G. T. (1994). *Developmental school counseling programs: From theory to practice*. Alexandria, VA: American Counseling Association. A compilation of developmental curriculum ideas and modules.

Palmer, P. (1998). *The courage to teach: Exploring the inner landscape of a teacher's life*. San Francisco: Jossey-Bass. A powerful discussion of what constitutes teaching with passion, combining pedagogy and learning into a "community of truth."

Root-Bernstein, R., & Root-Bernstein, M. (1999). *Sparks of genius: The thirteen thinking tools of the world's most creative people*. Boston: Houghton Mifflin. These authors present their ideas on creative thinking and the tools to enhance creativity in very practical terms, with many quotes and examples from science, the arts, and the humanities. Any classroom would be enriched by applying these ideas to modern education.

Collaboration and Consultation

LEARNING OBJECTIVES

By the end of this chapter, you will

1. Understand the value of collaboration and consultation

2. Have established an understanding of collaboration and reasons why collaboration is an effective way of working in schools

3. Have learned contemporary approaches to collaboration (e.g., Adelman and Taylor's model of collaboration)

4. Understand the ways in which family-school-community collaboration enhances students' development, well-being, and learning

5. Value the ways in which collaboration can engage parents, guardians, and families to promote the academic, career, and personal/social development of students

6. Have learned strategies to promote, develop, and enhance effective collaboration teams within the school and the larger community

7. Realize ways to build effective collaboration teams of school staff, parents, and community members to promote the academic, career, and personal/social development of students

8. Have discovered the importance of locating resources in the community that can be used in the school to improve student achievement and success

9. Be able to describe differences between consultation and other forms of helping

10. Understand systems theories, models, and process of consultation in school system settings

11. Understand ways in which consultation practices can assist students, parents, teachers, and all other partners to act on behalf of their children to address problems that affect student success in school

12. Have discovered the value of consulting with teachers, staff, and community-based organization to promote student academic, career, and personal/social development

13. Appreciate a variety of consultation models and processes, including a generic process model of consultation

14. Be able to identify which model of consultation will fit best with which situation

15. Understand resistance and ways to address resistance in consultation

CASE STUDY

Yer's Island

Yer and Peg meet for lunch every Friday. They are both high school counselors in neighboring districts, and find reciprocal support in their weekly lunch meetings. They talk about school-related and counseling issues freely, without fear of unprofessional disclosure. (Being aware of confidentiality, however, they never use names or details.)

Today Yer needed help with a problem she was encountering with a group of teachers, specifically, the Social Studies teachers. "Peg, you know me. I'm a patient woman—I'm fairly tolerant and accepting. But this group of teachers this is about to push me over the edge! I can't seem to get them to understand that they are not reaching the students or educating them like they should be. In fact, I think we have the weakest Social Studies department in the district."

"Whoa! Back up. You are really keyed up. Slow down. What are they doing, exactly?" Peg urged.

Yer continued, "You see, they send me through email the names of *all* these kids they want me to work with. The teachers state that the kids are doing poorly in class and will most likely fail if I don't do something. That's a good thing—at least they care. The problem is that I think part of the problem the teachers are having with the kids are the teachers themselves. They hound me with, 'Did you see her? Did you work with him?' and it's only been two days since they brought me the names."

"You know, Yer, that doesn't sound like a problem to me. . . ." Peg began.

"Peg, let me finish, please. There's more to the story. A few of the kids have told me that they are bored to tears in the classes. The students went on to tell me that they mainly watch films or work out of packets in class. They say it's not all the Social Studies teachers, just mainly the new ones, fresh out of their undergrad."

"Wow, that does seem like a situation where you could use additional information and a few conversations. Have you met with the department? Observed the classes these particular kids are in?" Peg offered gently.

"No, I haven't. I am leary to speak to the department and yet I know I must do something. I have a pretty good relationship with the chair of the Social Studies Department. However, I really haven't gotten to know the newer teachers yet. I think not having a relationship with them is what is preventing me from moving forward."

"Sounds to me like you want a stronger and more collaborative relationship with the new teachers, and the chair of the Social Studies Department, which would allow you to address the issues with the teachers and the students," Peg shared.

Yer stared into space thoughtfully, her mind heavy in wonder. "I'm going to have to really give this a lot of thought. Maybe I need to gather additional information, build stronger relationships with the teachers and the department so that together we can tackle this issue. Perhaps the teachers need support and assistance with their teaching that they are afraid to bring to the department. Maybe I can help bridge the teachers in a way that enhances both the teacher's and the students' experiences in the classroom," Yer expressed.

"What specifically do you think you might do? It might help to talk through you plan," Peg prompted.

"I'm not sure. This one's going to be tough. I'm going to have to find a good way to approach this so that everybody wins."

CHALLENGE QUESTIONS

1. Put yourself in Yer's position. What feelings emerge for you as you consider approaching this issue?
2. If you were Yer, how would you go about gathering additional information and moving forward? What specific steps would you take?
3. How do you see collaboration and consultation rectifying this situation? ■

COLLABORATION

Nowhere is the idea that it takes a village to raise a child more prominent than in today's schools. The vast array of multifaceted issues, needs, and twenty-first-century requirements renders collaboration a vital component in educating today's young people. Collaboration between groups, such as schools, universities, communities, and professions, appears to have a positive influence on student academic achievement and school experiences (Brabeck, Walsh, & Latta, 2003). Likewise, collaboration between administration, teachers, staff, paraprofessionals, pupil services professionals, and parents affects students' success in school. Schoffner and Briggs (2001) noted that collaboration brings with it its own unique challenges and hurdles, yet produces positive communication, services, and programming outcomes for students' personal and academic achievement. Thus, school counselors must enter their buildings embracing the knowledge, awareness, and skills of successful collaboration and see it as an essential professional school counseling service.

Collaboration, defined in several ways, takes the shape of a variety relationships and encounters. *Grolier-Webster International Dictionary of the English Language* (1975) defined "collaborate" as working together with others, cooperating. In his discussion of conditions that help students graduate, Drew (2004) elaborates further, defining collaboration as the building of interdependent systems to achieve a common goal that cannot be achieved by each entity working alone. ASCA (2005) highlights the role of collaboration in the National Model, stating that "school counselors build effective teams by encouraging genuine collaboration among all school staff to work toward the common goals of equity, access, and academic success of every student" (p. 25). Lawson (2003) identified connecting and communicating, cooperation, coordination, community building, and contracting as important components to successful collaboration. Furthermore, S. Baker, Robichaud, Westforth Dietrich, Wells, and Schreck (2009) noted that collaboration entails a process of discovering ways to unravel and decipher challenges together in cooperation.

C. B. Stone and Dahir (2004) emphasize that "effective collaboration begins with a sincere need to make collaboration work . . ." (p. 184). School counselors are perfect for collaboration because of the unique qualities and skills they possess. However, be aware that mobilizing people and bringing them together in a collaborative fashion is not for the "faint of heart" (p. 184). Effective collaboration requires courage, a willingness to risk, objectivity, ego strength, flexibility, adaptability, willingness to compromise, confidence, and a spirit and attitude of optimism that exudes cooperation and perseverance (C. B. Stone & Dahir, 2004).

School counselor collaboration generally involves three domains: with schools, with community agencies, and with families (Bemak, 2000). Examples of collaboration across these domains include serving on district and administrative councils, student IEP teams, and school climate initiatives; teaming with administration to decipher and interpret achievement data; working with teachers on the design and delivery of curriculum; and addressing *all* student concerns. Additional examples include joining with pupil services professionals on prevention initiatives or professional development workshops, working with parent-teacher associations, or collaborating with parents to address a concern they have with their child (Galassi & Akos, 2007).

REFLECTION MOMENT

Think about times when you were involved in collaborative relationships or teams. What worked? What did not work? What attitudes and feelings do you maintain toward collaboration, in general, based on your experiences with collaboration?

One of the more vital collaborative relationships within a school involves pupil services professionals (school counselors, school psychologists, school social workers, and school nurses), who collectively provide students with essential services and interventions (Staton & Gilligan, 2003). In recent years, the pupil services professions, particularly counselors, social workers, and psychologists, have experienced close alignment and overlap in their roles and functions. This evolution has strengthened the availability of services to students and families, but has resulted in confusion and barriers. A general lack of knowledge and comprehension of each profession's philosophies, roles, and functions, coupled with budget constraints and turf wars, have resulted in tension between pupil services professionals about their professional practice in the schools (Staton & Gilligan, 2003). Furthermore, Staton and Gilligan reported that the barriers that interfere with successful collaboration between school counselors and school psychologists most often include lack of time, administrative support, and/or resistance from either counselors or psychologists. With pupil services professionals spread thinly across buildings, it is no wonder that counselors and psychologists find little time to collaborate. Similarly, building and district administration often lack a clear understanding of the similarities and differences between pupil services professionals, which creates potential for role ambiguity and confusion between who does what when, where, and with whom. Resistance can often emerge due to numerous factors, including a lack of education and training in models of collaboration in school counseling programs. Incorporating the services of the school counselor with those of the school psychologist will reduce overlap and will draw on each other's professional expertise (Rowley, 2000).

Staton and Gilligan (2003) presented a model of collaboration training that focuses on supporting graduate students' development of a professional identity. School counselors who enter their buildings with a strong sense of self-efficacy and identity are better equipped to negotiate relationships with others; define, give voice to, and advocate for their professional role and function; and request time to collaborate with pupil services professionals and other vital stakeholders. Learning experiences for school counselors-in-training that promote professional identity include reflective journal writing, presenting workshops on collaboration to school staff during practicum or internship, and shadowing each pupil services professional. Teaching graduate students to think systemically is an additional way to promote collaboration and embed collaboration into the professional identity of new school counselors. These types of activities promote professional identity, break down barriers between services providers, and ultimately strengthen the services and programs provided to students. The authors stress the systemic nature of their model in helping graduate students develop their own sense of professional identity, gain an accurate understanding of other professions, and learn to communicate across professions effectively.

Additional options for collaborating within schools include:

1. Building collaborative teams to address the systemic issues of students who are at risk or who are not functioning effectively in the school (Bemak, 2000; Keys, Bemak, & Carpenter, 1998). This team approaches the discussion with a focus on cultural, community, and school issues that might interfere with the student's functioning, and brings the support of various school professionals to that discussion (Jackson & White, 2000).
2. Collaborating with special education experts and other professionals in the schools to
   a. support special education transition services for students who live with disabilities (Sitlington, Clark, & Kolstoe, 2000)
   b. support the holistic development of students with learning disabilities (Koehler & Kravets, 1998) and at-risk and violent youth (Barr & Parrett, 2001)
3. Merging the services of all school-based mental health providers in school-based health clinics, mental health clinics, and "multiple systems" clinics to provide one-stop access to assistance. Examples cited include integrating violence prevention, parent training, tutoring, daycare, and bereavement with medical services (Porter, Epp, & Bryant, 2000).
4. Collaborating with principals to evaluate the school climate for violence, racism, sexual harassment, and gang activity; to help in the selection of new teachers; to deal more effectively with discipline issues that affect the school by adding a counseling component to the school's discipline policy; to address issues raised by athletic programs in the school; and to assist with the development of the school's crisis plan (Niebuhr, Niebuhr, & Cleveland, 1999).

REFLECTION MOMENT

What is your understanding of the profession of school social worker, school psychologist, and school nurse? In what ways does each profession support the academic achievement and school success of students? What will you need to accomplish in order to prepare yourself to create effective collaborative pupil services relationships?

Besides collaborating with pupil services teams, building collaborative partnership with school staff, parents, and the community is a critical role and function of school counselors. The literature is growing in recognition of collaboration as an essential component to students' academic and personal/social success. Griffin and Galassi (as cited in Griffin & Farris, 2010) expressed the importance of a collaborative and integrated approach to addressing students' mental health and functioning. They went on to assert that "many parents and teachers are often unaware of the resources available and how to access those resources" (p. 249). To highlight the process of building those community collaborations, Griffin and Farris (2010) advocated that school counselors utilize *community asset mapping*, which pulls together existing community resources that all stakeholders can access. The authors detail a four-step process for creating a community asset map, which is: (1) Develop a multidisciplinary team (e.g., school counseling advisory council); (2) review a current list of identified community resources, programs, and services, including new ones; (3) contact individuals and resources; and (4) develop and maintain a resource guide and map the assets of each resource. Griffin and Farris encourage school counselors to start small and build the map over time, gradually adding new resources and updating the guide as necessary. The process of community asset mapping is invaluable because of the connections that school counselors make with community agencies, organizations, and professionals, which can assist and support all stakeholders in meeting the needs of students.

Community asset mapping is one means of collaboration that pulls together valuable resources for stakeholders and in the process immerses school counselors in their communities. School-family-community collaboration is yet another means of strengthening school counselors' connections with their community and valuable resources for meeting students' needs, as we will see below.

MODELS OF COLLABORATION

Adelman and Taylor Model of Collaboration

Sink (2002) conceptualized the school as a system. Likewise, "Schaef and Fassel (1992) described a school district as a mega system, a school as a system, and classrooms as subsystems" (as cited in Sink, 2002, p. 360). Pioneers in the discussion of systemic collaboration among all stakeholders and partners are Howard Adelman and Linda Taylor (Adelman & Taylor, 1994, 1997, 1998; Taylor & Adelman, 2000). This researcher/practitioner team outlined a model of collaboration that involves all stakeholders effectively in the process of educating young people. They based the foundation of their approach on three observations. First, school professionals do not integrate functions well. The school psychologist, the school social worker, the school nurse, and the school counselor have many overlapping duties and professional goals (helping students function in school). Adelman and Taylor noted that these professional services are fragmented and seldom coordinated. Professionals might feel territorial ownership; the importance of one's own role overshadows those of the other school professionals (Adelman & Taylor, 1994). Second, compounding this fragmentation, school professionals often feel threatened by the intrusion of community professionals in the school setting, creating alienation from community resources and isolating school professionals and students (Adelman & Taylor, 1998). Third, professionals and educators do not consider the needs of the vast majority of students in the design and delivery of programs and services.

Adelman and Taylor (1998) described the typical student population within a school on a continuum. At one end of the continuum, there are the few students who come to school "motivationally ready and able" to learn for that hour (Adelman & Taylor, 1998, p. 146). These students experience no barriers to their learning; they engage in the instructional component of the school (defined as classroom teaching and enrichment activities) and consequently experience the desired outcome of the instructional component (learning). At the other end of the continuum are the high-needs students who are "avoidant, very deficient in current capabilities, have a disability, or major health problems" (Adelman & Taylor, 1998, p. 146). Most school support services are designed in response to these students, the high-need students. However, the very intensity of these needs consume much of the school professionals' time, leaving little time for the needs of any other students.

The vast majority of students fall somewhere in the middle of the continuum and these are the students whose needs go unmet. In any given hour, many of these students are "not very motivated, lacking prerequisite knowledge and skills, possess different learning rates and styles, and experience minor vulnerabilities" such as emotional upsets, concerns about home functioning, minor health concerns, and so on (Adelman & Taylor, 1998, p. 146). For these students, school professionals and educators who happen to notice the barriers to their learning might address them in a piecemeal manner, but we have failed to design student support services to address the needs experienced by this considerable mass of students.

From their observations and awareness of student needs, Adelman and Taylor (1994, 1998; Taylor & Adelman, 2000) proposed the need for an "enabling component" that supports and enhances instruction built by collaboration among all educational professionals with support from the family and community. To implement this concept, schools must rethink how they design programs and provide services to students. Taylor and Adelman (2000) view collaboration as multidisciplinary, interdisciplinary, and transdisciplinary. To them, collaboration entails combining resources, programs, professionals, families, and volunteers to integrate services and programs to meet the needs of all students.

Adelman and Taylor call for school counselors to carry out new roles in this restructuring process, including increased coordination of programs and services within schools and communities, focus on learner support activities related to broad awareness of barriers to learning, and assuming leadership over the change process (Taylor & Adelman, 2000). They cite the Memphis School District as one example in which school counselors have been assigned leadership roles in "creating readiness for systemic change; mapping, analyzing, and redeploying relevant school resources; and working to strengthen connections between school, home, and other community resources" (p. 306). Clearly, this model of collaboration is very broad-based, suggesting how services can be meshed, how collaboratives can be transdisciplinary, and how schools can be transformed into caring, respectful places.

REFLECTION MOMENT

What comes to your mind when you envision engaging in collaboration based on the assumptions of Adelman and Taylor? What assets do you bring to their model? What challenges do you face in light of the Adelman and Taylor model?

CASTT a Wider Net through Partnering

C. B. Stone and Dahir (2006) created CASTT, the acronym for Community, Administrators, Students, Teachers, and Technology, to describe school counseling programs that base their success and achievement around the partnerships they have developed with their community, administrators, students, teachers, and technology. The phrase "CASTT a wider net" represents the ways in which CASTT partnerships extend services efficiently across domains or stakeholders with a minimum of duplicated efforts. The anticipated outcome is a strong and viable school counseling program that thrives from the investment and "wide" commitment of the represented partnerships. For example, community CASTT partnerships include parents, human services agencies, neighborhood associations and groups, businesses, colleges, universities, and other postsecondary institutions, and alumni (C. B. Stone & Dahir, 2006). This wide net of partnerships brings to the school counseling program rich resources, vast perspectives, and a variety of stakes in the education of students.

Collaborative Inclusion Model

Clark and Bremen (2009) created a collaborative model for school counselors and teachers that represent various consultation practices. The model recommends a seven-step inclusive intervention process—meaning, the teacher and counselor collaborate, plan, implement, and evaluate interventions in the classroom where *all* students can benefit. The seven recommended steps are:

1. Referral of the student to the school counselor that may come from a teacher, administrator, parent, or self-referring student.
2. Identification of the problem: Gathering information and a review of available records; talking with stakeholders, such as teacher(s), parents, and the administrator.
3. Classroom observation: Observing child's affective and academic status as well as interactions with teacher(s) and peers.
4. Plan in-class intervention: What goals and steps you, as the school counselor, hope to take. It will be optimal to involve the teacher at this stage. It is important to note the strengths of the student(s).
5. Implement intervention and modify as necessary. This step may also include the infusion of peer tutoring/mentoring to offer continued student support.
6. Develop a plan to leave with teacher and student(s) for ongoing follow-up after the counselor finishes the classroom intervention. This stage may include reinforcements, system of feedback, and a protocol to be followed.
7. Evaluate and monitor the intervention: The counselor may want to check in with the student(s) and teacher on a periodic basis or do a follow-up classroom observation. Student databases that are updated daily or weekly at the school level are becoming more readily accessible to school counselors and may be used to monitor discipline referrals, absences, and grades (pp. 87–88).

The school counselor and teacher may decide to implement one-on-one interventions, work with a few students at a time, or create small-group interventions, which is a shift from traditional school counseling interventions whereby the school counselor removes students from the classroom for services. The collaborative inclusion model supports the school counselor remaining in the classroom where *all* students can learn valuable lifelong skills, increase learning, and create a cooperative and cohesive classroom environment.

Collaborative Culturally Competent Schools

Simcox, Nuijens, and Lee (2006) proposed an ecological and culturally sensitive model of collaboration between school counselors and school psychologists to increase cultural competence in schools based on Murphy, DeEsch, and Strein's (1998) and Rowley's (2000) earlier ideas. The model presents a collaborative partnership between school counselors and school psychologists in the development, implementation, and evaluation of interventions at four primary levels of services for students, parents and families, educators, and the community. The four levels are:

> *Level I: Student-Centered Interventions:* entail promoting and supporting the academic success of *all* children and youth utilizing individual, small-group, and consultative interventions.
>
> *Level II: Family Empowerment:* focuses on empowering families through presentations and forums that include such topics as curriculum, school practices, assessment and placement, parent-teacher relations, and educational administration.
>
> *Level III: Collegial Consultation:* aims at creating professional development opportunities for educational staff and professionals in ways that promote culturally sensitive, response, and competent schools. Workshops and seminars might target dispelling cultural

myths, creating and maintaining culturally competent educational practices and strategies, or working with children and youth with limited English proficiency (LEP).

Level IV: Brokering Community Resources: whereby schools and communities can find common ground and come together in the education and school success of young people. Collaboration at this level might include increasing community awareness, getting community leaders involved with schools, developing supplemental community-based educational programming, and creating a community resource bank.

Each level outlines the roles and functions of the school counselor and school psychologist based on their areas of expertise, similarity, and differences. Challenges to implementing the model might include stakeholder resistance, logistics, and resources. The authors urge counselors and psychologists to view the components of the model as ideals and to select those components and elements of the model that fit best with their interests and expertise and the needs of their schools and communities. Ultimately, the model proposes that school counselors and school psychologists collaborate and use their complementary awareness, knowledge, and skills in transformative ways to promote the academic achievement and educational success of all children (Simcox et al., 2006).

REFLECTION MOMENT

Consider additional ways that you, the school counselor, could collaborate with teachers, staff, administration, pupil services professionals, community stakeholders, parents, and students to increase inclusiveness and culturally competent schools.

CONSULTATION

The importance of school counselors engaging in collaborative and consulting roles is well supported. Consultation is an essential service that school counselors provide that requires competent and effective collaboration. The Council for the Accreditation of Counseling and Related Educational Programs (CACREP) (2001, 2009) requires school counselors to demonstrate knowledge and skill in the consultation process, effectively consulting with teachers, administrators, parents, students, community groups, and agencies as appropriate. Likewise, the American School Counseling Association (ASCA) identifies consultation as "a *collaborative* partnership in which the counselor works with parents, teachers, administrators, school psychologists, social workers, visiting teachers, medical professionals and community health personnel in order to plan and implement strategies to help students be successful in the educational system" (American School Counselor Association, 1999; emphasis added). In the ASCA National Model (ASCA, 2005), consultation is presented as a responsive service within the delivery system component of the framework: "Counselors consult with parents or guardians, teachers, other educators, and community agencies regarding strategies to help students and families" (p. 42). Within the system support aspect of the delivery system component, consultation is associated with collaboration and teaming: "Through consultation, partnering, collaborating and teaming, school counselors provide important contributions to the school system" (p. 43). As a collaborative activity, consultation fits within the Themes of the ASCA National Model. It is one of the primary activities school counselors engage in with educational staff, parents, and colleagues, and is a critical way of working with students.

Research has established the amount of time that counselors spend in consultation in the schools. Burnham and Jackson (2000) found that counselors from all three levels spend from 1 to 80 percent of their time providing consultation, with a majority spending an average of 18 percent of their time in consultation. Those with whom counselors consulted, in descending rank order, were community agencies (professionals in hospitals, mental health, and social services), teachers, students, and parents (p. 45). The authors of this study expressed concern that "consultation, as an intervention, needs to be more well-defined for counselors. . . . [C]onsultation may be a 'catch-all' for services rendered" (Burnham & Jackson, 2000, p. 47). These authors pointed out that there is overlap between counseling and consulting skills and that counselors need a better understanding of consulting and the practice of consultation. More than just a theoretical aspect of school counseling, consulting is a crucial part of the counselor's job.

One of the challenges with clearly defining and grasping fully the consultation role could be the lack of available research that address "real needs of practices of school-based consultants" (Kampwirth, 2006, p. 19). Overall, studies have demonstrated that consultation does produce positive effects; however, additional studies, specifically targeting school consultation, are necessary to secure its effectiveness and then clearly define its role and function in school counseling. Moreover, the field needs studies that ask such questions as, "Which models of consultation work most effectively with which consultees and clients?" (Kampwirth, 2006). Research that addressed these specific questions is needed to strengthen our knowledge, skill, and application of school counselor consultation.

Most counselor education programs address consultation as part of school counselor training; in fact, many CACREP-accredited programs will offer a course in consultation. This chapter is not meant to suffice as your only exposure to consultation but as a supplement to focus and refine your consultative skills relative to your CSCP.

Definition of Consultation

When we examine consultation, we can see why it is so useful. There are various approaches to consultation, but all define consultation as interaction between the counselor and another person with the primary focus of assisting that other person to function more effectively with a third person or group within a work, school, or interpersonal system. Dougherty (1990) defines consultation as "a process in which a human services professional assists a consultee with a work-related (or caretaking-related) problem with a client system, with the goal of helping both the consultee and the client system in some specified way" (p. 8). Other common characteristics of consultation involve a professional, voluntary, tripartite, and temporary relationship, in which the consultant provides direct service to the consultee in problem solving and indirect service to the client by improving the situation for both (Parsons & Kahn, 2005). The relationship is confidential, collaborative, and collegial, without power differential or supervisory implications, where the consultee maintains responsibility for implementing the insights and outcomes of the consulting relationship (Dougherty, 1990; Dustin, 1992; Kahn, 2000; Kurpius & Rozecki, 1992; Mauk & Gibson, 1994; Parsons & Kahn, 2005).

This definition maintains a focus on the consultee as being another professional or adult (Dougherty, Dougherty, & Purcell, 1991; Erchul & Conoley, 1991; Hall & Lin, 1994; Kahn, 2000; Kurpius & Rozecki, 1992; Parsons & Kahn, 2005; J. White & Mullis, 1998) who works with the consultant on behalf of the client system. Inherent in this definition are three parties: the consultant (the school counselor), the consultee (the person who approaches the consultant for assistance), and the client (the third person, usually not present during the consultation, about whom the consultee has concerns). In schools, "client" usually means the student or the student's family; however, to effect systemic change mandated by the ASCA National Model, school counselors must also consider students as consultees.

For our purposes, we will use a broader definition of consultation provided by D. Brown, Pryzwanski, and Schulte (1998), while maintaining all the characteristics, conditions, and caveats of the relationship and goals of consultation outlined above. "Human service consultation is defined as a voluntary problem-solving process . . . engaged primarily for the purpose of assisting consultees to develop attitudes and skills that will enable them to function more effectively with a client, which can be an individual, group, or organization for which they have responsibility" (p. 6). The way consultants approach the consultee's issues is from a position of respect for the autonomy and independence of the consultee to see problems, generate and evaluate alternatives, and independently select appropriate change strategies.

Consultation provides many benefits to school counselors, the consultees, and the client/system. First, consultation is an efficient use of time, providing an opportunity for the counselor to intervene in a holistic, systemic way with the school, whole classrooms, students, and their families (J. White & Mullis, 1998). Furthermore, consultation empowers the consultee to address his or her own problems and work them through, providing long-term benefits to both the consultee and those with whom the consultee interacts (Hall & Lin, 1994). These benefits accrue to all parties, whether the counselor is consulting with students, families, teachers, administrators, or community members.

Although it is possible to see many similarities between counseling and consulting, the two processes are distinct and separate. In terms of their similarities, both counseling and consulting are predicated on a helping, genuine, respectful relationship, and both are focused on the goal of an independent, fully functioning helpee/consultee (D. Brown et al., 1998). Both may employ one-on-one meetings or group education as interventions, and both maintain confidentiality. However, there are substantial distinctions between them. Counseling is dyadic, involving only two parties, and is focused on the intrapsychic, personal problems of the client (Dougherty, 1990), with the goal of altering the behavior, feelings, or beliefs of the client in the deeply interpersonal counseling relationship (D. Brown et al., 1998). In Schmidt's (2008) view, "a counseling relationships assists an individual in making direct changes in his or her life" (p. 196).

Consultation, on the other hand, is always triadic, involving the consultant, the consultee, and the client (the person or group for whom the consultee *has* some responsibility [D. Brown et al., 1998; Dougherty, 1990] or toward whom the consultee *feels* some responsibility). Ultimately, the goal of consultation is to address a situation involving a consultee and a third party or system. The consultant collaborates with the consultee who then makes adjustments or intervenes with the third party or system. Furthermore, consultation focuses on systemic or work issues, not on the personal issues or private motives of the consultee (except as they may interfere with work issues) (D. Brown et al., 1998; Dougherty, 1990; Kurpius & Rozecki, 1992; Schmidt, 2008).

Another helping process that is often confused with consulting is advice giving. Just as there are important distinctions between counseling and advice giving, so too are there important distinctions between consulting and advice giving (D. Brown et al., 1998). Although as popularly used, the term "consulting" is often synonymous with "advice giving," the process of advice giving is not consulting. Because the advice giver assumes the role of an expert, there is no collegial relationship (if, indeed, there is any relationship at all) or collaboration. In addition, there is no assumption of respect or confidentiality. Finally, the goal of giving advice is not to improve the functioning of the helpee; it is on solving problems in the most expedient way possible. Advice giving is a casual, problem-focused, expert-to-neophyte interaction focused on expediency and convenience. Consultation is an intentional, professional, respectful, collegial, problem- and process-focused interaction to enhance the functioning of both consultee and client/system. When these processes are juxtaposed, it is easy to see the unique qualities of consultation.

Generic Process Model of Consultation

A variety of models outline the process of consultation, each with its own strengths and limitations. Similar to the search for a good match between a counselor's personal theory of change and various counseling theories, school counselors have a variety of consulting approaches that may match their personal styles. Rather than address all these various models, let's examine a generic model of the process of consultation (Hall & Lin, 1994). In this model,

Dougherty (1990) identified four major phases of consultation: entry, diagnosis, implementation, and disengagement. Adapted for school counselors, corresponding activities for each stage would include

I. Stage 1: Entry
   A. Establish a professional helping relationship with the consultee.
   B. Explore the needs of the consultee.
   C. Set tentative goal(s) with the consultee.

II. Stage 2: Diagnosis
   A. Gather information about the situation, the consultee, and the system about which the consultee has concerns.
   B. With the consultee, define the problem.
   C. Confirm goal(s) with the consultee.
   D. Generate possible interventions.

III. Stage 3: Implementation
   A. Facilitate consultee's selection of an intervention.
   B. Facilitate the consultee's creation of a plan of action.
   C. The consultee implements the plan.
   D. Together, the consultant and consultee evaluate the plan.

IV. Stage 4: Disengagement
   A. Formulate a contingency plan with consultee.
   B. Reduce involvement.
   C. Invite consultee back as needed to provide follow-up and support.

This model fits well with both Caplan's and Schien's models, which will be discussed later in this chapter. S. Baker et al. (2009) presented five modes of consultation that school counselors most frequently engage in with consultees. The modes are the prescription, provision, initiation, collaboration, and mediation.

Prescription Mode

School counselors are valuable assets to teachers and instructional staffs. They have a wealth of developmental, prevention, and intervention expertise to support students' academic and school success. When utilizing the prescriptive mode, the school counselor prescribes an intervention strategy to the consultee that targets a needed change in a client. For example, a teacher approaches the school counselor for assistance with students who are having difficulty getting along with peers in a middle school classroom. Because of the disruption they are creating, students are having difficulty concentrating and staying focused on tasks. The counselor comes into the classroom, unannounced, and observes the students in the classroom setting, analyzes the information gathered, and presents the teacher with a plan for addressing the students' behavior. In this example, the school counselors acts in a consulting role to assistance a teacher (consultee) with the behavior and academic achievement of students (the client) in her classroom (S. Baker et al., 2009).

Provision Mode

Occasionally, consultees are unable or unwilling to implement the intervention strategies that are recommended or proposed by the school counselor. Such circumstances might necessitate the school counselor implementing the proposed or recommended interventions directly. For example, if the consultee lacks confidence, experience, or time to implement the intervention strategy such as in the previous example, the school counselor then agrees to implement the plan with the students in the classroom (S. Baker et al., 2009). This would be an example of the counselor engaging in the provision mode. In this particular instance, we would highlight that the consultee would need to eventually gain the skills and confidence to implement future classroom interventions directly to strengthen his or her relationship with the students.

Initiation Mode

There are times when school counselors may notice circumstances or become aware of issues that a prospective consultee is not addressing successfully and will attempt to initiate assistance if they believe their involvement could be valuable. In the case of the middle school students described above, a school counselor would enter the initiation mode if the counselor overheard the teacher complaining about the classroom situation and the counselor approached the teacher to initiate assistance (S. Baker et al., 2009).

Collaboration Mode

Collaborative consultation engages school counselors and consultees in a process of trying to identify possible solutions to problems that consultees are experiencing. This consulting relationship and process would be the exact opposite from the prescriptive mode. Continuing with the example above, the counselor and the teacher would mutually join and work their way through the consultation process to arrive at a consensus as to what they believe is the best way to respond to the students' dilemma (S. Baker et al., 2009). We believe this is a win-win consulting relationship because of the buy-in that both the school counselor and the consultee have with the issue, the intervention plan, and the outcome. Likewise, Kampwirth (2006) indicated that studies over the past 20 years suggest an increase in the use of collaborative consultation over the more expert modes of consultation, such as prescriptive or provisional.

Mediation Mode

The mediation mode involves the school counselor taking on a mediation role and working with two or more individuals who need assistance in resolving disputes. In these situations, the school counselor attempts to facilitate open lines of communication between the disputing parties in hopes of achieving a mutual consensus. Consultants serving in a mediation mode may offer suggestions for shared consideration by the disputants and are not responsible for dictating solutions. If we refer to our example above, one of the students in the class requests that the school counselor mediate the dispute occurring with the other students. At this point, the first student is essentially the consultee and the remaining students are the client system. Likewise, the teacher might refer all of the students to the school counselor for mediation, thus becoming the consultee (S. Baker et al., 2009).

CONSULTING WITH STUDENTS

The reason for expanding our definition of consultation is that counselors do indeed consult with students as an appropriate part of the job (CACREP, 2001, 2009), in spite of what more traditional definitions of consultation might suggest. In fact, Burnham and Jackson (2000) found that counselors consulted with students more than with parents (p. 45).

In terms of the classical definitions of consulting, it is difficult to distinguish when a counselor is *consulting* with students about a third person for whom the student feels responsible, and when the counselor is *problem solving* with the student about a third person. In traditional definitions, problem solving with the student about a third person would not meet the criteria for consultation, because there is no responsibility for the third person; however, this issue does not diminish the counselor's ability to enhance the functioning and interaction of the consultee or the client. You are urged to consider that, as an appropriate extension of the advocate role of the counselor, consulting with students about ways to improve the school environment/system or the family environment/system is an appropriate use of consulting skills. In this view, the student is not responsible *for* the school or family system, but rather is responsible *to* that system, and student efforts to make change in that system require tremendous courage. Using this perspective, consulting with students about ways to facilitate positive change in family systems or school systems is not an option; it becomes a mandate. One example of this mandate would include sexual harassment (C. B. Stone, 2000) where a student may need consultation to understand how to address this serious issue.

Let's examine several situations germane to middle or high schools to understand how consulting works with students.

SCENARIO 1   A student comes to the counselor because the student is not getting along well with others on the student council. Rather than a friendship, this relationship with the other students is "work" related—addressing the work of the student council. The counselor consults with the student, helps him understand the context of student government, allows him to examine his interaction style relative to the group, and then asks him to let her know how it goes with the council. This is consultation, not counseling. If, however, the counselor and student examine why the student feels he must always have the approval of others, this is counseling.

SCENARIO 2   A student comes to the counselor because her family is dysfunctional, with alcohol addiction in both parents. The counselor provides counseling to the student to allow her to process her feelings of despair, grief, and frustration; then they brainstorm ideas for helping her make healthier choices for her own future. This is counseling, not consultation. If, however, the student wants to understand the implications of organizing a family intervention with the goal of helping her parents into treatment, this is consultation. There is no direct or sustained attention paid to the student's feelings about her parents' addiction.

SCENARIO 3   A student comes to the counselor with a problem with a teacher. The counselor provides counseling for the student to help him understand his feelings about the teacher's actions; they talk about perspective taking to help the student understand the teacher's perspective better. Then they brainstorm ways that the student can adjust his behavior to allow better interaction between teacher and student. This is counseling, not consulting. If, however, the behavior of the teacher becomes one of intimidation, or if the behavior of the teacher suggests serious impairment, the counselor may strategize with the student about how the student could take these concerns to the administration, with the goal of empowering the student to address his concerns directly. Indirectly, the school system may benefit from helping this teacher change his or her behavior. *Important Note*: this situation must be handled very professionally and carefully to avoid serious negative consequences to the student, the teacher, and the counselor.

SCENARIO 4   A student comes to the counselor with a problem with the assistant principal. The counselor tells the student to get over it, because the assistant principal is a powerful administrator, and the student has only two years to graduation. The counselor suggests that the student get a hobby to help with stress management. This is disrespectful advice giving, neither counseling nor consulting.

REFLECTION MOMENT

Can you think of a situation in which you have already provided consultation according to the definition of professional consultation outlined above? When consultation is not done appropriately, serious ramifications can result. Can you think of what some of those consequences might be? At what point does poorly done consultation become unhealthy triangulation? (Triangulation occurs when one person becomes involved in a problem between two others, taking sides in the conflict instead of encouraging direct communication between the two with the problem.)

CONSULTING WITH ADULT PARTNERS

Consultation does appear to be an increasingly important way for counselors to work with adult partners (Dustin, 1992; Parsons & Kahn, 2005). The advantages of using consultation as an approach to problems with parents, teachers, administrators, other pupil service professionals, and our community partners are numerous. Consultation provides a systemic intervention, allowing counselors to reach into the students' context and mobilize other persons in the students' support network. It is an efficient use of time, providing reinforcement and collaboration among all partners on behalf of the student, and it is proactive and preventive (J. White & Mullis, 1998). Furthermore, consultation is an important element of the advocate function of school counselors, in which the counselor helps parents, teachers, administrators, and community professionals understand students and their issues (Crespi & Howe, 2000). As a direct result of this enhanced understanding, these adult partners can work more effectively with and for students (Kurpius & Rozecki, 1992)—that is in line with the ASCA National Model's theme of systemic change.

A more detailed look at a model of consultation will help you understand all the forms consultation can take, specific to our adult partners. Caplan's model (1970; Caplan & Caplan, 1993; Erchul & Conoley, 1991) is of particular interest here, because it provides a framework for understanding various dimensions of consultation and strategies for facilitating change both for individuals and for organizations. (*Note*: Caplan's original model was designed for mental health consultation but will be modified here to focus on its application in the school setting.)

It is important to note that Caplan's approaches to consultation depend on accurate assessment of the consultee's and client's contexts in any consultation. Caplan (1970) cautions consultants to be very sensitive to the norms of the consultee's personal and professional context, so that the consultant does not suggest interventions that are contrary to community, professional, or organizational norms and mores. His insights are relevant for school counselors; success of the consultation will depend on the extent to which the consultant accurately understands the culture of the family (consulting with parents), the culture of the school (consulting with school colleagues), the culture of the district (consulting with student services partners), the culture of the agency (consulting with community professional service providers), and the culture of the community as a whole (consulting with community members). This is an important reminder to school counselors that foundation multicultural and multisystemic counseling skills are as essential in consultation as they are in counseling.

Caplan's (1970) model begins with two dimensions: focus on the individual (case consultation) versus the organization (administrative consultation), and focus on the single client (client centered or program centered) versus the consultee (consultee centered). As you can see from Figure 10.1, this results in a 2 × 2 grid with four possible consulting approaches, each with its own focus for intervention. Let's explore these four approaches one at a time.

Client-Centered Case Consultation (I)

According to Caplan (1970), client-centered case consultation is characterized by direct contact between the consultant and the *client* in which the consultant's primary goal is to develop a plan for dealing with the client's difficulties. Secondary to this goal is the goal of helping the consultee improve his or her skills. The consultant is an expert who assesses the environment of the client, the client's level of functioning, and all aspects of the problem in order to arrive at a diagnosis of the problem and a plan that the consultee will then implement. The consultant provides direction to the consultee in the implementation and monitors the progress of the client in this process.

The most common example of this type of consultation is when the school psychologist does assessment for special education referrals, recommending accommodations for teachers to follow. But school counselors also function within this type of consultation when they meet with a student, at the request of a teacher, to determine if a classroom behavior problem is one that

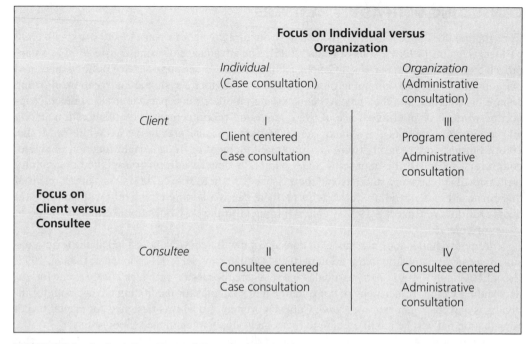

FIGURE 10.1 Caplan's Four Types of Consultation

should be addressed through counseling or through the disciplinary function of the administration. Similarly, a parent might request that the school counselor meet with a student to determine if counseling or alternative parenting strategies are warranted.

Consultee-Centered Case Consultation (II)

This type of consultation is the most sensitive and intricate of the four types presented by Caplan (1970). In this type of consultation, the consultant is assessing and addressing the functioning of the *consultee*, with the secondary goal of improving the interaction between the consultee and the client(s). The consultant rarely meets with the client(s) in this type of consultation, but deals directly with the consultee in the exploration of the problem and determination of interventions. This exploration of the problem centers around conceptual or affective distortions that the consultee exhibits while interacting with the clients.

Caplan (1970) identifies four sources of difficulties that consultees face, with increasing levels of anxiety and resistance: lack of knowledge, lack of skill, lack of confidence, and lack of objectivity. The first two sources of difficulty, and the easiest to address, are the lack of knowledge and the lack of skill. In these two sources of difficulty, the school counselor can address the challenge faced by the consultee by providing information and/or by providing practice in the missing skill. For example, school counselors may help teachers or parents address the needs of students by providing information relative to developmental issues and may provide role-playing practice with the consultees to improve their communication skills.

The third source of difficulty for the consultee may be lack of confidence. At its least problematic level, the consultant would provide feedback to help the consultee through early professional experiences, such as those experienced by first-year teachers who seek assurance that they are handling classroom management appropriately. Caplan (1970) suggests that consultants (school counselors) support consultees (first-year teachers) in this situation, while also evaluating the extent to which more senior members of the consultee's profession (experienced teachers) would provide long-term support. Another example of this type of situation might include parents who come to the school counselor for assurance that they have handled a rare occurrence, such as the death of their child's friend, appropriately. However, at its most problematic level, serious lack of confidence and resulting anxiety might prevent a consultee from functioning effectively; at this level, the consultant might refer the consultee for more intensive intervention, such as counseling and/or therapy.

The fourth source of difficulty for consultees is the most involved and sensitive. Lack of objectivity involves cognitive and affective distortions that limit the consultee's ability to function professionally. The five distortions described by Caplan (1970) are as follows:

1. *Direct personal involvement.*   This occurs when the consultee's professional relationship with the client is transformed into a personal relationship, such as when a teacher becomes romantically involved with a student.
2. *Simple identification.*   This occurs when the consultee loses professional perspective because the client represents a struggle in the consultee's personal life. For example, a parent who is ineffective in addressing a student's drinking may be struggling because of her own substance abuse issues.
3. *Transference.*   This occurs when the consultee transfers issues from other relationships onto the relationship with the client. An example of this would include a school social worker who has problems working with gay students because he has not yet worked through his own feelings about his gay son.
4. *Characterological distortions.*   If, in the previous example, the consultee has problems working with gay students because he believes all gays are disgusting, this is an example of the distortions coming from prejudicial attitudes and beliefs.
5. *Theme interference.*   "A theme represents an unsolved problem or defeat that the consultee has experienced, which influences his or her expectations concerning a client" (D. Brown et al., 1998, p. 31). In this case, the consultee expresses hopelessness that the situation with the client can be improved. An example of this type of interference would include a teacher who has problems working with attention-deficit students because she perceives them all as threatening and unpredictable, believing the "theme" that all ADD students will disrupt the classroom.

To address all five of these problems, Caplan (1970) believes that consultants should

1. Model professional objectivity and perspective
2. Refocus the consultee onto the issue(s) of the client
3. Unlink the distortions of the consultee from the reality of the client, so that the consultee can perceive the situation more objectively
4. Dispute the predetermined conclusions and themes by
   a. identifying possible outcomes other than those feared by the consultee ("Some ADD students might be disruptive, but let's also look at how much this student could contribute to the class through her humor and creativity.")
   b. relaying a "parable" about a situation in which the feared outcome did not manifest ("You have had Carla in your class and you didn't even notice she was diagnosed with ADD.")
   c. relaxing the focus on the situation to diffuse the anxiety ("We can talk any time you want about the situation, but I know we won't need to meet that often.")

If none of these strategies is successful with the consultee, a referral would be made to allow the consultee to work on these issues with a private counselor or therapist.

Program-Centered Administrative Consultation (III)

A parallel to the client-centered case consultation, program-centered administrative consultation occurs when a consultee calls on the consultant to provide assistance with a specific need or problem in an organization. In this situation, the focus remains on the need or problem and does not broaden to an examination of the entire organization. For example, a school counselor might be asked to provide a program audit (as discussed in the ASCA National Model) for another school, so that an informed but objective professional does the review of the comprehensive school counseling program. When the parent-teacher organization of the school invites the school counselor to present a program on substance abuse issues to the members, it is an example of program-centered administrative consultation. When the local social welfare agency invites the school counselor to work with its social workers to streamline referrals to the student assistance program in the school, this is also an example of this type of consultation.

Consultee-Centered Administrative Consultation (IV)

Caplan's (1970) final type of consultation involves efforts to improve the functioning of the organization as a whole. For example, a school might call in a school counselor from another district to provide consultation for communication problems between the administration and the teachers. (In this situation, the in-house school counselor would not be the ideal consultant. An outside professional would have the advantage of objectivity, having no history or preconceived ideas about the source of the problem.) In this example, the consultant would enter the system, diagnose the problem, make recommendations to the school administration to resolve the situation, and monitor the success of efforts to facilitate change. Another example of this situation might be a parent-teacher organization that invites the school counselor to provide consultation in the design of an internal structure of officers that can facilitate decision making.

As you can see, Caplan's model and the four types of consultation can be used to conceptualize and plan appropriate strategies for consulting with individuals, groups, or entire organizations of parents, teachers, administrators, pupil/student service professionals, and colleagues in the community. Let's now examine the school counselor's role providing consultation with each of these partners.

REFLECTION MOMENT

It's easy to see why many graduate programs in counselor education offer a separate class in consultation. If your program offers such a class, be sure to enroll in it. You are fortunate that you will have more time to absorb these various models. If your program does not offer a class in consultation, consider finding such a class online, from another university, or through independent study.

Can you think of examples in your own experience in which you provided consultation in each of Caplan's four types of consultation?

Consulting with Parents

In terms of Caplan's (1970) model, most of the work counselors do in providing consultation to parents is done either as client-centered case consultation or as consultee-centered case consultation. In these situations, the consultee is the parent or caregiver, and the client is usually the student. (Occasionally, other persons, such as a teacher, might be the client in the consultation.) The most common situation is client-centered case consultation, in which the parent approaches the school counselor for help with the student's behavior, attitudes, relationships, or other concern. In this type of consultation, the focus remains on the *student*, with the counselor meeting with the student and with the parent to assess the problem, identify possible solutions, and help the parent implement recommendations. In the case of consultee-centered case consultation, the focus is on helping the *parent* function more effectively with the student, addressing the parent's problem that interferes with the relationship with the student.

It is with these personal problems of the parent that we see how counseling and consultation can overlap. In fact, some models describe consultation with the family in the same terms as family counseling, to the point that some authors suggest that if the counselor isn't qualified to provide family counseling, the counselor would apply a model of family consultation and education (Magnuson & Norem, 1998; Nicoll, 1992).

Consulting with School Colleagues

Consultation with colleagues in the schools can focus on individuals (client-centered or consultee-centered case consultation) or on the school as a whole (program-centered or consultee-centered administrative consultation). One of the most common ways that counselors work with teachers and other student service professionals is as a consultant. If a teacher, school social worker, school psychologist, or school nurse were the consultee, a school counselor would use client-centered consultation to help that professional deal more effectively with students' attitudes or behaviors that are deemed problematic. If the problems seem to reside with the professional, a school counselor would use consultee-centered consultation to help that person deal more effectively with all students by working on that person's attitudes or behaviors. If the principal is the consultee, the tasks involved often require administrative consultation: program-centered consultation to design or deliver a specific program or consultee-centered administrative consultation addressing overall school issues such as school climate, communication, or morale among the staff.

If the school counselor is collaborating effectively with colleagues in the schools, much of that time will involve consulting with teachers. The importance of contact with teachers was highlighted in a study of teacher perceptions of counselors; the highest level of respect for the skills and dedication of the counselor was found "in those schools where counselors interacted with every teacher on a one-to-one basis at least once per semester" (R. L. Gibson, 1990, p. 254).

Consulting with Community Colleagues

School counselors frequently consult with community partners about schools and about the developmental issues of young people, blurring the lines between education, advocacy, and consultation. If we continue to use Caplan's (1970) model of consultation, we can see the many ways that school counselors consult with colleagues in the community. Individual client-centered or consultee-centered case consultation might take place with a colleague who is a professional in health care, mental health, or social services (physician, nurse, psychologist, psychiatrist, counselor, or social worker) who is working with an individual student or family. Program-centered administrative consultation might occur if a community law enforcement, mental health, or social service agency asked the school counselor to present a program on student development or work on ways to coordinate referrals. Consulting with general community members would most often consist of consultee-centered administrative consultation (for example, if the local chamber of commerce or service organization wanted to know how to support school efforts and an educational agenda).

We have seen that the integration of family, community, and school must be accomplished to support young people who have minimal support systems. The most important issues facing education—at-risk children and school-community integration, for example—will demand consultation with community colleagues (Dustin, 1992; Parsons & Kahn, 2005). This requires a very broad focus, the ability to see the big picture of a student's context, and skills in initiating community participation, but the overall benefits are immeasurable (Kurpius & Rozecki, 1992). Improved social and economic conditions can result through voluntary cooperation and self-help efforts (Kurpius & Rozecki, 1992), which can be initiated in the community by mobilizing the community's concern over its young people.

REFLECTION MOMENT

Can you see yourself providing consultation to parents, caregivers, teachers, administrators, school psychologists, school nurses, school social workers, community law enforcement, social welfare agency workers, and community health care and mental health professionals? Which of these groups will present the greatest challenge for you? Which one(s) will present the most comfort for you? Why?

GENERAL ISSUES: EXPERTISE AND RESISTANCE

In our discussion of the traditional definitions of consultation, we focused on the relationship between the consultant and the consultee as equal and collegial. When working in a school setting, it is likely that counselors might need to be flexible in how their expert status is factored into the relationship, to acknowledge the consultee's expectations of the counselor's expertise. To address these expectations, Schein (as cited in Dougherty, 1990, p. 196) described three templates for consultation in terms of the expectations of the consultee relative to the expert status of the consultant. Schein labeled these approaches as the purchase of expertise model, the doctor-patient model, and the process model of consultation.

In the purchase of expertise model, the consultant is an expert who is expected to provide a solution to a previously determined problem. In the doctor-patient model, the consultant is again an expert, but in this model, the consultant is expected to provide both a diagnosis of the situation and the solution. In contrast, the role of the consultant in the process model is not expert as in the other two models, nor is the consultant expected to provide a diagnosis or the solution. Rather, the role of the process consultant is egalitarian, and the consultant's job is to monitor and provide insights into the process of problem solving. In this model, the focus is on helping the consultee formulate his or her own solutions to the problem. Schien's process model has been the primary structure on which other authors (Dougherty, 1990; Dustin, 1992; Kahn, 2000; Kurpius & Rozecki, 1992; Mauk & Gibson, 1994) constructed the traditional definitions.

These templates provide useful perspectives from which to understand consultation in schools, where consultees come with varying levels of insight into the problem, the solutions, and the process to resolve any given dilemma. Many consultees come to the school counselor because they acknowledge the counselor's expertise in certain issues and seek out consultation with the counselor because of his or her expert status. Often, students want the counselor to provide some insights into the problem, the solutions, and the best process for problem resolution. Schein's insights allow counselors to accept that status as needed to facilitate the growth of the consultee and improvement of the client system.

In spite of the counselor's best efforts to establish and maintain an egalitarian and respectful posture relative to the consultee and the client, throughout consultation there is always the possibility that the consultee will resist the consulting efforts of the school counselor. As Caplan (1970) pointed out, consultants must understand the reality of the family, culture, and community of which consultees and clients are a part. Even with this sensitivity, there are many sources of resistance to consultation. Understanding these sources may help you design approaches to students, caregivers, teachers, and others in ways that reflect your sensitivity to their concerns.

There are many possible sources of resistance to consultation. Specifically, parents and caregivers might fear being blamed, fear a loss of privacy, or fear that the school will take over their authority (J. White & Mullis, 1998). These parents may have had negative experiences with schools in general or your school in particular or may resist consultation because they believe everything will work out without intervention (J. White & Mullis, 1998). Further, resistance may be triggered by consultant insensitivity, the consultant's style, or a dysfunctional consulting relationship (Parsons & Kahn, 2005).

In addition to these issues, school and community colleagues present a variety of fears and concerns in the face of consultation. These include fear of losing status with students, fear of blame, fear of being perceived as incompetent, fear of success (since success may result in more work), fear of change, and fear of the unknown (J. White & Mullis, 1998). Other possible sources of resistance include rigidity, discouragement, and hopelessness (J. White & Mullis, 1998).

Intrapsychic sources of resistance include the possibility that consultees may have serious personal problems impeding their efficacy with students, or they may not be able to overcome *your* racial, educational, or economic background (J. White & Mullis, 1998). Furthermore, all of the adult partners may experience cognitive distortions that can lead to defensiveness, such as overgeneralizing from past experiences to new experiences or from one group of students to another, catastrophizing that prior negative experiences will increase or reoccur, and blaming others for their own shortcomings (Dougherty et al., 1991).

Fortunately, there are a number of strategies to reduce resistance (Dougherty et al., 1991; Parsons & Kahn, 2005). First, counselors should recognize that resistance is normal and healthy (Dougherty, 1990; J. White & Mullis, 1998). Second, helping the consultee to understand the process of consultation, the role of the consultant, and the appropriate role of consulting within the professional purview of the counselor can increase cooperation. Third, establishing an open, respectful, and confidential relationship that fosters trust will provide comfort to consultees, which, in turn, will help them deal with the stress of change and fears of loss of control or of status. Fourth, counselors can increase cooperation by focusing on the positives of the situation and expressing support for the consultee (J. White & Mullis, 1998). Furthermore, consultants will find greater success when they remain objective, refrain from engaging in power struggles, use encouragement, and emphasize the control of the consultee in the implementation of the solution (Dougherty et al., 1991; J. White & Mullis, 1998).

COLLABORATION AND CONSULTATION IN ACTION

SEQUIOA MIDDLE SCHOOL   In Fontana, California, has many community partnerships/resource services, and collaboration is embedded throughout the school counseling program. These partners expose students to community resources, expand their understanding of future occupations, teach tolerance for others, and reward academic success. These services are critically important to students and families as the work is performed by providing academic student incentives, mentoring, tutoring, personal/social counseling services, curriculum training, peer leader training, and College Day information sharing. A special career education program called Lunch with Professionals Day invites members of the community to share their interests and profession with the students. Volunteers are valuable resources at Sequoia and the community is encouraged to continue their involvement through the website, newsletters, and participation in school activities and events. Community members are also encouraged to join the Guidance Advisory Committee, the School Site Council, and the English Language Advisory Committee.

Consultation with teachers, administrators, and parents provides many opportunities for counselors to advocate for students. The mentor/mentee program at Sequoia addresses the goals for No Child Left Behind by identifying students who are on the border of passing the state exams. Individual teachers work with 250 students for academic encouragement. Consultation and subsequent counseling referrals from these teachers can often lead to interventions that address attendance issues, basic school supply needs, peer conflicts, and family issues that prevent these students from performing to their greatest potential academically. As an Administrative Designee to the Exceptional Children's program, the counselors stay actively involved in consultation with teachers, parents, and community resources in meeting the needs of students.

Collaboration and consultation around school community and program needs occurs through meetings of the Guidance Advisory Committee (GAC), interaction with counselor websites, dissemination of the school counseling program brochures and peer program brochures, consultations with individual parents, and scheduled parent meetings. The Guidance Advisory Committee joins the counselors in the development of services for all students through collaboration among parents, students, community members, and staff. As mentioned previously in the Interdisciplinary Curriculum Development section, members of GAC consist of the school counselors, an administrator, parents, teachers, and students. The GAC meets three times a year to discuss student needs and assess the effectiveness of the counseling program. The GAC is divided into subcommittees that address issues and projects such as College Day organization, SPARC (Support Personnel Accountability Report Card) development, parent in-services, and revision of mission, goals, and objectives for the current and coming years.

Sequoia Middle School was recognized by the national organization "Do Something" (www.dosomething.org) for their service learning project of collecting 350 backpacks filled with school supplies and personal items for Hurricane Katrina victims. Each backpack also included a stuffed animal and a personal note from a student.

WAKEFIELD HIGH SCHOOL in Raleigh, North Carolina, school counselors engage in many collaborative activities to facilitate positive change in students. The SAP counselor often has representatives from community agencies share information or facilitate group meetings. School Business Alliance members help with the retained ninth-grader group on career development and work readiness topics. Some universities and colleges have held onsite admissions meetings with students in addition to the regular attendance of college representatives to share information with potential applicants. College and military representatives participated in a Junior Parent Post-Secondary Opportunities Night organized through Student Services. The career development counselor also works to pull in representatives from community businesses and training programs for the Friday Fairs available for students to see the kinds of careers that exist in different occupational cluster areas.

CASE STUDY REVISITED

Integration

Taking what you learned from this chapter about collaboration and consultation, let's revisit our original questions.

1. After reading the chapter, how do you see collaboration and consultation assisting with this situation and the relationships involved? In what ways?
2. Select models of collaboration and consultation you might use in this situation. Detail the specific steps you would work through with the Social Studies Department, with the new teachers, and to enhance the classroom environment for the teachers and the students. ∎

Suggested Readings

Baker, S., Robichaud, T., Westforth Dietrich, V., Wells, S., & Schreck, R. (2009). School counselor consultation: A pathway to advocacy, collaboration, and leadership. *Professional School Counseling, 12*(3), 200.

Brown, D., Pryzwansky, W. B., & Schulte, A. C. (1998). *Psychological consultation: Introduction to theory and practice* (4th ed.). Boston: Allyn and Bacon. A seminal text that outlines the variables and implications of the models, styles, skills, ethics, and legalities of consultation.

Caplan, G., & Caplan, R. B. (1993). *Mental health consultation and collaboration*. San Francisco: Jossey-Bass. This book provides a comprehensive and detailed overview of Caplan's model of consultation.

Clark, M., & Breman, J. (2009). School counselor inclusion: A collaborative model to provide academic and social-emotional support in the classroom setting. *Journal of Counseling & Development, 87*(1), 6–11. Retrieved from E-Journals database.

Dougherty, A. M. (1990). *Consultation: Practice and perspectives*. Pacific Grove, CA: Brooks/Cole. This text provides a generic model of consultation as well as an overview of models of consultation.

Kampworth, T. J. (2006). *Collaborative consultation in the schools: Effective practices for students with learning and behavior problems* (3rd ed.). Upper Saddle River, NJ: Prentice Hall.

Kurpius, D. J., & Rozecki, T. (1992). Outreach, advocacy and consultation: A framework for prevention and intervention. *Elementary School Guidance & Counseling, 26*, 176–189. This article outlines a framework for consultation based on the level of intervention needed in schools and communities.

Parsons, R. D., & Kahn, W. J. (2005). *The school counselor as consultant: An integrated model for school-based consultants*. Pacific Grove, CA: Brooks/Cole.

White, J., & Mullis, F. (1998). A systems approach to school counselor consultation. *Education, 119*, 242–253. This article provides an in-depth discussion of consultation with families.

CHAPTER

11

Leadership, Advocacy, and Coordination

LEARNING OBJECTIVES

By the end of this chapter, you will

1. Understand the definition of leadership and its role in effective comprehensive school counseling

2. Be able to challenge common myths about leadership to see that anyone can develop leadership skills

3. Understand and identify the personal qualities of a good leader

4. Understand and identify the professional skills of a good leader

5. Understand various models of leadership in school counseling

6. Have developed the ability to apply a model of leadership to school counseling

7. Understand the definition of advocacy and the importance of advocacy for systemic change

8. Understand the definition of coordination and its role in effective comprehensive school counseling

9. Be able to identify opportunities for leadership and advocacy with students, parents, school colleagues, and community colleagues

10. Be aware of the importance of the activities of the ASCA National Model that include leadership and advocacy of the delivery system, the management system, and the accountability system

11. Be able to discuss the advantages and disadvantages of various administrative activities that are often assigned to the school counselor

12. Be able to discuss ways that school counselors can challenge some of the administrative tasks that are inappropriately assigned to school counselors

CASE STUDY

Harmony's District and the Budget

Harmony threw her notes together at the last minute, even though she knew she would be speaking on behalf of school counseling programs in the district. She grabbed her coat and keys as she headed for her front door. "Don't wait up for me, dear. This may be a long meeting," she yelled. Then she was off to pick up two other district counselors to attend the school board meeting.

The boardroom was packed, full of teachers, parents, and students. No one was in a good frame of mind; the district had announced a large decline in enrollment for the third straight year, and the budget was to be slashed. As the meeting began, the district announced its position. Money was short for the coming year, and cuts were inevitable. The district had to find positions or programs that would be eliminated, period. They had already explored closing schools, cutting salaries, and a host of other options, but those possibilities had been blocked by overwhelming community reaction to school closings and by union reaction to the salary question. Last year's tax referendum was soundly defeated by the community, so there was no new money coming to the district to support the current buildings and teaching staff. Cuts had to be made.

One by one, programs came up for cutting. And one by one, teachers, parents, students, and administrators spoke on behalf of saving their programs. The vocational education program at the high school was in danger, but was then revived; the after-school tutoring program at the middle school was next, but was granted a reprieve. Transportation for after-school activities was discussed, but was spared. With each program and each voice, the level of tension increased. Something would be cut.

Finally, comprehensive school counseling was mentioned as a possible program to cut. Harmony braced herself and then asked for a turn to outline the importance of school counseling programs. She talked about the work counselors do with students, she outlined each school's counseling programs, she described how much the students need the developmental curriculum, and she ended by summarizing the administrative work counselors do. Feeling that she had concisely and objectively argued to keep the counseling program, she ended her comments and waited for the board's reaction.

"What data do you have that your work helps students?" was the only question.

A lump rose in her throat as she realized that she had no data. She had only her own subjective experience, and that was not going to be enough.

CHALLENGE QUESTIONS

1. It is common for schools to face financial problems. Considering that the funding for schools comes primarily from local taxes, what role do parents play in terms of taxes?
2. What is the connection between parents' willingness to pay for school funding and data about the comprehensive school counseling program?
3. How does leadership affect the collection of data, and the collection of data affect leadership?
4. How does the role as coordinator relate to collection of data?
5. In what way(s) is Harmony a leader? In what way(s) did she fail as a leader?
6. Is Harmony an effective advocate? What would have supported her advocacy efforts? ■

LEADERSHIP, ADVOCACY, AND COORDINATION IN A COMPREHENSIVE SCHOOL COUNSELING PROGRAM

Imagine that you're on a plane and there's engine trouble. But in our imaginary world, there is no captain or copilot on the plane, no one designated to make decisions about problems, advocate for the passengers, coordinate the operation of the plane, or be responsible for the welfare of the passengers. How safe would you feel? There may be 300 very nice people on board that plane, and you could all talk about how to come to a decision by consensus, but you would likely have 300 different ideas about what to do, each one as uninformed as the next. Without a trained, competent person to focus, coordinate, and lead those 300 nice people, there is likely to be a crash.

Schools are like that plane. The principal is responsible for the academic mission of the school—in a sense, the captain of the plane. But the copilot, while responsible to the captain, has responsibilities also—for many technical aspects of the flight, for communication with the ground, for helping the captain remain on course. The copilot advises the captain, problem solves with the captain, advocates for the passengers, but is also a leader in the eyes of the passengers and the flight crew. We believe that the school counselor is, in essence, the copilot of the school, responsible for the comprehensive school counseling program, the developmental curriculum, and the academic, career, and personal/social development of students. This means that the school counselor must also be aware of and prepared to accept the roles, duties, and responsibilities of being a leader and an advocate.

Think about the metaphor of school-counselor-as-copilot; there are many parallels. First, just as the copilot is responsible for advising, problem solving, communication, and direction for the pilot, the school counselor advises the principal, problem solves with that professional, communicates up and down the chain of command and to external constituencies, and helps the school remain "on course" in terms of developmental education, school climate, and the developmental needs of students and families. Second, the copilot is perceived by the passengers as part of the flight crew, as a leader in his or her own right, responsible to and for them. Third, the copilot acts within his or her own professional duties, ensuring that her or his own unique tasks are accomplished to keep the flight in the air, on time, and on course—in essence, a coordinator of his or her professional activities. Finally, the copilot functions as a problem solver along with the captain, as an expert colleague on whom the pilot depends for information, opinions, and discussion of options. In this sense, the copilot advises the pilot and functions as an independent advocate of flight-related issues. So too is the school counselor an independent auditor of school-related issues for the principal, and, in the capacity, functions as an advocate for students, their families, and the school community.

These professional activities for school counselors form the foundation of most graduate programs in counselor education. Typically, counselors are taught in graduate school how to build consensus, how to facilitate others' finding their own answers, how to foster communication within and between groups, and how to empower clients to embrace their own intuitive life direction while simultaneously evaluating their alternatives. With that training, you are now being asked to integrate a new way of viewing yourself as a professional—a leader and an advocate, a champion for students, their development, and their issues. You are being asked to help create the healthy school environment, healthy home environment, and healthy classroom environment that enables and empowers healthy student learning and development. In addition, you are asked to lead and coordinate bringing these new realities to fruition.

This might be a paradigm shift for you. But consider this. If there is no leader for the comprehensive school counseling program of a school, how will you know what your course is, much less whether you're still on it? Who will attend to the communication of constituencies and be responsible for the developmental agenda for students and families? Who will advocate for all students, who typically don't have much voice in schools? More critical still, who will advocate for diverse students, who are often marginalized in our schools? Who will lead the "heart" of the school?

When we return to the ASCA National Model (2005), we see that Leadership and Advocacy are two of the Themes of the Model. In addition, leadership and coordination as defined in this chapter will incorporate both the Management System and the Accountability elements of the Model. Many authors agree that school counselors must accept a leadership role in the school. Many authors have championed the call for school counselors to accept leadership in developing a professional image, accepting leadership roles in the school, providing staff development, and advocating for students (M. A. Clark & Stone, 2000a, 200b; Curry & DeVoss, 2009; Dollarhide, Gibson, & Saginak, 2008; McMahon, Mason, & Paisley, 2009; Sink, 2009). Furthermore, these authors cite the need for counselors to lead the school as advocates for student success, by leading various committees in terms of external constituencies (e.g., parent groups), multicultural awareness, pupil assistance committees, mentoring programs, student leadership, and political involvement (M. A. Clark & Stone, 2000a, 2000b). In a similar vein, Bemak (2000) "focuses on a critical redefinition of the future school counselor as a leader in promoting educational reform and meeting national and state educational objectives inclusive of creating healthy safe school environments." (p. 324).

Other authors have called for school counselors to become leaders in advocating for specific constituencies (partners in the terms of the DAP model in this book) or for certain issues. For example, Briggs, Stanton, and Gilligan (2009) described how a girls' leadership camp enhances training for new school counselors. Malott et al. (2010) described a group experience in which young Latinas explore their identities, and called for school counselors to be leaders and advocates for group counseling as a service venue. Kurpius and Rozecki (1992) suggested that school counselors should take leadership in advocating for students, families, and teachers and in advocating for general school improvement within the building and in the district by collaborating with mental health agencies and the community at large. Smaby and Daugherty (1995) called for school counselors to become leaders in the effort to free schools of drugs and violence. Cole and Ryan (1997) called for school counselors to take leadership in portfolio development and authentic assessment for students. All these authors agree that school counselors cannot be complacent in passively maintaining the status quo. School counselors *must* be leaders and advocates for students, families, issues of social justice, schools, and most of all, the developmental agendas of students and families.

In fact, the Education Trust (2001) elevates this function to the highest importance for successful school counseling (as defined by the DeWitt Wallace-Reader's Digest Fund, National Initiative for Transforming School Counseling). Founded to promote "educational equity, access, and academic success for all students K–12," the Trust holds that "the trained school counselor must be an assertive advocate creating opportunities for all students to nurture dreams of high aspirations. . . . The school counselor serves as a leader as well as an effective team member working with teachers, administrators, and other school personnel to make sure that each student succeeds" (The Education Trust, 2001). In the transformation from counseling as ancillary to counselor as leader, the Trust advocates that school counselors focus on the whole school and system concerns by performing the role of leader, planner, collaborator, service broker, and program developer as an integral member of the educational team and champion for creating pathways for all students to achieve (The Education Trust, 2009a, 2009b).

It takes courage, energy, and determination to be a leader and advocate. It takes true dedication and a higher purpose to swim against the tide of status quo—and you will meet some people in the schools who choose to float with the tide rather than try to effect change. But that's not what a professional school counselor does—and that's not what *you* will do when you are a professional school counselor.

SCHOOL COUNSELOR AS LEADER

Formal and Informal Power Structures

In any group of individuals, there exist power dynamics, from either formal or informal power structures or both. In order to understand leadership, you will want to understand power. In terms of formal power structures (organizational power), it is important to note that school districts and school buildings depend on organizationally defined "ladders" of power delegated, in theory, by the people of the district. In other words, the school board is elected by the people of the district, who then delegate power and authority to the superintendent, and through the superintendent and district administrators, to the principal of each building. Leadership may be a function of these formal power structures, but not necessarily, as authority, responsibility, and leadership do not always co-occur. Each of these three dynamics—authority, responsibility, and leadership—may appear in isolation, causing challenges along the way. In all cases, however, school counselors must be aware of authority and responsibility when attempting leadership, because the role of the school counselor does not usually provide formal schoolwide authority.

In terms of both formal and informal (interpersonal) power, French and Raven's (1959) typology of power provides important insights, all based on the perception of the follower (the person responding to the request for action). The five types of power and related dynamics inform our thinking about leadership. *Reward power* is the power to provide benefits perceived as valuable to the follower. *Coercive power* is the power to impose punishments or remove benefits, again as perceived by the follower. *Legitimate power* is used when the follower perceives that the leader has the right to make the request and the follower has the obligation to comply. *Expert power* is applied when the follower believes the leader has the expertise, knowledge, or training that will result in valued outcomes. Finally, *referent power* is based on the follower's admiration, liking, desire for approval, or identification with the leader, which prompts compliance.

School counselors seldom have formal organizational power unless there is a "director" position. Usually, leadership is exercised with parents, colleagues, and other adults on the basis of expert power or referent power, while leadership with students may include all five power bases, as school counselors may have sanctions they can impose for unacceptable behavior or rewards they can offer for compliance with requests.

Definition of Leadership

In a synthesis of what other authors have proposed as definitions of leadership, Hersey et al. (1996) defined leadership as "the process of influencing the activities of an individual or a group in efforts toward goal achievement in a given situation" (p. 91). Kouzes and Posner (1995) take the definition one step further, defining leadership as "the art of mobilizing others to *want* to struggle for shared aspirations" (p. 30; emphasis authors'). Their point in adding emphasis to the voluntary nature of the struggle is important. Although a person with extrinsic power (reward power or coercive power) can motivate someone to do something with the promise of rewards or the threat of retribution, this is not leadership according to their definition. Only when the leader is able to tap intrinsic motivators will there be true leadership. For school counselors, the issue of choice has important implications for their leadership; there must be attention paid to methods for tapping intrinsic motivators.

The methods for motivating others vary, depending on the context of leadership and the goals that are to be accomplished (Bolman & Deal, 1997; H. Gardner, 1995; Hersey et al., 1996). In fact, Bolman and Deal (1997) have identified four leadership "frames" or contexts of leadership: structural leadership, involving the building of viable organizations; human resource leadership, involving the empowerment and inspiration of followers; political leadership, involving the distribution of power; and symbolic leadership, involving the interpretation and reinterpretation of meaning within our society.

Each of these frames has implications for leadership within school counseling (Dollarhide, 2003b). The first frame, structural leadership, involves technical mastery, strategizing for change and growth, and implementation (Bolman & Deal, 1997). The insights from this leadership frame suggest that school counselors must be effective at their jobs and up-to-date with the "science" of counseling and education (Dollarhide, 2003b). For example, school counselors must be informed about innovations in counseling (new theories and strategies, new medications), informed about innovations in school counseling (new programs, new approaches to student issues), aware of the status of student issues (changing families, new drugs on the street, new ways students express their pain), and informed about innovations in schools (new programs and approaches to teaching and learning). School counselors must also be able to plan effectively for changes, both within the comprehensive school counseling program and in the school as a whole. Finally, school counselors must be accountable for implementation; all the good intentions in the world will not make change happen. Change happens only when action is taken in the desired direction. The power bases (French & Raven, 1959) tapped by this frame are *expert power*, as the highly effective school counselor will generate respect from demonstrating expertise in school counseling, and *legitimate power*, as others come to recognize the role of the school counselor that includes leadership.

The second frame, human resource leadership, involves believing in people and communicating that belief, being visible and accessible, and empowering others (Bolman & Deal, 1997). These are the strengths of most school counselors, so leading using these qualities is very comfortable (Dollarhide, 2003b). For school counselors, our belief in our students, families, and colleagues is one of the reasons for being a counselor and a source of passion and joy. Being visible and accessible, being around others, is also a natural part of being a counselor: being in the halls, out at the buses, in the lunchroom with the students. (Incidentally, we call this "counseling by walking around," a play on "management by walking around." The idea is that by being with the students and teachers, the school counselor is available for conversations with those who may not want to make an appointment but who need to talk with the counselor.) The power base (French & Raven, 1959) that undergirds this frame is that of referent power, the power of personal connection and influence.

The third frame, political leadership, addresses an area in which many counselors report high levels of anxiety and stress (Dollarhide, 2003b). This leadership context involves being realistic about what the leader wants and what she or he can get, being able to assess the distribution of power, building linkages to important stakeholders, and using persuasion and negotiation (Bolman & Deal, 1997). School counselors need to be realists, aware that change is incremental and often comes as a result of negotiation and compromise. School counselors also need to know who is in both formal and informal positions of power in the school and the district, knowing what those in power want and knowing how to overcome opposition by trading on the basis of those interests. School counselors need to know who important stakeholders are and how to connect with them on behalf of the school and the comprehensive school counseling program. Finally, school counselors need to be able to persuade others and to negotiate for benefits to the program, the school, and the students. (The advisory council will provide many benefits in this leadership frame.) In terms of French and Raven's (1959) five bases of power, leadership efforts in this frame would tap all five bases in service of programmatic goals.

The fourth and final leadership frame is symbolic leadership. Within this leadership context, leaders use symbols to capture attention, they frame experience in meaningful ways for the follower, and they discover and communicate a vision (Bolman & Deal, 1997). In addition, leaders have a relationship with and a conversation with the community they represent (the school, families, students) and they embody the story of healthy choices they seek to tell (Gardner, 1995). When a school counselor is an effective leader, the counselor symbolizes many things: mental health, the profession of counseling, the advocate for students, to name a few. We can use these symbols to help others understand our position in the school and our comprehensive programs (Dollarhide, 2003b). We can help others frame their experiences in a larger context, perhaps a spiritual context or a historical context. School counselors can lead others by articulating a vision of healthy, resilient students and by maintaining faith in that vision. School counselors must remember that leadership involves a constant conversation with all partners in the process. We must also always remember that we embody the story we tell about our students, our schools, and our profession, and as such, we are role models. In terms of the five bases of power (French & Raven, 1959), this frame would tap *legitimate power*, *expert power*, and *referent power*.

Participatory Leadership and Distributed Leadership

In the definition of leadership above, the leadership activity is described as the actions of one person. However, there are several models of leadership that involve more than one person: participatory leadership and distributed leadership.

Participatory leadership is when one person takes initiative for engaging in the change process, and she or he recruits others with similar vision and dedication to work together toward shared goals. As stated on the webpage for Participatory Leadership (2008, par. 1):

> The participatory leadership paradigm is based on *respect* and *engagement*. It constructively focuses *energy* in every human to human *encounter*. A more advanced, more democratic and more effective model of leadership, it *harnesses* diversity, *builds* community, and creates shared responsibility for action. It deepens individual and collective learning yielding *real* development and growth.

This concept resulted from the view that all participants—leaders and followers—have energy, insights, and potential to offer on behalf of shared goals. So in this perspective, leadership is not a top-down, compliance-oriented effort; rather, it is a web of relationships and efforts that are orchestrated by the leader, who engages all others in a collaboration-oriented effort. It is indeed, a more egalitarian, respectful way to engage others in attaining common goals—in this case, healthy schools, healthy classrooms, and healthy students.

Similar to participatory leadership, distributed leadership also views leadership as a shared endeavor (Janson et al., 2009). In this perspective, leadership is contextualized in the realization that multiple leaders exist in the schools, and that "leadership practices are 'stretched' over them" (p. 101). The *practice* of leadership is the focus, rather than the leader him or herself, and the leadership process is seen as the interactions among multiple leaders, their followers, and the situation itself. The emphasis is on interdependence of all persons in the situation, and their shared goals become mutually beneficial as they explore ways to collaborate and coordinate their activities.

Myths about Leadership

Kouzes and Posner (1995) described the outdated myths about leadership that discourage capable people from seeing themselves as leaders. Contrary to popular belief, leaders arise not from maintaining the status quo but from finding new ways to address old problems. They are not renegades who attract a lunatic following, but attract followers with their deep faith in the abilities of others. Rather than focus on the short term, they are able to maintain a long-term approach to problem solving, knowing that change is incremental and slow. But their future orientation is not superhuman; it evolves, as all good ideas, from original thinking or the inspiration of someone else.

According to Kouzes and Posner, the "most pernicious myth of all is that leadership is reserved for only a very few of us" (1995, p. 16). Are good leaders born, or are they made? Most authors agree that it is a combination of innate qualities and leadership skills that make an effective leader (Bolman & Deal, 1997; H. Gardner, 1995; Hersey et al., 1996; Kouzes & Posner, 1995), but that anyone can become a leader with training and practice. Leadership is an "observable, learnable set of practices" (Kouzes & Posner, 1995, p. 16) that enhances certain qualities. So what are those qualities and those practices?

Personal Qualities of Effective Leaders

In Chapter 1, we talked about personal qualities and professional skills that are needed by effective school counselors. In that discussion, we listed both intuition and training as necessary to this profession, and we defined intuition in terms of creativity and imagination, flexibility, courage and belief/faith, and passion. It is interesting to note that the qualities of effective leaders include those same qualities (Bolman & Deal, 1997; H. Gardner, 1995; Hersey et al., 1996; Kouzes & Posner, 1995).

In addition, many other qualities are necessary, including vision, strength, commitment (Bolman & Deal, 1997); adaptability, social awareness, achievement orientation, assertiveness, cooperation, decisiveness, dependability, energy, persistence, self-confidence, tolerance for stress, responsibility, intelligence, creativity, diplomacy and tact, persuasiveness, ability to be organized (Yukl, as cited in Hersey et al., 1996, p. 102); charisma, originality (Kirkpatrick and Locke, as cited in Hersey et al., 1996, p. 104); honesty, forward-looking (visionary), ability to be inspiring, competence, fairness, supportiveness, credibility, and broadmindedness (Kouzes & Posner, 1995).

It is important to note that this list is not exhaustive. It is not a list of qualities that only leaders possess, it is not a list of qualities that someone aspiring to be a leader must have, and it is not a list of qualities all leaders have. These qualities, however, are those that will serve any counselor or any school counselor well; in fact, we believe that we see these qualities in most school counselors in our training programs. The purpose of presenting this list is to challenge you to think about which of those qualities you currently possess and which qualities you might further develop as you move into leadership in your school.

REFLECTION MOMENT

What are the qualities you see in yourself? What qualities do others see in you? Which qualities would you like to develop more fully? What can you do now to begin your development in that area (or in those areas)?

Leadership Roles and Skills

Another way to understand leadership is to examine the roles that are a part of leadership. In a discussion of leadership roles within Character Education programs, DeRoche (2000) listed the following, which we have adapted to address the roles of leaders of comprehensive school counseling programs:

- Visionary for future directions for the program, the school, and the students
- Designer and author of the mission statement for the school counseling program
- Consensus builder for the importance of the school counseling program, the developmental domains, and the values and content of the developmental curriculum
- Information provider about the program, the school, the developmental issues of students and families, and current innovations in the field of education, counseling, and school counseling
- Standard bearer for the quality of the comprehensive school counseling program, including methods to "guide and judge the effectiveness of the implementation, maintenance, and evaluation of the program" (p. 43)
- Architect of implementation plans for the program
- Role model for the values and lessons of the developmental curriculum, comprehensive school counseling, and the counseling and mental health professions
- Risk taker and advocate for the development of all students (as stated by DeRoche, "The leader has to take a stand and bear witness to the proposition that there is more to educating children and youth than increasing their test scores" [2000, p. 44])
- Communicator, the voice of the program, to inform all partners about the program, the students, the school, and counseling as a profession
- Collaborator in efforts to implement the comprehensive school counseling program
- Resource provider, which may take the form of materials or ideas for ways to integrate the developmental curriculum into the classroom (see Chapter 9)

This list of professional leadership skills will also be familiar in many ways. You will notice a direct overlap with many of the skills you have been challenged to develop in this book.

According to Bolman and Deal (1997, pp. 297–298), the following are the most effective leadership skills:

- Establishing a vision for the program
- Setting standards for performance of tasks or excellence of endeavors
- Creating focus and direction for collective efforts
- Caring deeply about what the organization or group does
- Believing that doing the group's work well is important
- Inspiring trust
- Building relationships and empowering others
- Communicating the vision with passion to others

It is important to note that these skills are among the professional skills of counselors. Accepting that school counselors are leaders is not so much of a stretch when you think of the professional skills that you have developed and are currently developing. These skills and leadership skills are not so different after all. In fact, in a recent study, Dollarhide et al. (2008) studied the leadership efforts of five new school counselors, and found that success in leadership resulted from the following (p. 265):

1. Taking responsibility for change
2. Having courage in the face of doubts
3. Focused and clear school-based goals (as opposed to districtwide goals)
4. Self-defined role of school counselor (as opposed to other-defined)
5. Support from administration and others after some successes are demonstrated
6. Growth from self-reflection
7. Efforts that included and balanced all four leadership frames
8. Persistence in the face of feeling isolated

REFLECTION MOMENT

Have you used any of these skills? If so, where and when? How did that feel? If not, where are there opportunities for you to observe someone model these skills? Can you see yourself as a leader?

A Process Model of Leadership

Kouzes and Posner (1995) have described their "commitments of leadership" (p. 318) that outline five steps for leaders to follow:

1. Challenge the process.
2. Inspire a shared vision.
3. Enable others to act.
4. Model the way.
5. Encourage the heart.

These steps are not specific to the business world; according to Kouzes and Posner (1995), they are the means to make a difference in the world:

> Beyond the horizon of time is a changed world, very different from today's world. Some people see beyond that horizon and into the future. They believe that dreams can become reality. They open our eyes and lift our spirits. They build trust and strengthen our relationships. They stand firm against the winds of resistance and give us the courage to continue the quest. We call these people *leaders*. (p. 317; emphasis authors')

It is important to note that in a recent study, Mason and McMahon (2009) used this process model to measure what demographic variables would be correlated with leadership efforts. They found that older, more experienced counselors and those with smaller student populations "rated themselves higher on all or most leadership practices" (p. 112). They conjectured that older, more veteran counselors have more "work-related self-efficacy, which may lead to the stronger leadership identities evidenced" in the study (p. 113). What can you, the new school counselor, glean from this? That leadership must be started from your first day on the job.

SCHOOL COUNSELOR AS AN ADVOCATE

An advocate is a champion, a voice for those who are marginalized or excluded from decision making. In this sense, school counselors need to be aware of the context of students, parents, and colleagues, and be willing to serve as their voice if they have no voice. As one of the ASCA National Model (2005) Themes, the advocacy role is a critical one for social justice issues, school climate issues, closing the gap efforts, and situations in which there is a power differential that is being abused. It is easy to see how interrelated leadership and advocacy are.

Definition of Advocacy

"Advocacy" is defined by the *American Heritage Dictionary* (2001) as "to speak, plead, or argue in favor of; one that argues for a cause; one that pleads on another's behalf" (p. 14). Intertwined in these definitions are several concepts:

1. Advocacy involves *action* on the part of the advocate. Knowing that things should be different, but not acting to make things better, is not advocacy. It is advocacy only when it is external.
2. Advocacy involves conversation, interaction with others. In order to be an effective advocate, you must dialogue about the issues, listening as well as speaking.
3. A cause is involved—a higher purpose or goal. This means that advocacy is about justice, fairness, equality—all higher causes.
4. Pleading on another's behalf implies that someone is silenced or unable to plead on his or her own behalf. This means that the advocate—the school counselor—speaks for those whose voices are not heard.

Furthermore, the American Counseling Association's Advocacy Competencies (J. Lewis, Arnold, House, & Toporek, 2003) illustrate that advocacy is not only acting on *behalf of others* but includes empowerment, which means acting *with* others—empowering them to self-advocate and modeling effective advocacy. Expanding advocacy to include empowerment yields greater benefits for the disempowered and disenfranchised, as they then acquire skills for self-advocacy throughout their lives. (See *Professional School Counseling*, issue 8, number 5 [June 2005] for an extensive discussion about empowerment in schools).

Advocacy can take many forms, as you can see from the illustration of the Advocacy Competencies (Figure 11.1): private conversation, public presentation (as in presenting a developmental curriculum lesson or parent workshop), print form (as in a counselor's newsletter, teacher notice, newspaper article), and community advocacy. The key that makes communication "advocacy" is the reasoned, reasonable appeal to others' sense of social justice, fairness, equality, and democracy, and the modeling of communication approaches for disenfranchised students/families.

Advocacy for Systemic Issues: Social Justice

As indicated in the ASCA National Model (2005), school counselors are charged with addressing systemic issues that impede students' academic, career, and personal/social development. As we discussed in Chapter 2, respectful, inclusive environments are conducive to

ADVOCACY COMPETENCIES: Lewis, Arnold, House & Toporek

Endorsed by the ACA Governing Council March 20–22, 2003

Client/Student Empowerment

- An advocacy orientation involves not only systems change interventions but also the implementation of empowerment strategies in direct counseling.
- Advocacy-oriented counselors recognize the impact of social, political, economic, and cultural factors on human development.
- They also help their clients and students understand their own lives in context. This lays the groundwork for self-advocacy.

Empowerment Counselor Competencies

In direct interventions, the counselor is able to:

1. Identify strengths and resources of clients and students.
2. Identify the social, political, economic, and cultural factors that affect the client/student.
3. Recognize the signs indicating that an individual's behaviors and concerns reflect responses to systemic or internalized oppression.
4. At an appropriate development level, help the individual identify the external barriers that affect his or her development.
5. Train students and clients in self-advocacy skills.
6. Help students and clients develop self-advocacy action plans.
7. Assist students and clients in carrying out action plans.

Client/Student Advocacy

- When counselors become aware of external factors that act as barriers to an individual's development, they may choose to respond through advocacy.
- The client/student advocate role is especially significant when individuals or vulnerable groups lack access to needed services.

Client/Student Advocacy Counselor Competencies

In environmental interventions on behalf of clients and students, the counselor is able to:

8. Negotiate relevant services and education systems on behalf of clients and students.
9. Help clients and students gain access to needed resources.
10. Identify barriers to the well-being of individuals and vulnerable groups.
11. Develop an initial plan of action for confronting these barriers.
12. Identify potential allies for confronting the barriers.
13. Carry out the plan of action.

FIGURE 11.1 Advocacy Competencies

Community Collaboration

- Their ongoing work with people gives counselors a unique awareness of recurring themes. Counselors are often among the first to become aware of specific difficulties in the environment.
- Advocacy-oriented counselors often choose to respond to such challenges by alerting existing organizations that are already working for change and that might have an interest in the issue at hand.
- In these situations, the counselor's primary role is as an ally. Counselors can also be helpful to organizations by making available to them our particular skills: interpersonal relations, communications, training, and research.

Community Collaboration Counselor Competencies

14. Identify environmental factors that impinge upon students' and clients' development.
15. Alert community or school groups with common concerns related to the issue.
16. Develop alliances with groups working for change.
17. Use effective listening skills to gain understanding of the group's goals.
18. Identify the strengths and resources that the group members bring to the process of systemic change.
19. Communicate recognition of and respect for these strengths and resources.
20. Identify and offer the skills that the counselor can bring to the collaboration.
21. Assess the effect of counselor's interaction with the community.

Systems Advocacy

- When counselors identify systemic factors that act as barriers to their students' or clients' development, they often wish that they could change the environment and prevent some of the problems that they see every day.
- Regardless of the specific target of change, the processes for altering the status quo have common qualities. Change is a process that requires vision, persistence, leadership, collaboration, systems analysis, and strong data. In many situations, a counselor is the right person to take leadership.

Systems Advocacy Counselor Competencies

In exerting systems-change leadership at the school or community level, the advocacy-oriented counselor is able to:

22. Identify environmental factors impinging on students' or clients' development
23. Provide and interpret data to show the urgency for change.
24. In collaboration with other stakeholders, develop a vision to guide change.
25. Analyze the sources of political power and social influence within the system.
26. Develop a step-by-step plan for implementing the change process.
27. Develop a plan for dealing with probable responses to change.
28. Recognize and deal with resistance.
29. Assess the effect of counselor's advocacy efforts on the system and constituents.

Public Information

- Across settings, specialties, and theoretical perspectives, professional counselors share knowledge of human development and expertise in communication.
- These qualities make it possible for advocacy-oriented counselors to awaken the general public to macro-systemic issues regarding human dignity

Public Information Counselor Competencies

In informing the public about the role of environmental factors in human development, the advocacy-oriented counselor is able to:

30. Recognize the impact of oppression and other barriers to healthy development.
31. Identify environmental factors that are protective of healthy development.

FIGURE 11.1 (Continued)

32. Prepare written and multi-media materials that provide clear explanations of the role of specific environmental factors in human development.
33. Communicate information in ways that are ethical and appropriate for the target population.
34. Disseminate information through a variety of media.
35. Identify and collaborate with other professionals who are involved in disseminating public information.
36. Assess the influence of public information efforts undertaken by the counselor.

Social/Political Advocacy

- Counselors regularly act as change agents in the systems that affect their own students and clients most directly. This experience often leads toward the recognition that some of the concerns they have addressed affected people in a much larger arena.
- When this happens, counselors use their skills to carry out social/political advocacy.

Social/Political Advocacy Counselor Competencies

In influencing public policy in a large, public arena, the advocacy-oriented counselor is able to:

37. Distinguish those problems that can best be resolved through social/political action.
38. Identify the appropriate mechanisms and avenues for addressing these problems.
39. Seek out and join with potential allies.
40. Support existing alliances for change.
41. With allies, prepare convincing data and rationales for change.
42. With allies, lobby legislators and other policy makers.
43. Maintain open dialogue with communities and clients to ensure that the social/political advocacy is consistent with the initial goals.

FIGURE 11.1 (Continued)

learning, but not all schools provide such an environment for students. In fact, many school counselors report that they are not comfortable addressing multicultural issues; Holcomb-McCoy (2005) found that 209 surveyed school counselors rated themselves "somewhat competent" (a 2 on a 4-point Likert scale) for multicultural knowledge (knowledge of multicultural groups and issues), but self-rated "competent" on multicultural terminology and multicultural awareness. This would suggest that while school counselors know the terminology and are aware of other groups, their understanding of how discrimination manifests in the school is more limited.

This limited knowledge may result in the perpetuation of discrimination in the schools. Goodman and West-Olatunji (2010) argue that "systemic oppression may compound transgenerational trauma experienced by socially marginalized individuals because of endemic, long-term hegemony" (p. 178) and then detail how cultural hegemony manifests in schools. They draw strong connections between the symptomology of trauma and the behaviors of students labeled as "academic underachievement" (a term usually used to refer to the challenges of diverse students), and cite the traditional deficit-oriented explanations for this underachievement as perpetuation of the hegemony. They point out that "social action to counter educational hegemony is a necessary step in ameliorating the effects of traumatic stress and improving academic performance for African American and Latino American students" (p. 181), and urge counselors to develop advocacy skills to assist educational colleagues to become more aware of systemic oppression and its effect on classroom dynamics.

By being aware of diversity issues in the school, by monitoring the academic progress of students of diversity (poverty, cultural diversity, second-language issues, etc.), and by being in touch with the climate of the school in terms of inclusion/exclusion, school counselors can become aware of situations requiring advocacy and can then begin advocacy work.

The Advocacy Competencies

What does advocacy actually look like?

As you can see from the Advocacy Competencies (Figure 11.1; J. Lewis et al., 2003), the advocacy activities are those that are undertaken with or on behalf of others. For each of the advocacy activities, there is a description and a list of competencies that you can incorporate into your developing skill set.

REFLECTION MOMENT

Have you ever served as an advocate? Often, we advocate in informal settings around things that we feel passionate about—politics, family issues, relationship issues. Can you recall any similar situations or experiences? What can you learn from those situations or experiences that can help you develop and refine your advocacy skills?

Knowing that advocacy and leadership take courage and dedication on the part of the school counselor, what intrapersonal resources can you tap to strengthen your resolve to be the leader and advocate that your students need?

SCHOOL COUNSELOR AS COORDINATOR

Definition of Coordination

To understand why this coordination is essential for effective school counseling programs, we must explore what is meant by "coordination." Harrison (2000b) summed it up best in his definition: "Coordination is a *counselor initiated leadership process* in which the counselor helps organize and manage the comprehensive guidance program and related services" (p. 190; emphasis added). Within this definition are embedded several important concepts. First, coordination activities are connected to leadership. Second, coordination activities are counselor initiated, and therefore not a passive or second-rate function of the comprehensive school counseling program. Third, coordination is essential for the organization of the program and, finally, coordination is essential for the management of the program. Let's examine each of these observations separately.

The connection of leadership and coordination is important. Good leaders are involved in the day-to-day activities of their work, and so coordination of work, services, and programs is a natural part of effective leadership. This technical mastery increases trust in the professional skills of the leader, and the willingness to actually "get your hands dirty and work" increases everyone's trust in the credibility of the leader (recall that structural leadership—leading an effective school counseling program—is one of the four frames of leadership from earlier in this chapter). The fact that coordination is not passive but an active part of the school counselor's job is also important. As previously mentioned, good intentions alone do not get the job done; only active, goal-directed movement will lead to progress toward goals.

Counselors utilize coordination in the organization and management of the program. In fact, the Management System of the National Model (Chapter 5) addresses administrative agreements, coordination of the advisory council, action planning, use of time and calendars, and use of data—all of which require the coordination of the school counselor. In addition, the Accountability element of the National Model requires counselors to coordinate the collection, analysis, and dissemination of results reports and program audits to improve the program based on results. (For an excellent comprehensive discussion of accountability, see C. B. Stone and Dahir's [2007] *School Counselor Accountability: A MEASURE of Student Success*, 2nd ed.). In all of these activities, counselors coordinate ideas, resources, materials, and personnel to bring about the design and creation of the program, and then coordinate all those ideas, resources, materials, and personnel to make the program happen. In this view, the work counselors must do with personnel involves collaboration and cooperation to coordinate resources for the school counseling program. Recall the Themes of the ASCA National Model. In essence, the National

Model emphasizes that a program of effective leadership, collaboration, and advocacy will result in systemic change.

In case this all sounds very conceptual, rest assured, it's not. Much of the work of coordinating the comprehensive school counseling program is very practical. Examples of coordination include scheduling meetings (with counseling groups, advisory boards, teachers and parents), scheduling appointments (with students, teachers, parents), creating budgets, writing grants, documenting activities and achievements, compiling and analyzing data, evaluating the program in the program audit, scheduling facilities for events, securing donations for a program or event, typing flyers and creating brochures, stapling, sealing envelopes, and affixing stamps. Don't assume you will have clerical help in the school; many counselors do their own typing and answer their own phones.

REFLECTION MOMENT

What are those coordination activities at which you excel? Which ones challenge you?

LEADERSHIP ADVOCACY, AND COORDINATION: EXAMPLES AND ISSUES

Leadership, Advocacy, and Coordination with Students

Leadership, advocacy, and coordination are important activities with each of the partners in the DAP model. In terms of leadership and advocacy with students, the school counselor is looked to as the professional and personal leader of and advocate for programmatic efforts that focus on effective learning, mental health, respect, and healthy development. As we have discussed, these are important aspects of the learning that students must do to become healthy, functional adults in the community, to become healthy parents, significant life partners, contributors to the community in terms of work and/or employment, and community builders. As a visible leader and advocate in the school, the school counselor is the role model for students through his or her work in the school and in her or his own personal life and interactions with others.

As the leader and advocate of these programmatic efforts, school counselors coordinate programs and events for students in the three domains. Although not intended as an exhaustive list of events all counselors must coordinate, specific examples of possible programs and events in each domain might include the following (Bemak, 2000; Burnham & Jackson, 2000; M. A. Clark & Stone, 2000a, 2000b; Cole & Ryan, 1997; Fazio & Ural, 1995; Goodman & West-Olatunji, 2010; Harrison, 2000b; Smaby & Daugherty, 1995):

Academic Development

Academic excellence award programs

Peer tutoring

Academic Olympic games

New student orientation and transition programs

Academic intervention for nonpassing students

Portfolios and authentic assessments

Career Development

Mentoring programs in professions and trades

Career days and events

Career interest testing programs

School-to-work/career programs

Career Cluster programming

Personal/Social Development

Advisor for student groups

Peer mediation programs

Peer mentoring programs

Community service programs

Student recognition for campus/community service

Mental health issues (for example, National Depression Screening Day)

Support groups, crisis and loss groups

Support groups for diverse students

Substance abuse prevention, intervention, and referral programs

Referrals for therapeutic intervention and treatment

Leadership, Advocacy, and Coordination with Parents

School counselors are directed by professional ethics to involve, as appropriate, the student's family and enlist the family's support when working with students, according to both the American Counseling Association and the American School Counselor Association. In addition, we have identified competencies for our adult partners that appear in Appendix A. Many authors call for school counselors to take the lead in coordinating strong connections between schools and parents/caregivers (Bemak, 2000; Colbert, 1996; Jackson & White, 2000; L. S. Kaplan, 1997; Keys & Lockhart, 1999; Peeks, 1993) and call for counselors to advocate for diverse and/or disenfranchised parents.

These parent/family connections vary from coordination of events such as potluck suppers and community-building activities (Jackson & White, 2000), to academic interventions involving parents (L. S. Kaplan, 1997), to involving parents as a part of the school's organization and structure, such as in curriculum committees and as trainers of other parents (Colbert, 1996), to providing family services such as family health services, employment services, and lifelong training (Peeks, 1993). Bemak (2000) suggests that schools must develop flexible hours to meet the needs of working parents, develop family advocacy programs and parent inclusion programs within the school, and develop a family space within the school where parents and families can feel comfortable and safe. The extent of these parent and family connections with the school will be determined by a variety of factors, just as we have discussed in earlier chapters on counseling with adult partners, educating adult partners, and consulting/collaborating with adult partners. One thing is clear: school counselors must work extensively with parents/caregivers to be successful (Bemak, 2000).

Leadership, Advocacy, and Coordination with School Colleagues

Just as we have seen in our discussion of leadership, advocacy, and coordination with parents and caregivers, school counselors are often called upon to provide leadership and advocacy with our partners in the school and in the district, including:

1. Coordinating various teams to address the systemic issues of students who are at risk or who are not functioning effectively in the school (Bemak, 2000; Keys, Bemak, & Carpenter, 1998). This team approaches the discussion with a focus on cultural, community, and school issues that might interfere with the student's functioning, and brings the support of various school professionals to that discussion (Jackson & White, 2000).
2. Coordinating the work of special educators and other professionals in the schools to
   a. Support special education transition services for students who live with disabilities (Sitlington et al., 2000)
   b. Support the holistic development of students with learning disabilities (Koehler & Kravets, 1998) and at-risk and violent youth (Barr & Parrett, 2001)

3. Integrate services of all school-based mental health providers in school-based health clinics, mental health clinics, and "multiple systems" clinics to provide one-stop access to help. Examples cited include integrating violence prevention, parent training, tutoring, daycare, and bereavement with medical services (Porter et al., 2000).

4. Better integrate the services of the school counselor with those of the school psychologist to reduce overlap and to draw on each other's professional expertise (Rowley, 2000).

5. Lead and coordinate evaluations of the school climate for violence, racism, sexual harassment, and gang activity; to help in the selection of new teachers; to deal more effectively with discipline issues that affect the school by adding a counseling component to the school's discipline policy; to address issues raised by athletic programs in the school; and to assist with the development of the school's crisis plan (Niebuhr et al., 1999).

6. Lead and advocate for employee assistance-like services for school employees (A. J. Clark, 1995).

When a counselor thinks holistically about the best way to help students with their development, it would be impossible to ignore the need to coordinate efforts with partners in the school and in the district. Some counselors may be the only counselor in the school, but there are other counselors in other buildings, and there are other professionals who serve in student services (e.g., psychologists, nurses, social workers, and building police or safety officers). Don't let yourself become a "service silo" isolated from other professionals. Students need everyone in the helping professions to be focused on what is best for the students, and integrated services for students is clearly more effective and more efficient.

In addition, school counselors at all levels must be able to coordinate the collection of data that tell about the health of the school and that signal how well students are learning in all three domains—academic, career, and personal/social. As was discussed in Chapters 5 and 7, this data would include achievement data (grades, test data, promotion and retention rates) and competency-based data (number of students with academic plans, results data from developmental guidance programs). Through understanding how students are progressing, professional school counselors collect and analyze student data to lead and coordinate program direction, emphasis, and upon evaluation, revisions to the program.

In addition to coordinating data for program definition and revision, this data is essential for monitoring student progress. Issues such as choices of classes and equitable access to all educational benefits are also important and are the result of careful and intentional examination of data. Based on documented concerns for the education of all students, school counselors must also help schools design ways to address the achievement gap between students with resources and students without resources (parental, financial). This means that school counselors need to be involved in creating *systems* for monitoring student progress—predictable, regular access to data sources and a process by which the data are discussed and analyzed with others in school leadership to design plans for multisystemic (family, classroom, counseling) interventions.

VARIETY AS THE SPICE OF LIFE: ADMINISTRATIVE TASKS Another important concept in the discussion of coordination is that of using coordinating (administrative) activities as a smoke screen to avoid doing more personal (counseling) work with students (Myrick, 1997). Harrison (2000b, p. 191) also noted that some school counselors become involved in "noncounseling, administrator-driven" activities inappropriately. This situation may arise when the school counselor is not the leader of the comprehensive school counseling program, when the counselor's time and energies are defined by noncounselors. Although many counselors also coordinate administrative functions, there are examples of activities that have potential for contributing to out-of-balance conditions (American School Counseling Association, 2005; Burnham & Jackson, 2000).

The discussion of coordination must also include a discussion of administrative tasks, and this discussion inevitably leads us back to the importance of leadership, the vision of the mission of the comprehensive school counseling program, and advocacy, the ability to challenge the status quo regarding *inappropriate* administrative tasks.

Everyone who works in a school will have some administrative tasks to complete. These tasks provide information for the administration, contribute to the well-being and improvement of the school and the district, and enable the building to operate in a safe and orderly fashion. Called system support activities by ASCA (2005), these duties include many we have already discussed (research and development to evaluate and improve the program and program management activities), but they also describe duties relevant to this discussion such as service on committees and advisory boards and fair-share responsibilities. When we discuss leadership, advocacy, and coordination within the school and the district, it is essential that we include these activities also.

This is not to imply that all administrative activities must be eschewed by counselors, as there are many activities that on their surface seem to be administrative, but on closer examination, clearly provide substantial holistic benefits to the school, the students, and to the comprehensive school counseling program (ASCA, 2005). To help you understand this issue more clearly, let's take a look at the overall advantages of devoting time to these activities. When evaluating the benefits of academic activities such as writing curriculum guides, assessing transcripts, and designing the master schedule, some counselors believe that their participation cements their connection with the academic mission of the school, giving them greater credibility with teachers. When describing activities such as lunchroom duty, hall monitor, chaperoning dances, scheduling students, and serving as advisor for student groups, some counselors believe that the enhanced contact with students allows for conversation, trust, and greater awareness of student lives and issues. Some counselors simply believe they are "helping out" (Wiggins & Moody, 1987) and may feel more effective as a result.

The disadvantages of these activities are numerous, especially if these activities become out of balance. Counselors might find themselves perceived by teachers and students as being quasi-administrators, a role that compromises the counselor's credibility and impedes trust (Gibson, 1990). In addition, counselors may believe that they are helping out, but students and teachers may notice the counselor's avoidance of professional tasks (Wiggins & Moody, 1987). But the single biggest problem with out-of-balance clerical and administrative work is time. At all educational levels, administrative activities that do not contribute to the CSCP deplete the counselor's time for working on crucial CSCP activities. This concern is echoed by Gysbers and Henderson (2000, p. 76): "Care must be taken . . . to watch the time given to system support duties because the prime focus for counselors' time is the direct service components of the comprehensive guidance program." The loss of time to devote to the comprehensive school counseling program can leave counselors exhausted and incapable of responding appropriately to student needs (Burnham & Jackson, 2000).

ASCA (2005, p. 56) outlines activities that are, for the most part, outside the purview of a CSCP:

- Registration and scheduling of all new students
- Coordinating cognitive, aptitude, and achievement tests
- Responsibility for signing excuses for tardy or absent students
- Performing disciplinary actions
- Sending students home who are not appropriately dressed
- Teaching classes when teachers are absent
- Computing grade point averages
- Maintaining student records
- Supervising study halls
- Clerical record keeping
- Assisting with duties in the principal's office
- Preparation of individual education plans, student study teams, and school attendance review board
- Data entry

Each activity in this category siphons time from the activities of a CSCP; each must be weighed in terms of its unique advantages and disadvantages to the students and the comprehensive school counseling program. Then these must be weighed against the overall effect all these activities have on our ability to meet the goals and objectives of our program. If the activity does not directly contribute to the CSCP, it should be discussed with the principal and noted in the management agreement.

Assessment/Testing   When the counselor devotes time to serving as the testing coordinator for the building, many hours are lost that could more directly benefit the program's main focus (Burnham & Jackson, 2000; Gysbers & Henderson, 2000). Burnham and Jackson (2000) found that schoolwide testing programs were coordinated by 87.5 percent of their respondents, but in 2005, Dollarhide and Lemberger (2006) found that only 42 percent of responding counselors coordinated tests and another 11 percent were involved as proctors and academic remediators. Test interpretation with students and parents, however, would be an appropriate use of the counselor's training and within the scope of the academic, career, and personal/social development of students.

Discipline (Attendance, Hall Monitor, Conflict Resolution, Bus Duty)   There are good reasons that counselors become involved in helping students with attendance problems, observing student behaviors directly in the halls, and helping with conflict resolution between students. These benefits accrue directly to students when counselors are a part of the building discipline process. The key is for counselors to maintain a role in the prevention and intervention of the inappropriate behavior but to not be the primary disciplinarian of the school. That role is better handled by the principal, appropriate vice principal, school police/safety officer, or dean of students, as the case may be.

Role of Registrar: Scheduling, Transcripts, and Curriculum Guides   Many counselors are expected to schedule all students, evaluate and maintain transcripts, and prepare curriculum guides. Although ASCA (2005) indicates that it is appropriate for counselors to provide academic advice for students and that this role does require an understanding of the curriculum of the school, counselors should not be responsible for the activities of a registrar. These activities closely relate to the academic mission of the school and should be housed in the offices of academic leadership.

Environmental Assessment   As was presented in Chapter 2, school counselors can have a tremendous impact on the climate of the school when they are involved in efforts to monitor and improve the emotional environment of the school. In many schools, these conversations take place in committees charged with monitoring the school for "developmental assets," "positive behavior and energy," "inviting elements," or other similar terms. In a nutshell, when school counselors are involved in improving the level of respect, inclusion, and empowerment for all members of the school community, the school as a whole will benefit. We believe that this administrative duty could be an important way the school counselor leads and advocates for a healthy environment.

Special Education Case Management and IEPs   School counselors are an important part of the process of educating all students, including those identified as disabled according to PL 94-142 and the Americans with Disabilities Act (ADA) (Koehler & Kravets, 1998). In the process of educating students with disabilities, school counselors are appropriately involved in the process of referral for evaluation, conversations with parents and caregivers, and meetings to define appropriate accommodations. Counselors are also involved in many Individualized Educational Plan (IEP) multidisciplinary meetings that detail the services and programs the student must access to be successful in school. As the professional charged with leadership over the program to secure every student's academic, career, and personal/social development, the counselor must be involved in these meetings. In some cases, however, the school counselor is named the case manager or "lead," and given the responsibility of seeing that the student's IEP is followed and updated yearly. In this situation, the counselor is not the best professional for this role. Those with licensure in special education are specifically trained to understand the needs of students with IEPs, and these professionals are in the best position to handle this responsibility. For a more in-depth discussion of the school counselor's role with special education students, see Koehler and Kravets (1998).

ADDRESSING OUT-OF-BALANCE ADMINISTRATIVE TASKS   Researchers have consistently found that counselors are too often pulled away from professional programs focused on the academic, career, and personal/social development of students to perform non-CSCP tasks for the school (Burnham & Jackson, 2000; R. L. Gibson, 1990; Partin, 1993; Wiggins & Moody, 1987). When Burnham and Jackson (2000) surveyed counselors, they found that the average amount of time spent in nonguidance activities was 25.04 percent—slightly over one-quarter of the job. This means that out of every week, approximately 10 hours, or more than one day, was spent doing tasks not related to the comprehensive school counseling program. And these figures do not include the activity of testing, which we would argue constitutes another task that does not belong in the school counselor's list of responsibilities (Dollarhide & Lemberger, 2006).

How do you provide leadership and advocacy when discussing tasks that are not appropriate for the comprehensive school counseling program? There are a number of suggestions to follow, each specific to the situation.

First, if you are involved in the design of a new program, you would be able to challenge the imposition of those administrative tasks during the discussions about the design of the program. As you will recall from Chapter 5, the Foundation of your program includes philosophy, beliefs, and National Standards for Student Development. These inform the Delivery System and the Management System. As you design these elements in your CSCP, you must be able to discuss why certain administrative or noncounseling tasks would not be appropriate in your program, because the priority for time should be focused on meeting the needs of your student partners first. After student partners, the needs of parents and caregivers would be addressed next. Your stand on how to best meet these competing priorities must be based on the professional literature, your professional judgment, and resources from the profession such as textbooks and expert advice.

If you are employed at a school that has an existing program, Gysbers and Henderson (2000) discuss displacement as the means for finding a better fit between the tasks and the program (p. 202). They describe the displacement process as specifying the nonprogram responsibilities under discussion, broken down into small tasks, and "either eliminating them or shifting the responsibility for doing them to someone else" (p. 203). They believe that discussing smaller tasks, rather than entire functions, will enable others to accept them within their job duties. Also, they believe that it is the responsibility of the counselor to identify the person to whom the tasks should be assigned, determined on the basis of efficiency.

In some cases, the school will struggle to find the best professional to accept the responsibility. In other cases, the district will need to hire someone to perform the displaced activity. An example of this would be the hiring of a middle or high school registrar to handle student records, grades, transcripts, enrollment, withdrawal, registration for classes, and scheduling changes (from one section to another or from one time slot to another) that maintain the student's overall educational plan. (The comprehensive school counseling program would retain responsibility for academic advisement and help students establish the overall educational plan and program of study for each year, but it would no longer include responsibility for transcripts, grades, master schedules, or curriculum guides.)

If it is not possible to completely displace the noncounseling program activity, then Gysbers and Henderson (2000) suggest that counselors streamline these activities. In this process, the goal is to reduce the amount of time the counselors spend in the activity. This is useful for those activities in which counselor's involvement at some level is important, but not to the current extent. "Over time, counselors' involvement has become counselors' overinvolvement"

(Gysbers & Henderson, 2000, p. 206). One good example is testing. Counselors "fell into" this responsibility due to their training in the interpretation of assessment instruments; eventually, this became full responsibility for a horrendous and time-consuming task that belongs with the academic leadership of the school. The solution to this overinvolvement would be the hiring of a professional at the district level to coordinate and conduct the district's testing and academic assessment program; counselors' involvement would be streamlined to retain responsibility for the interpretation of the testing results.

In the third situation, the counselor might be approached by someone who thinks it would be a good idea for the counselor to accept another responsibility, one that does not already fall in the comprehensive school counseling program. In response, Partin (1993) recommended that counselors should ask "'In place of what?' Because time is finite, any additional task must be at the expense of something else" (p. 280). He urged counselors to maintain their focus on their program priorities. "If counselors quickly acquiesce to external pressures to take on new projects and duties, others may begin to assume that those counselors must not have had enough to do before or that what they were doing was not important" (p. 280). Clearly, counselors are reminded to focus on their program priorities and to not blindly accept new duties that do not enhance the program.

This is not to imply that new program priorities will never emerge, because new issues and new problems emerge all the time. Remember, though, that you will have an advisory committee and management agreements that can help you in the case of new program priorities or emerging student issues that must be addressed. If new priorities emerge, they should be discussed with your principal and advisory committee, and the discussions must clearly convey that you are asking for their input in the redefinition of the comprehensive school counseling program.

It is not sufficient for schools to argue that school counselors must continue doing non-CSPC activities because they have always done it, or because there is no one else to do it. These are not acceptable reasons. Ultimately, counselors must recognize that they must accept leadership of their comprehensive school counseling programs, and this leadership means setting program priorities to maximize student potential. Counselors must be willing to advocate on behalf of the school counseling profession and the comprehensive school counseling program. Counselors are not glorified secretaries, psychometrists, telephone operators, truancy officers, or registrars. They should keep their focus on their program priorities in terms of the developmental domains, the professional activities of school counselors, and their primary partners—students. As a counselor, dare to transform school counseling in your lifetime.

REFLECTION MOMENT

What are your reactions to the administrative functions discussed above? Do you believe these functions should be done by counselors? If so, which one(s)?

Leadership and Coordination with Community Colleagues

Powerful interventions result when community professionals join with school professionals to design comprehensive, wraparound services, as discussed in Chapter 10. Programs that utilize community resources to accomplish the goals of the school counseling program include mentoring programs (Brotherthon & Clarke, 1997), community mapping (Griffin & Farris, 2010), interagency collaboration (Price & Edgar, 1995), school/community collaboration (Ponec, Poggi, & Dickel, 1998), and youth services teams for at-risk youth (Hobbs & Collison, 1995). A case in point is the finding that school counselors in isolated rural communities need to coordinate services with professionals in the community due to limited resources within the school itself (Morrissette, 2000). In addition, the needs of the students are met with coordinated school-community partnerships, as evidenced by Luongo's (2000) argument that partnering child welfare, juvenile justice, substance abuse/mental health diagnostic and treatment services, and schools is essential to meet the needs of our most vulnerable youth.

It seems logical that school counselors would collaborate with community professionals to meet students' needs, but there are many barriers to such coordination of services. Outdated ideas about the role of the counselor and/or the role of schools, site-focused school administrators, turf issues, professional obsolescence, and overloads of "administrivia" are all impediments to moving forward to effect systemic change (Bemak, 2000). But if school counselors are indeed leaders and advocates, then it becomes our responsibility to move toward such change.

REFLECTION MOMENT

What issues do you feel passionate about—passionate enough to engage in advocacy, leadership for change, and coordination of resources? If you envision yourself working toward tangible results on the issue you are most passionate about, then you can begin to see where you can apply the skills and insights you developed in this chapter.

LEADERSHIP, ADVOCACY, AND COORDINATION IN ACTION

In the three RAMP schools we have introduced in this book, we can see leadership, advocacy, and coordination in action at each level. In Ford Elementary School (Tucson, Arizona), leadership is seen in the design of the management agreement with the principal. In additional leadership and advocacy efforts, the school counselor designed closing-the-gap programs to address attendance, targeting the students and the parents in her effort to increase attendance. This school counselor also coordinates outcomes data and uses that data to advocate for changes in the program.

At Sequoia Middle School (Fontana, California) the counselors lead their advisory council, the inclusion of Character Education lessons delivered in all classes, and various programs designed to transition new students, provide mentoring for incoming students, and recruit students into the tobacco-free programs (among others). Parents are also included in the counselors' leadership, and they advocate for healthy students through parent programs on bullying, academic improvement, and graduation requirements. CSCP materials are available in English and Spanish, another example of advocacy for diverse families. The counselors also coordinate program activities, funding, and data collection and analysis.

Finally, at Wakefield High School (Raleigh, North Carolina), the counselors serve in many leadership roles in the school. They serve on the leadership team and various administrative and student-oriented committees, in addition to leading efforts to revamp the class registration process. An example of leadership and advocacy, these counselors are also working to increase enrollment in AP courses among students of diversity by working with teachers and students. Further, advocacy efforts are infused into the work of all the counselors, which include outreach efforts to recruit students for programs, parent workshops for retained ninth-graders, outreach to parents of ESL students, and efforts to provide services for parents of diverse students. Leadership, advocacy, and provision of programs, needs and outcomes data, and program resources are all examples of the ubiquitous nature of coordination.

CASE STUDY REVISITED

Integration

Now that you have read the chapter, answer the following questions:

1. If you were on that school board, what questions would you have for Harmony?
2. How would you feel if you were one of the counselors in the audience listening to her presentation?
3. If you were in Harmony's place, what would you say to the board?

4. Now that you have read the chapter, what do you think the board is looking for?
5. On a more personal level, what questions would you ask a principal or interviewing committee about the school counseling program to help you understand who "leads" the program?
6. How would you establish yourself as the leader of your program? How would you blend the insights from each of the four contexts of leadership to maximize your ability to lead?
7. What leadership model would fit your personal style—the four "frames" of leadership, the participatory leadership model, or the distributed leadership model?
8. What advocacy skills do you think Harmony needs to polish? Looking at the Advocacy Competencies for her situation, what skills does she lack?
9. What functions do you see as appropriate in the coordination of your program? How would you go about establishing your leadership in terms of the programs and services you would coordinate within the structure of your program? ▪

Suggested Readings

Adelman, H. S., & Taylor, L. (1998). Reframing mental health in schools and expanding school reform. *Educational Psychologist, 33*(4), 135–152. This article lays the groundwork for the foundation of Adelman and Taylor's work in coordination and collaboration from a school perspective.

Barr, R. D., & Parrett, W. H. (2001). *Hope fulfilled for at-risk and violent youth: K–12 programs that work* (2nd ed.). Boston: Allyn and Bacon. This book provides examples of programs that have helped at-risk and violent youth to finish their secondary education. Counselors will find many ideas for collaboration with school and community professionals.

Bemak, F. (2000). Transforming the role of the counselor to provide leadership in educational reform through collaboration. *Professional School Counseling, 3*, 323–331. This article encourages school counselors to address the needs of young people who are most in danger of making unhealthy choices.

Bolman, L. G., & Deal, T. E. (1997). *Reframing organizations: Artistry, choice, and leadership* (2nd ed.). San Francisco: Jossey-Bass. These authors examine the four frames of leadership, applying these typologies to a variety of organizations and institutions. They also provide excellent ideas for developing leadership skills.

Burnham, J. J., & Jackson, C. M. (2000). School counselor roles: Discrepancies between actual practice and existing models. *Professional School Counseling, 4*, 41–49. A current study that describes the work that school counselors do (providing wonderful insights into how counselors actually spend their time) and then compares the findings to two existing models of comprehensive school counseling.

The Education Trust. (2001). Working definition of school counseling. Ed Trust: Transforming School Counseling. The DeWitt Wallace-Reader's Digest Fund, National Initiative for Transforming School Counseling. Retrieved March 2, 2001, from http://www.edtrust.org/main/school_counseling.asp. This organization has challenged school counselors to examine long-held, preconceived ideas of what school counseling

should be. There are many important insights into ways that school counselors can improve the quality of the work done in schools.

Keys, S. G., & Lockhart, E. J. (1999). The school counselor's role in facilitating multisystemic change. *Professional School Counseling, 3*, 101–107. In this article, the authors describe the role of the school counselor in collaboration and coordination across the student's subsystems of school, family, and community.

Koehler, M., & Kravets, M. (1998). *Counseling with secondary students with learning disabilities: A ready-to-use guide to help students prepare for college and work.* West Nyack, NY: Center for Applied Research in Education. The title describes this very useful book; a must-have for high school counselors.

Kouzes, J. M., & Posner, B. Z. (1995). *The leadership challenge: How to keep getting extraordinary things done in organizations.* San Francisco: Jossey-Bass. This book is full of exciting ways of viewing leadership that can help the reader understand the many skills that leaders employ in getting things done in organizations. An inspired and inspiring reading for anyone who hopes to get things done in the world.

Laveman, L. (2000). The Harmonium Project: A macrosystemic approach to empowering adolescents. *Journal of Mental Health Counseling, 22*(1), 17–32. This article describes the collaboration/coordination process from the community perspective, outlining how those in the community conceptualize their work with their school partners.

Professional School Counseling, volume 13, issue 2 [December 2009]: Special Issue on School Counselors and Leadership.

Professional School Counseling, volume 8, issue 5 [June, 2005]: Special Section on Empowerment.

Scruggs, M. Y., Wasielewski, R. A., & Ash, M. J. (1999). Comprehensive evaluation of a K–12 counseling program. *Professional School Counseling, 2*, 244–247. This article outlines the process of program evaluation, which will help to operationalize the section of this chapter on the leadership/management process.

Sitlington, P. L., Clark, G. M., & Kolstoe, O. P. (2000). *Transition education and services for adolescents with disabilities* (3rd ed.). Boston: Allyn and Bacon. This book provides an excellent overview of the need for transition services for students with disabilities and will generate many ideas for collaborating with special educators to facilitate the career development of these students.

Taylor, L., & Adelman, H. S. (2000). Connecting schools, families, and communities. *Professional School Counseling, 3,* 298–307. In this article, the Adelman and Taylor model of collaboration and coordination is specifically tied to the work of the school counselor.

Walsh, M. E., Howard, K. A., & Buckley, M. A. (1999). School counselors in school-community partnerships: Opportunities and challenges. *Professional School Counseling, 2,* 349–356. This article outlines many aspects of school-community partnerships and discusses variables that will improve the chances for these new models of collaboration to succeed.

12

The Delivery System in Action

LEARNING OBJECTIVE

By the end of this chapter, you will

1. Have examined the differences between the three levels of educational progression and understand the school counselor's main activities at each level

CASE STUDY

Kanika's Conundrum

Kanika just finished her graduate program and graduated with her master's in counseling with a school counseling emphasis. Even though she was certified K–12, her field experiences in her program had been at only the high school and middle school levels. By far, she preferred the high school level—she loved the high school age, she understood their issues, and she thought career exploration and college planning was exciting. It was her dream to work in a large high school, preferably in the district near her home town.

She was looking forward to becoming a school counselor, and had applied for every opportunity she heard about within a reasonable commuting distance. However, the economic situation in the state was not great and she knew that school counseling jobs would be scarce. A couple of districts had announced staffing cuts and had retracted the job postings announced earlier in the spring. Kanika was beginning to worry that she might not find what she wanted.

As the summer wore on, Kanika got very concerned. Would she have to take another waitressing job just to pay the rent? Then she heard that her favorite district might have an opening—but it was at the elementary level.

"Yikes!" she thought to herself. "Reading Mother Goose to kids all day? Using *puppets*? I don't know if I can do that!"

CHALLENGE QUESTIONS

How flexible are you in your thinking about the level you want to work? Is it true that elementary counseling consists of Mother Goose all day? What draws you to your favorite level, and what bothers you about your least favorite level? Can you see yourself working at all three levels? Why or why not? ■

SCHOOL COUNSELING ACROSS ELEMENTARY, MIDDLE, AND SECONDARY SCHOOLS: AN OVERVIEW

As we saw in the previous discussion on the National Model, school counselors in comprehensive school counseling programs work with all students in the school, providing all services in an environment of leadership, advocacy, and collaboration, with the goal of achieving systemic change and improvement. Exactly what that looks like will vary depending on a variety of factors. From the broadest source of variation to the most specific, these could include regional preferences, state department of education mandates, community and attendance zone issues, and building characteristics. Until now, we have been discussing school counseling as a whole, without making local/state distinctions or distinctions among the three educational levels. As a professional, you must attend to state and district mandates; you need to consult your state department of education for regulations and/or legislation and consult your district policy to understand local requirements and expectations.

The distinctions among school counseling activities at different grade levels are hard to identify; however, we can see distinctions among the three levels of educational progression: elementary, middle school, and secondary school. As we explored in depth in Chapter 2 in our discussion of developmentally appropriate education, schools should be built around an understanding of the development of young people; this understanding should include balanced consideration of academic, social, and emotional needs. Let's look at developmentally appropriate, comprehensive counseling at the three levels of elementary, middle, and secondary schools (Myrick, 1993). (First, though, a disclaimer: Different districts, for a variety of reasons, will configure schools in ways that are meaningful to that district. The following discussion will use grade levels that are most commonly associated with the three levels of schools: elementary, middle, and high schools.)

Elementary counseling encompasses the largest span of a young person's development. This span of development requires counselors to be sensitive to the needs of primary grade students (prekindergarten through third grade) as well as the needs of intermediate grade students (fourth through sixth grades). Elementary students in the primary grades are characterized by their strong ties to primary caregivers, the development of social skills, adjustment to nonhome environments and challenges, high need for physical activity, and rapid cognitive development (Charlesworth, 1996). Elementary students in the intermediate grades are characterized by the development of same-sex peer relationships, integration and solidification of prior learning, development of fine motor skills, and exploration of nonfamily adult relationships (Schickedanz et al., 1998). From these insights into development, it is easy to see why counselors in the elementary grades focus on building healthy self-concept, learning to get along with peers, developing morality and values, achieving personal independence, and developing healthy attitudes toward social groups (B. A. Snyder, 2000).

Both the focus of each activity and the amount of time devoted to each activity change according to the developmental level of the student. Overall, elementary counselors provide (1) behavioral counseling, with an emphasis on play and art in counseling, (2) small-group counseling focusing on issues and skills specific to elementary development, (3) classroom guidance in self-concept and adjustment issues, and (4) consultation for parents and teachers (Schmidt, 1999). The focus is more on personal/social development and academic development than on career development (Dollarhide, 2000b). According to Gysbers and Henderson (2000), elementary counselors ideally spend approximately 35 to 45 percent of their time in developmental guidance delivered in the classroom, with individual responsive services (counseling, consultation, and referrals) comprising approximately 30 to 40 percent of the counselor's time. Within this broad framework, elementary counselors adjust the amount of time providing individual counseling, depending on the level of language development and capacity for insight of the child (Schmidt, 1999). This would suggest that counselors generally spend more time counseling with intermediate students than with primary graders, due to the older students' greater abilities to understand themselves and their choices.

The middle school student is characterized by "transescence," being caught between childhood and adolescence (B. B. Baker, 2000). This educational phase involves multiple transitions: the transition from small neighborhood elementary schools to larger, more diverse middle or junior high schools, and the transition from childhood to adolescence. Young people at this stage of development struggle with their self-esteem, focus on their status relative to peers, begin to experiment with various behaviors, and develop formal thought processes (Schickedanz et al., 1998). It is at this point that many young people begin to exhibit the signs of troubles to come: eating disorders; unhealthy sexual choices; smoking, drug, and alcohol use; and lack of interest or motivation in schools (Schickedanz et al., 1998), increasing the need for counselors to be proactive and aware of each student's unique challenges.

To address these developmental needs, middle school counselors have to be as flexible and spontaneous as their students are. Typical activities include insight-oriented and rational individual counseling; group counseling (which, given the transescent's focus on peers, is usually highly effective); peer helping and mediation programming; transitional services to ease students from elementary to middle school and then from middle to high school; developmental curriculum on change, sexuality, healthy choices, and conflict resolution; and consultation with teachers, and to a lesser degree, with parents (Schmidt, 1999). Middle school counselors generally distribute their time equitably across issues addressing personal/social development, career development, and academic development (Dollarhide, 2000b). Other ways that middle school counseling will vary from elementary school counseling include more emphasis on crisis counseling and management and more developmental curriculum involving drug and alcohol education and prevention (B. B. Baker, 2000), realities shared by secondary school counselors.

The developmental issues of young people in secondary schools involve the search for identity, independence, self-definition, meaningful relationships, and ways to make a unique contribution to the world. In response, school counselors need to become more aware of their roles as student advocate and environmental assessor, working to enhance the climate of mutual respect in secondary schools. Coy and Sears (2000) identify the primary activities for secondary school counselors as individual counseling, group guidance, group counseling, career development and information services, placement, consultation, and coordination. Similarly, Schmidt (1999) found that counseling, decision making about postsecondary options, providing college information, and helping with class schedules were the most important counseling services as identified by students, parents, and teachers. The focus of secondary counselors often shifts away from personal/social development, to focus instead on career and academic development (Dollarhide, 2000b).

In a report funded by the Bill and Melinda Gates Foundation conducted by Public Agenda entitled *Can I get a little advice here? How an overstretched high school guidance system is undermining students'college aspirations* (Johnson, Rochkind, Ott, & DuPont, 2010), the issues of postsecondary advisement are examined. As highlighted in the title of the report, the findings suggest that high school counselors need to be more informed about colleges and more intentional about helping students, especially diverse students and first-generation college students, to consider college as their primary option after high school. The report blames inadequate high school advisement for low college attendance rates. This perspective is important to consider if you are thinking about becoming a high school counselor.

REFLECTION MOMENT

Can you see the different ways that school counselors function at various levels? With which age group do you see yourself functioning most effectively?

In this chapter, the ASCA National Model is seen at each of the educational levels as it is operationalized in an award-winning program. Each section of this chapter has been authored by a counselor educator who interviewed the professional school counselor in a RAMP school—a school in which the comprehensive school counseling program has been recognized as an exemplary ASCA National Model program. For the year in which these schools won this prestigious designation, there were only eight such honorees nationally.

In reviewing ASCA's website, the following statement introduces the Recognized ASCA Model Program, or RAMP, distinction:

> The RAMP designation, awarded to schools that align with the criteria set in the "ASCA National Model: A Framework for School Counseling," recognizes schools that are committed to delivering a comprehensive, data-driven school counseling program and an exemplary educational environment. (American School Counselor Association, November 22, 2005)

The purpose of this chapter is to give you an overview of what such exemplary programs involve and to provide an image of what the job, program, and counselor activities might include. After all, the journey to a destination is much smoother when you know where you're going— you need to be able to envision a model program in order to create your own.

THE ASCA NATIONAL MODEL IN THE ELEMENTARY SCHOOL

By Charles Lindsey,
University of Wisconsin, Oshkosh

PROFILE OF SCHOOL: Ford Elementary School, Tucson, Arizona

School Demographics

In looking at the socioeconomic status of the school population in terms of free and reduced lunch, the counselor indicates that of the 350 students, approximately 200 receive free lunch and 60 receive reduced lunch. Demographically, the majority (43.8 percent) of Ford Elementary School students are Caucasian. The second largest demographic is Hispanic (approximately 38.3 percent), with smaller percentages of African American, Native American, and Pacific Islander students comprising the remainder of the school population.

There are 14 full-time classroom teachers at Ford Elementary School, 1 counselor, and 1 administrator. There are approximately 25 total staff when support staff are included. Ford Elementary School is 1 of 74 elementary schools in the Tucson Unified School District (TUSD). In addition, Ford Elementary has implemented the counseling-related program entitled "Bully-Proofing Your School" and is a leader among elementary schools in the district in using and promoting this program.

Comprehensive Competency-Based School Counseling Program

The School Counseling Program at Ford Elementary

1. Serves all students
2. Is proactive and prevention based
3. Provides developmentally appropriate curriculum
4. Uses the American School Counseling Association National Standards for the elementary level
5. Can be objectively evaluated

The comprehensive competency-based guidance (CCBG) program is congruent with the school district's mission, philosophy, curriculum, and Arizona Academic Standards

(Tucson Unified School District, 2003). In addition, the guidance and counseling program at Ford Elementary School comprises a system of interconnected and interdependent elements, organized into four major areas:

1. *Foundation.* Elements that provide the framework for the counseling program and defines student results
2. *Delivery system.* Ways that the guidance program is delivered to students
3. *Management system.* The process by which the guidance program is managed for results
4. *Accountability.* Measurements of student results, the effectiveness of counselors, and overall program success

Foundation

The foundation provides the counseling program's framework and defines student results. Included in this component are such aspects as mission statement, philosophy, goals, and standards/competencies. The counselor approached building the foundation for her program by looking closely at the mission statements and philosophies of both the district and her school, then blended them to create counseling program mission and philosophy statements that fit well with her school specifically.

This counselor directly tied her foundational goals to the standards and competencies set forth in the American School Counselor Association National Model (2003a). In fact, the TUSD Elementary Standards are adapted from the ASCA National Standards, and these nine standards are organized in academic, career, and personal/social domains. Constantly looking at how various program components relate and interconnect is precisely the technique the counselor recommends not only for putting a comprehensive school counseling program together but also in formulating a RAMP application.

Delivery System

The delivery system includes the ways in which the guidance program is delivered to students and is further divided into the subcomponents of guidance curriculum, individual planning, responsive services, and system support.

GUIDANCE CURRICULUM AND INDIVIDUAL PLANNING Guidance curriculum includes classroom guidance lessons, large-group activities, and structured small-group guidance. The counselor describes spending a large part of her day in classrooms presenting on an array of CCBG developmentally appropriate topics usually selected with the input of teachers and relating directly to the overarching CCBG model. She is consequently able to connect topics directly with competencies outlined in the CCBG model.

Regarding school counseling curriculum lessons, the counselor states that the district has a number of counseling-based lessons online, and that this resource pool is continuously growing. Small-group work has decreased significantly due to the frequency with which she is delivering classroom guidance lessons. She does, however, spend a portion of each day working in smaller groups with children. She typically enters several different classrooms on a daily basis between 8 and 10 A.M.—what is called a "literacy block" period. During this time she provides individual planning, working individually or in small groups with children who are struggling with an array of issues having a negative impact on their academic performance.

RESPONSIVE SERVICES Responsive services include activities that meet the immediate needs and concerns of students and include consultation, personal counseling, crisis counseling, and referrals to community services. Because the counselor is the sole counselor at Ford Elementary School, she plays a significant role as a consultant working with teachers, administrators, parents, and counselor-colleagues within the district in determining how the needs of specific students might best be met. She is available if the need for crisis counseling surfaces and will make referrals to community services when warranted, often consulting with other elementary school counselors or the district counseling office to assess appropriate referrals.

SYSTEM SUPPORT   System support comprises management activities that support the guidance program through professional development, research and development, staff and community relations, and consultation activities with staff, parents, and the advisory council. In the Tucson Unified School District, school counselors are required to regularly update their professional knowledge and skills. The counselor places much personal importance on professional development and adds that she will take every continuing education opportunity available to her.

Consultation is another means by which the counselor develops system support for her school counseling program. She regularly consults with teachers, staff members, and parents in order to provide information, to support the school community, and to receive feedback on the emerging needs of students. One specific avenue for consultation that the counselor uses, and actually facilitates, is the Ford Elementary Site Council. This is a site-based advisory committee that includes and represents the students, parents, faculty, staff, members of the community, business partners, and the school principal (Inez C. Ford Elementary School, 2006). The goals of the council include providing a framework for site decision making; promoting an improved education process to meet the needs of students; facilitating communication between the site council, the school, community, and TUSD; and reviewing guidance program results and recommending priorities to the appropriate administrative bodies.

The counselor emphasizes that through the Ford Elementary Site Council, she is able to build positive relationships and convey vital information to stakeholders. Site council meetings occur on a monthly basis, and the counselor underscores that this team is highly "data-driven"; she typically presents some type of data to the group at each meeting and this requires her to constantly think about research and development within her program. Consequently, she has learned to delve into efforts such as guidance program evaluation, data analysis, follow-up studies, and the continued development and updating of guidance learning activities and resources.

Management System

The record keeping, documentation, and process evaluation component that reviews student results are included in the management system.

In the Tucson Unified School District, each counselor takes the initiative in developing a counselor-principal agreement. This agreement is essentially a statement of responsibility by each counselor specifying the results for which he or she will be accountable. The counselor-principal agreement is unique to the CCBG process in that it becomes the single most important document outlining outcomes to be attained with students, staff, parents, community, and the counselor's own professional development. Each TUSD counselor is also responsible for a school plan that addresses how the desired results for the counseling program will be achieved. The plan specifically contains the standards/competencies that will be addressed through the counseling program, in addition to anticipated completion dates. School counselors in the district must also develop a master calendar of guidance events they have planned throughout the school year.

Accountability

Accountability serves to measure the overall success of the counseling program. The counselor emphasizes that a primary benefit of the assessment system is to examine the needs in her school, as well as assess the gap between the desired results of the counseling program and results that are actually being achieved. She underscores the use of data to determine gaps in the program, and through assessment she is also able to make informed decisions regarding needed changes in the program.

Professional school counselors in the TUSD use a Needs Data Survey to assess what competencies need to be taught, to document the competencies in which students may already be proficient, and to gauge how effective counseling instruction and interventions have been (Tucson Unified School District, 2003). Needs data surveys may be given to students, parents, teachers, administrators, other school personnel, and community members. These surveys are available at all school counseling offices within the district and are also available in a Spanish-language version. Other forms of data typically used by TUSD counselors to plan and evaluate their programs include analysis of attendance rates, standardized test scores, performance objectives, mobility information, school quality surveys, and tracking the numbers of students who need additional tutoring. These data are collected, analyzed, and used to drive individual counseling programs.

The counselor states that she has used the district intranet as a tool in the "closing the gap" effort implemented at Ford Elementary School. By using data, she focused on students who were falling below a 90 percent attendance rate and developed interventions to increase attendance for these students. She reports that in a matter of months, the attendance rate for these specific students increased to above 95 percent. More specifically, during the first quarter of the school year, the counselor used the database to focus on students below a 90 percent attendance rate. She adds that she often couples the letter she sends to parents with a "check-in" group in which chronically truant students are required to report to the counselor before school begins. As part of this "check-in" process, students simply use a sticker chart to recognize when they are on time for school; when a certain number of on-time arrivals have been consistently achieved, students receive an attendance certificate celebrating their accomplishment.

Additional assessment system measures employed by school counselors in the TUSD include quarterly program audits of guidance activities and specific results of counseling programs; these audits are submitted by counselors to the district guidance office. Counselors are also responsible for annually assessing their programs by using a program evaluation instrument developed by the district. The program evaluation instrument helps counselors assess the level and quality of their programmatic implementation and the general effectiveness of their programs and provides a basis for considering program improvements.

The counselor states that TUSD school counselors are evaluated according to professional counselor performance standards that have been developed for the district. These performance standards serve both as a basis for counselor evaluation by their administrators and as a means for counselor self-evaluation. It is through these accountability components that the counselor is charged to continuously reflect on the caliber of her counseling program and the effect it is having on all students at Ford Elementary School, to consider how the program might be improved, and to envision ways to demonstrate the successes of her program to stakeholders.

Elementary Calendar Year Breakdown

SUMMER During the summer, the counselor focuses strongly on professional development and attempts to attend as many professional conferences as possible.

FALL As the school year begins, the counselor has learned to give teachers a couple of weeks to "settle in" with their students. She typically doesn't schedule much during the first two weeks of school and instead uses this time to assist with kindergarten students and to help with other issues that arise as the school year gains momentum. Each year during the first two weeks of school, a districtwide reading test is delivered, and the counselor is responsible for overseeing the testing for grades K–3.

After the first couple of weeks of school, the counselor then creates a sign-up sheet for teachers to indicate their time preferences for her to enter their classrooms, both to support the teachers during the morning 8–10 A.M. "reading-block period" and for regular CCBG programming. She adds that for school year 2005–2006, her schedule became so full that she had to create "A" and "B" schedules—alternating between them on a weekly basis. She asks teachers for feedback on the types of topics and issues that might be appropriate for their specific classrooms and in so doing attempts to maintain a level of flexibility in her program delivery.

SPRING   When school begins again in January, the counselor reports that her schedule typically will follow the same rhythm as that developed in the fall. This can change, however, depending on school needs based on an assessment of the fall semester. As an example, the counselor notes that when she moved into the spring of 2006, she focused greater attention on kindergarten and first-grade classes, because there seemed to be some significant issues surfacing in these grades. She emphasizes that each spring is unique for the counseling program because it is shaped by what occurred the previous fall. Importantly, each intervention that is implemented is evidenced based, and data collection is important as the counselor provides feedback to the school, district administrators, and the Ford site council.

The counselor underscores that by the spring, she usually knows every student on a first-name basis and has some rapport built with a majority of students. She reports that this also provides important insight into programming alterations that might be most appropriate for the latter part of the school year. She serves as the interim principal when the existing principal has to be away from the school. When asked if this proves to be a conflict for her, she stated, "I have a solid rapport with my students and they know that they can come to me, even though at times I must play an administrative role. I think it comes down to my knowing them on a personal level and relating to them primarily from a counseling perspective."

END OF YEAR   The end of the school year is again marked by a series of reading tests that are delivered schoolwide. This counselor, therefore, spends time engaging students in test-taking strategies, developing relaxation skills, and delivering transition lessons with students as they prepare to move to the next grade. The end of the year is also a time for her to reflect on the year as a whole and to assess both the strengths and the shortcomings within the program. In so doing, she strives to make continued improvements within the program and to honestly evaluate her role as an evolving professional.

THE ASCA NATIONAL MODEL IN THE MIDDLE SCHOOL

By Phyllis K. Robertson,
Western Carolina University

PROFILE OF SCHOOL: Sequoia Middle School, Fontana, California

School Demographics

The Sequoia Middle School counseling program has adopted the logo of the Eyrie—Where Eaglets Fledge. Like eagles caring for eaglets in a nest, the counseling team wants their students to be nurtured, secure, and respected, and given a safe place to spread their wings while learning the skills needed to succeed in life. The counseling program at Sequoia utilizes a comprehensive, developmental approach to delivering services to the entire school community. The concept of the eyrie supports the understanding of the middle school years as times of rapid growth and development in cognitive, emotional, and physical characteristics for students and the necessity for gentle support and guidance by knowledgeable and caring adults.

Sequoia MS is located in Southern California in Fontana, a suburban area of Los Angeles. Fontana has grown rapidly as people who work in Los Angeles and Orange counties found the housing more affordable in the former steel mill town. Many of the parents of Sequoia children commute to these two counties for work. The school operates on a trimester schedule and serves seventh- and eighth-graders with an enrollment approaching 1,400. Fifty-three percent of the students receive free or reduced lunch and 11 percent of the students receive special education services. Race/ethnicity percentages for students are Black, 3 percent; Asian, 1 percent; Native American, 0 percent; White, 7 percent; Hispanic, 88 percent; and Other, 1 percent. Of their students, 80 percent speak Spanish with the majority fluent in English as well. Students with limited English speaking, writing, and reading abilities are identified soon after enrollment and represent approximately 3.3 percent of the students.

Foundation

Through counselor leadership and collaboration, school administrators, faculty, parents, and students at Sequoia support the concept of the school counseling program and recognize the value of a comprehensive, developmental counseling program in the school. The school counseling program mission statement currently states:

> The mission of the Sequoia Middle School counseling program is to prepare Sequoia students for success in our ever changing world. Our comprehensive, developmental counseling program addresses academic, career, and personal/social development to assure high levels of learning for ALL students. Sequoia School Counselors advocate for the success of all students. Working with parents, students, staff, and the community, the School Counselors develop, implement, and evaluate programs to assure student success.

This mission statement is aligned with the school's and district's statements and will be updated as the school board revises its mission statement and goals. The counseling program philosophy is based on the ASCA model, national standards, and ethical guidelines. It states that all students are important; have the ability to be responsible, respectful, and successful; and have the right to participate in a school counseling program with access to a full-time credentialed professional school counselor. It includes a delivery system with guidance curriculum for all students as well as closing-the-gap activities, individual planning, responsive services, and system support.

Delivery System

There are 96 faculty and staff at Sequoia, and only two school counselors who serve an average of 700 students each. Students access the school counselors by alphabetical listing or by availability of the counselor. Delivery system domains of career and personal/social are divided by the two counselors and both work in the academic domain. The rationale for division of these duties was based on mutual agreement by the counselors and on the professional development experiences at the district and state level. One counselor is responsible for construction of the master schedule with teacher course assignments and student registration duties, and the other is responsible for coordinating the annual testing program.

The school counseling department is open for student/parent/teacher access from 7 A.M. to 2 P.M. The counselors work together to schedule activities and presentations so that a counselor is always available in the counseling department for responsive services. As the Sequoia counselors strive to meet the needs of all students, group counseling, large-group guidance, closing-the-gap activities, coordination activities, and peer leadership activities are scheduled and posted to allow for optimal interaction with students.

School counselors are also available during evening parent meetings. Programs and services presented and available to parents include guidance advisory committee, counselor websites, school counseling brochure, peer program brochure, consultation with parents, and scheduled parent meetings. Brochures and websites are available in Spanish and English.

The counseling department has a full-time guidance technician who completes data entry for scheduling and assists with the master schedule and schoolwide testing. The clerk also handles student records, grades and progress reports, and student study team paperwork. The school receptionist processes paperwork for new student enrollment.

Written survey needs assessments are given at the beginning of each school year to students, parents, and teachers, and during the parent orientation program. These surveys are also available throughout the school year in the counseling department and during additional parent meetings for parents to complete. The Support Personnel Accountability Report Card (SPARC) team examines the data and develops a comprehensive program that impacts the overall school climate and safety for all students. This team consists of administrators, counselors, faculty and staff, parents, and community members.

CLASSROOM INSTRUCTION   With the increased focus on classroom accountability in California, it was initially determined that counselors would provide curriculum through the elective and physical education classes. Seventh-grade competencies/indicators focus on study skills, and eighth-grade competencies/indicators focuses on decision-making skills. The same class and topic configuration is maintained so that all students enrolled for two consecutive years will receive all of the lessons.

The leadership team at Sequoia determined that ongoing Character Education lessons were needed throughout the year, which has led to all teachers providing Character Education sessions within their curriculum to promote positive behaviors and relationships on campus. This change has led to 90 percent of the school faculty, staff, and students participating in the Character Education program. In addition, faculty and staff help students beyond their regular academic responsibilities to include a variety of topics and support counselor-led guidance lessons.

INTERDISCIPLINARY CURRICULUM DEVELOPMENT   All strong counseling programs must have the support of an educated, active and responsible guidance advisory committee. This committee at Sequoia consists of the two counselors, one administrator, student peer leaders, four to five parents, and teachers. The chairperson is typically a parent, but for 2005, a student led the council. Meetings are held once a trimester in the morning and evening to accommodate member schedules. Meetings have been held later in the evening after parent conferencing nights to eliminate travel time for parents. The committee assists the school counselors in developing goals and objectives, planning and implementing College Day, planning parent trainings and in-services, and discussing and approving the Support Personnel Accountability Report Card. As opportunities arise, the guidance advisory committee is capable of becoming more involved in other areas of the program.

SCHOOLWIDE AND SMALL-GROUP ACTIVITIES   Make a Friend at Sequoia (MAFAS) day is part of the transition program from the elementary school to the middle school. Each sixth-grade teacher at the feeder schools selects a boy and a girl to spend an entire day with a seventh-grade boy or girl at the middle school. This allows for special attention to be given to students who may be at risk or experience difficulty with change.

Other programs include Kick Butts Day, a national day sponsored by Tobacco Free Kids Organization (2005) for increasing awareness of the dangers of tobacco use, in which peer leaders receive training on prevention activities and then deliver these activities to the rest of the school. On College Day, the faculty and staff wear college shirts and talk about positive college experiences, and the guidance advisory committee passes out college information to students. In addition to these events, Mix It Up Day is an international day sponsored through the Tolerance.org project by the Southern Poverty Law and Study Circles Resource Centers. At Sequoia, 200 students are chosen to go through trainings about diversity, communication skills, social boundaries, and cliques, and experience a variety of group activities. These students promote and participate in the Mix It Up at Lunch Day where students are encouraged to sit and talk with other students they would not normally socialize with at the lunch table. After the event, these students have a discussion and debriefing through the use of a postsurvey to determine areas of strength or concern they have for their school population on issues of tolerance and acceptance of differences. Administrators and teachers are actively involved in supporting the event.

Anger management, safety, and conflict resolution services are available for families and students from the school resource officer and campus security officers. These classes are for students who have been involved in a physical altercation at the school.

PARENT WORKSHOPS AND INSTRUCTION Parent workshops have been offered on the topics of bullying, academic improvement, and high school graduation requirements. Work and family demands placed on parents have led to low turnout for some evening workshops, so the counselors have now prepared a series of workshops that are held once a month on multiple topics at different times of day. This strategy allows for flexibility in the parents' work schedule and parents have direct input into topic choice for any of the sessions on the given day.

In addition, the website for the school counseling program provides parenting tips addressing such areas as drug and alcohol prevention, college information, community and national services for adolescents, information on teen health issues, and discipline and communication styles. The website includes a link to a parent conflict survey created by Positive Parenting for Teens on the University of Minnesota's Extension Service website. This survey is straightforward and convenient for parents to use in gaining understanding of their child(ren) and themselves by interpreting responses to communication and discipline conflicts.

As the number of non-English speaking families continues to increase, the school counseling and peer program brochures are published in English and Spanish.

INDIVIDUAL OR SMALL-GROUP APPRAISAL Counselor Catch is a program where the counselors try to "catch" their students being successful and recognize them with rewards. The counselors periodically ask teachers if students (randomly selected) have homework done, or the counselors may go into a classroom to see who has work written in their "planner" or dressed out for PE. In 2004 the school's accountability report card indicated that 66 percent of the students in the school were caught doing their homework.

The counselors have eighth-grade students examine their career aspirations by using the Career Cruising (2005) website in computer lab settings. The counselors monitor students in one class session for three weeks while they complete surveys on interests and skills while matching these to an extensive list of possible careers. The counselors take an active role in relating the career information to academics through completion of a worksheet and application of the information discussed in the recorded interviews with people from different career fields. An early development of student career portfolios is supported in these classes. The website program is offered in both English and Spanish.

INDIVIDUAL OR SMALL-GROUP ADVISEMENT Each counselor and administrator assumes the role of Administrative Designee for the Exceptional Children's program for involvement in IEP meetings and 504 plan development. Counselors serve the same role as administrators in these meetings and maintain active involvement in securing appropriate services for special needs students.

Prealgebra, algebra, and geometry courses are offered at the middle school with counselors having the chance to advocate for students enrolling in the higher math classes. Through this advocacy, in 2004 the number of eighth-graders has increased in algebra and geometry, and the number of seventh-graders in algebra. The counselors work with the math lead teachers to determine placement based on a set criteria, providing the opportunity for students to enroll in high school classes that will ensure that they meet college entrance requirements.

CONSULTATION Consultation with teachers, administrators, and parents provides many opportunities for counselors to advocate for students. The mentor-mentee program at Sequoia addresses the goals for No Child Left Behind by identifying students who are on the border of passing the state exams. Individual teachers work with 250 students for academic encouragement. Consultation and subsequent counseling referrals from these teachers can often lead to interventions that address attendance issues, basic school supply needs, peer conflicts, and family issues that prevent these students from performing to their greatest potential academically.

As an Administrative Designee to the Exceptional Children's program, the counselors stay actively involved in consultation with teachers, parents, and community resources in meeting the needs of students.

INDIVIDUAL AND SMALL-GROUP COUNSELING   While one counselor is delivering classroom guidance activities, the other is available for individual and small-group counseling. During lunchtime students can drop by the counseling offices for brief chats and schedule appointments. Scheduled small-group sessions include TEMP sessions (Together Everyone Makes Progress), which are offered each trimester for students who are experiencing some type of turmoil in their life. Such experiences can include divorce or separation, approaching death of a loved one, and domestic violence. The counselors also implement Youth Connections, which is a privately developed program adopted and required by the school district for small-group counseling. The curriculum for the program was created by Rainbow Days Youth Connection and has tested reliability. Seven groups of 8 to 14 students meet for 6 to 10 sessions each year. These students participate in sessions addressing identity development, handling anger, goal setting, decision making, dealing with peer pressure, and drug and alcohol prevention.

CRISIS COUNSELING   Each counselor participates in crisis intervention training designed and provided by the school district. This allows for uniformity of the delivery of services throughout the district.

REFERRALS   For internal school referrals for student services, counselors consult with the school psychologist, resource officer, speech and language specialist, physical and occupational therapist, adaptive physical education specialist, and a district counselor who works with teen parents. An approved list of external referral sources in the county is provided by the school district. Counselors can have input into this list of services but approval for contact remains with the district office.

PEER FACILITATION   Peer mediation is available daily for students. Peer leaders are trained in mediation and communication skills to encourage their peers to make positive choices when dealing with everyday conflict. A peer teacher meets with the students one class period per day to train them as peer helpers using the Peer Assistance Leadership (PAL) program and Schrumpf et al.'s (1997) peer mediation book. In the classes, seventh- and eighth-graders learn listening and attending skills, problem-solving strategies, and the mediation process, culminating in peer mediation certification. After one year of class work, students who have excelled are chosen to become peer leaders who are then assigned to the counselor one class period per day for the purpose of providing mediation, personal support, and educational programs for students. These students conduct these programs within the counseling program offices where they receive supervision by a counselor. Peer leaders use PowerPoint presentations to work with small groups of eighth-grade students to explain the high school registration process, graduation requirements, and college entrance requirements. These small-group meetings are held prior to the high school counselors' involvement in registering the students for high school courses. Another service the peer leaders give is a meet-and-greet experience for new students by providing a welcome and tour of the campus on their first day.

PROFESSIONAL DEVELOPMENT   The school counseling team partakes in professional development by participating in the American School Counselor Association conference and listserv discussions, the California Association of School Counselors conference and Leadership Development Institute, the Education Trust conference, district and regional workshops, and service on district and site committees. The school counselors participate in the California

Association for School Counseling Leadership Development Institute each year to become refreshed on innovative and reliable school counseling services. The school counseling department meets monthly among themselves, in faculty meetings, with administrators, and with the leadership team.

IN-SERVICE TRAINING   The lead counselor is actively involved in the school's leadership team monthly meetings where many site school decisions are deliberated. The leadership team members include administrators, the student body director, department chairpersons, and the lead counselor.

Relationship aggression staff in-service was provided for the faculty and staff at Sequoia. Several faculty members have had lunch discussions about books, which have now led to in-service programs after school in which faculty members get together to talk about the readings and their relationship to working with the students at Sequoia. On-site programs and services are presented and available to staff, which include adolescent development in-services, participation in leadership team meetings, and dissemination of research and current readings on adolescent development and best practices. All teachers, counselors, and administrators are fluent in Spanish, or are enrolled in Spanish classes, to meet the needs of Sequoia's Limited English Proficient (LEP) students.

Management System

Consultation about school community and program needs occurs through meetings of the Guidance Advisory Committee (GAC), interaction with counselor websites, dissemination of the school counseling program brochures and peer program brochures, consultations with individual parents, and scheduled parent meetings.

Sequoia Middle School has many community partnerships/resource services. These partners expose students to community resources, expand their understanding of future occupations, teach tolerance for others, and reward academic success. These services are critically important to students and families as the work is performed by providing academic student incentives, mentoring, tutoring, personal/social counseling services, curriculum training, peer leader training, and College Day information sharing.

Accountability

Funding resources supporting the school counseling program include school site funds, Safe and Drug-Free School funds, and tobacco use prevention funds. Data analysis for the counseling program consists of record keeping of individual and small-group contacts, where pre- and post-surveys are completed for all activities. The program uses an internal data collection system for obtaining information on attendance, GPA, and the number of discipline referrals.

Table 12.1 summarizes the responsive and support services and activities employed at Sequoia each trimester.

THE ASCA NATIONAL MODEL IN THE HIGH SCHOOL

By Robert I. Urofsky,
CACREP Director (formerly with Clemson University)

PROFILE OF SCHOOL: Wakefield High School, Raleigh, North Carolina

School Demographics

Wakefield High School is located in city of Raleigh, which is also the state capital. Wakefield High School is a comprehensive public secondary school located in the northern suburbs of Raleigh. The school is located in a fairly new community that saw a large growth in new homes

TABLE 12.1 Sequoia Middle School Program Calendar, 2004–2005

First Trimester	Second Trimester	Third Trimester
Seventh-grade orientation	Youth Connection group work	Personal/social guidance lessons
Career Plan Development	TEMP group counseling	Kick Butts Day
Character education lessons	Leadership meeting (3)	Leadership meetings (3)
Leadership meetings (3)	Mentor/mentee program starts	CAT testing
Guidance advisory committee management	Mix It Up Day	Staff meetings (3)
Academic development guidance lessons	Personal/social development guidance lessons	Career development guidance lessons
College Day	Second Youth Connection group	Staff in-service
Relationship aggression staff development	Second TEMP group	Make a Friend at Sequoia Day
Red Ribbon Week	Peer program training	Career plan development
Staff meetings (3)	College Day	Counselor Catch
Counselor Catch	Peer education of graduation and college entrance requirements	Guidance advisory committee management
Honor roll evening program	Staff meetings (3)	
	Guidance advisory committee management	
	High school registration	
	Counselor Catch	
	Honor Roll evening program	

beginning around 2000. The school opened in 1999 in response to growing population in the area. It had a total enrollment of 1,920 students in 2004–2005 and 2,156 students in 2005–2006. The 2005 senior class enrollment was 469 students. There are 516 Wakefield High School students identified as special education students and 239 students with Individualized Education Plans, as well as 277 considered academically gifted. The 2003–2004 school year saw the start of a Ninth-Grade Academy at Wakefield as part of a countywide Ninth-Grade Academy initiative.

The school's administration consists of a principal, an assistant principal for instruction, three assistant principals, and an assistant principal intern. In 2004–2005, the school had 175 full staff with 128 teachers and a support staff of 12 administrative and clerical assistants. The school's Counseling and Student Services Department consists of a Dean of Student Services, four school counselors, a Student Assistance Program counselor, a career development counselor, and an intervention coordinator.

The ethnic makeup of the school closely mirrors that of the county as a whole. Approximately 64 percent of the students are White, 23 percent African American, 6 percent Hispanic, and 4 percent Asian. Wake County employs districting or zoning to maximize the mix of socioeconomic status of students in the schools. Some students come from 15 to 20 miles away to attend Wakefield High School. Eighteen percent of students at Wakefield receive a free or reduced lunch. Wakefield has an English-as-a-second-language (ESL) student population of approximately 100 students from the northeast portion of the county. Not all schools in Wake County have these ESL programs.

The mission statement for Wakefield High School states, "The Wakefield High School educational community will work together to guide and encourage students to become lifelong learners and productive citizens of a global society." The school offers three courses of study: career prep, college tech prep, and college/university prep. Approximately 66 percent of students indicate plans to attend a four-year college, 23 percent plan to attend a two-year college, and 11 percent indicate plans for military/other. The 2005 average SAT score for Wakefield High School was 1057 (Verbal 518, Math 539), which was slightly lower than the Wake County total of 1075 and above the North Carolina total of 1010. The 2005 AP test averages data showed average scores above four in the areas of calculus AB, calculus BC, economics-macro, German language, and human geography; above three in art/drawing, biology, chemistry, English literature, European history, French language, government/politics U.S.; psychology, Spanish language, and statistics. In 2004, Wakefield met 100 percent of the target goals for Adequate Yearly Progress (AYP) standards for No Child Left Behind (NCLB), as well as ABC standards used with the North Carolina Department of Public Instruction.

Wakefield High School offers courses on a 4 × 4 block schedule. In line with its mission statement, Wakefield High School offers advanced placement and honors courses, as well as a vocational and business program designed to prepare students for the world of work. Coursework in this program includes drafting, carpentry, business education, and family and consumer science. The school has award-winning programs in instrumental music, chorus, theater, visual arts, and dance. Wakefield High School provides dual enrollment opportunities for selected elective courses not offered at Wakefield through cooperative arrangements with local universities and technical community colleges.

Program Context

Wakefield High School's Counseling and Student Services Department consists of a Dean of Student Services, four school counselors, a Student Assistance Program (SAP) counselor, a career development counselor, and an intervention coordinator. One counselor is assigned to the ninth grade and the remaining grades are split alphabetically among the other three counselors. The Dean of Student Services functions as a liaison between the counselors and the school administration, coordinates departmental activities and course registration, works with the assistant principal of instruction on curriculum and instruction matters, serves as the scholarship coordinator for Wakefield High School, and serves as the counselor for midyear graduates. The average number of students served by each counselor is approximately 450 students. The school is allotted counselors according to the number of students enrolled at the school. The school started in 1999 with two counselors. After two years, two more counselors were added and then another was added a year later. There is the possibility that another counselor will be added soon. In addition to the counseling staff, there are two full-time clerical assistants. The clerical assistants free up the counselors' time by taking care of many noncounseling tasks such as scheduling appointments, maintaining up-to-date information resources, and helping students locate information.

In addition to the school counselors, there are a number of other student service personnel providing support to students at Wakefield High School. There is a career development counselor included in the Counseling and Student Services Department, whose position is different from the other counselors. This counselor handles students who are participating in internships, coordinates a career fair, conducts career education with each grade, and works with a Business Alliance. There is also an intervention coordinator who works closely with ninth-graders who scored low on the eighth-grade end-of-year tests to develop personal education plans. This individual also works with the school's credit recovery program. A transition counselor is spread out over several schools in the district, working specifically with students who are suspended long-term. There are school-based mental-health personnel working with students with mental health needs who do not have insurance to cover a private therapist. In addition, Wakefield High School shares the services of a school psychologist, a school nurse, a speech pathologist, a physical therapist, and an academically gifted coordinator with other schools in the district. There are financial aid counselors who come in once per week to work with students and their families on completing FAFSA (free application for federal student aid) applications.

Foundation

The school counselors in the Counseling and Student Services Department at Wakefield High School connected to and built on the mission and values statements of the school in developing their own philosophy/vision, belief, and mission statements. The following philosophy/vision, belief, and mission statements guide the school counselors' actions and activities at Wakefield High School:

WAKEFIELD HIGH SCHOOL COUNSELING AND STUDENT SERVICES DEPARTMENT PHILOSOPHY AND VISION STATEMENT

The Counseling and Student Services Department of Wakefield High School will foster a learning environment and opportunities in which all students can achieve academically, socially, and prepare for postsecondary career options. This statement is consistent with the No Child Left Behind reform movement of the United States Government, the NC Accountability Plan (ABC Plan) and Wake County Public Schools' Goals 2008. The Wake County Schools Goal 2008 states: "By 2008, 95 percent of students in grades 3 through 12 will be at or above grade level as measured by the State of North Carolina End-of-Grade or Course tests, and all student groups will demonstrate high growth."

WAKEFIELD HIGH SCHOOL COUNSELING AND STUDENT SERVICES DEPARTMENT BELIEF STATEMENTS

The counselors in Wakefield High School believe

- All students can learn and should be given the opportunity to do so.
- All students have dignity and worth.
- All students have the right to participate in the school counseling program.
- All students' ethnic, cultural, racial, sexual differences and special needs are considered in planning and implementing the school counseling program.
- All students have access to a full-time, state-certified, master's degree level school counselor to deliver the counseling program.

The school counseling program should

- Be based on specified goals and developmental student competencies for all students
- Be based on the fact that learning requires the active participation, mutual respect, and individual accountability of students, teachers, staff, parents, and community members
- Include education that extends beyond the classroom environment allowing students to develop lifelong learning skills and encourage ethical and moral behavior
- Be based upon data, which will be used in assessing the needs of the school counseling program and will drive program development and evaluation

All counselors at Wakefield High School

- Will abide by the professional school counseling ethics as advocated by the American School Counselor Association
- Will participate in professional development activities essential to maintain a quality school counseling program

WAKEFIELD HIGH SCHOOL COUNSELING AND STUDENT SERVICES DEPARTMENT MISSION STATEMENT

The Counseling and Student Services Department of Wakefield High School will provide a comprehensive developmental counseling program addressing the academic, career, and personal/social development of all students. School counselors are professional school advocates who provide support to maximize student potential and academic achievement. In partnership with the local educational community including other educators, parents or guardians, and students, school counselors will facilitate the support system to assure that students of the Wake County Public School System have access to and are prepared to become lifelong learners and productive citizens of a global society.

The school's principal, all of the school counselors, a school board member, and an advisory council member all signed off in agreement to these philosophy/vision, belief, and mission statements.

Delivery System

GUIDANCE CURRICULUM   The Wakefield High School Counseling and Student Services Department uses the Wakefield High School Curriculum Crosswalking Tool once per year as an assessment tool to determine where they are meeting their curriculum goals. The standards used are from the ASCA National Model.

The school counselors do classroom guidance by grade level, generally beginning in November of the school year. By this time the counselors have already met individually with all seniors for senior interviews. As the school utilizes 4 × 4 block scheduling, the counselors meet for classroom guidance with half of all freshmen, sophomores, and juniors during the first semester and half during the second semester. Academic-related guidance is done through the English classes. Half of the students in the class are taken to the media center while the other half remain in the classroom focusing on their academic studies. During classroom guidance, the counselors focus on high school graduation requirements and the importance of academic success. These sessions are done in conjunction with the career development coordinator to make the idea of success more meaningful for the students. During the classroom guidance sessions, the students complete graduation plans and select their course of study. The counselors also provide copies and explain student transcripts in terms of college admissions. The counselors may also do some need-based lessons depending on teacher requests in certain classes.

Part of the classroom guidance includes career development activities. All students complete career interest inventories. The freshmen participate in a program called Futures for Kids. The juniors go to the College Foundation website where, in addition to completing interest inventories, they establish accounts at no charge with the College Foundation. This gives them access to information on careers, links to colleges and universities, and a universal college application. The counselors have the students take interest inventories online to infuse technology with the lessons.

INDIVIDUAL STUDENT PLANNING   Because Wakefield High School is so large and the caseload per counselor is approximately 450 students, individual planning is an area of challenge for the counselors. The counselors work to ensure that they see each student one to two times per year, but it is a challenge to personalize these meetings. The counselors meet with each senior for senior interviews during the first part of their senior year to begin to finalize postsecondary plans, and there is a freshman camp held at the beginning of the year to assist freshmen with the transition to high school. A significant portion of individual planning occurs during classroom guidance. The counselors hold a number of workshops throughout the year to provide information to students and parents on academic and postsecondary planning issues.

RESPONSIVE SERVICES   There is one counselor at Wakefield High School who is assigned to work with ninth-grade students in the Ninth-Grade Academy. The other counselors split up the remaining grades alphabetically. The counselors provide individual counseling to students on an as-needed basis. In addition, there are school-based mental health professionals who can provide services to qualifying students with Medicaid or Health Choice if the students do not have insurance coverage for private therapists. At times depending on a student's individual needs, the school-based mental health professional may obtain a release so that the school counselor can work with the student as well. The Student Assistance Program (SAP) counselor administers a needs assessment to students at Wakefield High School and then runs small groups to help meet identified needs. Target groups have included students who were newcomers to the area, children of divorce, substance abusers and their families, students interested in increased racial and ethnic understanding, gay and lesbian supporters, truancy, and retained ninth-graders.

SYSTEM SUPPORT   The Dean of Student Services acts as a liaison between the school counselors and the school's administration and helps coordinate many of the Counseling and Student Services Department's programmatic activities. There are a number of Management System activities (discussed later) that act to support the counseling program in place at Wakefield High School.

The Counseling and Student Services Department also engages in a number of public relations activities to help make various constituent groups aware of programs and services and to build support for and involvement in their programs, such as publishing a "Counselors Corner" in the PTSA newsletter, which is mailed to every household, putting scholarship information on the Student Services website, sending emails to parents of seniors, and putting notices in the local weekly newspaper.

Management System

AGREEMENTS   The school counselors at Wakefield High School work with the principal each year to create a Wakefield High School Counselor/Administrator Agreement.

SCHOOL IMPROVEMENT/CLOSING-THE-GAP GOALS   The following are examples of goals at address school improvement and closing the gap activities: Increase minority enrollment in AP English III by 5 percent; Increase parent involvement of LEP/ESL students by 20 percent, and Increase promotion rate of ninth-graders to 85 percent

PROGRAMS, INFORMATION, ASSISTANCE, OUTREACH

Teachers.   Closing-the-gap strategies for minority students at faculty meetings

Parents.   Parent open houses, topic-focused and grade-level parent nights

Community.   Business Alliance–Friday Career Fairs; PTSA Family Day

PROFESSIONAL DEVELOPMENT FOR SCHOOL COUNSELING STAFF   The school counseling team participates in professional development to increase their knowledge and skills.

COUNSELOR AVAILABILITY/OFFICE ORGANIZATION   The school counseling department will be open for students, parents, and teachers from 7:00 A.M. to 3:30 P.M. (with staggered hours during registration in March). The career center will be open from 10:30 A.M. to 3:00 P.M.

ADVISORY COUNCIL   Wakefield High School's Leadership Team functions as an advisory board for the Counseling and Student Services Department. The Leadership Team meets twice a month to focus on schoolwide issues and needs. It is composed of the school's administration, department chairs, the Dean of Student Services, and representative teachers and parents.

USE OF DATA   In determining their program goals, the Counseling and Student Services Department looks at school data. The Wake County School System is effective in gathering and presenting data on particular schools, and Wakefield High School has access to a statewide program called NCY through which they can obtain student information specific to Wakefield, including data on different groups of students. One purpose of this program is to ease a student's entry into a school if he or she transfers because the student's information can be transferred school-to-school quickly. In addition, the school system generates at-risk data on particular students identified on the basis of certain risk factors including suspensions, failed courses, and achievement on state exams. The school counselors get together at the beginning of every year and look at this collection of data to help determine their goals and objectives. In addition, they are able to review their results reports (discussed later) at the end of each year to help determine the effectiveness of activities and which activities to continue, discontinue, and/or modify.

ACTION PLANS   The Wakefield High School Counseling and Student Services Department generates action plans and results reports related to their program goals for each year. The Principal and the Dean of Student Services sign the action plan and results forms following submission and review.

USE OF CALENDARS   The Wakefield High School Counseling and Student Services Department uses and publishes a master calendar specifying important dates and deadlines, as well as counselor and program activities.

Accountability

The school counselors at Wakefield High School generate different types of data throughout the year including process data, perception data, and information on number of students affected by different programs. This information is put into results reports throughout the year. At the end of the year, the school counselors are able to review the results reports to determine how successful they were in achieving their goals and which programs they want to continue, discontinue, and/or modify.

RESULTS REPORTS   The Wakefield High School Counseling and Student Services Department generates action plans and results reports related to their program goals for each year. The following is an example of the action plan and results related to one of the 2004–2005 goals:

Target group: Minority students in rigorous courses

Target group selection is based upon the following criteria: percentage in honors and AP

Data that drove this decision: low enrollment of minority students in AP English III

Counselor: Dean of Student Services

Target group: Members of student group with one or more F's during high school who agreed to spend time after school to get help for academics and to prepare for college

Standards, competencies and indicators addressed: A:A1, A:A2, A:A3, A:B1, A:B2, A:C1, C:C1.1, PS:A1, PS:A2, PS:B1

Type of service delivered: facilitate monthly workshops with guest speakers on self-esteem, leadership, cultural code switching for survival, college visits to WSSU, NCSU, NCCU, UNCW, facilitate development and performance of Black History program, facilitate parent meetings that focus on course registration, graduation requirements

Start/end dates: 9/04–05/05

Number of students affected: 52

Perception data: 15 members participated in the WSSU trip, 8 participated in the NCSU trip, and 22 participated in the UNC-CH trip, 98 percent of members participate in the monthly workshops; other data in progress

Results data: 45 parents attended parent meeting; 22 responded to survey; 45 percent were not aware of credits their son or daughter already earned or courses and number of credits needed for graduation prior to the meeting, 40 percent knew nothing or little about the student information database and how to access it prior to the meeting; after the meeting 100 percent reported they knew how to access the database and knew the number of credits already earned and courses still needed for their son or daughter; other data in progress

Implications: Parent involvement, knowledge and participation in academic planning will be vital to student success. Monthly workshops are better attended than college tours. What other motivational strategies can be used for the students?

Leadership, Advocacy, Collaboration, and Systemic Change

LEADERSHIP   The Counseling and Student Services Department's involvement in leadership activities at Wakefield High School has positive effects for Wakefield's students. The counselors serve in many leadership roles throughout the infrastructure of the high school. Through their involvement in these committees and groups, the school counselors are able to contribute to schoolwide decisions and to consistently advocate for students.

The school counselors have also taken a leadership role in increasing minority student enrollment in AP courses. Beyond encouraging students who have performed well to move up to the higher AP course level, the counselors are working with the teachers to encourage them to identify students with the potential to succeed. The counselors noted that teachers had been hesitant to do so in fear that they would be held responsible if a student did not succeed. The counselors are advocating for the stance that until the students have a chance to participate in an AP class, they will not understand the amount of work and time necessary to succeed, and that this unknown may prevent the students from enrolling in the courses in the first place. The counselors and teachers are spending time with minority students sharing information about the courses and encouraging good work habits in the hopes of instilling the confidence needed to be successful in AP classes.

ADVOCACY   Advocacy efforts are infused throughout the work of the Counseling and Student Services Department at Wakefield High School. The SAP counselor conducts a needs assessment to help target small-group efforts toward the specific needs identified by the students. The school counselors have conducted outreach efforts to inform and update parents on the student assistance activities of the SAP program.

Advocacy is also evident in the Counseling and Student Services Department efforts to increase minority enrollment in AP courses and to increase the involvement of ESL students' parents. Beyond their own targeted programs, the school counselors are also encouraging faculty and administration to promote advanced courses to eligible students. The school counselors are now holding quarterly meetings with the parents of minority students to increase minority parent involvement in the life of the school and to keep them informed of pertinent information.

COLLABORATION   The counselors in the Counseling and Student Services Department engage in many collaborative activities to facilitate positive change in students. The SAP counselor often has representatives from community agencies share information or facilitate group meetings. School Business Alliance members help with the retained ninth-grader group on career development and work readiness topics. Some universities and colleges have held on-site admissions meetings with students in addition to the regular attendance of college representatives to share information with potential applicants. College and military representatives participated in a Junior Parent Post-Secondary Opportunities Night organized through Student Services. The career development counselor also works to pull in representatives from community businesses and training programs for the Friday Fairs available for students to see the kinds of careers that exist in different occupational cluster areas.

SYSTEMIC CHANGE   The push for greater minority student enrollment in AP courses is a prime example of the Counseling and Student Services Department's efforts to enact systemic change that makes a positive difference in student achievement. Because this is an approved goal with a written action plan, the school counselors are devoting their energies to making a change in the way teachers, students, and parents think about AP courses. This has resulted in a high level of support from faculty for the Counseling and Student Services Department to be more student centered and to follow national guidelines for comprehensive school counseling programs.

CSCP ACTIVITY TIME LINE

August, September, October

Parent Orientation, Freshman Camp/New Student Orientation, PTSA Newsletter deadline, High Five—High School Convocation, Senior Night, Senior interviews, PSAT info to juniors, PSAT registration, College board meeting, Scholarship nominations due, Official Rank for seniors due, Groups begin, Schedule evening parent conferences, PSAT testing, Senior workshop on resumes and essays, Senior workshop on choosing a college

November, December:

Small groups, ASVAB testing, Potential senior failures conferences, Failure letters to parents, College on-site interviews, Early financial aid interviews, PE classes for "Signs of Suicide," Meet with early graduating seniors, Closing-the-gap parent meeting/Business Alliance, Advisory Council Meeting

January, February, March:

High school registration meeting/Career Club, Schedule adjustments for second semester, PSAT Interpretation Night/Heritage Middle School visit, Early graduation rehearsal, Early Graduation ceremony, Financial Aid night, Middle school counselor registration breakfast, AP exam registration, Getting Off to a Fresh Start Program/Career Club, Closing-the-gap parent meeting, Open House/Curriculum Fair, Junior/Sophomore Night, Career Club

April, May, June:

Pyramid of intervention workshop, Course registration, Final senior GPA and rank for honors/report cards, Closing-the-gap parent meeting, Sophomore English class small groups, Freshman English class small groups, Promotions/retentions, Graduation, Final transcripts sent to colleges

---

CASE STUDY REVISITED

Integration

Kanika's dilemma is not unusual—often new school counselors think they would prefer one level, only to find that the other levels offer unique opportunities that they enjoy. What is your favorite level and why? What did you read in this chapter that confirms your target level? What caused you to rethink your favorite? What can you do now to expand your thinking about your future? ▪

Web Resources for These Ramp Programs

Elementary School:

City of Tucson. (2006). *Old pueblo, new Tucson.* Retrieved January 9, 2006, from http://www.tucsonaz.gov

Inez C. Ford Elementary School. (2006). *Ford Site Council.* Retrieved January 15, 2006, from http://edweb.tusd.k12.az.us/Ford/site_council.htm

Tucson Unified School District, Comprehensive Competency Based Guidance. (2003). *Program Handbook.* Retrieved January 12, 2006, from http://instech.tusd.k12.az.us/counseling/Documents/program/section1.PDF

Middle School:

Nancy Jarman-Dunn's counseling website at http://fusd.tv/sites/middle/jarman/IndexMain.html

Sequoia Middle School's website at http://www.fusd.net/schools/MiddleSchool/Sequoia/index.stm

SPARC (Support Personnel Accountability Report Card) for Sequoia Middle School at http://www.lacoe.edu/orgs/1077/index.cfm

Backpack collection for Hurricane Katrina Victims at http://dosomething.org

Career Cruising website at http://careercruising.com/default.asp

Kick Butts Day activities at http://TobaccoFreeKids.org

Mix It Up Day activities at www.tolerance.org/teach/mix_it_up/about.jsp

Rainbow Days Youth Connection has the Youth Connection small-group curriculum at http://www.rdikids.org/yc_c.shtml

High School:

About Wake County—Geographic facts. (n.d.). Retrieved January 18, 2006, from http://www.wakegov.com/about/geography.htm

U.S. Census Bureau—State and County Quickfacts. (n.d.). Retrieved January 18, 2006, from http://quickfacts.census.gov/qfd/states/37/37183.html

Wake County planning, land use and zoning—economy. (n.d.). Retrieved January 18, 2006, from http://www.wakegov.com/planning/demographic/dd_Economy.htm

Wake County planning, land use and zoning—education. (n.d.). Retrieved January 18, 2006, from http://www.wakegov.com/planning/demographic/dd_Education.htm

Wake County planning, land use and zoning—population. (n.d.). Retrieved January 18, 2006, from http://www.wakegov.com/planning/demographic/dd_Population.htm

13

Emerging Issues for Schools and Students

With contributions from Robert Urofsky, CACREP Director

LEARNING OBJECTIVES

By the end of this chapter, you will

1. Understand the mental health concerns faced by school counselors in the field

2. Appreciate the diversity in the schools and feel a renewed commitment to learn more about different persons

3. Understand the effect of poverty on our students and feel a renewed commitment to help every child succeed in school and life

4. Consider new forms and structures of schools relative to educational reform

5. Understand the connection between spirituality and mental health and the appropriate role school counselors can play in the development of students

6. Consider new ways of looking at educational structures

7. Understand the importance of technology in school counseling and the need to remain current with technological developments

8. Understand the process of collecting data through action research

9. Understand the various ways to secure alternative funding for programs

CASE STUDY

Samuel's Mother

Erin always participated in the events of her school, so that parents and teachers would see her as integral to the school community. So on Parent's Night at Gila Vista Elementary School, she walked from room to room as she always did, introducing herself and inviting parents to visit her counseling office before they left. Entering the second-grade classroom, she was surprised to hear a woman's voice screaming at the second-grade teacher about the progress of Samuel, a new student in the school. She was accusing the teacher of treating her son unfairly, holding him to higher behavioral and academic expectations than others. It was clear that the teacher was trying to escape the mother's tirade, as she nervously looked around the room at the embarrassed parents who were unwilling witnesses to this exchange. After a few minutes, Erin decided to intervene, to see if the parent might be interested in processing her concerns in private, but the mother yelled, "You're all a bunch of trained monkeys!" and left, slamming the door.

The next day, Erin approached the teacher to offer consultation. "Is there anything I can do to help you with her?"

The teacher shrugged. "I've worked with lots of parents like her. I'm not sure what I can do to help her or her son. They come from such a different world; I'm not even sure how to reach out to them. I don't think the mother had a good experience at school when she was young. I can't even begin to imagine why she's so angry." Erin felt a surge of pity for both Samuel and the second-grade teacher. She made a mental note to get him from class at the first opportunity.

CHALLENGE QUESTIONS

What was your reaction as you read this case study? What might be going on with this parent? What do you do to remind yourself to listen with compassion to someone who is so angry?

Most people will generate a mental image of the scene as they read. Being completely honest, attend to the image of the mother you "saw" as you read the case study. How did you imagine the mother looked? What was her culture, her age, her dress, her mental condition? What are all the things you would want to know about her? ■

EMERGING ISSUES IN SCHOOL COUNSELING

We wish we had a crystal ball to see into the future for our profession of school counseling; we would use it to help future counselors prepare for everything that the world will throw at them. We must be aware of what is happening in our communities and our schools to foresee answers to future needs. This is how we will survive as a profession—through being proactive, not reactive.

There are many issues emerging in the field that will affect school counseling but we will attend to those that are most critical for school counseling. If our programs are indeed comprehensive—holistic, systemic, balanced, proactive, integrated, and reflective—we will be well situated to address these emerging issues.

MENTAL HEALTH NEEDS OF STUDENTS

School counselors report that the frequency with which they encounter students with mental health issues is increasing at an alarming rate, and it has been posited that about "one in five children or adolescents in the U.S. manifests a diagnosable mental health or addictive disorder" (Cauce & Srebnik, 2003). In one study, only about 25 percent of those students who recognized they had a mental health problem sought out professional help (Saunders, 1994, as cited in Cauce & Srebnik, 2003). Of those seeking help, one study found that the most frequently used formal sources for mental health help were medical doctors (78 percent), school personnel (57 percent), school principals (36 percent), and sports team coaches (35 percent) (Dubow et al., 1990, as cited in Cauce & Srebnik, 2003). Think about what these statistics mean. Extrapolating from these studies, we can calculate that approximately 20 percent of young people need mental health assistance, indicating how prevalent the need is for mental health services for young people. But only a quarter of those students (meaning 25 percent of 20 percent, or 5 percent of all students) seek help from mental health providers, suggesting how important it is for mental health to be destigmatized. Of the 5 percent who come for help, only about half of them (2 to 3 percent) will come to school personnel (counselors or teachers) for that help. What does this say about this issue for professional school counselors?

Add to your consideration of these issues some information about psychotropic medication. In a national survey of school counselors, Bauer, Ingersoll, and Burns (2004) examined the experiences of school counselors with psychotropic medication in the schools. They found that of the 138 respondents, 42 percent estimated that between 1 and 10 percent of their students were taking these medications and 17 percent estimated that from 11 to 20 percent of their students were taking medications. When asked to identify all the diagnoses for which the medications were prescribed, 94 percent listed ADHD (attention-deficit hyperactivity disorder), 80 percent listed ADD (attention-deficit disorder) and depression, 69 percent listed hyperactivity, and 57 percent listed bipolar. Other diagnoses mentioned include anxiety, obsessive-compulsive disorder, mood disorder, oppositional defiance disorder, and posttraumatic stress disorder, among others. While the school nurse was most often identified as the professional responsible for the dispensation of medications in the school, other persons included school counselors, teachers, and office staff. Over half of the school counselors responded that they had received no formal training in psychopharmacology, yet 91 percent agreed or strongly agreed that it was important for school counselors to understand medication issues and 96 percent agreed that such training would be helpful in their work. The authors conclude that "school counselors need access to this information [diagnosis and treatment of childhood psychiatric disorders] to function effectively as child advocates and consultants in the school system" (p. 209).

These realities—the prevalence of mental health issues, the lack of help seeking, and the increasing reliance on psychotropic medication for youth—make mental health one of the most critical issues for school counselors. Counselors report that students with emotional disabilities, such as problems with depression, autism spectrum disorders, anger management, posttraumatic stress, reactive attachment disorder, and oppositional defiance disorder, are being increasingly diagnosed at all educational levels. It is crucial that counselors become knowledgeable about these issues to assist in the early assessment, identification, and referral of these students to school and community resources. Furthermore, school counselors must be able to provide counseling and support services for these students to facilitate their academic, social and emotional, and career development. A student's *DSM-IV* (*Diagnostic and Statistical Manual of Mental Disorders*, 4th ed.) diagnosis doesn't eliminate the counselor's vital role in promoting school success. School counselors must understand diagnostic, treatment, and special education terminology, legislation, and issues, since counselors must understand educational responses to a student's mental health status.

In addition to the life stressors, educational stressors, and physical stressors on youth, consider family stressors. According to the Forum on Child and Family Statistics (2010), today's youth also face significant family and systemic challenges. (The Federal Interagency Forum on Child and Family Statistics, or the Forum, is a working group of federal agencies that collect, analyze, and report data on issues related to children and families. The Forum has partners from 22 federal agencies as well as partners in private research organizations.) Their 2010 report states: "The percentage of children whose parents had secure employment was the lowest since 1996, and the percentage living in poverty was the highest since 1998. The percentage of children in food-insecure households was the highest since monitoring began" (par. 4). These systemic stressors place more households and more children than ever at risk from the economic fallout of world events.

Counselors must work to help students and families understand mental health issues and encourage them to access school and community resources as needed. They need to normalize both developmental struggles and mental health concerns so that students and families are more comfortable talking about their needs (with the reminder that there are often culturally determined preferences for sources of mental health assistance).

For those who come to school counselors for help, responses to these needs are shaped by the ASCA National Model and insights into comprehensive school counseling. In a comprehensive school counseling program, you would attend to the student's holistic development while working to support the learning process. You would demonstrate awareness of contextual implications with the student's diagnosis, evaluating the student's classroom context and family context to facilitate support for the student. You would balance your responses to the student to meet his or her needs, ranging from counseling, educating, and consultation, with an emphasis on proactive activities and advocacy that will mitigate the damaging effects of the diagnosis on all aspects of development. Finally, you would design feedback and documentation of your work with the student for reflection and accountability.

It is important to note that if counselors eschew their role in the mental health issues of students and walk away from the counseling foundation of our profession, we leave a void that others will fill. In many districts, school psychologists and school social workers also provide mental health support, and in a recent development, school nurses have been promoted as "well positioned to bridge school and community health activities" and to "facilitate medical/psychiatric intervention and alter the trajectories for students vulnerable to mental health problems and violence" (Hootman & DeSocio, 2004, p. 27). Our student support colleagues can be essential partners in providing help for all students. In a world of ever-growing mental health needs, ignoring the work we do as *counselors* in a comprehensive school counseling program will result in the loss of our roots and our identity. To create the best possible scenario for students, school counselors must continue to provide counseling for students, while concurrently emphasizing the importance of educating, consulting, collaboration, leading, advocacy, and coordinating for all our partners.

Crisis Counseling and Family Crisis Assistance

As a part of the discussion of mental health, it is important to mention the need for counselors to provide crisis counseling. Counselors must be able to work effectively with students who are in crisis and must be able to act decisively in cases of suicide risk. In a study done in 2000 of 186 secondary school counselors, researchers found that 87 percent of them felt that suicide work was part of the job, but only 38 percent of them felt they had the skills to be effective with suicidal students (K. A. King, Price, Telljohann, & Wahl, 1999, 2000). According to the Centers for Disease Control (2009), "a nationwide survey of youth in grades 9–12 in public and private schools in the United States (U.S.) found that 15% of students reported seriously considering suicide, 11% reported creating a plan, and 7% reporting trying to take their own life in the 12 months preceding the survey. Each year, approximately 149,000 youth between the ages of 10 and 24 receive medical care for self-inflicted injuries at Emergency Departments across the U.S." (par. 2). The number of lives lost each year is staggering: "For youth between the ages of 10 and 24, suicide is the third leading cause of death. It results in approximately 4400 lives lost each year" (par. 1). As discussed in Chapter 8, school counselors must have skills in the assessment of suicide potentiality. Furthermore, it is crucial that counselors know the answers to the following questions:

1. What are the expectations of the district and the school administrators in terms of notification of caregivers and school administration?
2. What are the processes and roles of social services, law enforcement agencies, school professionals, and counselors in terms of getting the student to a safe location?
3. How do you access local mental health emergency services? What is the location, address, phone, and placement procedures of the local mental health facility if a commitment becomes necessary?
4. What are the implications of transportation, information sharing, and notification of all parties (caregivers, administrators, law enforcement, and mental health professionals)?

In a comprehensive school counseling program at any educational level, counselors must anticipate the need for addressing students in crisis. In a proactive and preventive effort, counselors would educate all partners in the warning signs of crisis (as developmentally appropriate). Thinking systemically (because people in crisis often indicate their suicidal thoughts to friends), students would be trained to be aware of warning signs in their friends and the need to inform an adult of their concerns (Nelson & Galas, 1994). Parents, teachers, and administrators, also, would benefit from education in this area. Furthermore, prevention/intervention efforts would involve leadership activities in the school that would yield (1) the development of a plan for the eventuality of dealing with a student who is suicidal, (2) the documentation of a process that answers all the preceding questions, and (3) the provision of in-service training for the adult partners in the school to outline the plan.

Families also experience crises, potentially resulting in a self-injurious attempt. Resources for family members in the community must be made available, and postvention activities would involve educating family members about mental health issues and helping students know how to keep themselves safe.

Self-Destructive Behaviors

Along with mental health issues, school counselors are reporting increasing instances of unhealthy and self-destructive behaviors. According to McWhirter et al. (2007), young people are engaging in high-risk behaviors, such as intake of alcohol and other drugs, in alarming numbers. Along with these unhealthy and high-risk behaviors, some students express their pain in self-destructive behaviors such as self-mutilation, cutting, pinching, scratching, biting, self-hitting, burning, and interfering with wound healing (Kress, Gibson, & Reynolds, 2004). As an example of the need for reflection in a CSCP, counselors need to understand their own reactions to some nontraditional ways of self-decoration, such as tattooing, piercing, branding, and carving, to be able to understand when self-marking is self-destructive and when it is self-decoration. In addition, reflection and self-supervision is important when working with clients who self-injure, as clinical work with self-injurious students is identified as the most traumatizing to the professional (Kress et al., 2004).

One theory describing the etiology of cutting suggests that the intent of the behavior is not to die; rather, it is in response to a numbing dissociative state associated with psychological trauma. Sources of the trauma that often result in self-injury are identified as sexual and physical abuse, anxiety and depression, family violence, eating disorders, peer conflict, low impulse control, and traumatic loss (Kress et al., 2004; Levenkron, 1998). However, self-injurious behaviors are also known to be contagious; other adolescents, in what might be considered a "rite of togetherness" (Taiminen et al., as cited in Kress et al., 2004, p. 199), may engage in social self-mutilation as an outgrowth of psychological and social factors (Kress et al., 2004).

In a CSCP, counselors would attend to all self-destructive behavior in holistic, systemic, balanced, proactive, integrated, and reflective ways. It is important to note that this issue, due to its severity and safety issues, requires notification of parents and possible hospitalization; as such, the event must be handled with attention paid to informing students of confidentiality issues (Froeschle & Moyer, 2004). School counselors responding to these behaviors would examine the effect of the behavior on academic, career, and personal/social development, and would provide counseling, referrals, advocacy, and consulting as appropriate. Furthermore, counselors should take into account the student's family, school, and community contexts to examine prevention and intervention strategies that would provide the most support for the student's recovery and aftercare. Appropriate intent on the prevention/intervention/treatment continuum would suggest that activities would be balanced in terms of education of all partners (prevention efforts), counseling and advocacy for the student as well as consulting and leadership with all adult partners (intervention efforts), and referrals to the community (treatment efforts). Integrated efforts to inform students (as developmentally appropriate) of the dangers of self-mutilation might include presentations in health classes, for example. Finally, all efforts would be documented to provide data for accountability and reflection.

REFLECTION MOMENT

What is your level of knowledge about mental health diagnoses, medications, and the ways that counselors can support students with mental health issues in the schools? What do you know about crisis and crisis counseling? What do you know about self-destructive behaviors?

In addition, think about your feelings on these topics, as they generate reactions from us based on our values, our faith traditions, and our sociocultural background. How do you feel about these issues, and how do you react to young people who manifest these issues?

What are the resources in your community to assist you with these questions? What do you need to do to become more proficient in these topics?

BUILDING CRISIS MANAGEMENT

It seems an oxymoron to plan for a crisis, since crises are usually unforeseen. However, in order to ensure the safety of all persons in a school building, the need for building crisis response planning is essential. There are too many instances of unforeseeable events—from the death of a student to the death of a teacher or principal, to acts of violence perpetrated by students or against students—that make such crisis planning a necessity. In addition, world events (such as the attacks of September 11, 2001) also generate the need for crisis planning to assist the school community.

According to Kerr (2009), crisis planning is a multistep process. First, a planning committee is formed in which major stakeholders are involved. It is this committee that will research applicable state and district policies, and design responses for communication and support for various levels and types of crisis. Once a plan is in place, prevention efforts are also engaged with the knowledge that "an ounce of prevention is worth a pound of cure." After the crisis is over, the committee is then involved in providing support to those in the school and others on the committee itself during the postcrisis processing of the response. To mitigate the impact of the crisis, the committee calls rehearsals for all levels of crisis response and educates the school community on the plans and contingencies. During each of these steps, the school counselor is an integral part of the efforts to keep all persons safe, informed, and calm.

In many districts, counselors in the district are expected to respond during a crisis at another school. This highlights the need for you to collaborate closely with your counselor colleagues in other schools: you and they will rely on each other during times of crisis such as a suicide, a death of a student or school colleague, a building event such as a fire, or a community, national, or international event such as those on September 11, 2001. You may find that students seek out persons they know to talk to; if you don't find that you are needed by the students, seek out teachers or other adults in the building who need someone to talk to about their feelings after the crisis event.

REFLECTION MOMENT

Have you been in a building in which a viable crisis plan was in place? How did you know? What about when you were in your K–12 education: Do you remember fire drills? How safe did you feel after a drill? Reflect on these experiences as you think about your role in building crisis management.

MULTICULTURALISM AND DIVERSITY

Many excellent books have been written that explore this topic in detail, and this short discussion is not intended to convey all the subtleties and nuances of effective multicultural and multivalues interactions. The intent is to highlight the most salient issues relative to school counseling, especially as it relates to the ASCA National Model and the DAP model as discussed in this book. It is hoped that, as you come to better appreciate the need for advocacy, social justice, and systemic functioning in school counseling, you will cement your commitment to your education and experiences to foster healthy development for all students.

The importance of this topic cannot be understated; students of color and linguistic diversity are expected to comprise the majority of all students by the year 2020 (Holcomb-McCoy, 2004; Sue & Sue, 1999), and already constitute a numerical majority in many locations and communities in the country (Sue & Sue, 1999). Furthermore, there are many diversity constructs, including culture, ethnicity, gender, sexual orientation, ability and disability levels, religious/faith traditions, and age, among others. Each of these diversity constructs is interwoven into our values systems and merged with our unique personalities to yield our personal phenomenology and epistemology. As the world becomes more diverse, the assumptions that we hold as products of our own diversity constructs and values orientations must be amended to become more inclusive, more empowering, and more just.

Without exception, the need for *all* counselors—of all ethnic, cultural, and values statuses—to improve their skills in this area is paramount. As stated by Sue and Sue (1999), "If counselors and therapists are to provide meaningful help to a culturally diverse population, we must not only reach out and acquire new understandings, but develop new culturally effective helping approaches" (p. 10). But all counselors must also be aware that diversity comes from a variety of sources—linguistic, cultural, ethnic, gender, religious, sexual orientation, economics, national origin, ability level, among others—and make the commitment to value, learn about, and empower all others who might be different from ourselves. Awareness of one source of values orientations and resulting oppression (such as ethnicity or gender) cannot be substituted for the others (such as sexual orientation or ability level) (Helms, 1994). And we cannot forget that oppression comes in many forms, some of which are hidden, but nonetheless insidious and destructive. Examples of subtle oppression include silencing of females (Reinharz, 1994), denial of positive attributes in male identity development (McCarthy & Holliday, 2004), differential encouragement of postsecondary options based on learning disabilities (Durodoye, Combes, & Bryant, 2004), and lack of understanding of the needs of Muslim students (Carter & El Hindi, 1999).

This learning about others is also grounded in the need to learn about ourselves. The need to understand one's own diversity constructs is evident when you consider the implications of Embedded Intergroup Relations (Alderfer, 1994), which posits that interaction between people depends on (1) the unique personalities of the individuals, (2) the messages the individuals receive and internalize from their own group (defined as any diversity construct with which the person identifies), and (3) the present and historical relationships between the groups that the individuals represent (p. 221). Consider what this implies for communication, but most especially for counseling: if counselors are to truly counsel others (developing empathy, trust, unconditional positive regard, etc.), then counselors must reflect on and remain aware of the following:

1. The counselor's personality as shaped and defined by identity development processes and values development
2. The client's personality, as shaped by the same forces
3. The counselor's messages internalized from her or his own group
4. The client's messages from his or her group
5. The present relationship between the group of the counselor and the group of the client
6. The historical relationship(s) between the group of the counselor and the group of the client

Effective multicultural counseling begins with understanding ourselves and our identity development. Next, we must develop a visceral, personally derived understanding of others, which means understanding at the "gut" level, not just the intellectual level; it involves personal interaction with diverse others. Finally, we must recognize that the present *and* the past will affect how others perceive us and the groups to which we appear to belong. This has a direct impact on whether students of diversity and their families perceive the school counselor as someone to whom they can turn in times of need.

These insights provide a backdrop from which to better understand Holcomb-McCoy's (2004) list of multicultural counseling competencies for school counselors. These competencies include

- Competence in multicultural counseling. This means becoming aware of strategies and approaches that are relevant and appropriate for diverse students, rather than assuming that traditional strategies (which have been developed for nondiverse students) will suffice for all.
- Competence in multicultural consultation. As observed in the development of the DAP model, consultation is a crucial skill, and diverse students, families, and colleagues need consultation strategies that are appropriate. Furthermore, negative racial and/or cultural attitudes can and should be confronted using consultation.

- Competence in understanding racism and student resistance. In working toward a diverse and multiculturally appreciative and respectful school climate, school counselors must be aware of all forms of resistance to tolerance and inclusion. From rabid, overt racism to denial of the oppression of all forms of diversity, the spectrum of racism must be challenged when found in schools, colleagues, students, and families.
- Competence in understanding racial identity development. Most difficult for counselors from traditional White, middle-class backgrounds is understanding the anger (Sue & Sue, 1999) that is a natural part of being a member of a disenfranchised and oppressed group (person of color, female, gay/lesbian, for example). Added to this, of course, is the reminder that this includes the identity development process for all persons of diversity (Helms, 1994). The understanding of diversity identity development must then be applied to the issues and concerns of students and their families, as well as to colleagues.
- Competence in multicultural assessment. As high-stakes testing becomes more widespread and assessment becomes more ubiquitous, the adaptations needed by diverse students, in terms of language, testing environment (for students with attention issues), and content, become critical.
- Competence in multicultural family counseling. Awareness of contextual issues, including families of diversity, is imperative. As stated by Holcomb-McCoy (2004), "Counseling interventions with families must take into account its [*sic*] cultural kinship networks, socialization experiences, typical interactive patterns, and culturally linked attitudinal and behavioral arrangements" (p. 180).
- Competence in social advocacy. Social action and social advocacy are necessary for systemic change, and it is through these activities that schools can become inclusive, respectful places for learning that are safe for diverse students, families, and staff.
- Competence in developing school-family-community partnerships. Holcomb-McCoy (2004) suggests that counselors should take a leadership role in developing partnerships that empower families to access services in the school and community that can provide support for families in need.
- Competence in understanding interpersonal interactions. Issues of inclusion, respect, and valuing are communicated through words, voice, subject, and nonverbals. Counselors must be aware of their own attitudes and how those are communicated to diverse students, ensuring that the context of counseling is affirming, safe, and welcoming.

As you can see from the above competencies, leadership is a basic requirement for any meaningful change to take place. It is critical that counselors empower themselves to transform the climate of the school on behalf of students, to advocate for and create a welcoming environment in which everyone can learn, free from harassment and hatred.

REFLECTION MOMENT

Where are you in the evolution of your sense of social justice? What can you do to expand your awareness of persons from other diversity constructs?

Poverty

Although the issues of diversity and poverty are often interconnected, they are not synonymous. In many cases, economic realities transcend cultural ones; in other words, economic class can have a more defining impact on values development than culture or ethnicity. One study (Weis, as cited in Holcomb-McCoy, 2004) found that "teachers initiate more frequent and more varied interactions with students from middle and upper class backgrounds than they do with those from the poor and working classes" (p. 181). Payne (2003) discusses the "hidden rules" of economic classes (p. 59), and suggests that the rules of the middle class dominate our educational institutions. Because most educational professionals come from the middle class, educators presume that everyone knows the "rules": the value of education; an emphasis on future planning; the use of formal, written, sequential narrative structure; a belief in choice ("Good choices now can provide a better future"); and the certainty that hard work and achievement are the keys to success. In contrast, students from generational poverty live with the hidden rules of poverty: the value of entertainment; an emphasis on the present; the use of informal, spoken, circular narrative structure; a belief in fate ("That's the way life is; what can you do?"); and the certainty that survival depends on relationships that can change without notice. In the world of poverty, school is a source of entertainment, a time to be with friends; it is not a way out of poverty (p. 79).

Payne (2003) discusses educational strategies that can help mitigate the effects of poverty's rules and help teach students the value of education and career efforts. Recognition that these behaviors are not the result of flaunting of rules, but rather are manifestations of a unique value system, can reframe educators' frustrations with children from poverty. Mentoring, explicitly teaching alternatives to habituated behaviors, and recognition of underlying messages and needs can help further students' educational, career, and personal/social efforts. It is important to note that Payne's work has been criticized as being derived from personal anecdotal insights rather than based on research; for the school counselor, some of the insights have intuitive logic and appeal regardless of the source.

It is also important to note that generational poverty, which often derives from a lack of viable employment opportunities in impoverished neighborhoods or communities, may differ from situational poverty, which derives from temporary economic hardships experienced by the family. Contextual awareness and sensitivity is required to ascertain when students are struggling from the former versus the latter, and interventions vary based on this contextual assessment. In terms of a holistic, systemic, balanced, proactive, integrated, and reflective comprehensive school counseling program, recognition of the challenges of students of poverty come from this systemic awareness of students' lives. Balanced, proactive activities with all partners would involve the following:

- Counseling and educating students experiencing poverty to help them learn new behaviors and expand career options
- Educating parents about community resources and consulting with parents about the school system (since suspicion of authority in general, and schools in particular, is a legacy of generational poverty [Payne, 2003])
- Educating school and community colleagues on the effects of poverty, advocating for the families and children of poverty, and consulting with school colleagues to facilitate understanding in how to include ALL students in the educational process
- Leading the effort to transform the climate of the school toward respectful inclusion on the basis of income

In a CSCP, reflection is necessary to improve the program and the counselor's function within that program. In the case of families and students experiencing poverty, it is important that counselors examine their own assumptions and class-bound hidden prejudices to determine if such persons are treated with respect and to ensure that these students and families feel welcome and valued in the school counseling office.

REFLECTION MOMENT

What are the "rules" of the socioeconomic culture in which you were raised? How do those rules affect your perceptions today? What do you need to do to expand your awareness and understanding of those from other socioeconomic strata?

SPIRITUALITY

Meaningful learning cannot take place if the child does not feel safe emotionally in the learning environment, and emotional safety cannot happen without a sense of community in the school (Bluestein, 2001; National Research Council, 2000; Starkman et al., 1999). Research consistently shows that a sense of community—a climate of caring support, of sharing, of mutual respect— provides the setting in which a child can ask questions, take risks, and modify his or her cognitive and affective constructs to allow for change and growth. These descriptors have deepened the awareness of many education and counseling professionals that the conditions that foster a sense of community in a school also foster spirituality, because programs that nurture a sense of community in a school (hope, compassion, respect, honesty, integrity, service to others, purpose in life or career) also develop persons who are spiritually well (Ingersoll & Bauer, 2004, p. 304).

In this book, "spirituality" is defined as "humans' expressions of and attempts at meaning- making that are uniquely personal as well as communal or sociocultural" (Sink & Richmond, 2004, p. 291). Religion is an organized, communal or cultural expression of spiritual beliefs, but the two terms are not synonymous. As cited in MacDonald (2004), one survey found that 50 percent of those sampled in the United States said that religion was very important in their lives, whereas other surveys have found that 80 to 90 percent of U.S. respondents believe in a "spirituality that included a god or gods" (p. 293). It can be concluded that, for many persons, spiritual realities are not expressed in organized religions; yet, as Sink and Richmond (2004) point out, these realities may be expressed in simple activities such as career exploration, reflection on a poem, painting a pow- erful image, or taking a walk and reflecting on nature. As such, the topic of spirituality, once taboo due to the separation of church and state, is becoming an acceptable topic for school counselors to explore, as long as it is given careful consideration.

There are many reasons that counselors need an expanded awareness of the role of spiri- tuality in the lives of students. First, spiritual development is a crucial developmental issue, connected to cognitive development and moral reasoning skills (Ingersoll & Bauer, 2004; Sink, 2004); second, spiritual exploration and discussion are natural in the counseling process, as stu- dents need to examine the meaning of their lives and the events therein (Koch, 2003; Myers, Sweeney, & Witmer, 2000); third, as a diversity construct, it can be considered unethical if is- sues of oppression and exclusion on the basis of religion and spirituality are ignored (Carter & El Hindi, 1999; Hanna & Green, 2004; Ingersoll & Bauer, 2004; Koch, 2003; Lonborg & Bowen, 2004); fourth, knowledge of the student's spiritual traditions can enhance the counsel- ing relationship and engender trust with the student and his or her family (Hanna & Green, 2004). This would suggest that we, as school counselors, must prepare to counsel students in the spiritual context (1) through a deeper understanding of the role of spirituality in terms of development, (2) by exploring our own spirituality and resolving to live a more meaningful spiritual life, (3) by understanding our misconceptions and biases about other religions and spiritual traditions, and (4) by making the commitment to expand our understanding of other religious and spiritual traditions.

Once that "inner" work is done, counselors are ready to engage students on this topic. As outlined in the discussions of multiculturalism and poverty, comprehensive school counseling programs promote activities that enhance spirituality to facilitate academic, career, and person- al/social development, and maintain a broad systemic view of the student to interface effectively with peers, family, and friends. Balanced, proactive activities would include the following:

- Counseling students with a focus on understanding the student's meaning-making (spir- itual) structures and faith traditions, educating students in skills that enhance their own spiritual development (Koch, 2003; Sink, 2004), and educating students about other faith traditions
- Consulting with parents about the values or faith traditions of the family
- Educating school and community colleagues on various faith traditions or spiritual orienta- tions, advocating for the families and children of "minority" faith traditions, and consulting

with school colleagues to facilitate understanding in how these faith traditions may manifest in academic, career, or personal/social development

• Leading the effort to transform the climate of the school toward respectful inclusion on the basis of religion, faith tradition, and/or spirituality

And, as always, the need for self-examination is clear when evaluating one's own faith traditions and spiritual realities. As counselors, we cannot be unhealthy in our own lives and hope to have credibility as we try to help others become more healthy.

REFLECTION MOMENT

Where are you in the journey within your own spirituality, and what is your reaction when considering talking about these issues with others? What can you do to make yourself more at ease when talking about this topic?

EDUCATIONAL REFORM

In 1983, the National Commission on Educational Excellence published *A Nation at Risk*, a scathing report on the state of the educational system in the United States. The report warned that the United States was losing ground to foreign competition in commerce, industry, science, and technological innovation. Although the authors of the report recognized that there were many contributing factors, a great deal of responsibility was attributed to the failings of the educational system and society's handling of it:

> Our society and its educational institutions seem to have lost sight of the basic purposes of schooling, and of the high expectations and disciplined effort needed to attain them. . . . That we have compromised this commitment, is, upon reflection, hardly surprising, given the multitude of often conflicting demands we have placed on our Nation's schools and colleges. They are routinely called on to provide solutions to personal, social, and political problems that the home and other institutions either will not or cannot resolve. (National Commission on Educational Excellence, 1983)

The report warned of dire consequences for the health and prosperity of the United States if it did not enact significant educational reform.

The publication of *A Nation at Risk* sparked the current school reform movement in the United States (Estes, 2004). Although changes have occurred in the way that the U.S. educational system is organized and has operated since 1983, many reformers feel that not much has improved and that the current educational system requires significant overhaul. The depth of the feelings that underlie the educational reform debate can be seen in the Pacific Research Institute's (Riley, 2000) (a strong proponent of such an overhaul) assessment of the public school system:

> Despite tinkering with methodology, standards, class size, and other measures, the system remains a public utility with captive customers and guaranteed funding—a monopoly producing bad products at high prices—and has shown such resistance to change, some have argued for a different approach. (p. 1)

In 2001, the United States Congress enacted, at the urging of President George W. Bush, the No Child Left Behind Act of 2001, a broad-based reform of the Elementary and Secondary Education Act governing kindergarten through 12th-grade public education. This reform plan calls for "stronger accountability for results, expanded flexibility and local control, expanded options for parents, and an emphasis on teaching methods that have been proven to work" (U.S. Department of Education, Fact Sheet on No Child Left Behind, n.d.).

The No Child Left Behind Act (NCLB) is representative of several significant strands within the educational reform movement. NCLB requires all states to establish state-guided accountability programs that require yearly testing of students in grades 3–8 on progress in reading and math, and the dissemination of the results by school in yearly report cards. Individual states must also report on a yearly basis disaggregated data on student performance so they may demonstrate progress toward closing the achievement gap between disadvantaged students and other students in the public schools (U.S. Department of Education, Fact Sheet on No Child Left Behind, n.d.).

A second and related aspect of educational reform included in the No Child Left Behind Act is the call for comprehensive school reform efforts based on scientifically based research and effective practices. The Comprehensive School Reform (CSR) Program provides grants to schools, particularly Title I schools serving disadvantaged students, throughout the United States that enable them to enact "coherent school-wide improvements that cover virtually all aspects of a school's operations, rather than piecemeal, fragmented approaches to reform" (U.S. Department of Education, About CSR, n.d.). Whether the schools choose a nationally recognized comprehensive school reform program or choose to develop their own, the schools must integrate the following 11 components of reform. Each school must do the following:

- Employ proven methods and strategies based on scientifically based research.
- Integrate a comprehensive design with aligned components.
- Provide ongoing, high-quality professional development for teachers and staff.
- Include measurable goals and benchmarks for student achievement.
- Be supported within the school by teachers, administrators, and staff.
- Provide support for teachers, administrators and staff.
- Provide for meaningful parent and community involvement in planning, implementing, and evaluating school improvement activities.
- Use high-quality external technical support and assistance from an external partner with experience and expertise in schoolwide reform and improvement.
- Plan for the annual evaluation of strategies for the implementation of school reforms and for student results achieved.
- Identify resources to support and sustain the school's comprehensive reform effort.
- Be found to significantly improve the academic achievement of students or demonstrate strong evidence that it will improve the academic achievement of students (U.S. Department of Education, About CSR, n.d.).

The Northwest Regional Educational Laboratory (NWREL) offers a catalog of such reform models that currently contains 29 models that are either schoolwide or single-subject models implemented schoolwide (NWREL, n.d.).

Another important educational reform strand included in the No Child Left Behind Act is school choice. Fuller, Burr, Huerta, Puryear, and Wexler (1999) characterized the basic underlying concepts of the school choice movement as follows:

> Choice is founded upon a human-scale theory of accountability. Give parents the option to exit their neighborhood school and shop from a wider variety of alternatives. Or, bypass the school system entirely and give public dollars directly to parents via vouchers, boosting their purchasing power. Thus, school principals and teachers—if the theory's underlying assumptions are met—become directly accountable to parents, not to school boards or state education agencies. This market competition for parents, enacted by a more diverse set of schools, will raise the quality of public education. (p. 5)

There are a number of different types of school choice options for which reformers have advocated over the years, including charter schools, private voucher programs, site-based management, tax credits, home schooling choice, and public school choice, including magnet schools and open-enrollment options. Charter schools are public schools that agree to meet certain academic performance standards and accepts accountability for results while exercising greater variation in educational methods for achieving those results. While there is great variation in voucher programs, they are generally supported by individuals, businesses, and groups that give vouchers to low-income children to enable them to attend private schools. Under site-based management, decision-making authority rests with committees consisting of principals and teachers at a school rather than with school boards or central administrations (Rees, 2000). Magnet schools are public schools with a specific curricular focus, and open enrollment allows parents to enroll their child in a public school outside their immediate neighborhood (Fuller et al., 1999). School choice is evident in the No Child Left Behind Act in that parents whose children are in schools identified as failing may choose to transfer their child to another school or a charter school, and the act expands support for the creation of new charter schools (U.S. Department of Education, Fact Sheet on No Child Left Behind, n.d.).

Although the No Child Left Behind Act has had its critics, related, among other things, to the adequacy of its funding or its inadequate attention to social issues impacting achievement of students in the schools, it is clear that the act represents a number of components of the educational reform movement. Furthermore, the act and these components are having a significant effect on the current look and feel of public education in the United States, including school counseling (Dollarhide & Lemberger, 2006). A growing number of public educational options, new forms of accountability demands and approaches, increased opportunities for parental input and participation, an increased emphasis on standards and testing of progress toward meeting standards, and the enactment of research-supported comprehensive school reform programs are all part of the changing educational landscape in the early twenty-first century.

GENDER AND SCHOOLS

The No Child Left Behind Act of 2001 (NCLB), a broad-based reform of the Elementary and Secondary Education Act governing kindergarten through 12th-grade public education in the United States, calls for "stronger accountability for results, expanded flexibility and local control, expanded options for parents, and an emphasis on teaching methods that have been proven to work" (U.S. Department of Education, Fact Sheet on No Child Left Behind, n.d.). NCLB puts increased pressure on schools to be accountable for their student achievement outcomes. However, the law also contains provisions to assist schools in developing innovative ways to boost student achievement outcomes.

One provision within Title V of the Act, which addresses parental choice and innovative programs, allows local education agencies (LEAs) to use federal funds for developing innovative assistance programs including programs to provide same-gender schools and classrooms (V.A.3.5131[a][23]). As the U.S. Department of Education sought to provide additional information to the states regarding this provision, it acknowledged that single-sex classes or activities were generally prohibited under Title IX of the Education Amendments of 1972 prohibiting sex-based discrimination. However, it maintained that there were allowable instances and that an LEA could offer single-sex schools if the action constituted remedial or affirmative action. LEAs pursuing this option, it maintained, would need to be aware of the constitutional requirements in this area and that they could be challenged in court litigation.

Since that time, the Department of Education has worked to address some of the limitations on schools offering same-sex classes and schools, proposing Title IX amendments under which "single-sex classes would be permitted if they are part of an evenhanded effort to provide a range of diverse educational options for male and female students, or if they are designed to meet particular, identified educational needs of students (U.S. Department of Education, 2004). Rod Paige, then U.S. Secretary of Education, maintained that while the research in this area was "incomplete," there was evidence to suggest that single-sex education can help some students in some settings.

This component of NCLB is, in part, representative of a growing concern about a gender achievement gap in public education. M. A. Clark, Oakley, and Adams (2006) write

> In the United States, boys are achieving at lower levels than girls as shown by test scores, grades, and drop-out rates. They have a higher incidence of ADHD, discipline referrals, and special education referrals and placements. Reports show that boys represent more than two-thirds of high school students with disabilities, including physical, learning, and emotional. Women have surpassed men not only in high school graduation rates but in university enrollment and degree completion. In this country, girls capture more academic honors, outscore boys in reading and writing and score about as well on math at the three grade levels (fourth, eighth and 12th) tested by the National Assessment for Educational Progress exam. (par. 1)

It is important to recognize that this gender achievement gap is not without its controversy and critics. Rivers and Barnett (2006) state that the crisis is a "manufactured" one, "the product of both a backlash against the women's movement" and the media's tendency to report on the next big crisis for the nation (par. 6). These authors assert that when the data is disaggregated by race and class, the problem emerges as one for inner-city and rural boys.

Educator and therapist Michael Gurian (2001) maintains that there are important reasons to attend to differences between boys and girls in their education, because they have significantly different needs in certain areas. A one-size-fits-all approach to education, he maintains, is not appropriate as there are certain developmental and structural differences between male and female brains that may lead them to process emotional and cognitive input differently. In addition, he indicates there are a number of chemical differences, hormonal differences, and functional differences that may influence how males and females process information. These differences have significant implications for a learning environment and for the work of school counselors. Consider the following example provided by Gurian:

> The female brain processes more emotive stimulants, through more senses, and more completely than does the male. It also verbalizes emotive information quickly. Boys can sometimes take hours to process emotively (and manage the same information as girls). This lesser emotive ability makes males more emotionally fragile than we tend to think. A boy who has had a crisis at home this morning may come to school with a higher cortisone (stress-hormone) level than, say, his sister because he has held in, or not processed, the emotional stress of the crisis at home. He may be unable to learn for much of the morning, whereas his sister may quickly process and even talk out the hard edges of the stress so that she can learn efficiently the very same morning. The male is often, thus, intrinsically fragile because he cannot guide his own emotions to processing and to words as quickly as a female does, and his fragility may extend to his ability to learn that day. (pp. 31–32)

Gurian goes on to point out other brain differences affecting this type of processing, including evidence indicating female brains tend to move sensory information with emotive content up in the brain toward areas where thinking occurs whereas male brains tend to move such information down, to areas more likely to invoke a fight-or-flight response. Through understanding these and other differences, Gurian maintains, schools and teachers can develop organization and teaching strategies more likely to assist both males and females in achieving academic and personal/social success.

A number of other authors have begun to emphasize developmental issues unique to either males or females. Clinical psychologist Mary Pipher, in her best-selling book *Reviving Ophelia* (1994), presented numerous case studies chronicling the significant negative psychological changes occurring in girls as they transitioned from childhood to adolescence. Pipher attributed these changes to a "girl-poisoning culture" in which young girls were bombarded by negative media messages and images about females (p. 12). L. M. Brown and Gilligan (1992), likewise, chronicled the difficult transition females experience from childhood to adolescence. This passage, they assert, is a passage into silence, disconnection, and a loss of a sense of self. Wiseman (2002) and Simmons (2002) have brought attention to the relational nature of female interaction and assert that female adolescents may use this emphasis on relationships to wield power over one another and, potentially, to inflict psychological harm. Simmons encourages schools to view this relational aggression as a form of bullying. Similar to the work he has done with male development, Gurian (2003) details the impact biological factors and brain development have on female social and other forms of development.

Pollack (1999) and Gurian (1997) have chronicled the difficult developmental transitions boys experience as they progress from childhood into adolescence and on to adulthood. Similar to L. M. Brown and Gilligan's (1992) descriptions of female developmental challenges, Pollack (1999) asserts that the journey for boys is often one into sadness and disconnection as they are shamed from a very early age into conforming to an unwritten Boy Code. This code mandates that they must be tough, dominant, and unemotional, and leads them to hide their fears and feelings. Both Horne and Kiselica (1999) and Beymer (1995) have sought to offer strategies for counselors to use to meet the counseling and guidance needs of boys and adolescent males.

Whether or not there is a formal gender achievement gap, these and other authors make a compelling case for attending to differences between males and females that may help us to differentiate instructional and counseling strategies to maximize achievement and success for both genders.

REFLECTION MOMENT

What is your reaction to the concept of single-sex educational environments? Can "separate" be equal? What do you consider the advantages and disadvantages of both mixed-gender and single-gender classrooms? As a new school counselor, what are the implications you see for each?

TECHNOLOGY

Student Use of Technology

As new technologies become more affordable, students will need help understanding the power and the dangers of computers: how to use them as effective and efficient tools for learning and how to avoid the problems that new technologies might bring. Counselors are often the best resource for teachers and students to help humanize the school environment and to facilitate conversations among all persons in the school setting.

Current events highlight the concerns that many counselors, parents, and educators share about students' use of technology. The misuse of cell phones to harass or invade another's life is seen in students' texting sexually explicit material (or sexting) and cyberbullying. Such behaviors now may also carry legal implications, as there are a number of high-profile cases in which cyberbullies have been charged with harassment and identity theft. Privacy issues are raised when students post personal information on Facebook, Twitter, and other social sharing networks. Plagiarism is an example of academic misuse of technology, as term papers or research papers are readily available on the Internet. The key to these and other examples of misuse of technology is for the counselor to be aware of what kids are doing and how they are communicating with each other, and then design ways to educate students about these issues.

Counselor Use of Technology

In a survey of 92 school counselors from elementary, middle, secondary, and vocational schools, Owen and Weikel (1999) found that 88 percent of the counselors reported that a computer had been assigned to them to support the counseling program. (Logically, in the intervening years since this study was published, that number has risen dramatically.) They also found that middle and secondary counselors used computers more in their work than elementary counselors (an average of 12.5 and 14.5 hours per week, respectively). In terms of confidence in their computer skills, elementary counselors reported the lowest confidence, middle school counselors somewhat higher, and secondary school counselors reported the highest level of confidence. This same pattern described the reported level of agreement that their productivity had been enhanced by computers. When examining computer use for counselors at all levels, the results revealed computer use for routine word processing by 95 percent of respondents, grade/record keeping by 65 percent, class scheduling by 64 percent, statistical analysis by 33 percent, educational programs by 30 percent, email by 28 percent, Internet research by 13 percent, and teaching by 5 percent. The authors lamented the fact that counselors still were not using computers for activities directly related to student counseling functions.

Numerous authors call for counselors to become more computer-friendly. Sabella and Booker (2003) have identified numerous benefits of using computers: increasing administrative understanding of the work of the counselor, fostering greater respect for how counseling enhances student development, informing parents and teachers about the referral process, networking with other counseling professionals, interfacing with the local business community, informing student counselors about the field, and assisting student service personnel to learn how they can work more effectively with the school community. Some of the ideas to increase computer use include supervision with university, peer, and district professionals, as well as consultation among counselors (Myrick & Sabella, 1995); listserv discussions (Logan, 2001); instruction (Sampson & Krumboltz, 1991); promotion of the comprehensive school counseling program through multimedia presentations (Sabella & Booker, 2003); and student advocacy (through an examination of student data and the advocacy for the elimination of barriers to student success) (Hohenshil, 2000). In addition, new technologies exist to provide professional development such as podcasts, webinars, and virtual reality trainings. For example, Counselor Educators in Second Life, a virtual environment for free continuing education units (CEUs) for counselors on a variety of topics, can be found at http://sl.counseloreducation.org/. (Site url accessed on December 9, 2010.)

Furthermore, counselors could use computers to establish connections with students and families through a webpage or could use email with students and families. It is possible that a listserv could be used to conduct discussions with students after a developmental curriculum session or to foster communication with students who are in groups, especially with the advent of live video (such as Skype) communication. While there are numerous arguments against relying on computers for communication (confidentiality, security of communication, uncertain identity of communicator), computers are not going to go away. In fact, ACES, the Association for Counselor Education and Supervision, has identified 12 technical competencies that should be expected of counselor education students at the completion of their graduate program (Hohenshil, 2000). Counselors should be able to

1. Develop webpages, presentations, letters, and reports
2. Use audiovisual equipment
3. Use computerized statistical packages
4. Use computerized testing, diagnostic, and career decision-making programs
5. Use email
6. Conduct Internet searches

7. Subscribe to, participate in, and sign off counseling-related listservs
8. Access and use counseling-related CD-ROM databases
9. Know of legal and ethical codes related to counseling services via the Internet
10. Know strengths and weaknesses of counseling on the Internet
11. Use the Internet for finding and using continuing education opportunities in counseling
12. Evaluate the quality of Internet information

There are entire schools that exist on the Internet, and they employ school counselors to work with students, in many similar ways that school counselors work with students in person. One example of such a school is Ohio Connections Academy, which can be accessed at www.connectionsacademy.com/ohio-school/our-school/home.aspx (site accessed on July 28, 2010). According to the webpage, "Ohio Connections Academy (OCA) is a tuition-free, K–12 public eSchool that students attend from home. OCA brings a fully accredited public education directly to your family's door—anywhere in Ohio" (par. 1). This system of education differs from home schooling in that all educational material is determined by the Academy rather than by the parent-teacher, and all instruction is delivered via the Internet.

It is easy to see how useful computers would be in a CSCP, especially with the emphasis of the National Model on leadership, advocacy, collaboration, and systemic change. With the many uses of computers in today's world, the counselor who is not computer-savvy ignores a valuable resource. Computers can supplement all the counselor's activities in the DAP model (counseling, educating, consultation and collaboration, and leadership, advocacy, and coordination) to accomplish the systemic and proactive work of the counselor and can facilitate contact with all partners.

REFLECTION MOMENT

How comfortable are you with technology? What do you need to do to become more comfortable with technology as a school counselor?

ALTERNATIVE SOURCES OF FUNDING

Funding for schools will become more of an issue for taxpayers as the cost of living goes up, and even more so in the current economic climate since the "economic slowdown" of 2008. The answer for many educators, including counselors, is to seek outside funding from private and public granting sources. It is valuable to know about possible funding sources and the process for applying for grant funding.

There are distinct strategies for grant writing (Education World, 2004). Before you begin the search for external funds, you need three things: (1) permission to secure external funding from your administrator (building and/or district), (2) a project that is unique or innovative with documented efficacy, and (3) a detailed plan to implement your project. Specific to your project, you need (1) to document the need for the project (demographics, test results, evidence of current gaps in service); (2) a mission statement that clearly spells out the project's desired outcome; (3) measurable and specific goals and objectives; (4) a detailed project time line; (5) assessment tools to document and evaluate the attainment of your goals and objectives; (6) a list of all needed materials, personnel, and supplies; and (7) the total cost of your project.

In terms of process, you would:

1. Assemble a team (of teachers, fellow counselors, parents, students) to work on the grant application with you so that you can assign tasks (researching, writing, proofing, etc.) to share the burden of time devoted to this process
2. Research various funding sources to find one that best fits the project you have in mind
3. Collaborate with everyone involved in your project on the grant itself so that all parties are informed and supportive

4. Carefully read the call for proposals from your target funding source(s), following their directions exactly

5. Have someone who is not directly involved with the project read the proposal before submission to ensure accuracy, clarity, and consistency within the application.

When writing a grant, successful grant writers (Education World, 2004) encourage new writers to provide balanced attention to each of the three parts of the grant: the application form or forms, the narrative, and the budget. The application forms must be completed carefully, double-checking for accuracy. The narrative must be clearly written, based on evidence (research based), detailed, concise, and interesting to read. Finally, the budget should be reasonable, detailed, accurate, realistic, and flexible.

In addition to these insights, SchoolGrants (2006) emphasize that a "well documented needs statement is critical to your proposal" (p. 5). They recommend that you examine previous funded programs to gain a better understanding of your potential funding source, and if you are not funded, they recommend that you request reviewer comments so that you can improve your next grant application.

The Internet is a rich source of information on educational grants that would be of particular interest for school counselors. Consider corporate or private philanthropic organizations in addition to federal, state, or local funds.

REFLECTION MOMENT

What has been your experience with grants? Is there a way to gain grant experience while you are still in graduate school? People in charge of hiring, such as principals, are always impressed with a candidate who is able to demonstrate grant experience.

CASE STUDY

Integration

Now that you have read the chapter, go back and reread the Case Study. What guesses do you have about this child and his mother? What would you want to know about Samuel? What would you want to know about his mother and/or any other relatives? His support system? His school experiences thus far?

Based on what you want to know, what would you do with the information? Using the DAP model as a template for planning your response, identify actions you could take in each block, based on your best guesses about the situation. Remember to be holistic, systemic, balanced, proactive, integrated, and reflective.

How might technology be useful in your work with this family? What grant ideas might be generated from knowing Sam and his mother attend your school?

Suggested Readings

Bauer, A. L., Ingersoll, E., & Burns, L. (2004). School counselors and psychotropic medication: Assessing training, experience, and school policy issues. *Professional School Counseling, 7,* 202–211. This article presents important research into the prevalence and issues of the administration of psychotropic medications in the schools.

Hohenshil, T. H. (2000). High tech counseling. *Journal of Counseling and Development, 78,* 365–369. This article outlines some important information about computers and counselors, including suggestions about ways that counselors could infuse computers into their work. It also contains an appendix in which the Technical Competencies for Counselor Education Students are presented.

Holcomb-McCoy, C. (2004). Assessing the multicultural competence of school counselors: A checklist. *Professional School Counselor, 7,* 178–186. This article is a comprehensive overview of the literature discussing multicultural skills in the schools. Furthermore, it includes a checklist of multicultural competencies that will enable the reader to reflect on current skill levels and plan for professional development.

Kerr, M. M. (2009). *School crisis prevention and intervention.* Upper Saddle River, NJ: Merrill. This useful book provides a great resource for building crisis prevention, intervention, and postvention.

Kress, V. E. W., Gibson, D. M., & Reynolds, C. A. (2004). Adolescents who self-injure: Implications and strategies for school counselors. *Professional School Counselor, 7,* 195–201. This article provides an excellent overview of the current literature and thinking about etiology and interventions for self-injurious behaviors and then extrapolates from these insights various intervention strategies appropriate for school counselors.

Payne, R. K. (2003). *A framework for understanding poverty* (3rd ed.). Highlands, TX: aha! Process. The second book: *Bridges Out of Poverty.* Both books provide much-needed insights into the issues facing students of poverty and use compassion and empathy in outlining school-appropriate interventions.

Spirituality and School Counseling [Special issue] (2004, June). *Professional School Counseling, 7*(5). This entire issue is devoted to the topic of spirituality in comprehensive school counseling programs and represents an important discussion on the issues of addressing spirituality in the schools.

Stone, C. B., & Dahir, C. A. (2007). *School counselor accountability: A MEASURE of student success* (2nd ed.). Upper Saddle River, NJ: Pearson/Merrill/Prentice-Hall. This book presents the rationale, strategies, and examples of documents that comprise school counselor accountability.

Additional readings in gender issues would include the following:

Gurian, M. (1997). *The wonder of boys: What parents, mentors, and educators can do to shape boys into exceptional men.* New York: Penguin.

Gurian, M. (2001). *Boys and girls learn differently! A guide for teachers and parents.* San Francisco: Jossey-Bass.

Gurian, M. (2003). *Wonder of girls: Understanding the hidden nature of our daughters.* New York: Simon and Schuster.

Pollack, W. S. (1999). *Real boys: Rescuing our sons from the myths of boyhood.* New York: Owl Books.

Simmons, R. (2002). *Odd girl out.* Orlando, FL: Harcourt.

Wiseman, R. (2002). *Queen bees and wannabes.* Norwalk, CT: Crown.

14

Personal and Professional Issues

LEARNING OBJECTIVES

By the end of this chapter, you will

1. Understand the challenges of comprehensive school counseling in terms of holistic life management

2. Understand the relationship between personal balance and professional health

3. Understand the limitations of school counselors and how to deal with those limitations

4. Have some concrete strategies for addressing the stress of professional school counseling

5. Be able to discuss the development of professional identity

6. Be able to identify the need for professional supervision

7. Understand how consultation and networking can alleviate feelings of isolation

8. Be able to discuss the need for continued education as a professional school counselor

9. Understand the role of involvement with professional associations in terms of membership, leadership, conference attendance, and contributing to the profession through conference presentations

10. Be able to identify the benefits of involvement with action research for district information as well as professional publications

11. Understand the strategies for locating and engaging a mentor to enhance your professional development as well as understanding the benefits of serving as a mentor to other professionals

CASE STUDY

Emily's Turn to Learn

Emily's week was not turning out as she had hoped. Here it was, only Wednesday, and she was already looking forward to the weekend; spring break was a distant memory, and the year seemed like it would never end. She came out of the building to go home, only to find she had a flat tire on her car. She waited in her car for the repair truck and thought about her week so far.

On Monday, she had gotten the first bit of bad news; the district was not going to replace Jose's position, so they were going from four counselors down to three. And student needs were higher than ever—with rezoning this year, several high-needs elementary schools were now part of the middle school's attendance district. Then, with the homeless shelter opening up down the street from the middle school, they had several students in and out within weeks—a lot of time spent there with scheduling and transition services, only to have them leave within a couple of days. Every year, the counselors worked with more students with greater needs but weren't going to have one-fourth of their staff next year.

Then, yesterday, Emily had gotten her annual professional performance review. She was not pleased with her review. She was supposed to learn email and the new school registration and student record package, but she had not had enough time last year to learn those things. The final report on the grant funds from last year still wasn't done. She was also supposed to conduct an in-service for the staff on the workshop she attended on reactive attachment disorder, but she never got around to that either. And even though she was elected to serve on the state's advisory council for professional school counseling, she had not attended any meetings. Emily thought she worked hard enough; she deserved the time she took off to relax. Besides, she was trying to spend more time with students, but there were so many other things that got in the way. The director of pupil services for the district had judged her too harshly for these other minor failings. Didn't central office care about the professional counselors at all?

Now this flat. Sighing, she checked her watch. Another 20 minutes before the tow truck would come. She decided to go back into the building to go to the restroom. Inside, she ducked into the closest girls' bathroom. Within seconds, several girls entered, and Emily became an unwilling witness to the conversation.

One voice said, "Yeah, she said the counselor didn't really understand anything she was telling her. Ms. Dorado just kept pushing her to tell her mother, tell her mother, you know? She said it really made her mad that Ms. Dorado wasn't listening to her. I thought counselors were supposed to listen to you!"

The second voice laughed. "Maybe it's just a problem with time. I know every time I go to talk to Ms. Dorado, she has about five minutes for me, then she has to go to another meeting, or whatever it is that counselors do. No one can ever find her. No one seems to know what the heck she does. I see her in the faculty lounge all the time."

"'Look at me—I'm so overworked I need a break!'" Both voices giggled. "No one I know has ever gotten any help from her. They should fire her. Everyone always goes to the other counselors. She's a big joke. She never does what she says she's going to do. That new kid said she was supposed to get back to him with changes in his schedule, but she never did . . ." The voices moved toward the door, then faded as the conversation moved out into the hallway.

Emily wanted to cry. She waited until the voices were out in the hall, then she went back out to wait in her car. Deep in thought, she didn't even see the repair truck arrive. She jumped a mile when the driver came to her window and asked, "Are you Emily Dorado? You called for a tire repair?"

CHALLENGE QUESTIONS

What was your reaction as you read the scenario? What conclusions did you come to about the counselor's job performance? What were some areas for potential improvement that you could see?

If you were this counselor, you could choose to ignore the feedback or you could choose to learn from it. What would your choice be? ▪

PERSONAL MENTAL HEALTH: THE SEARCH FOR BALANCE

Life is a series of choices, and we are all responsible for our choices. We can choose to live life out of balance, either self-focused and self-absorbed (me-first) or other-focused ("I'll give you my soul if you will just approve of me"). Both of these lifestyles are out of balance and unhealthy, causing problems in both work and personal life. One is no better than the other.

In Chapter 4, we discussed the need for balance in a CSCP in terms of balanced activities based on the need of the partner. In this current chapter, we are shifting the concept of balance to focus on the life of the counselor. In this context, "balance" can be conceptualized as the means by which the needs of the internal reality (the counselor's personal needs) and the external reality (the needs of all partners of the CSCP) are brought into alignment. We will use the metaphor of a *boundary*, where the needs of the self and the needs of others meet. It is often here that creativity emerges and we bring out the best in ourselves. In research describing creative thinking, this boundary causes contact between imaginary and visceral, between logical and intuitive, between body and mind, between science and art (DeBono, 1992; Gruber, 1993; Morris, 1992; Root-Bernstein & Root-Bernstein, 1999). For the purposes of this book, we will view balance as the need to nurture both the personal needs and the professional needs of the counselor, to the benefit of both aspects of existence. To function well as a counselor, you need to understand how to take care of your personal issues and needs while simultaneously taking care of the needs of your partners in the DAP model. Without balance, your personal needs will drive your professional choices, or your professional needs will compromise your personal self mentally, physically, and/or emotionally. Counselors are the models for mental health in the schools; counselors living with these out-of-balance conditions compromise their own and other counselors' credibility and ability to function.

In general, there are many sources of stress for a school counselor. Stress comes from working with others who don't understand the work that counselors do, from struggles of the students, and from budgets that do not keep up with needs. Other stressors include a lack of privacy and anonymity due to heightened visibility as a mental health professional and feelings of isolation resulting from a lack of professional peers within the school setting (Morrissette, 2000). We cannot change the context or realities of the job; what we can do is understand and prepare for ways to counteract these stressors.

In Chapter 1, we discussed the professional competencies for school counselors as outlined by the American School Counselor Association (ASCA) and the Council for the Accreditation of Counseling and Related Educational Programs (CACREP), and the rest of this book has been designed to help you to develop those competencies. In Chapter 1, we also outlined the personal qualities that professional school counselors need: creativity and imagination, flexibility, courage and belief, and passion. These are the antidotes for the stressors of working as a school counselor. This chapter is devoted to helping you to evaluate and refine those personal qualities that typify the best school counselors.

Where do these qualities come from? They are partly the result of temperament and they are partly the result of personal and professional health. We can't change temperament, but we can maximize our personal and professional health.

Finding Your Center

The term "center" is used in this context to refer to various aspects of our existence. It is used to refer to a spiritual center, involving our relationship with a higher power or higher purpose, and to a moral center, involving our relationship with our own values and morals.

Our awareness of our own values and morals is a crucial piece of being able to understand ourselves and, by extension, our students and partners. Since many concepts within our traditional definitions of "mental health" resonate with Western values of individualism, autonomy, environmental mastery, self-acceptance, happiness, and purpose in life, we must understand our own moral center and openly dialogue with clients about the "ongoing interpretive process" between our moral center and theirs (Christopher, 1999, p. 150). We can expand these values to include intrapersonal and interpersonal peace, compassion for all living things, and finding ways to help others and the planet. This reflective work has implications both for helping our students and for helping us work on our own issues. It is necessary for our connection with our students; it is also necessary for our connection with our inner resources. In this context, finding our moral center involves reflection and insight, which requires quiet reflection, compassion, patience, and a commitment to deepening our self-understanding.

Palmer refers to this as "sounding our own depths" (1998, p. 31). Deep self-knowledge facilitates the creation of a learning community. Palmer reinforces the connection between our inner reality and our outer work (counseling or educating), and challenges us to develop an ongoing dialogue with our own inner teachers. These inner teachers are the source of our professionalism, our desire to help others grow, and ultimately, our wisdom.

Other authors use the terms "spirit" and "wisdom" to describe this sense of connection between self, others, and higher purpose. Fox (1994) suggests that education of the whole person—heart, body, mind, and spirit; books and life; intellect and imagination—should be a part of our curriculum, where students learn awe, wisdom, compassion, and inner growth. This vision of education would transform the role of counselors, giving additional support to the idea that counselors must know their own center to help students locate and nurture theirs.

In another context, Young-Eisendrath and Miller (2000) examine the connection between spiritual development and health. "We regard spiritual development to be a necessary component of a healthy, effective life as a human being. . . . Mature spirituality is the honing of integrity, wisdom, and transcendence in the service of the question of what it means to be human. . . ." (p. 5). As counselors, educators, and human beings, there is support for the idea that being centered fosters the elements needed to maintain balance in life. It is from our "center," or core, that we find the spring from which creativity, imagination, flexibility, courage, belief, faith, and passion flow. If we drain this spring dry, we have nothing left to give others. If we dam the flow to save all these precious qualities, we are no longer of service to our CSCP partners. We must be able to dip from the spring as needed to replenish ourselves, while monitoring the flow to ensure enough reserves for the future.

REFLECTION MOMENT

Where do you go to get centered? How often do you go there? Do you need to go there more often?

Doing Your Best, Then Letting Go

One of the most difficult lessons for new counselors is learning when to let go. When do you know you've done all you can to help a student, parent, coworker? When is enough *enough*? In general, as with any counseling situation, the first step comes with the recognition that each of us is responsible for our own choices in life. As counselors, it is our job to make sure the door to change is open and that the client's movement toward healthy choices is applauded and commended. We can open the door, we can make the "healthy" side of the door attractive and appealing, we can point out the costs of remaining on the other side of the door, but we cannot force anyone to walk through the door. We are only human, with all the limitations that implies. But we are obligated by profession and training to give 100 percent in these efforts to persuade someone to make healthy choices.

With adults, most counselors feel comfortable leaving the choice with the client. However, with young people, give extra effort to helping them. In keeping with the metaphor, consider giving 110 percent. School counselors should open the door, encourage students to walk through the door, make the other side of the door very unappealing, and invite them again to walk over that threshold. When does enough constitute enough? Only you can answer that for yourself. What can you live with, without compromising your own personal and professional health?

"Letting go" involves an additional concept inherent in counseling in general—that of time. Change takes place when the client is ready, and not a moment before. The student needs time to evaluate the risks and benefits of walking through the door to change. If a student, in spite of the counselor's best efforts in giving 110 percent, chooses not to walk over the threshold, "letting go" involves the recognition that the student, for his or her own reasons, is not ready to change yet. Many of the most meaningful conversations counselors have with students are those that take place years after students have left school, in which students share with counselors how meaningful the counselors' interventions were all those years ago.

In this way, there is a strong similarity between counseling and parenting. Often, it's not until we reach our 20s that we realize what our parents were trying to tell us in our teens, that the lessons they were trying to teach us really did have value after all. Just as good parents must let go of their children to allow them to learn their lessons, so too must good counselors. Sometimes the best lessons come from bruised knees or bruised egos, and we can't save them from the lessons life has to teach them.

REFLECTION MOMENT

Have you had experience with finding the limit of your professional endurance? Have you had to make the difficult choice to let go? What was that experience like for you?

Stress Management Strategies

As school counselors, you will have many opportunities to talk with your DAP partners about stress. Children, adolescents, and adults can benefit tremendously from understanding how stress affects decision making; physical, emotional, and spiritual health; and relationships. Stress compromises performance, erodes stamina, and disables the natural resilience of both body and spirit. But stress cannot be avoided; it is a natural part of our everyday existence and keeps us striving to improve ourselves and our lives (Seaward, 1994). The best we can do is understand and manage stress, because it cannot be eradicated.

First, it is important to understand that stress comes from the way we interpret and internalize events in our lives. Events themselves do not cause stress; the emotions we experience as a result of our *beliefs* about these events are the sources of stress. Our beliefs about the "fairness" of life, our "right" to happiness, the way we "deserve" to be treated by life and others, often result in anger, frustration, fear, and indignation. Of these, the strongest stress triggers are the emotions of anger and fear (Seaward, 1994). These emotional states, in turn, trigger physiological responses that involve the nervous system and the immune system, which in turn telegraph our internal emotional states into physical reality (Seaward, 1994).

The ultimate antistress weapon, according to Seaward (1994), is self-esteem. It is strong self-esteem that allows us to keep fear from hijacking our nervous and immune systems. With strong self-esteem, we are less likely to catastrophize events in our lives, and we are better able to bounce back from life's inevitable disappointments and frustrations. You will undoubtedly notice that many of the strategies for managing stress are designed to enhance this fragile and elusive quality.

Managing stress can be accomplished in a variety of ways. The following stress management strategies are adapted from Seaward (1994):

1. Enhance your spiritual connection with your internal reality. Be centered within all elements of your identity. Get to know yourself well and explore your inner reality with compassion.
2. Enhance your spiritual connections with however you perceive and define the divine. Seaward provides an excellent reading list, including various perspectives on spirituality—Carl Jung, M. Scott Peck, Black Elk, Matthew Fox, Joan Borysenko, Jesus Christ, Lao Tzu, and Albert Einstein—that are then woven into some common themes of spirituality.
3. Enhance your spiritual connections with loving others, to increase healthy bonding, acceptance, peace, compassion, and respect in your daily life.
4. Explore and define your personal value system, so that you live with greater congruence and authenticity within that value system.
5. Explore and define a meaningful purpose for your life. Have goals to achieve, serve to promote love and respect in the world, or have some purpose to fill. This helps you keep your life in perspective and allows you to better handle disappointments and pain.
6. Explore the connection between your thoughts, expectations, and experiences to determine if you could restructure your cognitions to reduce your experience of stress.
7. Learn and practice assertiveness skills to help you maintain healthy boundaries.

8. Consider journaling as a means of exploring your feelings and experiences.

9. Use art therapy to tap, explore, and/or release your feelings about your experiences.

10. Use humor therapy to cope with disappointments and frustrations. It is important to recognize that there are healthy and unhealthy applications of humor. Those that enhance connection, compassion, and relief are healthy; those that ridicule or demean others are not healthy. To foster stress relief, humor used in a healthy way can build connections with others, reframe experiences, and allow us to view ourselves, others, and our world with more hope and compassion.

11. Use creative problem-solving strategies, such as brainstorming, clustering, and metaphors. Effective problem solving fosters self-efficacy and self-esteem.

12. Enhance your communication skills. Much of the stress of life comes from difficult relationships with others; communicating more effectively can substantially improve our relationships.

13. Improve your time management skills. Having an efficient means of allocating and accounting for time can help you manage the busy schedule of a school counselor. Recall that the establishment and maintenance of a calendar is a part of the ASCA National Model.

14. Consider a support group to help you cope with your own unique life situation.

15. Having a hobby can increase your social connections and creativity.

16. Consider the practice of forgiveness to manage your stress.

17. Taking care of your body is also essential. The primary strategies for taking care of yourself involve a three-pronged approach:
    • Exercise with a physician's approval
    • Proper nutrition that supports a healthy lifestyle
    • Relaxation, including diaphragmatic breathing, meditation, Hatha yoga (meditation, breathing, and various body postures), mental imagery (taking a mental vacation), music, massage, T'ai Chi Ch'uan (movement, breathing, and concentration), progressive muscular relaxation, autogenic training, and biofeedback

These ideas are offered as a means of promoting your holistic well-being and health. After all, if you're not healthy, you will not be of much use to your students or adult partners.

REFLECTION MOMENT

How do you know when you're having problems with your stress level? How do you deal with stress? Are there stress management strategies that you can put into place now to help you deal with the stress of graduate school?

PROFESSIONAL HEALTH

A counselor's professional health is also an issue of this chapter. Although there is substantial overlap between your personal and professional health, the strategies of this section are designed to help you address the work-related challenges of school counselors. Many of the challenges faced by school counselors have already been discussed, but an overview here might help you understand the context of this discussion.

1. Counselors often feel isolated since there is a limited number of counselors in any given district or building.

2. The role of the counselor is not well understood by parents, students, teachers, or administrators.

3. Counselors are often defined as ancillary services, not central to the functioning of the school.

4. Counselors' time often is eroded by activities that are not essential for the effective functioning of the comprehensive school counseling program.
5. There is little recognition for the hard work counselors do.
6. There may be little privacy for school counselors and their families in communities where school professionals are well known.
7. There are tremendous needs among all the partners, and students, families, coworkers, and entire communities look to the school counselor to address a variety of problems.
8. Information about ways of helping, perspectives on new or emerging problems, and technology are always evolving.
9. Burnout is high in the helping professions, and opportunities to "recharge one's batteries" are few.

Following are some ideas to help you mitigate the effects of these challenges.

Professional Identity

In Chapter 5, we talked about the professionalization of school counseling and the development of professional identity for school counselors, which resulted in the development of the ASCA National Model. Similarly, school counselors undergo a personal process in the development of a professional identity. It is helpful to have an overview of this process to understand how unique and diverse school counseling programs evolve. According to Brott and Myers (1999), this process involves the slow internalization of external standards and priorities. At first, the school counselor defines his or her role solely in external terms, derived first from graduate training and secondarily from the school and/or district administrators, other counselors, and existing programs. In the middle of this developmental process, school counselors interact with a variety of perspectives that provide feedback about the school counseling program and the role and skills of the school counselor. In other words, the counselor confronts a wide variety of evaluative voices (p. 344). In the final stage of professional development, the school counselor uses personal judgments in the definition of the role of the school counselor and in the design and definition of the comprehensive school counseling program. These personal judgments are now defensible as coming from professional experience and perspective, as professional and personal identities merge, unify, and solidify.

Another process model for the development of professional identity comes from Gibson, Dollarhide, and Moss (2010). In this model (see Figure 14.1), the professional counselor develops a professional identity when she or he is able to accomplish three tasks: define counseling for oneself, internalize responsibility for one's learning about counseling, and see oneself as part of a professional community to which and for which one is responsible. These three tasks take place across time, in which the new professional counselor moves from seeking external validation, through coursework and commitment, to an internal sense of professionalism.

This process explains why it is difficult for new counselors to engage in strong advocacy for the professional identity of all school counselors. For the most part, the development of this professional "voice" does not manifest until one has internalized a sense of professionalism, or until the third stage of the process as outlined by Brott and Myers (1999) and by Gibson et al. (2010). In spite of how difficult advocacy may be, one of the most important ways school counselors can work to mitigate the problems of the profession is through enhancing the identity and professionalism of the counseling profession in general, and the school counseling profession in particular. L. S. Johnson (2000) argues that school counselors must "refine their professional identity as highly trained practitioners, whose goal is to facilitate all students to become effective learners through the provision of a contemporary, integrated school counseling program that promotes the achievement of developmentally based competencies across academic, career, and personal/social domains. . . . [T]heir operational identity needs to be shifted from focusing on the individual services they provide to focusing on the integrated school counseling program as a whole. Similarly, their . . . target of services needs to move from being the individual student to

FIGURE 14.1 A Process Model of Professional Identity Development

the school system as a whole. . . ." (p. 32). To accomplish this, school counselors must align their mission as congruent with the academic mission of the school and document ways in which their work helps students to become effective learners (L. S. Johnson, 2000). In the terms of Gibson et al. (2010), school counselors must internalize their place in the professional community, and remain grounded in their professional identity. Education of the DAP partners, advocacy for the role of the school counselor, and leadership of the program will help provide a common ground from which school counselors can establish their contribution to students and the school.

Portfolios

Documentation of your contributions is essential, and there are a variety of ways to do this. In addition to the Results Report and the Program Audit of the National Model (see Chapter 5 for these topics), the professional portfolio provides a venue for that documentation (Boes, VanZile-Tamsen, & Jackson, 2001; James & Greenwalt, 2001; Johnson, 2000), which would be appropriate for the School Counselor Performance evaluation (ASCA National Model) that could reflect the ASCA School Counselor Competencies (Appendix B). Portfolios are the compilation and maintenance of various "artifacts" (documents, photographs, letters, disks, audio- and videotapes, computer disks—any work-related product) that describe and validate one's work history. James and Greenwalt (2001) refine this definition even further, describing the elements of a "working portfolio" as the documentation of one's entire professional development, and the "presentation portfolio" as a select portion of the working portfolio that is used for a specific purpose (a job interview or a consulting presentation, for example).

These portfolio artifacts are selected and/or designed to illustrate what you can do as a professional school counselor. Elements of the working portfolio could include the following (adapted from Boes et al., 2001; James & Greenwalt, 2001; L. S. Johnson, 2000):

1. Your philosophy of education
2. Your philosophy of comprehensive school counseling (citing the ASCA National Model and the Education Trust' *New Vision for School Counseling* (2009b)

3. Curriculum vitae (a comprehensive overview of all work locations, dates, and duties, and all educational experiences, courses, workshops, and conferences)

4. Resume (a summary of those work and educational experiences)

5. Practicum and internship experiences, with pictures of you with students (without revealing student identities) or pictures of student artwork

6. Results of work projects (such as new programs, surveys, grant proposals, needs assessments, outcomes assessments, reports)

7. Professional credentials, such as licenses, certifications, or endorsements

8. Continuing education courses, workshops, or presentations you have attended, with dates, locations, and presenters noted

9. Presentations you've made (including developmental curriculum lessons, workshops, in-services, and/or groups you have conducted)

10. Publications you have authored (including in-house publications such as brochures, flyers, or handbooks for students, parents, faculty, etc.)

11. Professional memberships, including dates and offices held

12. Service to school, district, and/or community in terms of committee membership, volunteer positions, and so on

Presentation portfolios, as mentioned, are selected artifacts from the work portfolio that serve to document a selection of your professional history. For example, if your state has specific competencies that must be documented for licensure, you might use a presentation portfolio for that purpose. Boes et al. (2001) suggest that you organize this special portfolio using the ASCA National Standards for Student Academic, Career, and Personal/Social Development, and include a reflective self-evaluation. It could make sense to structure your portfolio around the School Counselor Performance Standards (Appendix B) and include artifacts that document your attainment of each performance standard. A more common example of a presentation portfolio is one that is used for purposes of a job search, in which the applicant takes the presentation portfolio to the interview to share with the search committee. *Note*: electronic portfolios, those stored on a disk or CD, or available on a webpage, are increasingly viewed as "cutting edge" for counselors who must be able to function in this age of technology.

Supervision

It is clear from the literature that there are problems in the field in terms of supervision of counselors (Dollarhide & Miller, 2006). Supervision can be conceptualized in terms of three functions:

1. Administrative supervision, involving accounting for time, daily attendance, communication skills, adherence to school policies; may be provided by building or district administrator (these are articulated in the management agreements described in the National Model)

2. Program supervision, involving feedback relative to the progress of the comprehensive school counseling program; may be provided by district pupil services administrator or a counselor supervisor within the building

3. Technical, clinical, or counseling supervision, involving feedback on counseling, intervention, and developmental curriculum delivery skills; best if provided by a more experienced counselor (E. B. Roberts & Borders, 1994; Schmidt, 1990)

It is important that you understand that each of the three supervision venues listed above is designed to accomplish a unique purpose. The first is to help you function in the school setting; the second, to help you function in an effective comprehensive school counseling program; and the third, to help you function effectively with students, families, and colleagues.

As a counselor trainee, you will receive supervision from a supervising counselor. As a professional, you will be supervised by a number of supervisors, depending on the way the district designates personnel for the three supervision functions listed above. The most common scenario is supervision by a senior counselor for clinical and program supervision, and supervision by the principal for the administrative supervision. Depending on the district, the district pupil services director may also provide program supervision (which is good if this person has a counseling background). It is a challenge when a noncounselor is designated for any other type of supervision than administrative supervision, for good reason. Noncounselors usually do not have adequate understanding of the counseling profession, and it will be up to you to educate that person about counseling.

Although there is no shortage of people in the schools who will give you feedback about how you are doing your job, there is a general hands-off philosophy among counselors in terms of clinical supervision. But this kind of supervision, especially for new professionals in the field, can be extremely helpful in your development of a sense of professional efficacy (Crespi, Fischetti, & Butler, 2001; Dollarhide & Miller, 2006). In spite of a lack of supervisors in the field who have received training in supervision (Kahn, 1999; W. B. Roberts & Morotti, 2001), you are urged to voluntarily solicit clinical feedback. The ideal situation would involve obtaining this supervision from an experienced counselor (Dollarhide & Miller, 2006), but a study of peer-group supervision suggested substantial professional advantages accrued to the participants (Agnew, Vaught, Getz, & Fortune, 2000). Specifically, 97 percent of the 29 participants cited positive growth in clinical skills, increased sense of professionalism, increased consultation and referral skills, increased confidence, increased comfort with the job, decreased feelings of burnout, and increased professional validation. In addition, supervision is an important strategy to improve ethical counseling (American Counseling Association, 2005; Herlihy & Corey, 1996).

As you progress through your graduate training to become a school counselor, you will receive supervision in your field experiences (termed "practicum" and/or "internship" in most programs). According to Miller and Dollarhide (2006), you can begin your own professional development as a supervisee, by attending to and learning about supervision *while you are experiencing it*. Although formal training in supervision is usually reserved for doctoral-level students, you can explore the possibility of taking the class and/or read the professional literature in supervision, because it will enhance your ability to gain the maximum benefit from the supervision you receive. In addition, it will increase your ability, once you have been a professional for a couple of years (two years of experience is mandated by the Council for Accreditation of Counseling and Related Programs [CACREP, 2000]), to serve as a supervisor for upcoming counselor trainees.

Colleague Consultation and Networking

There is very little in this world that can help us feel better about our situation than consulting and networking with others. Although there may be few formal opportunities to network with your school counseling colleagues, nothing prevents you from initiating a "counselors' lunch" once a month or once a semester. Some counselors take advantage of in-service time provided by the district to call a meeting of the counselors and/or pupil services professionals to discuss issues of importance in the district and community. In this situation, the director of pupil services is usually involved to design the official agenda.

In addition, one-on-one consultation with your peers can establish resources and expertise that can help you do your job more effectively. This consultation is not limited to counselors; other pupil services professionals provide a rich source of perspectives and expertise. Access the expertise you will find in the teachers, school social worker, school psychologist, and others. In addition, there are many resources in the community with whom you could consult to enhance your functioning in your CSCP.

Both formal and informal networks are essential to your professional survival. It is important that you have opportunities to understand the challenges facing the school, the district, and the entire community. After all, how can you design systemic interventions and build community in your school if you can't build it among your colleagues and peers?

Lifelong Continuing Education

All counselors are in need of lifelong professional training and education, a position supported in the professional ethics of both ACA and ASCA. School counselors in the field sometimes lament that their districts won't pay for their ongoing educational needs. But note that you should not wait for your district to pay for your continued education. That is not the district's responsibility—it is your professional responsibility to remain up-to-date with the innovations in the field. In addition, new perspectives on important topics, such as multicultural counseling strategies (Constantine & Yeh, 2001), keep skills fresh and enhance self-efficacy.

There are many opportunities for continuing education. These include

1. In-service topics offered by the district
2. University classes
3. Continuing education programs offered by universities
4. Presentations by local mental health organizations and hospitals
5. Online programs for continuing education
6. Webinars, podcasts, and virtual training opportunities such as those offered by Counselor Educators in Second Life (found at http://sl.counseloreducation.org/) (accessed on December 9, 2010),
7. Conferences offered by national and state professional associations (American Counseling Association, American School Counselor Association, and their state affiliates)

In addition, you will want to remain up-to-date with the professional literature from your professional associations. You must read new books that address the issues your students, families, and community are facing. Remain aware of new music, movies, TV shows, and images pervading our culture that send messages to students about how they should be—how they should act, feel, think, and look—and that send messages about how their families, schools, and community should be. You must commit to your own lifelong learning.

Professional Associations

Membership and active involvement in your national, state, and local professional associations will provide you with a number of substantial benefits that will directly enhance the work you do in the schools. Networking with colleagues either online or in person at conferences, professional journals with current perspectives on the field, professional liability insurance, and opportunities for continuing education through conferences are the benefits of membership in professional associations. In addition, your contribution to those associations in terms of your time and involvement provides you with a greater connection to other dedicated professionals. Service in a leadership capacity in an association can range from being a member of a committee to running for office; a wide range of talents and perspectives is necessary for these associations to function effectively. And this does not supplant the need for counselors to be involved in terms of legislative and social activism, supporting legislation that enhances the professionalization of counseling or that provides support for schools. In addition, professional associations rely on their members to share their expertise in the form of conference presentations. Consider membership, service, involvement, activism, leadership, and presentations when you join the professional ranks of school counselors in the field.

Action Research

If your program is comprehensive, you will be structuring your program to conform to the ASCA National Model, and as such, you will use data for management and accountability. It is important to note that this information could also be invaluable to your colleagues in other schools, districts, and locations. Action research refers to insights gained by professionals in the field—data collected from students, schools, teachers, programs, activities—any source of information in your job or school. Such information is vital for understanding individual schools in context, providing a basis for locating your situation relative to another's situation. Are your students experiencing something different from those at another school, community, or state? Is there a program that works better than this one to address these issues? How might your students react to this new program? Are the needs of your students and families different from those elsewhere? If so, how are they different? What have others learned about this resource, this counseling strategy, this approach to parents? These questions can be answered only by practicing professionals who are in the field, working directly with students, resources, and parents.

When you initiate a new program and compile your data for your outcomes assessments and results reports, consider how your data might help others in the field. Don't hide behind "No one would want to read anything written by little ol' me." Consider sharing with others through a district newsletter, state association newsletter or journal, or national association newsletter or professional journal.

Just as geese flying in a V-shape benefit from the uplift of the wings of the goose in front, as professionals, we benefit from the wisdom of those who have come before us.

Being Mentored and Mentoring Others

Mentoring provides numerous benefits to both the person being mentored and the mentor. For the mentor, the benefits include opportunities for self-reflection and the positive feelings about making a contribution (VanZandt & Perry, 1992). Overall, mentoring provides an orientation for new professionals that helps them grow in their sense of intellectual competence, sense of purpose, feelings of autonomy, and personal integrity (Bova & Phillips, 1984). It is a forum in which mentees learn

1. Risk-taking behaviors: dealing with failure, dealing with risk
2. Communication skills
3. Political skills: how/where to get jobs, inside information about people in power, and the organization's values (a socialization function)
4. Specific professional skills: putting theory into practice, getting the big picture, professional skills, and learning how to put problems into context (Bova & Phillips, 1984)

If mentoring is such a wonderful thing, why doesn't everyone do it? There are a number of reasons that mentoring is not a universal experience. These reasons usually include lack of time, lack of a direct payoff with so many professional priorities, lack of interest in that kind of relationship with coworkers, and lack of knowledge or expertise in mentoring another person. It is important to recognize that locating a mentor is often a challenge, but it must be voluntary. Too much structure can kill the instinctive and voluntary commitment of mentors and the interest of mentees (Bennetts, 1995; Blunt, 1995).

TABLE 14.1 Roles of Mentors

Role:	**Consulting**	**Mentoring**	**Counseling**
Focus:	Answers to problems	Balance between solutions and exploration	Personal issues

FIGURE 14.2   Focus of the Relationship

Mentoring is a new way of thinking about a professional relationship. It is a connection between learner and teacher, centering around the teaching of meaning within the context of a professional setting. In this relationship, the goal is to help the new professional develop a professional identity in an environment of support and challenge. To help you understand what makes mentoring unique, consider the following illustrations. In Table 14.1, various roles are described in terms of support and challenge. In Figure 14.2, the three roles of mentor, consultant, and counselor are located on a continuum describing the focus of the relationship.

Tentoni (1995) outlined a number of activities of mentors. These include sponsoring the mentee's involvement in the environment, supporting the mentee, encouraging and affirming the mentee's independence and professionalism, and inspiring the new professional to work hard. In addition, mentors provide problem solving, listening, clarifying, and advising, similar to an effective counselor. The mentor also befriends the new professional, accepting new ideas and relating to the new professional. Finally, the mentor is also a teacher, modeling professional behavior and informing the mentee about the job. It is also important to recognize that there are four phases of the mentoring relationship: initiation, cultivation, separation, and ending, in which the relationship is redefined as that of colleagues (Daloz, 1988; Parks, 1990).

To help you determine if you want to seek out a mentor and to help you decide if you would like to mentor others, the following are traditional strategies for mentoring (Borman & Colson, 1984). It is important to note that these strategies about mentoring must be balanced with information about the mentoring needs of women and persons of color (Christopher, 1996; Hawks & Muha, 1991; Heinrich, 1995; E. P. Smith & Davidson, 1992). Some of these traditional strategies for mentoring are premised on a male, Eurocentric value system, which may pose certain challenges for women and persons of color who are not necessarily socialized to be comfortable with these behaviors. These potentially challenging strategies are italicized.

1. Encourage a positive attitude.
2. Encourage the mentee to establish personal values and goals.
3. Encourage the mentee to maintain an open mind to new ideas.
4. Interactions should be that of sharing, caring, and empathizing.
5. Encourage the mentee to use creative problem-solving processes.
6. Encourage the mentee to be an attentive listener and *an assertive questioner*. (Being too assertive might be contrary to cultural norms to be passive in relationships.)
7. Encourage the mentee to be an *independent thinker*. (Some people are socialized to consider the needs of others before self.)
8. Encourage the mentee to *recognize individual strengths and uniquenesses* and build on them. (Independent thinking and focus on individual strengths presumes an individualistic worldview versus a collectivistic worldview.)
9. Assist the mentee in developing *confidence*. (For those from a more collective worldview, this process involves more support and less challenge.)

10. Stress that the mentee should be aware of the environment, *intuitive* (intuition could be culturally or gender-influenced), problem-sensitive, and ready to make the most of *opportunities*. (There are implications in terms of competitive versus cooperative cultural norms).
11. Encourage the mentee to be an *active participant*, not a spectator. (This may depend on the action orientation of the mentee's culture in a new setting; for example, many Native American cultures stress patient observation of a new environment before becoming actively involved.)
12. Encourage the mentee to be a risk taker.
13. Encourage the mentee to be flexible and adaptable in attitudes and actions, looking for alternatives, and seeing situations/persons from different perspectives.

In addition to these traditional strategies, the following are suggestions for mentoring based on recent research:

14. Encourage your mentee to be flexible in the expectations of the mentoring relationship. Not all mentoring needs can or should be met through one mentoring relationship.
15. Strive to minimize dependence. Encourage the mentee to try it on his or her own, just as a good parent's goal is to help a child live his or her own life.
16. Monitor your own attachment to the relationship. Recognize that all mentoring relationships must eventually end to be healthy.

If you decide that you are interested in locating a mentor, you will want to look for a seasoned counselor who is not your direct supervisor. This will reduce dual-relationship issues with a supervisor and will enable you to more freely share your concerns and lack of confidence. Trust is an important part of the mentoring relationship (Heinrich, 1995), so you will want to get to know the potential mentor well to determine if you would have a good match between personality, trustworthiness, and personal style. Often you do not need a formal request of the mentor to determine if that person is interested in mentoring you; usually the best mentoring relationships evolve naturally between a novice and a seasoned professional.

As you mature in your own professional identity, remember that new, incoming professionals could also benefit from your support in their professional journey. Just as you are being encouraged to consider involvement in research and association leadership, you are also urged to consider mentoring new professionals.

REFLECTION MOMENT

Each of these topics for your professional health is important to your professional future. Which ones can you make a commitment to at this point in your training?

CASE STUDY REVISITED

Integration

Now that you have read the chapter, consider again Emily's situation.

1. As you review the topics of this chapter, what activities would help Emily do her job better?
2. Apply each of these topics to her situation, one at a time. In what ways would her situation have been different had she followed all the suggestions in this chapter?
3. Do you believe that she can turn this around and salvage her career? To do that, what does she need to do differently with students? With the district administration? With her colleagues in the school?
4. If you were Emily, what would you do first? ■

Suggested Readings

Boes, S. R., VanZile-Tamsen, C., & Jackson, C. M. (2001). Portfolio development for the 21st century school counselor. *Professional School Counseling, 4*, 229–231. This article outlines a very comprehensive approach to the creation of a professional portfolio for school counselors.

Brockman, J. (Ed.). (1992). *Creativity*. New York: Simon and Schuster. This book presents perspectives on creativity written by authors from many different fields, including science, art, medicine, and psychology. These perspectives help the reader consider ways to increase creativity in one's own life.

Brott, P. E., & Myers, J. E. (1999). Development of professional school counselor identity: A grounded theory. *Professional School Counseling, 2*, 339–348. This article outlines the process and stages of development of a professional identity for school counselors. This perspective can help new counselors understand their feelings of confusion and being overwhelmed by the role ambiguity of school counselors.

Seaward, B. L. (1994). *Managing stress: Principles and strategies for health and wellbeing*. Boston: Jones & Bartlett. This book outlines the sources and mechanisms of stress and then takes a broad and holistic look at the strategies for managing stress. It is an excellent tool for counselors who are providing developmental curriculum programs and/or group counseling experiences on stress management, as well as a wonderful tool for counselors to manage their own stress.

APPENDIX A

Program Goals for Adult Partners in the DAP Model

In a comprehensive school counseling program, counselors have primary responsibility for the growth and development of the student partners of the Domains/Activities/Partners model. But the ASCA National Model mandates that counselors also work toward systemic change, meaning counselors must also work systemically and holistically to address the systems in which our students are embedded. We must be aware of the needs of all partners in the education of young people. A comprehensive school counseling program, therefore, will also include systemic work with all the adult partners of the DAP model: parents and caregivers, teachers, administrators, other student services professionals (school psychologists, nurses, and social workers), and community colleagues (community mental health professionals, physical health professionals, social service and law enforcement professionals, employers, etc.).

For the work done with our adult partners, goals must be defined that will guide these interactions and provide outcomes that can be measured. This appendix contains some ideas for goals for adult partners, which could become part of the comprehensive school counseling program. These goals are presented here as a beginning for discussions, and should be modified based on local needs and priorities as established by the professional school counselor, in consultation with advisory groups. See Chapters 5 and 6 for a discussion of advisory groups and the program design process.

A. GOALS FOR ALL ADULT PARTNERS

Goal A.1 All partners will understand the developmental needs of students from a holistic perspective.

Goal A.2 All partners will understand the systemic elements of families, schools, and communities that facilitate student development.

Goal A.3 All partners will understand the systemic elements of families, schools, and communities that impede student development.

Goal A.4 All partners will understand the academic development process of students and will understand strategies to help students in that process.

Goal A.5 All partners will understand the career development process of students and will understand strategies to help students in that process.

Goal A.6 All partners will understand the personal/social development process of students and will understand strategies to help students in that process.

Goal A.7 All partners will understand their role in the development of students.

Goal A.8 All partners will demonstrate basic strategies for communicating with students in developmentally appropriate ways.

Goal A.9 All partners will understand the role of the other partners in the developmental process of students.

Goal A.10 All partners will understand the role of the school counselor and the role of comprehensive school counseling programs in the developmental process of students.

Goal A.11 All partners will feel comfortable approaching the school counselor with questions or concerns about students, families, schools, human development, or other topics.

Goal A.12 All partners will find the school counselor helpful in answering those questions and/or resolving those concerns about students, families, schools, and so on.

Goal A.13 All partners will understand the role of schools in educating young people for life, learning, and working.

Goal A.14 All partners will feel a part of the school community and the larger community and will share responsibility for, responsibility to, and will respond to the needs of those communities.

B. GOALS FOR PARENTS AND CAREGIVERS

Goal B.1 Parents/caregivers will feel welcome in the school environment.

Goal B.2 Parents/caregivers will feel included and invested in the work done with students in the comprehensive school counseling program.

Goal B.3 Parents/caregivers will understand the crucial effects that family can have on the development of young people.

Goal B.4 Parents/caregivers will acquire strategies for creating a healthy family environment for students.

Goal B.5 Parents/caregivers will foster positive interactions between families, schools, and the community on behalf of students.

C. GOALS FOR COLLEAGUES IN THE SCHOOLS

Goal C.1 Colleagues in the schools will understand the philosophy of developmentally appropriate education.

Goal C.2 Colleagues in the schools will feel included and invested in the work of the school counselor in the comprehensive school counseling program.

Goal C.3 Colleagues in the schools will understand the critical effect that schools can have on the development of young people.

Goal C.4 Colleagues in the schools will understand the need for an environment of respect in the school.

Goal C.5 Colleagues in the schools will acquire strategies for promoting an environment of respect in the school.

Goal C.6 Colleagues in the schools will foster positive interactions between families, schools, and the community on behalf of students.

D. GOALS FOR COLLEAGUES IN THE COMMUNITY

Goal D.1   Colleagues in the community will feel welcome in the school.

Goal D.2   Colleagues in the community will feel included and invested in the work of the school counselor in the comprehensive school counseling program.

Goal D.3   Colleagues in the community will understand the critical effect that neighborhoods and communities can have on the development of young people.

Goal D.4   Colleagues in the community will understand that civility and respect in the community will have a profound impact on the climate of the school.

Goal D.5   Colleagues in the community will acquire strategies for creating that environment of civility and respect in the community.

Goal D.6   Colleagues in the community will foster positive interactions between families, schools, and the community on behalf of students.

APPENDIX B

School Counselor Competencies

HISTORY AND PURPOSE

The American School Counselor Association (ASCA) supports school counselors' efforts to help students focus on academic, personal/social, and career development so they achieve success in school and are prepared to lead fulfilling lives as responsible members of society. In recent years, the ASCA leadership has recognized the need for a more unified vision of the school counseling profession. "The ASCA National Model: A Framework for School Counseling Programs" was a landmark document that provided a mechanism with which school counselors and school counseling teams could design, coordinate, implement, manage, and enhance their programs for students' success. The ASCA National Model® provides a framework for the program components, the school counselor's role in implementation, and the underlying philosophies of leadership, advocacy, collaboration, and systemic change.

The School Counselor Competencies continue the effort for a unified vision by outlining the knowledge, attitudes, and skills that ensure school counselors are equipped to meet the rigorous demands of our profession and the needs of our pre-K–12 students. These competencies are necessary to better ensure that our future school counselor workforce will be able to continue to make a positive difference in the lives of students.

DEVELOPMENT OF THE COMPETENCIES

The development of the School Counselor Competencies document was a highly collaborative effort among many members of the school counseling profession.

A group of school counseling professionals that included practicing school counselors, district school counseling supervisors, and counselor educators from across the country met in January 2007 to discuss ways to ensure that school counselor education programs adequately train and prepare future school counselors to design and implement comprehensive school counseling programs. The group agreed that the logical first task should be the development of a set of competencies necessary and sufficient to be an effective professional school counselor.

The group created a general outline of competencies and asked ASCA to form a task force to develop draft School Counselor Competencies supporting the ASCA National Model. The task force used sample competencies from states, universities, and other organizations to develop a first draft, which was presented to the whole group for feedback. After comments and revisions were incorporated, the revised draft was released for public review and comment. Revisions through the public comment were incorporated to develop the final version. The School Counselor Competencies document is unique in several ways. First, this set of competencies is organized around and consistent with the ASCA National Model. Second, the competencies are comprehensive in that they include skills, knowledge, and attitudes necessary for meritoriously performing the range of school counselor responsibilities (e.g., counseling, coordinating, consulting, etc.) in all components of comprehensive school counseling programs: foundation, management, delivery, and accountability. These competencies have been identified as those that will equip new and experienced school counselors with the skills to establish, maintain, and enhance a comprehensive, developmental, results-based school counseling program addressing academic achievement, personal and social development, and career planning.

APPLICATIONS

ASCA views these competencies as being applicable along a continuum of areas. For instance, school counselor education programs may use the competencies as benchmarks for ensuring students graduate with the knowledge, skills, and dispositions needed for developing comprehensive school counseling programs. Professional school counselors could use the School Counselor Competencies as a checklist to self-evaluate their own competencies and, as a result, formulate an appropriate professional development plan. School administrators may find these competencies useful as a guide for seeking and hiring highly competent school counselors and for developing meaningful school counselor performance evaluations. Also, the School Counselor Competencies include the necessary technological competencies needed for performing effectively and efficiently in the twenty-first century.

I. SCHOOL COUNSELING PROGRAMS

School counselors should possess the knowledge, abilities, skills, and attitudes necessary to plan, organize, implement, and evaluate a comprehensive, developmental, results-based school counseling program that aligns with the ASCA National Model.

I-A. Knowledge

ASCA's position statement, The Professional School Counselor and School Counseling Preparation Program, states that school counselors should articulate and demonstrate an understanding of:

I-A-1. The organizational structure and governance of the American educational system as well as cultural, political and social influences on current educational practices

I-A-2. The organizational structure and qualities of an effective school counseling program that aligns with the ASCA National Model

I-A-3. Impediments to student learning and use of advocacy and data-driven school counseling practices to act effectively in closing the achievement/opportunity gap

I-A-4. Leadership principles and theories

I-A-5. Individual counseling, group counseling, and classroom guidance programs ensuring equitable access to resources that promote academic achievement; personal, social, and emotional development; and career development including the identification of appropriate postsecondary education for every student

I-A-6. Collaborations with stakeholders such as parents and guardians, teachers, administrators, and community leaders to create learning environments that promote educational equity and success for every student

I-A-7. Legal, ethical, and professional issues in pre-K–12 schools

I-A-8. Developmental theory, learning theories, social justice theory, multiculturalism, counseling theories, and career counseling theories

I-A-9. The continuum of mental health services, including prevention and intervention strategies to enhance student success

I-B. Abilities and Skills

An effective school counselor is able to accomplish measurable objectives demonstrating the following abilities and skills.

I-B-1. Plans, organizes, implements, and evaluates a school counseling program aligning with the ASCA National Model

I-B-1a. Creates a vision statement examining the professional and personal competencies and qualities a school counselor should possess

I-B-1b. Describes the rationale for a comprehensive school counseling program

I-B-1c. Articulates the school counseling themes of advocacy, leadership, collaboration, and systemic change, which are critical to a successful school counseling program

I-B-1d. Describes, defines, and identifies the qualities of an effective school counseling program

I-B-1e. Describes the benefits of a comprehensive school counseling program for all stakeholders, including students, parents, teachers, administrators, school boards, department of education, school counselors, counselor educators, community stakeholders, and business leaders

I-B-1f. Describes the history of school counseling to create a context for the current state of the profession and comprehensive school counseling programs

I-B-1g. Uses technology effectively and efficiently to plan, organize, implement, and evaluate the comprehensive school counseling program

I-B-1h. Demonstrates multicultural, ethical, and professional competencies in planning, organizing, implementing, and evaluating the comprehensive school counseling program

I-B-2. Serves as a leader in the school and community to promote and support student success

I-B-2a. Understands and defines leadership and its role in comprehensive school counseling programs

I-B-2b. Identifies and applies a model of leadership to a comprehensive school counseling program

I-B-2c. Identifies and demonstrates professional and personal qualities and skills of effective leaders

I-B-2d. Identifies and applies components of the ASCA National Model requiring leadership, such as an advisory council, management system, and accountability

I-B-2e. Creates a plan to challenge the noncounseling tasks that are assigned to school counselors

I-B-3. Advocates for student success

I-B-3a. Understands and defines advocacy and its role in comprehensive school counseling programs

I-B-3b. Identifies and demonstrates benefits of advocacy with school and community stakeholders

I-B-3c. Describes school counselor advocacy competencies, which include dispositions, knowledge, and skills

I-B-3d. Reviews advocacy models and develops a personal advisory plan

I-B-3e. Understands the process for development of policy and procedures at the building, district, state, and national levels

I-B-4. Collaborates with parents, teachers, administrators, community leaders, and other stakeholders to promote and support student success

I-B-4a. Defines collaboration and its role in comprehensive school counseling programs

I-B-4b. Identifies and applies models of collaboration for effective use in a school counseling program and understands the similarities and differences between consultation, collaboration and counseling, and coordination strategies.

I-B-4c. Creates statements or other documents delineating the various roles of student service providers, such as school social worker, school psychologist, and school nurse, and identifies best practices for collaborating to affect student success

I-B-4d. Understands and knows how to apply a consensus-building process to foster agreement in a group

I-B-4e. Understands how to facilitate group meetings to effectively and efficiently meet group goals

I-B-5. Acts as a systems change agent to create an environment promoting and supporting student success

I-B-5a. Defines and understands system change and its role in comprehensive school counseling programs

I-B-5b. Develops a plan to deal with personal (emotional and cognitive) and institutional resistance impeding the change process

I-B-5c. Understands the impact of school, district, and state educational policies, procedures, and practices supporting and/or impeding student success

I-C. Attitudes

School counselors believe:

I-C-1. Every student can learn, and every student can succeed.

I-C-2. Every student should have access to and opportunity for a high-quality education.

I-C-3. Every student should graduate from high school and be prepared for employment or college and other postsecondary education.

I-C-4. Every student should have access to a school counseling program.

I-C-5. Effective school counseling is a collaborative process involving school counselors, students, parents, teachers, administrators, community leaders, and other stakeholders.

I-C-6. School counselors can and should be leaders in the school and district.

I-C-7. The effectiveness of school counseling programs should be measurable using process, perception, and results data.

II. FOUNDATIONS

School counselors should possess the knowledge, abilities, skills, and attitudes necessary to establish the foundations of a school counseling program aligning with the ASCA National Model.

II-A. Knowledge

School counselors should articulate and demonstrate an understanding of:

II-A-1. Beliefs and philosophy of the school counseling program that align with current school improvement and student success initiatives at the school, district, and state level

II-A-2. Educational systems, philosophies, and theories and current trends in education, including federal and state legislation

II-A-3. Learning theories

II-A-4. History and purpose of school counseling, including traditional and transformed roles of school counselors

II-A-5. Human development theories and developmental issues affecting student success

II-A-6. District, state and national student standards and competencies, including ASCA Student Competencies

II-A-7. Legal and ethical standards and principles of the school counseling profession and educational systems, including district and building policies

II-A-8. The three domains of academic achievement, career planning, and personal and social development

II-B. Abilities and Skills

An effective school counselor is able accomplish measurable objectives demonstrating the following abilities and skills.

II-B-1. Develops the beliefs and philosophy of the school counseling program that align with current school improvement and student success initiatives at the school, district, and state level

II-B-1a.   Examines personal, district, and state beliefs, assumptions, and philosophies about student success, specifically what they should know and be able to do

II-B-lb.   Demonstrates knowledge of a school's particular educational philosophy and mission

II-B-1c.   Conceptualizes and writes a personal philosophy about students, families, teachers, school counseling programs, and the educational process consistent with the school's educational philosophy and mission

II-B-2. Develops a school counseling mission statement aligning with the school, district, and state mission.

II-B-2a.   Critiques a school district mission statement and identifies or writes a mission statement aligning with beliefs

II-B-2b.   Writes a school counseling mission statement that is specific, concise, clear, and comprehensive, describing a school counseling program's purpose and a vision of the program's benefits for every student

II-B-2c. Communicates the philosophy and mission of the school counseling program to all appropriate stakeholders

II-B-3. Uses student standards, such as the ASCA Student Competencies, and district or state standards, to drive the implementation of a comprehensive school counseling program

II-B-3a. Crosswalks the ASCA Student Competencies with other appropriate standards

II-B-3b. Prioritizes students standards that align with the school's goals

II-B-4. Applies the ethical standards and principles of the school counseling profession and adheres to the legal aspects of the role of the school counselor

II-B-4a. Practices ethical principles of the school counseling profession in accordance with the ASCA Ethical Standards for School Counselors

II-B-4b. Understands the legal and ethical nature of working in a pluralistic, multicultural, and technological society

II-B-4c. Understands and practices in accordance with school district policy and local, state, and federal statutory requirements

II-B-4d. Understands the unique legal and ethical nature of working with minor students in a school setting.

II-B-4e. Advocates responsibly for school board policy, local, state, and federal statutory requirements that are in the best interests of students

II-B-4f. Resolves ethical dilemmas by employing an ethical decision-making model appropriate to work in schools

II-B-4g. Models ethical behavior

II-B-4h. Continuously engages in professional development and uses resources to inform and guide ethical and legal work

II-B-4i. Practices within the ethical and statutory limits of confidentiality

II-B-4j. Continually seeks consultation and supervision to guide legal and ethical decision making and to recognize and resolve ethical dilemmas

II-B-4k. Understands and applies an ethical and legal obligation not only to students but to parents, administration, and teachers as well

II-C. Attitudes

School counselors believe:

II-C-1. School counseling is an organized program for every student and not a series of services provided only to students in need.

II-C-2. School counseling programs should be an integral component of student success and the overall mission of schools and school districts.

II-C-3. School counseling programs promote and support academic achievement, personal and social development, and career planning for every student.

II-C-4. School counselors operate within a framework of school and district policies, state laws and regulations, and professional ethics standards.

III. DELIVERY

School counselors should possess the knowledge, abilities, skills, and attitudes necessary to deliver a school counseling program aligning with the ASCA National Model.

III-A. Knowledge

School counselors should articulate and demonstrate an understanding of:

III-A-1. The concept of a guidance curriculum

III-A-2. Counseling theories and techniques that work in school, such as solution-focused brief counseling, reality therapy, and cognitive-behavioral therapy

III-A-3. Counseling theories and techniques in different settings, such as individual planning, group counseling, and classroom guidance

III-A-4. Classroom management

III-A-5. Principles of career planning and college admissions, including financial aid and athletic eligibility

III-A-6. Principles of working with various student populations based on ethnic and racial background, English-language proficiency, special needs, religion, gender, and income

III-A-7. Responsive services

III-A-8. Crisis counseling, including grief and bereavement

III-B. Abilities and Skills

An effective school counselor is able to accomplish measurable objectives demonstrating the following abilities and skills.

III-B-1. Implements the school guidance curriculum

    III-B-1a. Crosswalks the ASCA Student Competencies with appropriate guidance curriculum

    III-B-1b. Develops and presents a developmental guidance curriculum addressing all students' needs, including closing-the-gap activities

    III-B-1c. Demonstrates classroom management and instructional skills

    III-B-1d. Develops materials and instructional strategies to meet student needs and school goals

    III-B-1e. Encourages staff involvement to ensure the effective implementation of the school guidance curriculum

    III-B-1f. Knows, understands, and uses a variety of technology in the delivery of guidance curriculum activities

    III-B-1g. Understands multicultural and pluralistic trends when developing and choosing guidance curriculum

    III-B-1h. Understands the resources available for students with special needs

III-B-2. Facilitates individual student planning

    III-B-2a. Understands individual student planning as a component of a comprehensive program

    III-B-2b. Develops strategies to implement individual student planning, such as strategies for appraisal, advisement, goal setting, decision making, social skills, transition, or postsecondary planning

III-B-2c. Helps students establish goals, and develops and uses planning skills in collaboration with parents or guardians and school personnel

III-B-2d. Understands career opportunities, labor market trends, and global economics, and uses various career assessment techniques to assist students in understanding their abilities and career interests

III-B-2e. Helps students learn the importance of college and other postsecondary education and helps students navigate the college admissions process

III-B-2f. Understands the relationship of academic performance to the world of work, family life, and community service

III-B-2g. Understands methods for helping students monitor and direct their own learning and personal/social and career development

III-B-3. Provides responsive services

III-B-3a. Understands how to make referrals to appropriate professionals when necessary

III-B-3b. Lists and describes interventions used in responsive services, such as consultation, individual and small-group counseling, crisis counseling, referrals, and peer facilitation

III-B-3c. Compiles resources to utilize with students, staff, and families to effectively address issues through responsive services

III-B-3d. Understands appropriate individual and small-group counseling theories and techniques such as rational emotive behavior therapy, reality therapy, cognitive-behavioral therapy, Adlerian, solution-focused brief counseling, person-centered counseling, and family systems

III-B-3e. Demonstrates an ability to provide counseling for students during times of transition, separation, heightened stress, and critical change

III-B-3f. Understands what defines a crisis, the appropriate response and a variety of intervention strategies to meet the needs of the individual, group, or school community before, during, and after crisis response

III-B-3g. Provides team leadership to the school and community in a crisis

III-B-3h. Involves appropriate school and community professionals as well as the family in a crisis situation

III-B-3i. Develops a database of community agencies and service providers for student referrals

III-B-3j. Applies appropriate counseling approaches to promoting change among consultees within a consultation approach

III-B-3k. Understands and is able to build effective and high-quality peer helper programs

III-B-3l. Understands the nature of academic, career, and personal/social counseling in schools and the similarities and differences among school counseling and other types of counseling, such as mental health, marriage and family, and substance abuse counseling, within a continuum of care

III-B-3m. Understands the role of the school counselor and the school counseling program in the school crisis plan

III-B-4. Implements system support activities for the comprehensive school counseling program

III-B-4a. Creates a system support planning document addressing the school counselor's responsibilities for professional development, consultation and collaboration, and program management

III-B-4b. Coordinates activities that establish, maintain, and enhance the school counseling program as well as other educational programs

III-B-4c. Conducts in-service training for other stakeholders to share school counseling expertise

III-B-4d. Understands and knows how to provide supervision for school counseling interns consistent with the principles of the ASCA National Model

III-C. Attitudes

School counselors believe:

III-C-1. School counseling is one component in the continuum of care that should be available to all students.

III-C-2. School counselors coordinate and facilitate counseling and other services to ensure all students receive the care they need, even though school counselors may not personally provide the care themselves.

III-C-3. School counselors engage in developmental counseling and short-term responsive counseling.

III-C-4. School counselors should refer students to district or community resources to meet more extensive needs such as long-term therapy or diagnoses of disorders.

IV. MANAGEMENT

School counselors should possess the knowledge, abilities, skills, and attitudes necessary to manage a school counseling program aligning with the ASCA National Model.

IV-A. Knowledge

School counselors should articulate and demonstrate an understanding of:

IV-A-1. Leadership principles, including sources of power and authority, and formal and informal leadership

IV-A-2. Organization theory to facilitate advocacy, collaboration, and systemic change

IV-A-3. Presentation skills for programs such as teacher in-services and results reports to school boards

IV-A-4. Time management, including long- and short-term management using tools such as schedules and calendars

IV-A-5. Data-driven decision making

IV-A-6. Current and emerging technologies such as use of the Internet, web-based resources, and management information systems

IV-B. Abilities and Skills

An effective school counselor is able to accomplish measurable objectives demonstrating the following abilities and skills.

IV-B-1. Negotiates with the administrator to define the management system for the comprehensive school counseling program

    IV-B-1a. Discusses and develops the components of the school counselor management system with the other members of the counseling staff

    IV-B-lb. Presents the school counseling management system to the principal, and finalizes an annual school counseling management agreement

    IV-B-1c. Discusses the anticipated program results when implementing the action plans for the school year

    IV-B-1d. Participates in professional organizations

    IV-B-1e. Develops a yearly professional development plan demonstrating how the school counselor advances relevant knowledge, skills, and dispositions

    IV-B-1f. Communicates effective goals and benchmarks for meeting and exceeding expectations consistent with the administrator-counselor agreement and district performance appraisals

    IV-B-1g. Uses personal reflection, consultation, and supervision to promote professional growth and development

IV-B-2. Establishes and convenes an advisory council for the comprehensive school counseling program

    IV-B-2a. Uses leadership skills to facilitate vision and positive change for the comprehensive school counseling program

    IV-B-2b. Determines appropriate education stakeholders who should be represented on the advisory council

    IV-B-2c. Develops meeting agendas

    IV-B-2d. Reviews school data, the school counseling program audit, and school counseling program goals with the council

    IV-B-2e. Records meeting notes and distributes as appropriate

    IV-B-2f. Analyzes and incorporates feedback from the advisory council related to school counseling program goals as appropriate

IV-B-3. Collects, analyzes, and interprets relevant data, including process, perception, and results data, to monitor and improve student behavior and achievement

    IV-B-3a. Analyzes, synthesizes, and disaggregates data to examine student outcomes and to identify and implement interventions as needed

    IV-B-3b. Uses data to identify policies, practices, and procedures leading to successes, systemic barriers, and areas of weakness

    IV-B-3c. Uses student data to demonstrate a need for systemic change in areas such as course enrollment patterns: equity and access; and the achievement, opportunity, and information gap

    IV-B-3d. Understands and uses data to establish goals and activities to close the achievement, opportunity, and information gap

    IV-B-3e. Knows how to use and analyze data to evaluate the school counseling program, research activity outcomes, and identify gaps between and among different groups of students

IV-B-3f.   Uses school data to identify and assist individual students who do not perform at grade level and do not have opportunities and resources to be successful in school

IV-B-3g.   Knows and understands theoretical and historical bases for assessment techniques

IV-B-4.   Organizes and manages time to implement an effective school counseling program

IV-B-4a.   Identifies appropriate distribution on school counselor's time based on delivery system and school's data

IV-B-4b.   Creates a rationale for school counselor's time to focus on the goals of the comprehensive school counseling program

IV-B-4c.   Identifies and evaluates fair-share responsibilities, which articulate appropriate and inappropriate counseling and noncounseling activities

IV-B-4d.   Creates a rationale for the school counselor's total time spent in each component of the school counseling program

IV-B-5.   Develops calendars to ensure the effective implementation of the school counseling program

IV-B-5a.   Creates annual, monthly, and weekly calendars to plan activities to reflect school goals

IV-B-5b.   Demonstrates time management skills including scheduling, publicizing, and prioritizing time and task

IV-B-6.   Designs and implements action plans aligning with school and school counseling program goals

IV-B-6a.   Uses appropriate academic and behavioral data to develop guidance curriculum and closing-the-gap action plan and determines appropriate students for the target group or interventions

IV-B-6b.   Identifies ASCA domains, standards, and competencies being addressed by the plan

IV-B-6c.   Determines the intended impact on academics and behavior

IV-B-6d.   Identifies appropriate activities to accomplish objectives

IV-B-6e.   Identifies appropriate resources needed

IV-B-6f.   Identifies data-collection strategies to gather process, perception, and results data

IV-B-6g.   Shares results of action plans with staff, parents, and community

IV-C. Attitudes

School counselors believe:

IV-C-1.   A school counseling program and guidance department must be managed like other programs and departments in a school.

IV-C-2.   One of the critical responsibilities of a school counselor is to plan, organize, implement, and evaluate a school counseling program.

IV-C-3.   Management of a school counseling program must be done in collaboration with administrators.

V. ACCOUNTABILITY

School counselors should possess the knowledge, abilities, skills, and attitudes necessary to monitor and evaluate the processes and results of a school counseling program aligning with the ASCA National Model.

V-A. Knowledge

School counselors should articulate and demonstrate an understanding of:

V-A-1. Basic concept of results-based school counseling and accountability issues

V-A-2. Basic research and statistical concepts to read and conduct research

V-A-3. Use of data to evaluate program effectiveness and to determine program needs

V-A-4. Program audits and results reports

V-B. Abilities and Skills

An effective school counselor is able to accomplish measurable objectives demonstrating the following abilities and skills.

V-B-1. Uses data from results reports to evaluate program effectiveness and to determine program needs

    V-B-1a.   Uses formal and informal methods of program evaluation to design and modify comprehensive school counseling programs

    V-B-1b.   Uses student data to support decision making in designing effective school counseling programs and interventions

    V-B-1c.   Measures results attained from school guidance curriculum and closing-the-gap activities

    V-B-1d.   Works with members of the school counseling team and with the administration to decide how school counseling programs are evaluated and how results are shared

    V-B-1e.   Collects process, perception, and results data

    V-B-1f.   Uses technology in conducting research and program evaluation

    V-B-1g.   Reports program results to professional school counseling community

    V-B-1h.   Uses data to demonstrate the value the school counseling program adds to student achievement

    V-B-1i.   Uses results obtained for program improvement

V-B-2. Understands and advocates for appropriate school counselor performance appraisal process based on School Counselor Competencies and completion of the guidance curriculum and agreed-upon action plans

    V-B-2a.   Conducts self-appraisal related to school counseling skills and performance

    V-B-2b.   Identifies how school counseling activities fit within categories of the performance appraisal instrument

    V-B-2c.   Encourages administrators to use the performance appraisal instrument reflecting appropriate responsibilities for school counselors

V-B-3. Conducts a program audit

    V-B-3a.   Completes a program audit to compare current school counseling program implementation with the ASCA National Model

V-B-3b.   Shares the results of the program audit with administrators, the advisory council, and other appropriate stakeholders

V-B-3c.   Identifies areas for improvement for the school counseling program

V-C. Attitudes

School counselors believe:

V-C-1. School counseling programs should achieve demonstrable results.

V-C-2. School counselors should be accountable for the results of the school counseling program.

V-C-3. School counselors should use quantitative and qualitative data to evaluate their school counseling program and to demonstrate program results.

V-C-4. The results of the school counseling program should be analyzed and presented in the context of the overall school and district performance.

REFERENCES

Ackoff, R. L. (1989). From data to wisdom. *Journal of Applied Systems Analysis, 16*, 3–9.

Adelman, H. S., & Taylor, L. (1994, October). *Pupil services and education reform.* Paper presented at the Safe Schools, Safe Students: A Collaborative Approach to Achieving Safe, Disciplined, and Drug-Free Schools Conducive to Learning conference, Washington, DC. ERIC No. 383955. Retrieved April 18, 2000, from http://webnf2.epnet.com (the EBSCO database).

Adelman, H. S., & Taylor, L. (1997). Addressing barriers to learning: Beyond school-linked services and full service schools. *American Journal of Orthopsychiatry, 67*, 408–421.

Adelman, H. S., & Taylor, L. (1998). Reframing mental health in schools and expanding school reform. *Educational Psychologist, 33*(4), 135–152.

Agnew, T., Vaught, C. C., Getz, H. G., & Fortune, J. (2000). Peer group clinical supervision program fosters confidence and professionalism. *Professional School Counseling, 4*, 6–12.

Alderfer, C. P. (1994). A white man's perspective on the unconscious processes within Black-White relations in the United States. In E. J. Trickett, R. J. Watts, and D. Birman (Eds.), *Human diversity: Perspectives on people in context* (pp. 201–229). San Francisco: Jossey-Bass.

Alexander, W. M., & George, P. S. (1981). The exemplary middle school. In R. D. Myrick (Ed.), *Developmental guidance and counseling: A practical approach* (2nd ed.). Minneapolis, MN: Educational Media.

American Association of Suicidology. (n.d.) *Know the warning signs.* Retrieved August 4, 2010, from http://www.suicidology.org/web/guest/stats-and-tools/warning-signs

American Counseling Association. (2005). *Code of ethics and standards of practice.* Alexandria, VA: Author.

American Heritage Dictionary. (2001). New York: Dell.

American School Counselor Association. (1999). *The role of the professional school counselor.* Alexandria, VA: Author. Retrieved May 31, 2000, from http://www.schoolcounselor.org/ role.htm

American School Counselor Association. (2003). *The ASCA National Model: A framework for school counseling programs.* Alexandria, VA: Author.

American School Counselor Association. (2004). *Ethical standards for school counselors.* Alexandria, VA: Author.

American School Counselor Association. (2005). *The ASCA National Model: A framework for school counseling programs* (2nd ed.). Alexandria, VA: Author.

American School Counselor Association. (2010). Careers and roles of the school counselor. Retrieved November 26, 2010, from http://www.schoolcounselor.org/content.asp?pl=325&sl=133&contentid=133

American School Counselor Association. (2008, July/August). School counselor competencies. *ASCA School Counselor, 45*(6), 64–73.

American School Counselor Association. (2009). *The role of the professional school counselor.* Retrieved October 29, 2009, from http://www.schoolcounselor.org/content.asp?pl=325&sl=133&contentid=240

Arredondo, P., Toporek, M. S., Brown, S., Jones, J., Locke, D. C., Sanchez, J. & Stadler, H. (1996). *Operationalization of the multicultural counseling competencies.* Alexandria, VA: Association for Multicultural Counseling and Development. Retrieved July 1, 2010, from http://www.amcdaca.org/amcd/competencies.pdf

Association for Specialists in Group Work. (2007). *Best practices*. Retrieved November 26, 2010, from http://www.asgw.org/PDF/Best_Practices.pdf

Atkinson, D. R., Morten, G., & Sue, D. W. (1989). *Counseling American minorities: A cross-cultural perspective*. Dubuque, IA: Brown.

Baker, B. B. (2000). Middle school counseling in the new millennium: A practitioner's perspective. In J. Wittmer (Ed.), *Managing your school counseling program: K–12 developmental strategies* (2nd ed., pp. 49–55). Minneapolis, MN: Educational Media.

Baker, S. B. (2000). *School counseling for the twenty-first century* (3rd ed.). Upper Saddle River, NJ: Merrill.

Baker, S., Robichaud, T., Westforth Dietrich, V., Wells, S., & Schreck, R. (2009). School counselor consultation: A pathway to advocacy, collaboration, and leadership. *Professional School Counseling, 12*(3), 200. Retrieved from MasterFILE Premier database.

Ball, J. D., & Meck, D. S. (1979). Implications of developmental theories for counseling adolescents in groups. *Adolescence, 14*, 528–534.

Bandura, A. (1977). *Social learning theory*. Englewood Cliffs, NJ: Prentice-Hall.

Barr, R. D., & Parrett, W. H. (2001). *Hope fulfilled for at-risk and violent youth: K–12 programs that work* (2nd ed.). Boston: Allyn and Bacon.

Bauer, A. L., Ingersoll, E., & Burns, L. (2004). School counselors and psychotropic medication: Assessing training, experience, and school policy issues. *Professional School Counseling, 7*, 202–211.

Beale, A. V. (1995). Selecting school counselors: The principal's perspective. *School Counselor, 42*, 211–217.

Bemak, F. (2000). Transforming the role of the counselor to provide leadership in educational reform through collaboration.

Professional School Counseling, 3, 323–331.

Bemak, F., & Keys, S. (2000). *Violent and aggressive youth: Intervention and prevention strategies for changing times*. Thousand Oaks, CA: Corwin Press.

Bennetts, C. (1995). The secrets of a good relationship. *People Management, 1*(13), 38–40.

Berens, L. V. (1988). *Please understand me: Empowering students of the 90's*. Huntington Beach, CA: Temperament Research Institute.

Beymer, L. (1995). *Meeting the guidance and counseling needs of boys*. Alexandria, VA: American Counseling Association.

Bilynsky, N. S., & Vernaglia, E. R. (1999). Identifying and working with dysfunctional families. *Professional School Counseling, 2*, 305–314.

Blackwell, T. L., Martin, W. E., Jr., & Scalia, V. A. (1994). *Ethics in rehabilitation: A guide for rehabilitation professionals*. Athens, GA: Elliott & Fitzpatrick.

Bluestein, J. (2001). *Creating emotionally safe schools: A guide for educators and parents*. Deerfield Beach, FL: Health Communications.

Blunt, N. (1995). Learning from the wisdom of others. *People Management, 1*(11), 38–40.

Blustein, D. L., & Noumair, D. A. (1996). Self and identity in career development: Implications for theory and practice. *Journal of Counseling & Development, 74*, 433–441.

Boes, S. R., VanZile-Tamsen, C., & Jackson, C. M. (2001). Portfolio development for the 21st century school counselor. *Professional School Counseling, 4*, 229–231.

Bolman, L. G., & Deal, T. E. (1997). *Reframing organizations: Artistry, choice, and leadership* (2nd ed.). San Francisco: Jossey-Bass.

Borman, C., & Colson, S. (1984). Mentoring—an effective career guidance technique. The *Vocational Guidance Quarterly, 32*(3), 192–197.

Bova, R. M., & Phillips, R. R. (1984). Mentoring as a learning experience for adults. *Journal of Teacher Education, 35*(3), 16–20.

Brabeck, M. M., Walsh, M. E., & Latta, R. E. (Eds.). (2003). *Meeting at the hyphen: Schools-universities-communities-professions in collaboration for student achievement and well being.* 102nd Yearbook of the National Society for the Study of Education. Chicago: University of Chicago Press.

Brammer, L. M., & McDonald, G. (1999). *The helping relationship: Process and skills* (7th ed.). Boston: Allyn and Bacon.

Brand, S., Felner, R., Seitsinger, A., Burns, A., & Bolton, N. (2008). A large scale study of the assessment of the social environment of middle and secondary schools: The validity and utility of teachers' ratings of school climate, cultural pluralism, and safety problems for understanding school effects and school. *Journal of School Psychology, 46*(5), 507–535.

Branden, N. (1994). *The six pillars of self-esteem.* New York: Bantam.

Briggs, M. K., Staton, A. R., & Gilligan, T. D. (2009). The girls' leadership experience camp: A parallel process of leadership skill development for school counselors-in-training. *Professional School Counseling, 13*, 125–134.

Brigman, G., & Campbell, C. (2003). Helping students improve academic achievement and school success behavior. *Professional School Counseling, 7*, 91–98.

Brigman, G., & Goodman, B. E. (2001). *Group counseling for school counselors: A practical guide* (2nd ed.). Portland, ME: J. Weston Walsh.

Brotherthon, W. D., & Clarke, K. A. (1997). Special friends: The use of community resources in comprehensive school counseling programs. *Professional School Counseling, 1*, 41–45.

Brott, P. E., & Myers, J. E. (1999). Development of professional school coun-selor identity: A grounded theory. *Professional School Counseling, 2*, 339–348.

Brown, D., Pryzwansky, W. B., & Schulte, A. C. (1998). *Psychological consultation: Introduction to theory and practice* (4th ed.). Boston: Allyn and Bacon.

Brown, D., & Trusty, J. (2005). *Designing and leading comprehensive school counseling programs: Promoting student competence and meeting student needs.* Belmont, CA: Brooks/Cole.

Brown, L. M., & Gilligan, C. (1992). *Meeting at the crossroads: Women's psychology and girls' development.* Boston: Harvard University Press.

Brown, O. S., & Peterkin, R. S. (1999). Transforming public schools: An integrated strategy for improving student academic performance through districtwide resource equity, leadership accountability, and program efficiency. *Equity and Excellence in Education, 32*(3), 37–52.

Bruner, J. S. (1961). The act of discovery. *Harvard Educational Review, 31*, 31–32.

Burnham, J. J., & Jackson, C. M. (2000). School counselor roles: Discrepancies between actual practice and existing models. *Professional School Counseling, 4*, 41–49.

Butler, E. R. (1993, March). *Basic principles for ethical decision making.* Paper presented at the meeting of the National Association for Student Personnel Administrators, Boston.

Campbell, C. A., & Dahir, C. A. (1997). *Sharing the vision: The national standards for school counseling programs.* Alexandria, VA: American School Counselor Association.

Canon, H. J., & Brown, R. D. (Eds.). (1985). *Applied ethics in student services.* San Francisco: Jossey-Bass.

Caplan, G. (1970). *The theory and practice of mental health consultation.* New York: Basic Books.

Caplan, G., & Caplan, R. B. (1993). *Mental health consultation and collaboration.* San Francisco: Jossey-Bass.

Capuzzi, D. (2009). *Suicide prevention in the schools: Guidelines for middle and high school settings* (2nd ed.). Alexandria, VA: American Counseling Association.

Carey, J., Carey, D., Hatch, T., Lapan, R., & Whiston, S. (2008). Report of the National Panel for Evidence-Based School Counseling: Outcome research coding protocol and evaluation of student success skills and second step. *Professional School Counseling, 11*(3), 197–206.

Carkhuff, R. R. (1987). *The art of helping* (6th ed.). Amherst, MA: Human Resource Development Press.

Carlson, J., Watts, R. E., & Maniacci, M. (2006). *Adlerian therapy: Theory and practice.* Washington, DC: American Psychological Association.

Carroll, B. (1993). Perceived roles and preparation experiences of elementary counselors: Suggestions for change. *Elementary School Guidance and Counseling, 27,* 217–224.

Carter, R. B., & El Hindi, A. E. (1999). Counseling Muslim children in school settings. *Professional School Counseling, 2,* 183–188.

Cassillius, B. (2006, May). Using relationships, responsibility, and respect to get from "good to great" in Memphis middle schools. *Middle School Journal, 37*(5), 4–15.

Cauce, A. M., & Srebnik, D. (2003). Before treatment: Adolescent mental health help-seeking. *The Prevention Researcher, 10*(4), 6–9.

Centers for Disease Control. (2009). *Youth suicide.* Retrieved July 28, 2010, from http://www.cdc.gov/violenceprevention/pub/youth_suicide.html

Charlesworth, R. (1996). *Understanding child development* (4th ed.). Albany, NY: Delmar.

Charney, R. S. (2002). *Teaching children to care: Classroom management for ethical and academic growth, K–8* (rev. ed.). Turner Falls, MA: Northeast Foundation for Children.

Chen, G., & Weikart, L. (2008). Student background, school climate, school disorder, and student achievement: An empirical study of New York City's middle schools. *Journal of School Violence, 7*(4), 3–20. Retrieved from Academic Search Complete database.

Christiansen, J. (1997). Helping teachers meet the needs of students at risk for school failure. *Elementary School Guidance & Counseling, 31,* 204–211.

Christopher, J. C. (1996). Counseling's inescapable moral visions. *Journal of Counseling & Development, 75,* 17–25.

Christopher, J. C. (1999). Situating psychological well-being: Exploring the cultural roots of its theory and research. *Journal of Counseling & Development, 77,* 141–152.

Clark, A. J. (1995). Rationalization and the role of the school counselor. *The School Counselor, 42,* 283–291.

Clark, M. A., & Breman, J. C. (2009). School counselor inclusion: A collaborative model to provide academic and social-emotional support in the classroom setting. *Journal of Counseling & Development. 87,* 6–11.

Clark, M. A., Oakley, E., & Adams, H. (2006, January 1). The gender achievement gap challenge. *ASCA School Counselor* [Electronic version]. Retrieved April 5, 2006, from http://www.schoolcounselor.org/printarticle.asp?article=822

Clark, M. A., & Stone, C. (2000a). The developmental school counselor as educational leader. In J. Wittmer (Ed.), *Managing your school counseling program: K–12 developmental strategies* (2nd ed., pp. 75–82). Minneapolis, MN: Educational Media.

Clark, M. A., & Stone, C. (2000b, May). Evolving our image: School counselors as educational leaders. *Counseling Today, 42,* 21, 22, 29, 30, 46.

Clinchy, B. (1989). On critical thinking and connected knowing. *Liberal Education, 75*(5), 14–19.

Cobia, D. C., & Henderson, D. A. (2007). *Developing an effective and accountable school counseling program* (2nd ed.). Upper Saddle River, NJ: Pearson.

Colbert, R. D. (1996). The counselor's role in advancing school and family partnerships. *School Counselor, 44*(2), 100–104.

Cole, D. J., & Ryan, C. W. (1997). Leadership in portfolio development: The school counselor's role. *Guidance & Counseling, 12*(4), 10–14. Retrieved November 28, 2000, from wysiwyg://bodyframe.9/http://ehostv (the EBSCO database)

Committee for Children. (2002). *Second step: Violence prevention curriculum.* Seattle, WA: Author.

Constantine, M. G., & Yeh, C. J. (2001). Multicultural training, self-construals, and multicultural competence of school counselors. *Professional School Counseling, 4,* 202–207.

Cook, A. L., & Houser, R. A. (2009). ASCA Ethical Standards and the relevance of Eastern ethical theories. *Journal of School Counseling, 7,* 1–24. Retrieved March 25, 2010, from Education Research Complete.

Corey, G. (2004). *Theory and practice of counseling and psychotherapy* (7th ed.). Pacific Grove, CA: Brooks/Cole.

Corey, G. C. (2009). *Theory and practice of counseling and psychotherapy* (8th ed.). Belmont, CA: Brooks/Cole.

Corey, G. C., Corey, M. S., & Callanan, P. (1993). *Issues and ethics in the helping professions.* Pacific Grove, CA: Brooks/Cole.

Cormier, S., & Hackney, H. (1999). *Counseling strategies and interventions* (5th ed.). Boston: Allyn and Bacon.

Council for Accreditation of Counseling and Related Educational Programs. (2000). *The 2001 standards: CACREP accreditation standards and procedures manual.* Alexandria, VA: Author.

Council for Accreditation of Counseling and Related Educational Programs. (2001). *The 2001 standards: CACREP accreditation standards and procedures manual.* Alexandria, VA: Author.

Council for Accreditation of Counseling and Related Educational Programs. (2009). *The 2009 standards: CACREP accreditation standards and procedures manual.* Alexandria, VA: Author. Available from http://www.cacrep.org.

Cowie, K., & Quinn, K. (1997). Brief family therapy in the schools: A new perspective on the role of the rural school counseling professional. *Family Journal, 5*(1), 57–69.

Coy, D., & Sears, S. (2000). The scope of practice of the high school counselor. In J. Wittmer (Ed.), *Managing your school counseling program: K–12 developmental strategies* (2nd ed., pp. 56–67). Minneapolis, MN: Educational Media.

Craig, G. J. (1996). *Human development* (7th ed.). Upper Saddle River, NJ: Prentice-Hall.

Crespi, T. D., Fischetti, B. A., & Butler, S. K. (2001, January). Clinical supervision in the schools. *Counseling Today, 43,* 7, 28, 34.

Crespi, T. D., & Howe, E. A. (2000, March). Families in crisis: Considerations and implications for school counselors. *Counseling Today, 42,* 6, 36.

Curry, J. R., & DeVoss, J. A. (2009). Introduction to special issue: The school counselor as leader. *Professional School Counseling, 13,* 64–67.

Cuthbert, M. I. (2000). Large group developmental guidance. In J. Wittmer (Ed.), *Managing your school counseling program: K–12 developmental strategies* (2nd ed., pp. 123–134). Minneapolis, MN: Educational Media.

Dahir, C. A. (2004). Supporting a nation of learners: The role of school counseling in educational reform. *Journal of Counseling & Development, 82,* 344–353.

Dahir, C. A., Sheldon, C. B., & Valiga, M. J. (1998). *Vision into action: Implementing the National Standards for School*

Counseling Programs. Alexandria, VA: American School Counselor Association.

Dahir, C. A., & Stone, C. (2003). Accountability: A M.E.A.S.U.R.E of the impact school counselors have on student achievement. *Professional School Counseling, 6*(3), 214.

Daloz, L. (1988). Into the trenches: A case study in mentorship. *Management of Lifelong Education Alumni Bulletin, 1*(2), 1–3.

D'Andrea, M., & Daniels, J. (1996). Promoting peace in our schools: Developmental, preventive, and multicultural considerations. *School Counselor, 44*, 55–64.

Dansby, V. S. (1996). Group work within the school system: Survey of implementation and leadership role issues. *The Journal for Specialists in Group Work, 21*, 232–242.

D'Augelli, A. R. (1994). Identity development and sexual orientation: Toward a prototype of lesbian, gay, and bisexual development. In E. J. Trickett, R. J. Watts, & D. Birman (Eds.), *Human diversity: Perspectives on people in context* (pp. 312–333). San Francisco: Jossey-Bass.

Davis, K. M. (2001). Structural-strategic family counseling: A case study in elementary school counseling. *Professional School Counseling, 4*, 180–186.

Davis, K. M., & Lambie, G. W. (2005). Family engagement: A collaborative, systemic approach for middle school counselors. *Professional School Counseling, 9*, 144–151.

Davis, T., & Ritchie, M. (1993). Confidentiality and the school counselor: A challenge for the 1990s. *The School Counselor, 41*, 23–30.

DeBono, E. (1992). *Serious creativity: Using the power of lateral thinking to create new ideas*. New York: HarperCollins.

DeRoche, E. F. (2000). Leadership for character education programs. *Journal of Humanistic Counseling, Education, and Development, 39*, 41–47.

DeVoss, J. A., & Andrews, M. F. (2006). *School counselors as program leaders*. Boston: Houghton Mifflin.

Dilley, J., Foster, W., & Bowers, I. (1973). Effectiveness ratings of counselors without teaching experience. *Counselor Education and Supervision, 13*, 24–29.

Dimmitt, C. (2009). Why evaluaton matters: Determining effective school counseling practices. *Professional School Counseling, 12*(6), 395–399.

Dimmitt, C., Carey, J. C., & Hatch, T. (2007). *Evidence-based school counseling: Making a difference with data-driven practices*. Thousand Oaks, CA: Corwin Press.

Dinkmeyer, D. C., Dinkmeyer, D. C., Jr., & Sperry, L. (1987). *Adlerian counseling and psychotherapy* (2nd ed.). Columbus, OH: Merrill.

Dollarhide, C. T. (1997). Counseling for meaning in work and life: An integrated approach. *Journal for Humanistic Education and Development, 35*, 178–187.

Dollarhide, C. T. (2000a). Career process and advising: Tools for the advisor. *NACADA Journal, 19*(2), 34–36.

Dollarhide, C. T. (2000b, April). *How do school counselors allocate their time?* Paper presented at the meeting of the Tri-County School Counselors Consortium, Whitewater, WI.

Dollarhide, C. T. (2003a). Comprehensive school counseling program and the domains/activities/partners model. In C. T. Dollarhide & K. A. Saginak (Eds.), *School counseling in the secondary schools: A comprehensive process and program* (pp. 81–103). New York: Allyn and Bacon.

Dollarhide, C. T. (2003b). School counselors as program leaders: Applying leadership contexts to school counseling. *Professional School Counseling, 6*, 304–309.

Dollarhide, C. T., Gibson, D. M., & Saginak, K. A. (2008). Leadership in school counseling: A year-long qualitative study. *Professional School Counseling, 11*(4), 262–271.

Dollarhide, C. T., & Haxton, R. (1999). Generations Theory: Counseling using generational value systems. *The CACD Journal, 19*, 21–28.

Dollarhide, C. T., & Lemberger, M. L. (2006). "No Child Left Behind": Implications for school counseling. *Professional School Counselor, 9*, 295–304.

Dollarhide, C. T., & Miller, G. M. (2006). Supervision for preparation and practice of school counselors: Pathways to excellence. *Counselor Education and Supervision, 45*, 242–252.

Dollarhide, C. T., & Saginak, K. A. (2003). *School counseling in the secondary schools: A comprehensive process and program.* New York: Allyn and Bacon.

Dollarhide, C. T., & Scully, S. (1999). The counseling/learning model: Using epistemological theory in college counseling. *The Journal of the Pennsylvania Counseling Association, 2*, 3–18.

Dougherty, A. M. (1990). *Consultation: Practice and perspectives.* Pacific Grove, CA: Brooks/Cole.

Dougherty, A. M., Dougherty, L. P., & Purcell, D. (1991). The sources and management of resistance to consultation. *The School Counselor, 38*, 178–186.

Drew, S. F. (2004). The power of school-community collaboration in dropout prevention. In J. Smink and F. P. Schargel (Eds.), *Helping students graduate: A strategic approach to dropout prevention* (pp. 65–78). Larchmont, NY: Eye on Education.

Dubelle, S. T., & Hoffman, C. M. (1984). *Misbehavin': Solving the disciplinary puzzle for educators.* Lancaster, PA: Technomic.

Dubelle, S. T., & Hoffman, C. M. (1986). *Misbehavin' II: Solving more of the disciplinary puzzle for educators.* Lancaster, PA: Technomic.

Dunn, R., Dunn, K., & Price, G. E. (1996). *Learning Styles Inventory.* Lawrence, KS: Price Systems.

Dunn, R., & Griggs, S. A. (1988). *Learning styles: Quiet revolution in American secondary schools.* Reston, VA: National Association of Secondary School Principals.

Durodoye, B. A., Combes, B. H., & Bryant, R. M. (2004). Counselor intervention in the post-secondary planning of African American students with learning disabilities. *Professional School Counseling, 7*, 133–140.

Dustin, D. (1992). School consultation in the 1990s. *Elementary School Guidance & Counseling, 26*, 65–76. Retrieved November 13, 2000, from http://webnf1.epnet.com (the EBSCO database).

Duttweiler, P. C. (2004). Systemic renewal: What works? In J. Smink & F. P. Schargel (Eds.), *Helping students graduate: A strategic approach to dropout prevention* (pp. 53–63). Larchmont, NY: Eye on Education.

The Education Trust. (2001). *Working definition of school counseling. Ed Trust: Transforming School Counseling.* The DeWitt Wallace-Reader's Digest Fund, National Initiative for Transforming School Counseling. Retrieved March 2, 2001, from http://www.edtrust.org/main/school_counseling.asp

The Education Trust. (2003). Transforming school counseling. Retrieved May 22, 2006, from http://www.2.edtrust.org/EdTrust/Transforming+School+Counseling/main

The Education Trust. (2009a). *National Center for Transforming School Counseling.* Retrieved August 4, 2010, from http://www.edtrust.org/dc/tsc

The Education Trust. (2009b). *The new vision for school counseling.* Retrieved July 2, 2010, from http://www.edtrust.org

Education World. (2004). Show me the money: Tips and resources for successful grant writing. Retrieved February 14, 2006, from http://www.educationworld.com/a_curr/profdev/profdev.039.shtml

Eggen, P., & Kauchak, D. (1994). *Educational psychology: Classroom connections* (2nd ed.). New York: Merrill.

Eisner, E. W. (1985). *The educational imagination: On the design and evaluation of school programs* (2nd ed.). New York: Macmillan.

Elliott, D. S. (1998). *Prevention programs that work for youth: Violence prevention.* Boulder, CO: Center for the Study and Prevention of Violence.

Ellis, A. (1973). *Humanistic psychotherapy: The rational emotive approach.* New York: McGraw-Hill.

Erchul, W. P., & Conoley, C. W. (1991). Helpful theories to guide counselors' practice of school-based consultation. *Elementary School Guidance & Counseling, 25,* 204–212. Retrieved November 13, 2000, from http://webnf1.epnet.com (the EBSCO database).

Erikson, E. H. (1963). *Childhood and society.* New York: Norton.

Erk, R. R. (1999). Attention deficit hyperactivity disorders: Counselors, laws, and implications for practice. *Professional School Counseling, 2,* 318–326.

Esters, I., & Ledoux, C. (2001). At-risk high school students' preference for counselor characteristics. *Professional School Counseling, 4,* 165–170.

Esters, I. G., & Ittenbach, R. F. (1999). Contemporary theories and assessments of intelligence: A primer. *Professional School Counseling, 2,* 373–376.

Estes, M. B. (2004). Choice for all?: Charter schools and students with special needs. *The Journal of Special Education, 37*(4), 257–267.

Evans, W. P., & Carter, M. J. (1997). Urban school-based counseling: Role definition, practice applications, and training implications. *Journal of Counseling & Development, 75,* 366–375.

Farwell, G. F. (1961). The role of the school counselor. *Counselor Education and Supervision, 1,* 40–43.

Fay, J., & Cline, F. (1986). *The science of control.* Golden, CO: Cline/Fay Institute.

Fay, J., & Funk, D. (1995). *Teaching with love and logic.* Golden, CO: Love & Logic Press.

Fazio, T. J., & Ural, K. K. (1995). The Princeton peer leadership program: Training seniors to help first year students. *NASSP Bulletin, 79*(5), 57–60.

Fleming, V. M. (1999). Group counseling in the schools: A case for basic training. *Professional School Counseling, 2,* 409–413.

Fontes, L. A (2000). Children exposed to marital violence: How school counselors can help. *Professional School Counseling, 3,* 231–237.

Forum on Child and Family Statistics. (2010). *America's children in brief: Key national indicators of well-being, 2010.* Retrieved July 28, 2010, from http://www.childstats.gov/americaschildren/index.asp

Foster-Harrison, E. S. (1995). Peer helping in the elementary and middle grades: A developmental perspective. *Elementary School Guidance and Counseling, 30*(2), 94–104.

Fox, M. (1994). *The reinvention of work: A new vision of livelihood for our time.* San Francisco: Harper.

Frankl, V. E. (1984). *Man's search for meaning* (rev. ed.). New York: Washington Square.

Fredrickson, R. H., & Pippert, R. R. (1964). Teaching experience in the employment of school counselors. *Counselor Education and Supervision, 4,* 24–27.

French, J. & Raven, B. H. (1959). *Studies of social power.* Ann Arbor, MI: Institute for Social Research.

Frey, K., & Sylvester, L. (1997). *Research on the Second Step Program: Do student behaviors and attitudes improve? What do teachers think about the program?* Seattle, WA: Committee for Children.

Froeschle, J., & Moyer, M. (2004). Just cut it out: Legal and ethical challenges in counseling students who self-mutilate. *Professional School Counseling, 7*, 231–235.

Fuller, B., Burr, E., Huerta, L., Puryear, S., & Wexler, E. (1999). *School choice: Abundant hopes, scarce evidence of results*. Berkeley, Stanford, and Los Angeles: Policy Analysis for California Education. (ERIC Document Reproduction Service No. ED 476 193)

Galassi, J. P., & Akos, P. (2007). *Strengths-based school counseling: Promoting student development and achievement*. Mahwah, NJ: Lawrence Erlbaum Associates.

Gardner, D. (1983). *A nation at risk: The imperative for educational reform*. Report of the National Commission on Excellence in Education. Washington, DC: U.S. Government Printing Office.

Gardner, H. (1983). *Frames of mind: The theory of multiple intelligences*. New York: Basic Books.

Gardner, H. (1995). *Leading minds: An anatomy of leadership*. New York: Basic Books.

Gardner, H., & Hatch, T. (1989). Multiples intelligences go to school: Educational implications of the theory of multiple intelligences. *Educational Researcher, 18*(8), 4–10.

Gellatt, H. B. (1991). *Creative decision making using positive uncertainty*. Los Angeles: Crisp.

Gellatt, H. B. (1996). Developing a future sense. In R. Feller and G. Walz (Eds.), *Career transitions in turbulent times: Exploring work, learning, and careers* (pp. 387–394). Greensboro, NC: ERIC Counseling and Student Services Clearinghouse.

Geltner, J. A., & Clark, M. A. (2005). Engaging students in classroom guidance: Management strategies for middle school counselors. *Professional School Counseling, 9*, 164–166.

Geroski, A. M., & Knauss, L. (2000). Addressing the needs of foster children within school counseling programs. *Professional School Counseling, 3*, 152–161.

Gibbs, J. (1995). *Tribes: A new way of learning and being together*. Sausalito, CA: Center Source Systems.

Gibson, D. M., Dollarhide, C. T., & Moss, J. (2010). Professional identity development: A grounded theory of transformational tasks of new counselors. *Counselor Education and Supervision, 50*(1), 21–38.

Gibson, R. I., Mitchell, M. H., & Higgins, R. E. (1983). Development and management of counseling programs and guidance services. In D. Brown & J. Trusty (Eds.), *Designing and leading comprehensive school counseling programs: Promoting student competence and meeting student needs* (pp. 78–106). Belmont, CA: Brooks/Cole.

Gibson, R. L. (1990). Teachers' opinions of high school counseling and guidance programs: Then and now. *The School Counselor, 37*, 248–256.

Gilchrist, S. (2006). S.O.A.R.I.N.G. In C. Holcomb-McCoy, *School counseling to close the achievement gap: A social justice framework for success* (pp. 89–91). Thousand Oaks, CA: Corwin Press.

Glasser, W. (1965). *Reality therapy: A new approach to psychiatry*. New York: Harper & Row.

Glasser, W., & Wubbolding, R. (1997). Beyond blame: A lead management approach. *Reaching Today's Youth, 1*(4), 40–42.

Goetz, E. T., Alexander, P. A., & Ash, M. J. (1992). *Educational psychology: A classroom perspective*. New York: Merrill.

Golderberger, N. R., Clinchy, B. M., Belenky, M. F., & Tarule, J. M. (1987). Women's ways of knowing. In P. Shaver & C. Hendrick (Eds.), *Sex and gender* (pp. 201–228). London: Sage.

Goldstein, A. P. (1999). *The Prepare curriculum: Teaching prosocial competencies* (rev. ed.). Champaign, IL: Research Press.

Goleman, D. (1995). *Emotional intelligence: Why it can matter more than IQ*. New York: Bantam.

Gonzalez, G. M., & Myrick, R. D. (2000). The Teacher as Student Advisors Program (TAP): An effective approach for drug education and other developmental activities. In J. Wittmer (Eds.), *Managing your school counseling program: K–12 developmental strategies* (2nd ed., pp. 243–252). Minneapolis, MN: Educational Media.

Goodman, R. D., & West-Olatunji, C. A. (2010). Educational hegemony, traumatic stress, and African American and Latino American students. *Journal of Multicultural Counseling and Development, 38*, 176–186.

Gordon, R. L. (1997). How novice teachers can succeed with adolescents. *Educational Leadership, 54*(7), 56–58.

Granello, D. H., & Granello, P. F. (2007). *Suicide: An essential guide for helping professionals and educators*. Boston: Pearson.

Griffin, D., & Farris, A. (2010). School counselors and collaboration: Finding resources through community mapping. *Professional School Counseling, 13*, 248–256.

Grolier-Webster international dictionary of the English language. (1975). New York: Grolier.

Gruber, H. E. (1993). Aspects of scientific discovery: Aesthetics and cognition. In J. Brockman (Ed.), *Creativity* (pp. 48–74). New York: Simon and Schuster.

Guerra, N. G., & Williams, K. R. (1996). *A program planning guide for youth violence prevention: A risk-focused approach*. Boulder, CO: Center for the Study and Prevention of Violence.

Guiffrida, D. A., & Douthit, K. Z. (2010). The Black student experience at predominantly White colleges: Implications for school and college counselors. *Journal of Counseling & Development, 88*, 311–318.

Gurian, M. (1997). *The wonder of boys: What parents, mentors and educators can do to shape boys into exceptional men*. New York: Penguin.

Gurian, M. (2001). *Boys and girls learn differently! A guide for teachers and parents*. San Francisco: Jossey-Bass.

Gurian, M. (2003). *The wonder of girls: Understanding the hidden nature of our daughters*. New York: Simon and Schuster.

Gysbers, N. C. (2004). Comprehensive guidance and counseling programs: The evolution of accountability. *Professional School Counseling, 8*, 1–14.

Gysbers, N. C. (2008). Evaluating school guidance and counseling programs: Past, present, and future. In H. L. K. Coleman & C. Yeh (Eds.), *Handbook of school counseling* (pp. 739–749). New York: Routledge.

Gysbers, N. C., & Henderson, P. (2000). *Developing and managing your school guidance program* (3rd ed.). Alexandria, VA: American Counseling Association.

Gysbers, N. C., Lapan, R. T., & Jones, B. A. (2000). School board policies for guidance and counseling: A call to action. *Professional School Counseling, 3*, 349–355.

Hackney, H., & Cormier, S. (1987). *The professional counselor, a process guide to helping*. Englewood Cliffs, NJ: Prentice-Hall.

Hall, A. S., & Lin, M. J. (1994). An integrative consultation framework: A practical tool for elementary school counselors. *Elementary School Guidance & Counseling, 29*, 16–28. Retrieved November 13, 2000, from http://webnf1.epnet.com (the EBSCO database).

Hall, A. S., & Lin, M. (1995). Theory and practice of children's rights: Implications for mental health counselors. *Journal of Mental Health Counseling, 17*, 63–80.

Hanna, F. J., & Bemak, F. (1997). The quest for identity in the counseling profession. *Counselor Education and Supervision, 36*, 194–206.

Hanna, F. J., & Green, A. (2004). Asian shades of spirituality: Implications for multicultural school counseling. *Professional School Counseling, 7*, 326–333.

Hanna, S. M., & Brown, J. H. (1999). *The practice of family therapy: Key elements across models* (2nd ed.). Belmont, CA: Brooks/Cole.

Harrison, T. C. (2000a). Brief counseling in the K–12 developmental counseling program. In J. Wittmer (Ed.), *Managing your school counseling program: K–12 developmental strategies* (2nd ed., pp. 85–94). Minneapolis, MN: Educational Media.

Harrison, T. C. (2000b). The school counselor as consultant/coordinator. In J. Wittmer (Ed.), *Managing your school counseling program: K–12 developmental strategies* (2nd ed., pp. 183–191). Minneapolis, MN: Educational Media.

Hawks, B. K., & Muha, D. (1991). Facilitating the career development of minorities: Doing it differently this time. *The Career Development Quarterly, 39*(3), 251–260.

Heinrich, K. T. (1995). Doctoral advisement relationships between women: On friendship and betrayal. *Journal of Higher Education, 66*(4), 447–469.

Helms, J. E. (1994). The conceptualization of racial identity and other "racial" constructs. In E. J. Trickett, R. J. Watts, and D. Birman (Eds.), *Human diversity: Perspectives on people in context* (pp. 285–311). San Francisco: Jossey-Bass.

Henderson, S. J. (2000). "Follow your bliss": A process for career happiness. *Journal of Counseling & Development, 78*, 305–315.

Herlihy, B., & Corey, G. (1996). *ACA ethical standards casebook* (5th ed.). Alexandria, VA: American Association for Counseling and Development.

Hersey, P., Blanchard, K. H., & Johnson, D. E. (1996). *Management of organizational behavior: Utilizing human resources* (7th ed.). Upper Saddle River, NJ: Prentice-Hall.

Hine, T. (1999). *The rise and fall of the American teenager*. New York: Bard.

Hinkle, J. S. (1993). Training school counselors to do family counseling. *Elementary School Guidance and Counseling, 27*, 252–258.

Hobbs, B. B., & Collison, B. B. (1995). School-community agency collaboration: Implications for the school counselor. *The School Counselor, 43*, 58–65.

Hohenshil, T. H. (2000). High tech counseling. *Journal of Counseling & Development, 78*, 365–369.

Holcomb-McCoy, C. (2001). Exploring the self-perceived multicultural counseling competencies of elementary school counselors. *Professional School Counseling, 4*, 195–201.

Holcomb-McCoy, C. (2004). Assessing the multicultural competence of school counselors: A checklist. *Professional School Counselor, 7*, 178–186.

Holcomb-McCoy, C. (2005). Investigating school counselors' perceived multicultural competence. *Professional School Counselor, 8*, 414–423.

Holcomb-McCoy, C. (2007). *School counseling to close the achievement gap: A social justice framework for success*. Thousand Oaks, CA: Corwin Press.

Holcomb-McCoy, C., & Mitchell, N. (2005). A descriptive study of urban school counseling programs. *Professional School Counseling, 8*, 203–208.

Holsen, I., Iversen, A. C., & Smith, B. (2009). Universal social competence programme in school: Does it work for children with low socio-economic background? *Advances in School Mental Health Promotion, 2*(2), 51–60.

Holsen, I., Smith, B., & Frey, K. S. (2008). Outcomes of the social competence program SECOND STEP in Norwegian elementary schools. *School Psychology International 29*(1), 71–88.

Hootman, J., & DeSocio, J. (2004, July/August). School nurses' important mental health role. *Behavioral Health Management, 24*(4), 25–29.

Horne, A., & Kiselica, M. S. (Eds.). (1999). *Handbook of counseling boys and adolescent males: A practitioner's guide*. Thousand Oaks, CA: Sage.

Hoyt, K. B. (1993). Guidance is not a dirty word. *The School Counselor, 40,* 267–273.

Huber, C. H., & Baruth, L. G. (1987). *Ethical, legal, and professional issues in the practice of marriage and family therapy.* New York: Merrill.

Hudson, G. R. (1961). Counselors need teaching experience. *Counselor Education and Supervision,* 24–27.

Hunter, M., & Russell, D. (1981). *Planning for effective instruction: Lesson design increasing your teaching effectiveness.* Palo Alto, CA: The Learning Institute.

Huss, S. N., Bryant, A., & Mulet, S. (2008). Managing the quagmire of counseling in a school: Bringing the parents onboard. *Professional School Counseling, 11,* 362–367.

Hutchins, D. E., & Cole, C. G. (1992). *Helping relationships and strategies* (2nd ed.). Pacific Grove, CA: Brooks/Cole.

Hutchins, D. E., & Vaught, C. C. (1997). *Helping relationships and strategies* (3rd ed.). Pacific Grove, CA: Brooks/Cole.

Hutchinson, R. L., & Bottorff, R. L. (1986). Selected high school counseling services: Student assessment. *The School Counselor, 33,* 350–354.

Ingersoll, R. E., & Bauer, A. L. (2004). An integral approach to spiritual wellness in school counseling settings. *Professional School Counselor, 7,* 301–308.

Isaacs, M. (2003). Data-driven decision making: The engine of accountability. *Professional School Counseling, 6*(4), 288. Retrieved from Academic Search Complete database.

Isaacs, M. L., & Stone, C. (1999). School counselors and confidentiality: Factors affecting professional choices. *Professional School Counseling, 2,* 258–266.

Ivey, A. E. (1986). *Developmental therapy.* San Francisco: Jossey-Bass.

Jackson, S. A., & White, J. (2000). Referrals to the school counselor: A qualitative study. *Professional School Counseling, 3,* 277–286.

James, S. H., & Burch, K. M. (1999). School counselors' roles in cases of child sexual behavior. *Professional School Counseling, 2,* 211–217.

James, S. H., & Greenwalt, B. C. (2001). Documenting success and achievement: Presentation and working portfolios for counselors. *Journal of Counseling & Development, 79,* 161–165.

Janson, C., Stone, C., & Clark, M. A. (2009). Stretching leadership: A distributed perspective for school counselor leaders. *Professional School Counseling, 13,* 98–106.

Johnson, C., & Johnson, S. (1998). *Results-based student support programs.* Training manual for California Counselor Leadership Academy. San Juan Capistrano, CA: Professional Update.

Johnson, D. W., & Johnson, F. P. (2000). *Joining together: Group theory and group skills* (7th ed.). Boston: Allyn and Bacon.

Johnson, L. S. (2000). Promoting professional identity in an era of educational reform. *Professional School Counseling, 4,* 31–40.

Johnson, R. S. (2002). *Using data to close the achievement gap: How to measure equity in our schools.* Thousand Oaks, CA: Corwin Press.

Johnson, S., & Johnson, C. D. (2003). Results-based guidance: A systems approach to student support programs. *Professional School Counseling, 6*(3), 180–184.

Johnson, S., Johnson, C., & Downs, L. (2006). *Building a results-based student support program.* Boston: Lahaska Press.

Kaffenberger, C., & Davis, T. (2009). Introduction to special issue: A call for practitioner research. *Professional School Counseling, (12)*6, 392–394.

Kahn, B. B. (1999). Priorities and practices in field supervision of school counseling students. *Professional School Counseling, 3,* 128–136.

Kahn, B. B. (2000). A model of solution-focused consultation for school counselors. *Professional School Counseling, 3,* 248–254.

Kalafat, J. (2006). Youth suicide prevention programs. *The Prevention Researcher, 13*(3), 12–15.

Kampwirth, T. J. (2006). Collaborative consultation in the schools: Effective practices for students with learning and behavior problems (3rd ed.). Upper Saddle River, NJ: Pearson Merrill/Prentice Hall.

Kaplan, D., & Allison, M. C. (1994). Family ethics. *Family Journal, 2*(1), 54–57.

Kaplan, L. S. (1996). Outrageous or legitimate concerns: What some parents are saying about school counseling. *The School Counselor, 43,* 165–170.

Kaplan, L. S. (1997). Parents' rights: Are school counselors at risk? *The School Counselor, 44,* 334–343.

Kegan, R. (1982). *The evolving self: Problem and process in human development.* Cambridge, MA: Harvard University Press.

Kerr, M. M. (2009). *School crisis prevention and intervention.* Upper Saddle River, NJ: Merrill.

Keys, S. G., Bemak, F., & Carpenter, S. L. (1998). Collaborative consultant: A new role for counselors serving at-risk youths. *Journal of Counseling & Development, 76,* 123–133.

Keys, S. G., Bemak, F., & Lockhart, E. J. (1998). Transforming school counseling to serve the mental health needs of at-risk youth. *Journal of Counseling & Development, 76,* 381–388.

Keys, S. G., & Lockhart, E. J. (1999). The school counselor's role in facilitating multisystemic change. *Professional School Counseling, 3,* 101–107.

King, K. A. (2006). Practical strategies for preventing adolescent suicide. *The Prevention Researcher, 13*(3), 8–11.

King, K. A., Price, J. H., Telljohann, S. K., & Wahl, J. (1999). How confident do high school counselors feel in recognizing students at risk for suicide? *American Journal of Health Behavior, 23,* 457–467.

King, K. A., Price, J. H., Telljohann, S. K., & Wahl, J. (2000). Preventing adolescent suicide: Do high school counselors know the risk factors? *Professional School Counseling, 3,* 255–263.

King, P. M., & Kitchener, K. S. (1994). *Developing reflective judgment.* San Francisco: Jossey-Bass.

Kirschenbaum, H. (2000). From values clarification to character education: A personal journey. *Journal of Humanistic Counseling, Education and Development, 39,* 4–20.

Kiselica, M. S., & Pfaller, J. (1993). Helping teenage parents: The independent and collaborative roles of counselor educators and school counselors. *Journal of Counseling & Development, 72,* 42–49.

Kline, W. B. (2003). *Interactive group counseling and therapy.* Upper Saddle River, NJ: Merrill Prentice Hall.

Koch, G. (2003). Adolescent spirituality: An oxymoron? In C. Dollarhide & K. Saginak (Eds.), *School counseling in the secondary school: A comprehensive process and program* (pp. 361–372). Boston: Allyn and Bacon.

Koehler, M., & Kravets, M. (1998). *Counseling with secondary students with learning disabilities: A ready-to-use guide to help students prepare for college and work.* West Nyack, NY: Center for Applied Research in Education.

Kottler, J. A. (1991). *The compleat therapist.* San Francisco: Jossey-Bass.

Kottler, J. A. (1993). *On being a therapist* (rev. ed.). San Francisco: Jossey-Bass.

Kouzes, J. M., & Posner, B. Z. (1995). *The leadership challenge: How to keep getting extraordinary things done in organizations.* San Francisco: Jossey-Bass.

Kress, V. E. W., Gibson, D. M., & Reynolds, C. A. (2004). Adolescents who self-injure:

Implications and strategies for school counselors. *Professional School Counselor, 7,* 195–201.

Krumboltz, J. D., & Thoresen, C. E. (Eds.). (1976). *Counseling methods.* New York: Holt, Rinehart and Winston.

Kurpius, D. J., & Rozecki, T. (1992). Outreach, advocacy and consultation: A framework for prevention and intervention. *Elementary School Guidance & Counseling, 26,* 176–189. Retrieved November 13, 2000, from http://webnf1.epnet.com (the EBSCO database).

LaFountain, R. M., & Garner, N. E. (1996). Solution-focused counseling groups: The results are in. *The Journal for Specialists in Group Work, 21*(2), 128–143.

Lambie, G. W. (2005). Child abuse and neglect: A practical guide for professional school counselors. *Professional School Counseling, 8,* 249–258.

Lapan, R. T. (2001). Results-based comprehensive guidance and counseling programs: A framework for planning and evaluation. *Professional School Counseling, 4,* 289–299.

Lawrence, G., & Kurpius, S. E. R. (2000). Legal and ethical issues involved when counseling minors in nonschool settings. *Journal of Counseling & Development, 78,* 130–136.

Lawson, H. A. (2003). Pursuing and securing collaboration to improve results. In M. M. Brabeck, M. E. Walsh, & R. E. Latta (Eds.), *Meeting at the hyphen: Schools-universities-communities-professions in collaboration for student achievement and well being* (pp. 45–73). 102nd Yearbook of the National Society for the Study of Education. Chicago: University of Chicago Press.

Lazear, D. (1999). *Eight ways of teaching: The artistry of teaching with multiple intelligences* (3rd ed.). Arlington Heights, IL: SkyLight Training & Publishing.

Lazovsky, R. (2008). Maintaining confidentiality with minors: Dilemmas of school counselors. *Professional School Counseling, 11,* 335–345.

Ledyard, P. (1998). Counseling minors: Ethical and legal issues. *Counseling and Values, 42*(3), 171–198.

Levenkron, S. (1998). *Cutting: Understanding and overcoming self-mutilation.* New York: Norton.

Lewis, A. C. (1994). Expectations for schools. *Education Digest, 60*(4), 72–74.

Lewis, J., Arnold, M. S., House, R., & Toporek, R. (2003). *The Advocacy Competencies.* American Counseling Association. Retrieved July 23, 2010, from http://www.counseling.org/Resources/Competencies/Advocacy_Competencies.pdf

Lickona, T., & Davidson, M. (2005). *Smart & good high schools: Integrating excellence and ethics for success in schools, work, and beyond.* Cortland, NY: Center for the 4th and 5th Rs (Respect and Responsibility). Washington, DC: Character Education Partnership.

Lipsitz, J. (1984). *Successful schools for young adolescents.* New Brunswick, NJ: Transaction Books.

Loesch, L. C., & Goodman, W. J. (2000). The K–12 developmental school counselor and appraisal. In J. Wittmer (Ed.), *Managing your school counseling program: K–12 developmental strategies* (2nd ed., pp. 204–210). Minneapolis, MN: Educational Media.

Loesch, L. C., & Ritchie, M. H. (2005). *The accountable school counselor.* Austin, TX: CAPS Press.

Logan, R. (2001, March/April). Creating a listserv—a key to communication. *The ASCA Counselor, 38,* 12.

Lonborg, S. D., & Bowen, N. (2004). Counselors, communities, and spirituality: Ethical and multicultural considerations. *Professional School Counseling, 7,* 318–325.

Love, N. (2002). *Using data/getting results: A practical guide for school improvement in mathematics and science*. Norwood, MA: Christopher-Gordon.

Luongo, P. F. (2000). Partnering child welfare, juvenile justice, and behavioral health with schools. *Professional School Counseling, 3*, 308–314.

MacDonald, D. (2004). Collaborating with students' spirituality. *Professional School Counseling, 7*, 293–300.

Mager, R. F. (1997). *Preparing instructional objectives: A critical tool in the development of effective instruction* (3rd ed.). Atlanta, GA: The Center for Effective Performance.

Magnuson, S., & Norem, K. (1998). A school counselor asks: "Am I prepared to do what I'm asked to do?" *Family Journal, 6*(2), 137–140.

Maliszewski, S., & Mackiel, J. (2002). Comprehensive guidance results-based evaluation: Developing a practical approach. Retrieved from ERIC database (ED461793).

Malott, K. M., Paone, T. R., Humphreys, K., & Martinez, T. (2010). Use of group counseling to address ethnic identity development: Application with adolescents of Mexican descent. *Professional School Counseling, 13*, 257–267.

Maslow, A. H. (1970). *Motivation and personality* (2nd ed.). New York: Harper.

Mason, E. C. M., & McMahon, H. G. (2009). Leadership practices of school counselors. *Professional School Counseling, 13*, 107–115.

Masten, A. S., Herbers, J. E., Cutuli, J. J., & Lafavor, T. L. (2008). Promoting competence and resilience in the school context. *Professional School Counseling, 12*, 76–84.

Mauk, G. W., & Gibson, D. G. (1994). Suicide postvention with adolescents: School consultation practices and issues. *Education and Treatment of Children, 17*, 468–484. Retrieved November 13, 2000, from http://webnf1.epnet. com (the EBSCO database).

McCall-Perez, Z. (2000). The counselor as advocate for English Language Learners: An action research approach. *Professional School Counseling, 4*, 13–22.

McCarthy, J., & Holliday, E. L. (2004). Help-seeking and counseling within a traditional male gender role: An examination from a multicultural perspective. *Journal of Counseling & Development, 82*, 25–30.

McFarland, W. P., & Dupuis, M. (2001). The legal duty to protect gay and lesbian students from violence in school. *Professional School Counseling, 4*, 171–179.

McGlothlin, J. M. (2008). *Developing clinical skills in suicide assessment, prevention, and treatment*. Alexandria, VA: American Counseling Association.

McMahon, H. G., Mason, E. C. M, & Paisley, P. O. (2009). School counselor educators as educational leaders promoting systemic change. *Professional School Counseling, 13*, 116–124.

McWhirter, J. J., McWhirter, B. T., McWhirter, A. M., & McWhirter, E. H. (2007). *At-risk youth: A comprehensive response for counselors, teachers, psychologists, and human service professionals* (4th ed.). Pacific Grove, CA: Brooks/Cole.

Meier, S. C., & Davis, S. R. (1997). *Elements of counseling* (3rd ed.). Pacific Grove, CA: Brooks/Cole.

Mellin, E. A. (2009). Responding to the crisis in children's mental health: Potential roles for the counseling profession. *Journal of Counseling & Development, 87*, 501–506.

Metcalf, L. (1995). *Counseling toward solutions: A practical, solution-focused program for working with students, teachers, and parents*. San Francisco: Jossey-Bass.

Miller, G. M., & Dollarhide, C. T. (2006). Supervision in schools: Building pathways to excellence. *Counselor Education and Supervision, 45*, 296–303.

Morris, J. (1992). *Creative breakthroughs: Tap the power of your unconscious mind*. New York: Warner.

Morrison, G. S. (1997). *Teaching in America.* Boston: Allyn and Bacon.

Morrissette, P. J. (2000). The experiences of the rural school counselor. *Professional School Counseling, 3,* 197–208.

Muller, L. E. (2000). A 12-session, European-American-led counseling group for African American females. *Professional School Counseling, 3,* 264–269.

Muro, J. J., & Kottman, T. (1995). *Guidance and counseling in the elementary and middle schools: A practical approach.* Madison, WI: Brown & Benchmark.

Murphy, J. P., DeEsch, J. B., & Strein, W. O. (1998). School counselors and school psychologists: Partners in students services. *Professional School Counseling, 2,* 85–87.

Muuss, R. E. (1988). *Theories of adolescence* (5th ed.). New York: Random House.

Myers, J. E., Sweeney, T. J., & Witmer, J. M. (2000). The Wheel of Wellness counseling for wellness: A holistic model for treatment planning. *Journal of Counseling & Development, 78,* 251–266.

Myrick, R. D. (1987). *Developmental guidance and counseling: A practical approach.* Minneapolis, MN: Educational Media.

Myrick, R. D. (1993). *Developmental guidance and counseling: A practical approach* (2nd ed.). Minneapolis, MN: Educational Media.

Myrick, R. D. (1997). *Developmental guidance and counseling: A practical approach* (3rd ed.). Minneapolis, MN: Educational Media.

Myrick, R. D. (2003). *Developmental guidance and counseling: A practical approach* (4th ed.). Minneapolis, MN: Educational Media.

Myrick, R. D., Merhill, H., & Swanson, L. (1986). Changing student attitudes through classroom guidance. *The School Counselor. 33*(4), 244–252.

Myrick, R. D., & Myrick, L. (1990). *The teacher advisor program: An innovative approach to school guidance.* Ann Arbor: University of Michigan, ERIC Counseling and Personnel Services.

Myrick, R. D., & Sabella, R. A. (1995). Cyberspace: New place for counselor supervision. *Elementary School Guidance and Counseling, 30,* 35–45.

Nassar-McMillan, S. C., & Cashwell, C. S. (1997). Building self-esteem of children and adolescents through adventure-based counseling. *Journal of Humanistic Education and Development, 36,* 59–67.

National Board for Certified Counselors. (2005). *Code of ethics.* Retrieved March 25, 2010, from http://www.nbcc.org/AssetManagerFiles/ethics/nbcc-code-ofethics.pdf

National Board for Certified Counselors. (n. d.). *The practice of Internet counseling.* Retrieved March 25, 2010, from http://www.nbcc.org/AssetManagerFiles/ethics/internetCounseling.pdf

National Board for Professional Teaching Standards. (2006). *Home page.* Retrieved August 4, 2006, from http://www.nbpts.org

National Career Development Association. (2007). *Code of ethics.* Retrieved March 25, 2010, from http://associationdatabase.com/aws/NCDA/asset_manager/get_file/3395/code_of_ethicsmay-2007.pdf

National Commission on Educational Excellence. (1983). *A nation at risk.* Retrieved April 22, 2006, from http://www.ed.gov/pubs/NatAtRisk/risk.html

National Research Council. (2000). *How people learn: Brain, mind, experience, and school* (expanded ed.). Washington, DC: National Academy Press.

Nelson, R. E., & Galas, J. C. (1994). *The power to prevent suicide: A guide for teens helping teens.* Minneapolis, MN: Free Spirit.

Newman, J. W. (1994). *America's teachers: An introduction to education* (2nd ed.). New York: Longman.

Nichols, M. P., & Schwartz, R. C. (1991). *Family therapy concepts and methods* (2nd ed.). Boston: Allyn and Bacon.

Nicoll, W. G. (1992). A family counseling and consultation model for school counselors. *The School Counselor, 39*, 351–361.

Niebuhr, K. E., Niebuhr, R. E., & Cleveland, W. T. (1999). Principal and counselor collaboration. *Education, 119*, 674–679. Retrieved November 13, 2000, from http://webnf2.epnet.com (the EBSCO database).

Noble, J. (2000). Students' educational achievement: What helps or hinders? *The ASCA Counselor, 38*, 14–15.

Northwest Regional Educational Laboratory. (n.d.). The catalog of school reform models. Retrieved April 22, 2006, from http://www.nwrel.org/ scpd/catalog/ index.shtml

Nystul, M. S. (1993). *The art and science of counseling and psychotherapy*. New York: Merrill.

Olson, L. (1999, April 21). Tugging at tradition: Lessons of a century. *Education Week*, pp. 25–29, 30–31.

Olson, M. J., & Allen, D. N. (1993). Principals' perceptions of the effectiveness of school counselors with and without teaching experience. *Counselor Education and Supervision, 33*, 10–21.

Owen, D. W., & Weikel, W. J. (1999). Computer utilization by school counselors. *Professional School Counseling, 2*, 179–182.

Paisley, P. O., & Hubbard, G. T. (1994). *Developmental school counseling programs: From theory to practice*. Alexandria, VA: American Counseling Association.

Paisley, P. O., & Peace, S. D. (1995). Developmental principles: A framework for school counseling programs. *Elementary School Counseling & Guidance, 30*(2), 85–93.

Palmer, P. J. (1998). *The courage to teach: Exploring the inner landscape of a teacher's life*. San Francisco: Jossey-Bass.

Park, N. & Peterson, C. (2008). Positive psychology and character strengths: Application to strengths-based school counseling. *Professional School Counseling, 12*, 85–92.

Parker, L. J. (1998). *Mythopoesis and the crisis of postmodernism: Toward integrating image and story*. New York: Brandon House.

Parks, S. D. (1990, Fall). Social vision and moral courage: Mentoring a new generation. *Cross Currents, 40*(3), 350–367.

Parsons, R. D., & Kahn, W. J. (2005). *The school counselor as consultant: An integrated model for school-based consultation*. Belmont, CA: Thomson.

Participatory Leadership. (2008). *A definition of participatory leadership*. Retrieved July 21, 2010, from http://www.participatory-leadership.com/Site/A_definition_of_Parti cipatory_Leadership_.html

Partin, R. L. (1993). School counselors' time: Where does it go? *The School Counselor, 40*, 274–281.

Payne, R. K. (1996). *A framework for understanding poverty* (3rd ed.). Highlands, TX: aha! Process.

Payne, R. K. (2003). *A framework for understanding poverty* (3rd rev. ed.). Highlands, TX: aha! Process.

Pedrotti, J. T., Edwards, L. M., & Lopez, S. J. (2008). Promoting hope: Suggestions for school counselors. *Professional School Counseling, 12*, 100–107.

Peeks, B. (1993). Revolutions in counseling and education: A systems perspective in the schools. *Elementary School Counseling and Guidance, 27*, 245–252.

Peer counselors help kids with problems, study shows. (2000). *The National Certified Counselor, 16*, 16.

Perry, N. (1992). *Educational reform and the school counselor* (Report No. EDO-CG-92-25). Washington, DC: Office of Educational Research and Improvement. (ERIC Document Reproduction Service

No. ED 347 491). Retrieved April 18, 2000, from http://webnf2.epnet.com (the EBSCO database).

Perry, W. G., Jr. (1981). Cognitive and ethical growth. In A. Chickering (Ed.), *The modern American college* (pp. 76–116). San Francisco: Jossey-Bass.

Personal liability insurance: Do you need your own policy? (2000, March/April). *The ASCA Counselor, 37,* 24.

Peterson, J., Goodman, R., & Keller, T. (2002, October). *A comparison of school counseling students with and without teaching background: Perceptions of the internship experience.* Paper presented at the meeting of the Association for Counselor Education and Supervision, Park City, UT.

Pipher, M. (1994). *Reviving Ophelia: Saving the selves of adolescent girls.* New York: Ballantine.

Pittman, D. (n.d.). *Preventing problems or promoting development: Competing priorities or inseparable goals.* Retrieved April 18, 2000, from http://www.iyfnet.org/document.cfm/22/general/51

Pollack, W. (1998). *Real boys: Rescuing our sons from the myths of boyhood.* New York: Holt.

Pollack, W. (1999). *Real boys: Rescuing our sons from the myths of boyhood.* New York: Owl Books.

Ponec, D. L., & Brock, B. L. (2000). Relationships among elementary school counselors and principals: A unique bond. *Professional School Counseling, 3,* 208–217.

Ponec, D. L., Poggi, J. A., & Dickel, C. T. (1998). Unity: Developing relationships between school and community counselors. *Professional School Counseling, 1,* 95–103.

Ponton, L. E. (1997). *The romance of risk: Why teenagers do the things they do.* New York: Basic Books.

Porter, G., Epp, L., & Bryant, S. (2000). Collaboration among school mental health professionals: A necessity, not a luxury. *Professional School Counseling, 3,* 315–322.

Posthuma, B. W. (1999). *Small groups in counseling and therapy: Process and leadership* (3rd ed.). Boston: Allyn and Bacon.

Poynton, T., & Carey, J. (2006). An integrative model of data-based decision making for school counseling. *Professional School Counseling, 10*(2), 121.

Price, L., & Edgar, E. (1995). Developing support systems for youth with and without disabilities. *Journal for Vocational Special Needs Education, 18*(1), 17–21.

Quarto, C. J. (1999). Teachers' perceptions of school counselors with and without teaching experience. *Professional School Counseling, 2,* 378–383.

Rak, C. F., & Patterson, L. E. (1996). Promoting resilience in at-risk children. *Journal of Counseling & Development, 74,* 368–373.

Rayle, A. D. (2005). Cross-gender interactions in middle school counselor-student working alliances: Challenges and recommendations. *Professional School Counseling, 9,* 152–155.

Rees, N. S. (2000). *School choice 2000: What's happening in the states.* Heritage Foundation Report. (ERIC Document Reproduction Service No. ED 440 176)

Reinharz, S. (1994). Toward an ethnography of "voice" and "silence," In E. J. Trickett, R. J. Watts, and D. Birman (Eds.), *Human diversity: Perspectives on people in context* (pp. 178–200). San Francisco: Jossey-Bass.

Remley, T. P., & Herman, M. (2000). Legal and ethical issues in school counseling. In J. Wittmer (Ed.), *Managing your school counseling program: K–12 developmental strategies* (2nd ed., pp. 314–329). Minneapolis, MN: Educational Media.

Reynolds, S. E., & Hines, P. L. (2001). *Vision-to-action: A step-by-step activity guide to systemic education reform* (6th ed.). Bloomington, IN: American Student Achievement Institute.

Rice, G. E., & Smith, W. (1993). Linking effective counseling and teaching skills. *The School Counselor, 40*, 201–206.

Rico, G. L. (1983). *Writing the natural way: Using right-brain techniques to release your expressive powers*. Los Angeles: Tarcher.

Riley, P. A. (2000). A charter school survey: Parents, teachers, and principals speak out. Retrieved February 16, 2005, from http://www.pacificresearch.org/pub/sab/educat/chartersurvey.pdf

Ritchie, M. H., & Partin, R. L. (1994). Parent education and consultation: Activities of school counselors. *The School Counselor, 41*, 165–170.

Rivers, C., & Barnett, R. C. (2006, Apr. 9). The myth of "the boy crisis." *Washington Post*. Retrieved April 9, 2006, from http://www.washingtonpost.com/wpdyn/content/article/2006/04/07

Roberts, E. B., & Borders, L. D. (1994). Supervision of school counselors: Administrative, program, and counseling. *The School Counselor, 41*, 149–157.

Roberts, W. B., Jr., & Morotti, A. A. (2001). Site supervisors of professional school counseling interns: Suggested guidelines. *Professional School Counseling, 4*, 208–215.

Robinson, E. H., III, Jones, K. D., & Hayes, B. G. (2000). Humanistic education to character education: An ideological journey. *Journal of Humanistic Counseling, Education and Development, 39*, 21–25.

Roby, D. (2004). Research on school attendance and student achievement: A study of Ohio schools. *Educational Research Quarterly, 28*(1), 3–14. Retrieved from Academic Search Complete database.

Rochester, D. E., & Cottingham, H. F. (1966). Is teaching experience necessary? Counselor educators speak out. *Counselor Education and Supervision, 5*, 175–181.

Root-Bernstein, R., & Root-Bernstein, M. (1999). *Sparks of genius: The thirteen thinking tools of the world's most creative people*. Boston: Houghton Mifflin.

Rowell, L. L. (2006). Action research and school counseling: Closing the gap between research and practice. *Professional School Counseling, 9*(5), 376–384.

Rowell, L., & Carey, J. (2009). Action research, outcome research and evidence-based school counseling practice. *Counseling Today, 51*(10), 56–57.

Rowley, W. J. (2000). Expanding collaborative partnership among school counselors and school psychologists. *Professional School Counseling, 3*, 224–228.

Sabella, R. A., & Booker, B. L. (2003). Using technology to promote your guidance and counseling program among stake holders. *Professional School Counseling, 6*, 206–213.

Saginak, K. A. (2003). A systems view of adolescents: The student in context. In C. T. Dollarhide and K. A. Saginak (Eds.), *School counseling in the secondary school: A comprehensive process and program* (pp. 49–62). Boston: Allyn and Bacon.

Sampson, J. P., Jr., & Krumboltz, J. D. (1991). Computer-assisted instruction: A missing link in counseling. *Journal of Counseling and Development, 69*, 395–397.

San Antonio, D. M., & Gamage, D. T. (2007). Building trust among educational stakeholders through participatory school administration, leadership and management. *Management in Education, 21*(1), 15–22. DOI: 10.1177/0892020607073406.

Schaef, A. W., & Fassel, D. (1992). *The addictive organization*. San Francisco: Harper Collins.

Scheer, J. (1994). Culture and disability: An anthropological point of view. In E. J. Trickett, R. J. Watts, & D. Birman (Eds.), *Human diversity: Perspectives on people in context* (pp. 244–260). San Francisco: Jossey-Bass.

Schickedanz, J. A., Schickedanz, D. I., Forsyth, P. D., & Forsyth, C. A. (1998). *Understanding children and adolescents* (3rd ed.). Boston: Allyn and Bacon.

Schickedanz, J. A., Schickedanz, D. I., Forsyth, P. D., & Forsyth, G. A. (2001).

Understanding children and adolescents (4th ed.). Boston: Allyn and Bacon.

Schmidt, J. J. (1990). Critical issues for school counselor performance appraisal and supervision. *The School Counselor, 38,* 86–94.

Schmidt, J. J. (1999). *Counseling in schools: Essential services and comprehensive programs* (3rd ed.). Boston: Allyn and Bacon.

Schmidt, J. J. (2003). *Counseling in the schools: Essential services and comprehensive programs* (4th ed.). Boston: Allyn and Bacon.

Schmidt, J. J. (2006). *Social and cultural foundations of counseling and human services: Multiple influences on self-concept development.* Boston: Allyn and Bacon.

Schmidt, J. J. (2008). *Counseling in schools: Comprehensive program of responsive services for all students* (5th ed.). Boston: Allyn and Bacon.

Schmoker, M. (2004, September). Learning communities at the crossroads: Toward the best schools we've ever had. *Phi Delta Kappan, 86,* 84–88.

School Mental Health Project/Center for Mental Health in Schools. (1999, Fall). Promoting youth development and addressing barriers. *Addressing Barriers to Learning,* 1–8.

SchoolGrants. (2006). 10 grant writing hints. Retrieved February 14, 2006, from http://www.schoolgrants.org/tips/10_tips.htm

Schrumpf, F., Crawford, D., & Usadel, H. C. (1997). *Program guide peer mediation: Conflict resolution in the schools.* Champaign, IL: Research Press.

Sealander, K. A., Schwiebert, V. L., Oren, T. A., & Weekley, J. L. (1999). Confidentiality and the law. *Professional School Counseling, 3,* 122–127.

Search Institute. (2010). *40 Developmental Assets.* Retrieved July 1, 2010, from http://www.search-institute.org/developmental-assets/lists

Seaward, B. L. (1994). *Managing stress: Principles and strategies for health and wellbeing.* Boston: Jones & Bartlett.

Shaffer, D. R. (1999). *Developmental psychology: Childhood and adolescence* (5th ed.). Pacific Grove, CA: Brooks/Cole.

Shechtman, Z., & Bar-El, O. (1994). Group guidance and group counseling to foster social acceptability and self-esteem in adolescence. *The Journal for Specialists in Group Work, 19,* 188–196.

Shechtman, Z., Bar-El, O., & Hadar, E. (1997). Therapeutic factors and psychoeducational groups for adolescents: A comparison. *The Journal for Specialists in Group Work, 22,* 203–213.

Sheldon, K. M., & Biddle, B. J. (1998). Standards, accountability, and school reform: Perils and pitfalls. *Teachers College Record, 100*(1), 164–180.

Sherman, L. W., Gottfredson, D. C., MacKenzie, D. L., Eck, J., Reuter, P., & Bushway, S. D. (1998). *Preventing crime: What works, what doesn't, what's promising.* National Institute of Justice Research in Brief. Washington, DC: U.S. Department of Justice.

Shoffner, M. F., & Briggs, M. K. (2001). An interactive approach for developing interpersonal collaboration: Preparing school counselors. *Counselor Education and Supervision, 40*(3), 193–202.

Simcox, A., Nuijens, K., & Lee, C. (2006). School counselors and school psychologists: Collaborative partners in promoting culturally competent schools. *Professional School Counseling, 9*(4), 272–277. Retrieved from Academic Search Premier database.

Simmons, R. (2002). *Odd girl out.* Orlando, FL: Harcourt.

Simon, C. A. (1999). Public school administration: Employing Thompson's Structural Contingency Theory to explain public school administrative expenditures in Washington State. *Administration & Society, 31,* 525–542.

Simpson, M. D. (1999, February). Student suicide: Who's liable? *NEA Today, 17,* 25–26.

Sink, C. A. (2002). Comprehensive guidance and counseling programs and the development of multicultural student-citizens. *Professional School Counseling, 6,* 130–137.

Sink, C. A. (2004). Spirituality and comprehensive school counseling programs. *Professional School Counseling, 7,* 309–317.

Sink, C. A. (2005). Fostering academic development and learning: Implications and recommendations for middle school counselors. *Professional School Counseling, 9,* 128–135.

Sink, C. A. (2009). School counselors as accountability leaders: Another call to action. *Professional School Counseling,13,* 68–74.

Sink, C. A., & Richmond, L. J. (2004). Introducing spirituality to professional school counseling. *Professional School Counseling, 7,* 291–292.

Sitlington, P. L., Clark, G. M., & Kolstoe, O. P. (2000). *Transition education and services for adolescents with disabilities* (3rd ed.). Boston: Allyn and Bacon.

Slavin, R. E. (1994). *A practical guide to cooperative learning.* Boston: Allyn and Bacon.

Smaby, M. H., & Daugherty, R. (1995). The school counselor as leader of efforts to have schools free of drugs and violence. *Education, 115,* 612–622.

Smink, J. & Schargel, F. P. (2004). *Helping students graduate: A strategic approach to dropout prevention.* Larchmont, NY: Eye on Education.

Smith, E. P., & Davidson, W. S., II. (1992). Mentoring and the development of African-American graduate students. *Journal of College Student Development, 33,* 531–539.

Smith, S. L., & Archer, J. (2000). The developmental school counselor and mental health counseling. In J. Wittmer (Ed.), *Managing your school counseling program: K–12 developmental strategies* (2nd ed., pp. 68–74). Minneapolis, MN: Educational Media.

Smith, T. B. (2004). *Practicing multiculturalism: Affirming diversity in counseling and psychology.* Boston, MA: Allyn and Bacon.

Snyder, B. A. (2000). Managing an elementary school developmental counseling program: The role of the counselor. In J. Wittmer (Ed.), *Managing your school counseling program: K–12 developmental strategies* (2nd ed., pp. 37–48). Minneapolis, MN: Educational Media.

Snyder, C. R. (1994). *The psychology of hope.* New York: Free Press.

Snyder, C. R., & Lopez, S. J. (2007). *Positive psychology: The scientific and practical explorations of human strengths.* Thousand Oaks, CA: Sage.

St. Clair, M. (1996). *Object relations and self psychology.* Pacific Grove, CA: Brooks/Cole.

Stadler, H. A. (1985). *Confidentiality: The professional's dilemma: Participant's manual.* Alexandria, VA: American Counseling Association.

Starkman, N., Scales, P. C., & Roberts, C. (1999). *Great places to learn: How asset-building schools help students succeed.* Minneapolis, MN: Search Institute.

Staton, A., & Gilligan, T. (2003). Teaching school counselors and school psychologists to work collaboratively. *Counselor Education and Supervision, 42*(3), 162. Retrieved from Academic Search Premier database.

Stone, C. B. (2000). Advocacy for sexual harassment victims: Legal support and ethical aspects. *Professional School Counseling, 4,* 23–30.

Stone, C. B., & Dahir, C. A. (2004). *School counselor accountability: A measure of student success.* Upper Saddle River, NJ: Pearson Education.

Stone, C. B., & Dahir, C. A. (2006). *The transformed school counseling.* Boston: Lahaska Press.

Stone, C. B., & Dahir, C. A. (2007). *School counselor accountability: A MEASURE of student success* (2nd ed.). Upper Saddle River, NJ: Pearson.

Stone, G., & Peeks, B. (1986). The use of strategic family therapy in the school setting: A case study. *Journal of Counseling & Development, 65*, 200–203.

Strawser, S., Markos, P. A., Yamaguchi, B. J., & Higgins, K. (2000). A new challenge for school counselors: Children who are homeless. *Professional School Counseling, 3*, 162–171.

Street, S. (1994). Adolescent male sexuality issues. *School Counselor, 41*, 319–325.

Strein, W., & Hershenson, D. B. (1991). Confidentiality in nondyadic counseling situations. *Journal of Counseling & Development, 69*, 312–316.

Strong, S. R. (1968). Counseling: An interpersonal influence process. *Journal of Counseling Psychology, 15*(3), 215–224.

Sue, D. W., & Sue, D. (1990). *Counseling the culturally different* (2nd ed.). Somerset, NJ: Wiley.

Sue, D. W., & Sue, D. (1999). *Counseling the culturally different: Theory and practice* (3rd ed.). New York: Wiley.

Sugai, G. (n.d.). *School-wide positive behavior support: Overview.* OSEP Center on PBIS, U.S. Department of Education. Retrieved on August 3, 2006, from http://www.pbis.org/pastconferencepresentations.htm

Sullivan, S., & Shulman, V. (2005). Managing change: The superintendent as line director of instruction. *International Journal of Leadership in Education, 8*(2), 123–143.

Talleyrand, R. M. (2010). Eating disorders in African American girls: Implications for counselors. *Journal of Counseling & Development, 88*, 319–324.

Taylor, L., & Adelman, H. S. (2000). Connecting schools, families, and communities. *Professional School Counseling, 3*, 298–307.

Tentoni, S. C. (1995). The mentoring of counseling students: A concept in search of a paradigm. *Counselor Education and Supervision, 35*, 32–42.

Thorn, A. R., & Contreras, S. (2005). Counseling Latino immigrants in middle school. *Professional School Counseling, 9*, 167–170.

Tolan, P., & Guerra, N. (1994; 1998). *What works in reducing adolescent violence: An empirical review of the field.* Boulder, CO: Center for the Study and Prevention of Violence.

Tompkins, L., & Mehring, T. (1993). Client privacy and the school counselor: Privilege, ethics, and employer policies. *The School Counselor, 40*, 335–342.

Tooker, E. D. (1957). Counselor role: Counselor training. *Personnel and Guidance Journal, 36*, 263–267.

Torbert, W. R. & Rook, D. (2005, April). Seven transformations of leadership. *Harvard Business Review,* 15 pages. Downloaded December 17, 2009, from http://hbr.org/product/seven-transformations-of-leadership/an/R0504D-PDF-ENG

Travers, J. F., Elliott, S. N., & Kratochwill, T. R. (1993). *Educational psychology: Effective teaching, effective learning.* Madison, WI: Brown & Benchmark.

Uellendahl, G., Stephens, D., Buono, L., & Lewis, R. (2009). Support Personnel Accountability Report Card (SPARC): A measure to support school counselor accountability efforts. *Journal of School Counseling, 7*(32), 71–31. Retrieved from Education Research Complete database.

U.S. Department of Education. (n.d.) About CSR. Retrieved April 22, 2006, from http://www.ed.gov/programs/compreform/2pages.html

U.S. Department of Education. (n.d.). Fact sheet on No Child Left Behind. Retrieved April 22, 2006, from http://www.ed.gov/print/nclb/overview/intro/factsheet.html

U.S. Department of Education. (2001). *United States Public Law PL 107-110, the No Child Left Behind Act of 2001*. Retrieved October 28, 2009, from http://www.ed.gov/policy/elsec/leg/esea02/index.html

U.S. Department of Education. (2004, March 3). Department to provide more educational options for parents. Retrieved April 22, 2006, from http://www.ed.gov/print/news/pressreleases/2004/03/03032004.html.

Valde, G. (2000). [Student reactions to the approach of educators]. Unpublished raw data.

van Hoose, W. H., & Kottler, J. A. (1988). *Ethical and legal issues in counseling and psychotherapy*. San Francisco: Jossey-Bass.

VanZandt, C. E., & Perry, N. S. (1992). Helping the rookie school counselor: A mentoring project. *The School Counselor, 39*, 158–163.

Wall, S., & Arden, H. (1990). *Wisdomkeepers: Meetings with Native American spiritual leaders*. Hillsboro, OR: Beyond Words.

Watson, C. H. (1990). Gossip and the guidance counselor: An ethical dilemma. *The School Counselor, 38*, 35–39.

Wellman, F. E. (1962). Vocational counseling of adolescents: A critical look. *Chronicle Guidance*, 1–7.

Wells, M. E., & Hinkle, J. S. (1990). Elimination of childhood encopresis: A family systems approach. *Journal of Mental Health Counseling, 12*, 520–526.

White, J., & Mullis, F. (1998). A systems approach to school counselor consultation. *Education, 119*, 242–253. Retrieved November 13, 2000, from http://webnf1.epnet.com (the EBSCO database).

White, R. (1981). Guaranteed services for counseling and guidance: A model for program development. In S. Johnson, C. Johnson, & L. Downs (2006). *Building a results-based student support program*. Boston: Lahaska Press.

Wiggins, J. D., & Moody, A. H. (1987). Student evaluations of counseling programs: An added dimension. *The School Counselor, 34*, 353–361.

Wilcoxon, S. A., & Magnuson, S. (1999). Considerations for school counselors serving non-custodial parents: Premises and suggestions. *Professional School Counseling, 2*, 275–280.

Williams, M. M. (2000). Models of character education: Perspectives and developmental issues. *Journal of Humanistic Counseling, Education and Development, 39*, 32–40.

Williamson, E. G. (1939). How to counsel students: A manual of techniques for clinical counseling. In D. Brown & J. Trusty (Eds.), *Designing and leading comprehensive school counseling programs: Promoting student competence and meeting student needs* (pp. 78–106). Belmont, CA: Brooks/Cole.

Wiseman, R. (2002). *Queen bees and wanna bes*. Norwalk, CT: Crown.

Wittmer, J. (1993). Implementing a comprehensive developmental school counseling program. In J. Wittmer (Eds.), *Managing your school counseling program: K–12 developmental strategies* (pp. 191–200). Minneapolis, MN: Educational Media.

Wittmer, J. (2000a). Counseling the individual student student. In J. Wittmer (Ed.), *Managing your school counseling program: K–12 developmental strategies* (2nd ed., pp. 95–110). Minneapolis, MN: Educational Media.

Wittmer, J. (2000b). Section one: Developmental school counseling: History, reconceptualization, and implementation strategies. In J. Wittmer (Ed.), *Managing your school counseling program: K–12 developmental strategies* (2nd ed., pp. 1–34). Minneapolis, MN: Educational Media.

Young-Eisendrath, P., & Miller, M. E. (2000). Beyond enlightened self-interest: The psychology of mature spirituality in the twenty-first century. In P. Young-Eisendrath & M. E. Miller (Eds.), *The psychology of mature spirituality: Integrity, wisdom, transcendence* (pp. 1–7). Philadelphia: Routledge.

Zimmerman, J. E. (1964). *Dictionary of classical mythology*. New York: Bantam.

Zinck, K., & Littrell, J. M. (2000). Action research shows group counseling effective with at-risk adolescent girls. *Professional School Counseling, 4,* 50–59.

INDEX